Gender, Race, and Ethnicity
in the Workplace

Gender, Race, and Ethnicity in the Workplace

*Issues and Challenges
for Today's Organizations*

VOLUME 1

*Management, Gender, and
Ethnicity in the United States*

EDITED BY
Margaret Foegen Karsten

PRAEGER PERSPECTIVES

Westport, Connecticut
London

Library of Congress Cataloging-in-Publication Data

Gender, race, and ethnicity in the workplace: issues and challenges for today's
organizations / edited by Margaret Foegen Karsten.
   p.   cm.
   Includes bibliographical references and index.
   ISBN 0-275-98802-3 (set: alk. paper)—ISBN 0-275-98803-1 (v. 1: alk. paper)—
   ISBN 0-275-98804-X (v. 2: alk. paper)—ISBN 0-275-98805-8 (v. 3: alk. paper)
   1. Diversity in the workplace—United States.   I. Karsten, Margaret Foegen
   HF5549.5.M5G46   2006
   658.3008—dc22   2006010950

British Library Cataloguing in Publication Data is available.

This book is included in the African American Experience database from
Greenwood Electronic Media. For more information,
visit www.africanamericanexperience.com.

Library of Congress Catalog Card Number: 2006010950
ISBN: 0-275-98802-3 (set)
      0-275-98803-1 (vol. 1)
      0-275-98804-X (vol. 2)
      0-275-98805-8 (vol. 3)

First published in 2006

Praeger Publishers, 88 Post Road West, Westport, CT 06881
An imprint of Greenwood Publishing Group, Inc.
www.praeger.com

Printed in the United States of America

The paper used in this book complies with the
Permanent Paper Standard issued by the National
Information Standards Organization (Z39.48-1984).

10 9 8 7 6 5 4 3 2 1

Ideas and opinions expressed in the chapters of volumes 1, 2, and 3 of
Gender, Race, and Ethnicity in the Workplace are those of the authors and
do not necessarily reflect views of the set editor or the publisher.

In gratitude to all the women of strength—colleagues, relatives,
and friends both living and deceased—who have
influenced my life.

Contents

Acknowledgments

I gratefully acknowledge the University of Wisconsin-Platteville for granting a sabbatical leave that ultimately led to this project and Nicholas Philipson, senior editor, Business and Economics at Praeger, for all his assistance. Furthermore, I thank the contributors for the ideas and insights they shared in their chapters. Dealing with them to complete this set has been a pleasure. Finally, I want to express appreciation to Mary Christoph Foegen for her counsel; J. H. Foegen for instilling in me the desire to write; and my immediate family: children in their birth order, John, Kathryn, and Amy, and my husband, Randy, for their support as I completed two major writing projects in eighteen months.

Margaret Foegen Karsten
March 2006

Introduction

Two generations have grown to adulthood since sweeping federal laws were passed to end employment discrimination based on race, color, religion, sex, and national origin and to ensure that women and men were paid equally for doing the same or substantially similar jobs. Why, then, is it still necessary—even compelling—to have a diverse group of practitioners, academics, and theorists in business, psychology, and related disciplines address issues related to gender, race, and ethnicity in the workplace?

Three reasons, *not* in order of importance, are money, power, and ethics. Women in management and the professions supposedly experience a $2 million lifetime income disparity vis-à-vis their male counterparts.[1] Economists indicate that white women experience a 7 percent wage penalty for *each child* they have.[2] Though no wage penalty is attached to motherhood for black women, they unfortunately tend to be paid significantly less than whites.

Though the sexes have reached numerical parity in management overall, scarcely more than a handful of women lead the powerful Fortune 500 firms in the United States. As of this writing, only one is a woman of color. And 95 percent of top executives in U.S. corporations are white males, though no appreciable difference exists in the percent of women and men who aspire to become chief executives.[3]

If those facts are not persuasive enough, consider that from 2000 through the first half of 2001, twenty-five cases filed with the Equal Employment Opportunity Commission involved egregious racial harassment—the use of nooses reminiscent of lynching.[4] Not in out-of-the way rural areas, the sites of such despicable incidents were cities such as San Francisco and Detroit. Those are only the overt acts; columnist Leonard Pitts commenting on the death of civil rights advocate Rosa Parks in 2005 said, "Racism that was once brazen enough to demand a black woman's bus seat is covert now, a throw-the-rock-and-hide-your-hand charade, its effects as visible as ever, its workings mostly hidden."[5]

How long will it take before repugnant incidents and effects—blatant and subtle—are abolished? When will future U.S. citizens wonder why publications in the early twenty-first century found it necessary to create lists of the top fifty women or blacks in major firms? Those from cultures characterized by extreme time consciousness, a strong streak of individualism, and a desire to pursue promotions into the pinnacles of power have become impatient with the slow pace of change. Incrementalists might urge them to learn from those of other cultural traditions that social change occurs slowly and that forty to fifty years, though a large portion of any person's life, is very little time in the context of social institutions that have existed for centuries. Others are not convinced that change must be slow. They argue that any additional time is too long to wait for those who have been deprived of full participation in and equal benefits of their work in this society.

Corporate downsizing notwithstanding, the United States may again face a shortage of highly skilled professionals. Baby Boomers, born between 1946 and 1964, are starting to retire in record numbers and will be replaced by the much smaller Baby Bust and Generations X and Y. Record numbers of women are in the labor force already, so they will not be a ready supply of additional labor, but women and people of color who are currently marginalized and underutilized may be.[6]

Twenty-five percent of U.S. firms do not have diversity programs.[7] Of those that do, only about one-third succeed; 20 percent fail.[8] This abysmal track record does not promote positive relations among people of various races and ethnicities. The road to a multicultural workplace is uneven and full of potholes; temporary spikes in dysfunctional conflict are to be expected. Miscommunication and misunderstanding even among people of similar backgrounds can result in serious organizational problems. Without honest, open face-to-face dialogue, which presupposes self knowledge such that people can explain who they are, their worldviews, and the factors, including ethnicity and race, that have shaped them, U.S. firms face trying times. Progressing from different starting points on the continuum ranging from monolithic to pluralistic to multicultural organizations will be challenging.

Stereotypes and the debate over the extent to which gender differences in behavior exist and their causes affect the enthusiasm with which workplace diversity is embraced. A 2005 Catalyst study showed that although few managerially relevant behavioral differences exist between the sexes, men are still viewed as more likely to "take charge" and women to "take care" of situations and people.[9] The consequences of such deeply embedded false mindsets are horrendous for women pursuing upward mobility, yet they are as likely to believe the stereotypes as men. A steady stream of contrary information must be presented to root out stereotypes if gender parity is to be a reality by 2019, as the optimistic Committee of 200, an elite group of powerful U.S. women, forecasts.[10] Otherwise, predictions of those who say gender equity will not occur for another 475 years may prove more accurate.[11]

Equity may not be achieved quickly if behavioral variations are primarily attributed to innate sex-based differences. Despite profuse apologies, former Harvard president Lawrence Summers, who resigned from that position on June 30, 2006, unleashed a controversy the previous spring by suggesting that the shortage of female science professors may be due to such distinctions. This rationale alarmed people who believe that nurture or socialization has far more to do with occupational choice than any internal differences, which they maintain are insignificant.

Baron-Cohen, who studies differences in empathizing and systematizing human brains that he believes are hard-wired but that appear in both women and men thinks the situation of those studying biological differences has improved since the 1960s and 1970s. In those days, serious researchers who recognized the role of socialization but wanted to study the impact of biology on sex differences in behaviors were "accused of oppression and of defending an essentialism that perpetuated inequalities between the sexes." Baron-Cohen argues that now the "pendulum has settled sensibly in the middle of the nature-nurture debate."[12]

His assessment is disputed by other researchers, notably Janet Hyde. Her meta-analysis revealed that gender-related behavioral differences long assumed to exist may not or may be highly exaggerated. She found few differences between the sexes and still fewer that were relevant to leadership or management in her studies of gender similarities.[13] False assumptions nonetheless persist and harm both sexes. Women who are not perceived as nice may be penalized in important selection and evaluation decisions; men may be perceived incorrectly and may see themselves as incapable of nurturing.[14]

Implications of many other factors based on which humans experience different workplace opportunity and treatment could have been explored; these volumes address only gender, race, and ethnicity for reasons of relative brevity. The socially constructed term *race* is used reluctantly, recognizing that it is not synonymous with skin color, differs from ethnicity, and may be unrelated to objective reality. The human race truly is the only one that exists.

Over the past two generations, much progress has been made. Things *have* changed, yet some issues in vogue today—such as "on-" and "off-ramps" for those who wish to step out of the fast track to provide care or get more education[15]—are essentially concerns from a quarter century ago that have been repackaged significantly.

A shortage of ideas for creating harmonious diverse workplaces in which all employees flourish is not the problem. We know what to do; now we must figure out how to do it. Ways to implement greater organizational equity must be considered carefully after they have been interiorized and are given high priority. Evaluation, accountability, and follow-up also are crucial to long-term success of equal opportunity efforts.

Consequences of failing in this endeavor could be dire. Some believe corporations are immune from the short-lived social disintegration and racial tension following Hurricane Katrina in 2005, but they may be deluded. Growing gaps between haves and have-nots in the United States, if not remedied, could result in chaos affecting all institutions, including businesses. Though many blacks have increased their incomes, their wealth trails that of the majority group.[16] Native Americans are virtually off the radar in terms of management of major firms, but the underlying leadership principles of some tribal nations are consistent with contemporary management theories, such as stewardship and servant leadership. Continuing to marginalize these and other racial and ethnic minorities is costly and must end.

This comprehensive set examines the status of women and racial/ethnic minorities and discusses challenges they face and the psychological, sociological, and legal contexts in which change must occur. It then suggests actions that organizations and individuals can take to deal with such challenges.

VOLUME 1

Volume 1 sets the stage for in-depth treatment of causes and consequences of workplace and leadership inequity. Perspectives of those who feel disconnected from or outside of the Eurocentric corporate mainstream in the United States, such as Asian Americans, Native American women, and black and white women are explored. Employment statistics pertaining to a spectrum of racial and ethnic minorities and to women are analyzed, as are those focused more narrowly on subgroups of Latinas.

Disaffection is expressed poignantly in the stories of those whose backgrounds would uniquely qualify them to make culturally rich, if thus far unrecognized and unrewarded, contributions to workplace management but for artificial barriers. This illustrates the amount of progress that must be made before those with different but equally valid and valuable perspectives become full partners in societal and business leadership.

Chapters in Volume 1 range from theoretical reflections on leadership to pragmatic analyses of employment statistics. The volume begins with conceptual discussions of leadership that draw on but go beyond experiences of diverse groups, including African American executives and entrepreneurs, skilled tradeswomen who perform managerial functions daily, Asian Americans, and Native American women. Advocated are flexible, holistic, situational leadership approaches that "give voice" to the marginalized, "give back" to the community, add value to society, and distance themselves from either/or dichotomies.

As a group, contributors largely reject hierarchical leadership but reach no consensus about what must replace it. Such agreement may be impossible if leadership depends on the circumstances. Leader effectiveness may demand both meticulous preparation through the study of related disciplines and a simultaneous willingness to "let go" and creatively combine a kaleidoscope of possibilities in new, different ways. The most fitting leadership analogy may be that of the artist whose painting-in-process evolves on an ever-changing canvas, suggested by Adler.

Though technically not managers, skilled craftswomen who eschew the title fulfill leadership roles and engage in traditional management functions of planning, organizing, directing, and controlling. The lack of attractiveness of management as an occupation is not an obstacle that the Glass Ceiling Commission of the 1990s envisioned but is nonetheless problematic. For most skilled tradeswomen, promotions to management would entail less flexible schedules, relative job insecurity associated with nonunionized supervisory positions, and short-term pay cuts due to necessary but unpaid overtime. Thus the short-run lack of incentives for tradeswomen to cross over to management may perpetuate occupational segregation at higher levels.

Such occupational segregation is the topic of later chapters in Volume 1. Contributors differ markedly in their views of this problem and related concepts. For example, Kim decries occupational segregation for its inefficiency in the use of human resources in a meritocracy where rewards are to be based on performance rather than on uncontrollable factors. Rosette, on the other hand, questions the existence of meritocracy due to unearned privilege, which gives advantages to some based on race, ethnicity, or gender.

VOLUME 2

Many legal, judicial, psychological, and sociological forces affect the treatment and advancement prospects of employees and executives based on their gender, race, and ethnicity. This volume discusses selected laws related to equal employment opportunity, affirmative action programs, and the relationship of the relatively neglected topics of racial and ethnic harassment to the more widely researched issue of sexual harassment and of the latter to workplace incivility (rudeness) and violence. The impact of stereotypes, socialization, and power-related concerns on the disenfranchised also are presented.

Twenty-five percent of human resource managers surveyed attribute sexual harassment lawsuits to failed romantic relationships in the workplace.[17] This worries some employers enough to ask the parties to sign so-called love contracts to release their firms from liability for harassment when or if the relationship ends. Unlike harassment, incivility, or violence, however, workplace romances may have a positive side, improving morale and satisfaction of the participants, possible charges of favoritism from co-workers notwithstanding. Romantic workplace relationships are addressed in Volume 2.

Though office romance may have unanticipated favorable effects on those directly involved, many laws and programs designed to rectify employment inequity have unintended harmful effects. For example, affirmative action has been wildly successful at opening previously closed doors for women and minorities — particularly white women — but also has led to consequences that some fear have hampered additional progress.

Furthermore, other equal employment opportunity–related programs focus on superficial problems and fail to discern (let alone address) their root causes. For example, Nydegger and coauthors point out in Volume 2 that workplace incivility and sexual harassment sometimes occur together. Rudeness at work, however, has been virtually ignored. Later, Callahan indicates that sexual harassment training implemented to deal with sexual assault by males in one branch of the military disregards the fact that its higher incidence and an increase in eating disorders among females in the same branch could be caused by perceived loss of personal control due to institutionalized resocialization practices.

In the first chapter of Volume 2, Heilman and Haynes argue that affirmative action may have unintended consequences that should be dealt with. The effects of the Pregnancy Discrimination Act of 1978 (PDA), intended or otherwise, could not be adequately assessed or addressed for many years due to different judicial interpretations. Not until enactment of the Family and Medical Leave Act in 1993 (FMLA) did the debate subside.

At issue was whether the PDA required employers to provide minimum job-protected leave when a woman was physically incapacitated during childbirth and recovery. In some jurisdictions, women could be fired for absenteeism associated with complications of pregnancy or time off for childbirth if their employers lacked temporary disability insurance. Those interpreting the PDA narrowly argued that pregnant women had to be treated only as well or as poorly as "nonpregnant persons" who were disabled for a time, assuming that their employers offered insurance or had other temporary disability policies. Even then, the controversy was resolved only for employees who met eligibility standards and worked for firms covered by the FMLA. Those employed by organizations not required to comply with the FMLA still may have to contend with such interpretations if their state laws provide no additional protection.

The FMLA allows all eligible employees, regardless of sex, unpaid, job-protected leave in an attempt to dispel gender stereotypes about responsibilities for caregiving. Some employees, however, fear their career commitment will be questioned if they take FMLA leave; others cannot afford to do so. Ironically, the FMLA, which was to protect employees' job rights when they needed time off work for caregiving, may deter employees—particularly women wishing to bear children—from job changes needed to advance in their careers because of its restrictive eligibility requirements.

Stereotypes about the career commitment of pregnant women harm all employed women. Such mindsets, though incorrect, readily extend to all in the same general category when they are grouped together based on one uncontrollable factor instead of viewed as individuals.

More than forty years after the *Harvard Business Review* published "Are Women Executives People?"[18] and over twenty-five years after "Women and Men as Managers: A Significant Case of No Significant Difference" appeared in *Organizational Dynamics*,[19] the perception (though not the reality) of a link between management and masculinity persists. Several contributors deal with these stereotypes and the difficulty in eradicating them despite evidence that any true gender differences in leadership are small and situational.[20] Such stereotypes may be all but intractable until women, who now represent half of all managers, professionals, and administrators, are no longer numerical tokens in the executive suite.

Tokenism is another subject examined in this volume. Though much empirical evidence describes the organizational consequences of tokenism for women, the few existing studies on the impact of racial and ethnic minorities are narrow. More should be conducted. Those researching women who are tokens believe the same concepts may apply to minorities and have seen positive results among token women in powerful positions when the organization employing them purposely legitimated their authority.

Any token group has far less power than the dominant class, but power can also be systematically taken from the numerical majority as is done in the military to resocialize recruits. Callahan's previously mentioned chapter illustrates how power and control of one's own life are systematically removed from both male and female air force cadets, resulting in dysfunctional consequences as both strive to regain it. An important distinction is that the women cadets seem to bear the brunt of the negative impact; not only do they experience eating disorders at a higher rate than other female college freshmen as they seek to control their bodies, but they also are targets of sexual assault by men cadets who react to being stripped of power by asserting control over women.

Whether they are military recruits or powerful corporate CEOs, women and men still seem to be evaluated differently. This occurs despite the notion that U.S. institutions including the judiciary are gender-neutral and fair. Those who do not conform to intensified gender-related prescriptions for behavior, which are especially strong stereotypical expectations based on gender, are punished harshly.[21] On the other hand, infractions of those violating relaxed gender-based proscriptions, or behaviors considered inappropriate for any U.S. adult but less so for males, may be dealt with less severely.[22] Though the final verdict is still out at this writing, these findings may be relevant in the respective cases of Martha Stewart and Ken Lay of Enron, discussed in the last chapter of Volume 2.

VOLUME 3

Organizational and individual strategies for dealing with challenges faced by people of color and women based on case studies, personal reflections, and research are presented in Volume 3. Face-to-face interpersonal communication is proposed as the new frontier in which the promised benefits of diversity management will be delivered as individuals begin to know and trust one another. Other chapters dealing with diversity focus on the path Shell Oil U.S. took to become a model firm in terms of not only cultivating a heterogeneous workforce but also using each employee's unique talents fully and best practices in diversity management, which include built-in accountability, top executive support, and aggressive promotion of diversity during recruitment.

Today's diverse workforce consists of about equal percentages of women and men. As the percent of sexual harassment cases filed by men increases, some might think harassment policies should be gender-neutral, but the authors of "Dirty Business," a chapter in Volume 3, disagree. They discuss why sexual objectification of women—even if it occurs off the job—has devastating effects on the workplace, what can be done to change the culture that perpetuates objectification, and who should be involved in effecting such widespread organizational change.

Another change in the workforce with implications for women and minorities involves career planning models. Vestiges from a bygone era that assume uninterrupted vertical movement within one company must be replaced by models with multiple career paths featuring flexible on- and off-ramps, lateral moves, and continuous learning.

Crucial to career advancement of women and racial/ethnic minorities is the cultivation of social capital through developmental opportunities. Those who have lower positions or have been historically underrepresented may need to temporarily gain legitimacy by reflecting that of more powerful organizational members. Role modeling, another avenue for development, deserves more study. Being perceived as and serving as role models also may affect women and minorities positively.

New forms of developmental relationships, such as a network of mentors, may be appropriate for a workplace in which demands for knowledge quickly outpace capabilities of any human, regardless of gender, race, or intellectual endowment. Other alternatives to the master-apprentice model are needed to ease the burden on executive women and minorities who are expected to help others advance but whose ability to sponsor protégés is limited due what has been dubbed a time famine.[23] Some options are virtual-, peer-, and co-mentoring, and mentors-for-hire.

If research supports the importance of developmental relationships for women and people of color, so does the life experience of contributors to this volume. Evans advocates greater use of peer mentoring and coaching and defines networking as "putting people together" for business reasons. Gee lists networking along with self-knowledge and reflection as strategies for dealing with gendered racism.

Though the business literature focuses on developmental relationships and activities occurring at work, one's personal life also can enhance leadership. Too often, personal life is assumed to detract from work, but that occurs only if resources are assumed to be limited. To the extent that multiple roles are energizing,[24] the net result of personal experiences that teach skills transferable to the workplace may be positive, especially for those who have lacked equal access to company-sponsored development programs historically.

Equal access and treatment are necessary but insufficient to create employment equity if certain groups face unequal limitations.[25] All organizations, including those in higher education, must seriously consider personal and professional needs and realities of the employees they seek to attract and retain when formulating work-life policies and programs to minimize disparities in constraints.

Perceived inequities may create stress. Thus, people of color and women are more likely than white male counterparts to encounter gender- and race-related stressors. Glass and concrete ceilings, manifestations of individual and institutional racism, and historical traumas deep enough to wound the soul represent unequal constraints.

The resilience some people of color and women exhibit in coping successfully with profound challenges or stressors is remarkable. It may lead to unparalleled gains in hardiness, self-efficacy, self-esteem, and empathy, qualities that can only help in future personal and professional endeavors. However, not all those in the workplace who have been harmed by "isms" related to gender, race, or ethnicity are gifted with such resilience. They must not be abandoned, nor must their possible future contributions as employees or executives be dismissed. Rather, organizations must fully commit not only to stress-reduction strategies but also to creation of an environment that optimizes the talents of all.

NOTES

1. E. Murphy, *Getting Even: Why Women Don't Get Paid Like Men—And What to Do about It* (New York: Touchstone, 2005).

2. S. A. Hewlett, "Executive Women and the Myth of Having it All," *Harvard Business Review* 80 (2002): 66–74.

3. J. S. Lublin, "Women Aspire to Be Chief as Much as Men Do," *Wall Street Journal* (2004, June 23): D2.

4. A. Bernstein, "Racism in the Workplace: In an Increasingly Multicultural U.S., Harassment of Minorities Is on the Rise," *Business Week* (2001, July 30): 37–43, 64–67.

5. L. Pitts, "Rosa Parks: She Taught Us the Power of One," *Wisconsin State Journal* (2005, Oct. 31): A6.

6. S. A. Hewlett and C. B. Luce, "Off-Ramps and On-Ramps: Keeping Talented Women on the Road to Success," *Harvard Business Review* (March 2005): 43–46, 48, 50–54.

7. T. Joyner, "Ethnicity, Gender Bias Remain Common at Work," *Wisconsin State Journal* (2005, April 15): C9.

8. S. Rynes and B. Rosen, "A Field Survey of Factors Affecting the Adoption and Perceived Success of Diversity Training," *Personnel Psychology* 48 (1995): 247–71.

9. Catalyst, *Women "Take Care," Men "Take Charge": Stereotyping of U.S. Business Leaders Exposed* (New York: Catalyst, 2005).

10. M. Llewellyn-Williams, *The C200 Business Leadership Index 2004: Annual Report on Women's Clout in Business* (Chicago: Committee of 200, 2001–2004).

11. D. L. Corsun and W. M. Costen, "Is the Glass Ceiling Unbreakable? Habitus, Fields, and the Stalling of Women and Minorities in Management," *Journal of Management Inquiry* 10 (March 2001): 16–25.

12. S. Baron-Cohen, "The Essential Difference: The Male and Female Brain," *Phi Kappa Phi Forum* 85(1) (2005): 23.

13. J. S. Hyde, "The Gender Similarities Hypothesis," *American Psychologist* 60 (2005): 581–92.

14. Ibid.

15. Hewlett and Luce, "Off-Ramps and On-Ramps: Keeping Talented Women on the Road to Success," 43–46, 48, 50–54.

16. D. Hajela, "The Color of Money Still Divides Blacks and Whites," *Wisconsin State Journal* (2005, January 18): D1, D9.

17. Society for Human Resource Management, "Workplace Romance Survey (item no. 62.17014)," Alexandria, VA: SHRM Public Affairs Department.

18. G. Bowman, N. Worthy, and S. Greyser, "Are Women Executives People?" *Harvard Business Review* (July–August 1965): 15–28, 164–78.

19. S. M. Donnell and J. Hall, "Men and Women as Managers: A Significant Case of No Significant Difference," *Organizational Dynamics* (Spring 1980): 71.

20. Hyde, "The Gender Similarities Hypothesis."

21. D. A. Prentice and E. Carranza, "What Women and Men Should Be, Shouldn't Be, Are Allowed to Be, and Don't Have to Be: The Contents of Prescriptive Gender Stereotypes," *Psychology of Women Quarterly* 26 (2002): 269–81.

22. Ibid.

23. L. A. Perlow, "The Time Famine: Toward a Sociology of Work Time," *Administrative Science Quarterly* 44 (1999): 57–81.

24. R. Barnett and G. Baruch, "Social Roles, Gender, and Psychological Distress," in R. Barnett, L. Biener, and G. Baruch, eds., *Gender and Stress* (New York: Free Press, 1987), pp. 122–41.

25. L. Bailyn, *Breaking the Mold: Women, Men, and Time in the New Corporate World.* (New York: Free Press, 1993).

1

Women Leaders in Corporate America: A Study of Leadership Values and Methods

Patricia H. Werhane, Margaret Posig, Lisa Gundry,
Elizabeth Powell, Jane Carlson, and Laurel Ofstein

Despite enormous strides in the status of women in U.S. corporations, as of 2006, only ten women are CEOs in the Fortune 500 companies and twenty in the Fortune 1000 firms. In 2004, the last year for which we could obtain data, women made up 16.9 percent of the boards of Fortune 500 and 10 percent of Fortune 1000 firms. In 2004, women earned seventy-seven cents for every dollar earned by men.[1] Only 81 representatives in the U.S. Congress (out of 535 seats) are women, and so far no woman has been elected vice president or president of the United States.[2]

These daunting statistics, however, belie another phenomenon: the growing importance of women in leadership positions in U.S. corporations. This chapter is a qualitative study of some of those women, their achievements, and the value-added contributions they have made in their leadership positions. For this study we have chosen eighteen women from a variety of for-profit sectors of the economy. Some have started from the bottom of an organization; others have moved from one organization to another; still others have started their own businesses. Included in our study are women in finance, retail, service industries, education, labor, banking, accounting, consulting, architecture and design, energy, marketing, and health care. The data were collected from a series of personal interviews conducted in 2004 and 2005.

This study is flawed in several respects. Our selection criteria were based on women who represented different sectors of the economy and those to whom we had access. Many women in this study are or were members of the Chicago Network, a selective organization of women leaders in Chicago. Others are graduates of the Darden Graduate School of Business at the University of Virginia. So our sample is small and hardly representative of a good cross-section of American women leaders. Second, merely because we have limited our study of leadership to women, we cannot conclude that the motivations, background, traits, and qualities of leadership we found are unique to women. At best, we can presume that the leadership stories these women tell display some commonalities among successful business women leaders, which might be factors in their careers. Studies of male leaders may reveal parallel factors and similar leadership styles, but that is not our concern in this chapter. Rather, we want to tell stories about women who have been successful and who are role models for other women still struggling in their careers.

Third, this study deliberately focuses on women in business. Much has been written about women who are political or religious leaders, for example, Eleanor Roosevelt, Margaret Thatcher, Mother Teresa, and Hillary Clinton. Less has been written about successful women in the for-profit sector. As an increasing number of women enter the workforce and strive for leadership positions, our study may be helpful to them.

Although the women in our study are exemplary, our aim is to do more than just celebrate their achievements. We were searching for common leadership styles as models for women now entering the workforce. Although we have selected women in a variety of sectors of the economy, we have found recurring themes—repeatedly similar styles of leadership. Each woman we have chosen to study has a different story to tell. Each comes from a different background, has had a variety of opportunities, and evaluates herself and her achievements from a unique perspective. Yet some similarities are striking.

The women included in this chapter are models of a leadership style that Judith Rosener has labeled "nontraditional" or "transformational."[3] Unlike leaders in hierarchically structured organizations, these women do not view their authority as a matter of power. They do not think of themselves as persons in superior positions of formal authority. These women are not transactional leaders who view leadership as a series of transactions between managers and employees, a trade of promotion or salary for good performance, or a punishment of demotion or firing for poor performance. Rather, they see leadership as an ongoing give-and-take process. They often see themselves as team leaders, as inspirational rather than directive. Their interactions with managers and employees are seldom transactional exchanges of rewards or demotions for superior or inferior performance. Instead, these women see themselves as working to coordinate and balance their interests and those of their employees, transforming these into shared corporate goals. This is usually translated into forms of interactive and participatory leadership that empower employees while achieving corporate ends. Often this leadership style is not aimed at transforming employees to adopt the values and goals of the company. Instead, leadership is thought of as a two-way interaction where both managers and employees are motivated and sometimes even changed.[4] So the leadership style is more like coaching than directing; more participative than hierarchical.

All speak of adding value in their organizations through a participatory inclusive style of leading their employees as colleagues rather than as subordinates or followers. Indeed, the terms *subordinate* and *follower* seldom surfaced in the interviews we conducted.

As already stated, every woman in our study has a different story. Like leaders cited in Howard Gardner's work, *Leading Minds*, they all weave narratives, or "identity stories," that tell us something about themselves and, more important, communicate what they value.[5] None are hypocritical: They lead from whom they are and what they stand for, and that transparency becomes obvious to those they lead.

Each woman interviewed exhibits an absolute sense of self-confidence. Despite various struggles and challenges and even discriminatory treatment, each is very sure of herself and her abilities. This is not merely a mentality of survival; it demonstrates a positive view of capabilities, a disregard for discriminatory practices, and optimism that these challenges can be overcome. That optimism stems from a firm belief deeply embedded in the psyche of each woman that she is as talented and capable as her male counterparts and superiors, and indeed, that turns out to be the case. Are such traits genetically coded so that we can sort them out as evident in all women who are leaders? That conclusion is highly questionable and impossible to prove. What we found is that each of the leaders in this collection is extremely smart and, in the case of Eva Maddox, aesthetically gifted. These talents are necessary for the kinds of leadership that are manifested by these women. However, they are not sufficient to account for their successes. The evidence of self-confidence or self-assurance, the ability to address obstacles in a variety of situations, and the ways in which each has overcome a disparate set of difficulties are learned from their experiences and from those who have (or have not) mentored these leaders.

One standard explanation for leadership success is related to well-developed mentoring experiences. Yet many of these women have *not* had positive mentoring experiences. At the same time they repeatedly speak of the importance of mentoring their managers and employees. Many have worked in hierarchical organizations where they were ignored. Yet they emphasize the importance of collaboration, listening, and inclusion in decision making.

Is the leadership success these women exhibit due primarily to the situations in which they find themselves? Is their success contingent on particularly favorable circumstances, so that in other situations they would not have had opportunities? Or, given their talents, would they have been unsuccessful in other industries or under other market conditions? Of course the context in which one finds oneself plays a critical role in one's ability to succeed or fail. And there is always a bit of luck involved. Anne Arvia's appointment as CEO of ShoreBank, for example, was due to the death of her mentor. Had Maddox not come into contact with architect Stanley Tigherman, her creative path would have been quite different. But these women and the others we have studied also demonstrate the ability to make the most of their talents given their situations, and many demonstrate the ability to redefine that context.

Communication as well as collaboration—communicating to and with managers and employees—is another theme running through the stories of these women. Transparency—sharing information and eliciting new ideas—is emphasized repeatedly. Although some of these women have been passed over for executive positions in the past, we find that each emphasizes the importance of hiring, promoting, and including managers who seem to be more capable than the leader. Thus there is an absence of fear of being second-guessed, sharing power, or being replaced.

Many of these women have found themselves in difficult economic situations either because the company they are leading has experienced tough economic times, such as those occurring after 2001, or because they found themselves in a leadership position in an organization that had not been well led in the past. But rather than get discouraged, the women we interviewed saw these problems as challenges and attacked them with enthusiasm and intelligence. Women who have not experienced these challenges have become change agents in their organizations. Thus we see restlessness with the status quo and a quest for excellence.

We had a selection bias: Each woman we have chosen to study has been a success in her organization or in multiple organizations. Failure seemed not to be an option, although there were (and still are) plenty of chances for failure for all the women in this study. Part of the many reasons for this may be because these leaders are "first-class noticers."[6] That is, they listen, are attentive to context, and observe well. Noticers are skillful at recognizing talent, identifying opportunities, and grasping the economic context in which their company finds itself. So noticers can often identify good managers. They often have a good sense of "smell" for opportunities and potential pitfalls, and thus many have been able to guide their organizations to avoid some economic disasters as well as add value. This sort of talent was evident in almost every leader in our study.

Finally, in different ways, each woman we studied exhibits what has been called elsewhere "ethical leadership." That is, each integrates her values with those of her organization and "embodies the purpose and values of the organization and of employees within the understanding of ethical ideals.... She connects the goals of the organization with those of the internal constituents and the community."[7] This principles-based ethical leadership was evidenced in every leader we interviewed.

THE ROLE OF INTELLIGENCE

In *Leading Minds* Gardner argues that two conditions for leadership in any venue are intelligence, what he calls "the attainment of expertise in various domains,"[8] and a strong "sense of self," which manifests itself in leaders as self-confidence. We see both of these characteristics in all the leaders we studied. We leave it to the reader to decide whether they are inherited or learned, but obviously not all smart people or even smart and self-confident people are leaders. The consistent evidence of self-confidence that we found, however, will become apparent as we unfold the stories of each woman.

It was also obvious that being smart is universally a characteristic of the women we studied. However, some literature links intelligence with education; in business it is often linked to undergraduate degrees in business or, better, MBAs. But our study does not verify that link to education or to management education in every case. Some anomalies are striking. Two subjects, Caroline Sanchez Crozier and Margaret Blackshere, were the first in their families to go to college.

Eva Maddox is an internationally recognized interior designer. In 1975, she started and headed her own design firm, which she sold to Perkins and Will, one of the largest architecture firms in the United States, in 2002. Then with architect Stanley Tigherman, she founded Archiworks, an interdisciplinary school of environmentally sustainable design. Yet Maddox's background and training as a designer belies her abilities as a manager, a founder, and the president of a large design firm. She studied design at the University of Cincinnati and spent several years selling design ideas for another firm. From her modest beginnings in a small town in middle Tennessee, she has become one of the top commercial designers in the United States today. As founder and president of Eva Maddox Associates, she provided leadership, motivation, design direction and overall vision for her firm while working with clients such as DuPont, Tootsie Roll, Hallmark, and Ogilvy & Mather. But Maddox never studied management or had a course in leadership.

Phyllis Apelbaum's background is even more dramatic. She left school after eighth grade to earn money for herself and her family. She began with a Chicago messenger service and after thirteen years, in 1973, quit to start her own firm, Arrow Messenger Service, now one of the largest messenger services in the country. Yet she never finished high school and has no formal management training. In her words, "My desire was to earn a living—nothing more, nothing less. I wasn't looking for power. I was looking to earn a living. I was looking to be the master of my own fate." Yet today Arrow has over 200 employees, and Apelbaum's aim is to grow the company to at least 300. Interestingly Apelbaum, using herself as an example, tries to hire the less educated, whom she finds to be honorable and loyal as well as capable.

"SURVIVE AND THRIVE"

Apelbaum exhibits a common trait we found evident in most of the women we interviewed: a survival instinct coupled with a drive to succeed—the ability to survive and thrive in difficult environments under pressing economic circumstances. Another survivor-thriver is Paula Sneed, senior vice president for Global Marketing at Kraft Foods. Sneed grew up in Boston in a supportive family and attended Simmons College and Harvard Business School. She began her career at General Foods as an assistant manager. One of Sneed's mantras is to "always have a ridiculous dream." Her ridiculous dream at Kraft when she first started there, as she puts it, "was to be a general manager [GM] and there'd never been a black woman promoted above the first-level promotion and between that and the GM was something like nine slots. But my attitude was, 'I want to do that,' and by having that in my life I knew I would have to work like a dog or I would never get there. [But] I didn't think I would see a woman GM in my lifetime." Today Sneed is the only high ranking African American executive at Kraft and one of the few women in a senior position.

A third example is Sondra Healy. She especially likes Winston Churchill's dogged approach regarding failure: "When you fail, just continue and don't have less enthusiasm going forward." Healy grew up in Chicago and studied art and theater. As she worked to make a career in theater, her father, the founder of Turtle Wax, died suddenly. Despite her training and career aspirations, Healy began working at Turtle Wax as director of public relations. Later, with her new husband, she took over the management of that firm and has served as co-chair for the past thirty years. Possibly the best-known supplier of car care products in the United States, Turtle Wax has the majority of the market share.

What does a survive and thrive instinct have to do with leadership? We argue that like intelligence, it is necessary for any leader. Having to survive in difficult environments or under stress or because of tragedy is one of many mechanisms that can push potential leaders into leadership positions. This does not imply that all those in such situations will become leaders. Such challenges, however, are prods and set the stage for those who are capable to become leaders.

Part of the survive and thrive instinct is often coupled with a determination to never give up and a passion for achieving a goal. Mary Ann Leeper is a co-founder, president and chief operating officer of the Female Health Company. When Leeper, a pharmaceutical chemist who had risen through the management ranks of several pharmaceutical companies, set out with her partners to create a company around a new product—the female condom—she knew her business had strong social goals, but she never envisioned herself as a social entrepreneur. In the mid-1980s, Leeper recognized women's need to protect themselves from HIV/AIDS and found a Danish physician, Lasse Hessel, who had invented a prototype female condom. The company formed to market this product faced two almost insurmountable hurdles. First, the U.S. Food and Drug Administration was very slow in approving this device, despite the fact that male condoms and diaphragms had been on the market for many years. This process of approval almost bankrupted the company. Second, Female Health Company executives mistakenly thought that because male condoms were so popular, marketing female condoms would be equally successful. This proved to be untrue. Most women in the United States were not interested in that kind of protection.

As the company struggled to survive with large debts and without a market share, on Easter Sunday 1991 Leeper received a call from a woman identifying herself as "Anna." Anna, who identified herself as an HIV-positive African American living in Harlem, had called to thank Leeper personally for creating a product that would protect her "sisters" from her fate. Leeper describes that moment as transformational. The company was no longer just another business, but now one with a deep and serious mission—to help women protect themselves against HIV transmission. Today, the female condom is sold commercially in 17 countries and distributed by public sector agencies in over 100 countries, most of which are in the developing world. In 2005, for the first time, the Female Health Company, a publicly-traded for-profit corporation, did not lose money.

CONTINGENT AND SITUATIONAL LEADERSHIP

Some leaders in this study appear to be what Northouse and others have called "contingent leaders." That is they have happened to be in the right place at the right time with talents that matched the situation.[9] Healy might appear to be a contingent leader. Yet what is striking is that *despite* her background and studies in drama and art, she has been a very successful CEO.

More of the women in our study appear to be situational leaders, adapting and readapting themselves to new and changing situations.[10] Deborah DeHaas began as an auditor at Arthur Andersen and is now managing partner at Deloitte Touche with a concentration in consulting. Donni Case, retired president of the Financial Relations Board (FRB), began as a student of history and economics. The FRB concentrates on the application of communication, message, and positioning of public companies' corporate or financial brands and communicating that positioning to the largest portfolio managers in the world. It has offices throughout the globe, and until 2005, when she took early retirement, Case was responsible for its North American operations. Yet as she says, she was never groomed for the CEO position and learned how to lead only by observing models of leadership in her organization, some of which she rejected as not worthwhile.

Margaret Blackshere, the first woman president of the Illinois AFL-CIO, is another example of a situational leader, someone who has stepped into various roles, all successfully. Blackshere was originally a schoolteacher. She says,

> I went to school to become a teacher in the '60s and we thought we could do anything, improve things, and make life better. I was making $3,000 a year, we built a new school, and they didn't consult the teachers. Teachers didn't get treated with respect. I looked around in my community in southern Illinois and there were steelworkers, mineworkers, industrial unions that were really doing well because they belonged to a union and worked together. We formed a union and went to our superintendent, arguing that we deserved some respect and to be paid adequately. He seemed to agree and then later he said he couldn't do it—we were outraged that he had lied to us. This was a good lesson for me—I realized that not everyone agreed with you. I couldn't understand if you were doing something good why people disagreed with you.

Later Blackshere became a lobbyist for the teachers' union and then began working for other unions. Eventually she became secretary treasurer at the AFL.

> I felt that I had a role to play. The labor movement traditionally does a wonderful job on legislation, collective bargaining, and politics. I thought we should do more—coalition building, community effort...so that was my campaign. If we want to grow this labor movement then we would need to expand what we do; we can't just take care of our current members, and we need to take care of working people.

Blackshere is now trying to change the culture at the AFL-CIO, traditionally an all-male organization. The board of AFL-CIO now has seven African Americans, two Latinos, and five women. Her goal is "to grow the labor movement and make it comfortable with all working people, immigrants, women, gays. This is a struggle because we have a lot of [members] who think they're doing OK but their organization isn't. [We have] high-priced labor leaders making $300,000 a year. I make $125,000. They told me that this was the upper salary."

THE QUESTION OF POWER

How are these leaders motivated? Because each holds or has held positions of great power, one would imagine that personal or professional power would be a strong motivating theme. But it is not. Healy is primarily motivated to preserve what her father had started; Cynthia Sanchez Crozier, founder and CEO of Computer Services and Consulting, had created a family business and is motivated by concerns for the long-term viability of keeping the business going for all those who are employed. Cathy Calhoun, president of Weber Shandwick, a division of Interpublic Group, the largest public relations and management communication company in the world, says her greatest accomplishment was when the company was named the fourth-best place to work in Chicago. She comments, "What we've tried to do is to provide our clients excellence by selling our people and their skills—our intellectual capital. We've had to work really hard so that people want to stay and be creative. [Our aim is] to make this place better and make it an employer of choice in our industry."

For Donna Zarcone, president and COO of Harley-Davidson Financial Services (HDFS),

> I love to grow organizations; I love to grow things; I love to garden. That's just who I am. I love to lead; it's very energizing for me to be able to take a group of people, to build a team and then set a common purpose for that team to go accomplish and then go and make it happen and be part of that, whether it's problem solving or leadership development or communication with employees or just all the different things of communicating and working with customers,

I enjoy that, and I get a lot of personal satisfaction from that. So my motivation was to be able to lead. I really admire this company and found that this was a good fit for me because it is a very values-based company. People are held accountable for their expectations; the behaviors resonated very well with me, so I wanted to be part of this organization, and I wanted to help make it more successful.

These are not the traditional definitions of power, particularly for heads of large corporations.

An interesting case of power management is Apelbaum's approach at Arrow Messenger Service. The company had only been in business a few years when Apelbaum received the opportunity of a lifetime. A company she knew well was setting up package pick-ups nationwide, and she was approached to be the Chicago vendor with a contract worth $500,000. That was a lot of money eighteen years ago when Arrow was still a start-up. She agonized over how she could make it work but quickly realized that at that time, her company was simply too small to take the business on. She went back to the company and said that although she appreciated the opportunity, Arrow was not the right vendor for them. It was one of her most painful decisions but she knew she would not have been able to do a good job in the time frame the contract needed to be done.

Apelbaum is, however, a firm believer in destiny. "When you turn business down for the right reason and in the right way, very often it will come back to you." And it did. A few years after the fateful $500,000 question, Apelbaum got to bid on another large contract. Neiman Marcus was coming to Chicago and needed a courier company. Apelbaum's anecdote proved to be a great selling point. She convinced the department store that she understood what it took to service a big account and even offered the company she had originally turned down as a reference.

Others describe their motivation in terms of servant leadership. R. K. Greenleaf contends that a great leader is a servant first, and the conscious choice of wanting to serve *first* makes one want to lead. The ultimate goal of a servant leader is fulfilling others' needs. "Exemplary leaders use their power in service of others" and enable them to act by strengthening them and developing them into leaders."[11] This approach is in sharp contrast with a traditional transactional style of leadership that emphasizes power and control. Servant leaders serve followers to promote their empowerment and enable them to accomplish organizational goals.[12]

Dess and Picken have also noted that a great leader is a great servant. Servant leaders may be effective in providing keys to empowerment, such as flexible resources for employees, depending on their needs. For example, leaders may be coaches, listeners, or providers of information, if that is what their followers need. Servant leaders also facilitate the growth of their employees, both professionally and emotionally. They enable others to discover their own inner spirit and potential to make a difference and ultimately to develop into servant leaders themselves.[13]

Deborah DeHaas is the managing partner of Global Strategic Clients for the Midwest region of Deloitte Touche, one of the big four global accounting groups operating in over 120 countries. DeHaas exemplifies servant leadership both inside and outside of the workplace, and the roots of this leadership style may be seen in her upbringing and in the values that were ingrained in her. She puts those values into practice while serving her employees, clients, and community. "My roots are very much in client service. My job is all about helping other people be more effective in what they need to do in serving our clients." DeHaas is motivated by opportunities to make a difference and help impact people in a positive way. She likes to get the best out of her people. What she calls her golden rules include being a good communicator with the people around her and treating them with dignity and respect and in a fair-minded way. She engages them in the consultation process and encourages them to come to conclusions that create solutions for the stakeholders. Unlike leaders who are driven by huge power needs, servant leaders like DeHaas make a conscious choice to serve others first; that is their primary motivation for leading.[14]

True to the servant leadership style, DeHaas helps the group find the best course of action, and in doing so helps others discover their potential to make a difference. In a service environment, DeHaas believes that it is important to have a servant mentality. "I practice servant leadership and am here to serve people. My position at Deloitte has given me tremendous opportunity to help the service, because I am in a service business that helps to make things better for the client."

Another outstanding servant leader is Paula Sneed. Sneed has worked for Kraft Foods for the past twenty-eight years and recently achieved the top position of senior vice president, Global Marketing Resources and Initiatives, having held numerous assignments in brand and business management, including leadership of the company's Foodservice and Desserts division in the United States. This new position is the pinnacle of a career for which Sneed strived from the beginning. Despite her determination and a smart, competitive spirit, Sneed sees herself as a servant leader rather than as head of global marketing at Kraft.

> Power is something to be used very wisely. A leader should be a servant, and if a leader is not a servant in some meaningful way then [she is] not a good leader. You ought to be serving the people that you're working with; you want to be encouraging them to reach to a higher level than they could imagine and to perform at that level, and you want to be, in addition, setting the role model. My model[s] of leadership [are] people like Gandhi and Jesus Christ who really provided leadership, both moral and personal. This kind of leadership makes a difference in the way people feel about what they do.

Case summarizes this absence of a quest for power as the ultimate goal: "There was no way that I was ever groomed to be a leader. I wasn't ever interested in being a CEO."

ROLE MODELS AND MENTORING

As we mentioned in the introduction to this chapter, positive mentoring is often assumed to play an important (if not essential) role in developing leadership talent. In cultivating trust if not absolute loyalty, strong mentor relationships are very important. Experts such as Julie Indvik who have studied mentoring experiences argue that "one of the critical types of relationships for career advancement is a *mentor relationship*, in which a senior individual provides task coaching, emotional encouragement, and sponsoring the protégé with top level decision makers."[15]

Mentoring can make a significant difference in developing leaders, creating bonds between present and future leaders, and helping ensure the long-term leadership in a company. Part of being a successful leader is the ability to mentor and to develop other leaders in the organization. Yet "several studies have documented that women leaders have experienced *lower support* throughout their careers than similarly employed males."[16] These studies show that in many companies women managers are mentored significantly less either by men or women. It is not surprising, then, that in 2005 where our data end, very few women are CEOs in the Fortune 1000 organizations and on corporate boards.

We asked each woman about her mentors or role models from whom she developed her leadership opportunities and style. The responses were quite diverse, but we did not find consistently that every woman had a role mentor in her organization or profession. Many listed a parent or teacher as their most important role model rather than a mentor in their organization. So although many of these women exhibit the kind of mentoring leadership that Indvik describes in their organizations, in over half the cases leadership development did not uniformly come from a positive organizational culture or a strong managerial mentor.

That this is unfair and discriminatory and that it creates unequal opportunities at the top of organizations should be obvious. But suppose you are a woman manager who finds herself in such an organization? How can one take the absence of mentoring or a negative mentoring relationship and use it to one's own competitive advantage to develop survival techniques and leadership skills? Case, retired CEO of the FRB, is an example of someone who did this. She reports,

My father was my big role model. . . . I honestly looked, and I tried to find role models that were in business. When I started out there weren't any women, so that was something a little bit against me. I could never relate to the celebrity

CEO types, and there are a lot of other scary characters. I realized very early as a result of my father's incredible ethical behavior that I could never follow those types of people. My father was vice president of manufacturing of a small family-owned company, and he had to deal with family politics, unions, dumping, questionable incentives and other such practices.

She continues,

The people I worked for were brilliant businesspeople, so you have to separate their ability to make and do business and to identify new opportunities in the marketplace from their people skills. A lot of people would say that that was a style of leadership, but I think that many of these leaders when I came to the industry had a kind of "George Patton" approach to leadership. They would stand there and command the troops and tell them what to do. They didn't really want to invite opinion, and they didn't really want to have any kind of a democratic forum. They pretty much thought that they knew it all already, and they even told you how they wanted you to say it. It was that type of thing.

As a result, as a woman in a man's profession she received virtually no positive mentoring as she worked her way up the organization. Indeed, she found that some of the managers and executives to whom she reported became negative mentors. They not only did not help her; they discouraged her progress and demeaned her as a woman. Rather than becoming discouraged, however, Case used the negative mentoring she was receiving as data for ways *not* to manage and lead. Thus she turned what for most women are negative experiences that become detrimental to their careers into learning experiences from which she could develop her own leadership style as antithetical to that of these nonmentors.

Seconding this, Donna Zarcone concludes: "You can learn as much from a bad leader as you can from a good leader. You just take it as a learning experience and say, 'I'm never going to do that.' I know how damaging it was for me to be working for a leader like that." Fortunately, Zarcone and some other leaders in our study have had positive mentoring experiences. Zarcone talks in detail about one of her bosses at NF Computer Sales and Leasing Co. (NFC), where she was executive vice president and CFO with responsibility for accounting, treasury, legal, information systems, and other administrative areas. "He was a genius," she says, "He had a photographic memory, understood detail, understood risk, and understood the structure of transactions in a way that made him a wonderful teacher for me because he would teach me and say, 'You're looking at it wrong; this is how you look at it.' So his ability to take me under his wing and really help me understand was great."

An amazing mentor and role model to Pamela Strobel, who until 2005 was executive vice president and chief administrative officer of Exelon, was her grandmother. (Exelon is a large energy company and the holding company for Commonwealth Edison [ComEd], Chicago area's largest source of electrical energy.) The first woman to earn an undergraduate degree in physics from the University of Illinois in 1918, Strobel's grandmother went on to get her master's degree in the same field and began working at ComEd in the early 1920s. It was fascinating and instructive to Strobel that in 1920, according to her grandmother, there was no better place in the world to work because you were part of bringing the most important thing into people's lives—electricity. It was changing the world, and to be working at ComEd was, according to her grandmother, tremendously exciting. High growth and energized and extremely satisfied employees were the order of the day under the leadership of Samuel Insull, then the preeminent utility manager in the United States. Over time, of course, that euphoria got lost as the company, like any other in the economically depressed 1930s, encountered severe challenges. Strobel's grandmother lived until 1999, which allowed Strobel six years of sharing what she was living through at ComEd and comparing it with her grandmother's experiences. Because of her grandmother, Strobel decided that one of her missions at Exelon was to reinvigorate that culture of enthusiasm. Her motto is, "Every day, there's more to do, so let's do it."

Blackshere's favorite role models are Eleanor Roosevelt and Mary Quinn, another teacher she met in her early teaching days. Quinn always reminded Blackshere of her roots and was a true stabilizing force. She taught Blackshere that you have to win before you can make changes. Interestingly, Blackshere has become a role model and mentor to other women in trade unions. She was thanked on innumerable occasions by letter and in person as other women recognized that she was an enabler and had broken through a male-dominated world and had the staying power to stick with a difficult situation. She gave other women hope and inspiration. Blackshere's mantra is, "Take advantage of every opportunity, just do it because it will lead to something and make you a better person."

Cathy Calhoun describes her "really wonderful mentor, Barbara Molansky, who brought me along and made me her partner and when she decided to retire, I was the heir apparent. So I had good mentoring, good luck, and some skills that were valuable."

Anne Arvia, the current CEO of ShoreBank, was assistant controller of ShoreBank when her mentor and bank CEO, Margaret Cheap, was diagnosed with cancer and later died. As her mentor, Cheap was grooming Arvia for the CFO of the bank, but when she died, Arvia, then under age forty, was appointed to Cheap's position. Arvia says of Cheap,

> It was a short time that I actually worked with her, but we were very close, and she was extremely visionary and strategic, and playful. She was that person who walked into a room and just lit up the whole room. You just knew that Margaret had arrived. And she wasn't the center of attention or anything; she just had a tremendous presence about her that made people be drawn to her, in a very down-to-earth way. I learned a lot about business from her, about how to handle [difficult] situations.

Without that kind of mentoring, Arvia admits, she would not be successful in her new role as CEO.

Many women we studied, whether or not they were well mentored in their organization, speak of the importance of mentoring and in particular of mentoring women. Beth Prichard, former CEO of OrganizedLiving, says,

> In terms of mentors, I grew up before that was even invented—especially at Johnson Wax because I worked in the world of men. I'd never had a female peer until I went to work. At Johnson Wax I was the first woman they hired, the first woman manager, the first woman officer and never had a peer until the last year I was there. I remember when I was promoted to a manager in market research, and it was the first time that a man ever had to work for a woman, and I wondered if they said the same thing to men.
>
> I finally did have a mentor, the president and CEO of Johnson Wax. He was the group product manager of Household, and he took me on as his administrative assistant, which was not secretarial. It gave me all different jobs across the company, international and domestic, but what he really taught me was how to manage. I would do my work at night and I would follow him to meetings during the day, and he would tell me why he made decisions and what he looked for, and it was two years of the most incredible training so that was the mentor from heaven. I was doing two jobs—shadowing him plus doing my job.
>
> One of the things I've got pleasure out of is mentoring a lot of young women, some young men, too. I keep telling them, "You have choices and it's your choice to go and work someplace where you will not have a life. It means that when you have to get things done, you'll get things done at all costs, but it also means you make the right choice in terms of when something has to give or something has to go."

DeHaas summarizes the responsibility for mentoring. "I always look for opportunities to help mentor and develop people around me. It is a very strong responsibility to help women be successful. Madeleine Albright once said, 'There's a special place in Hell for women who don't help other women.'"[17]

OPERATING IN A MALE-DOMINATED ENVIRONMENT

Several women in our study were and still are in work environments that have been traditionally male-dominated. The women in financial services (Donni Case, Ellen Carnahan, and Anne Arvia), Margaret Blackshere in the AFL-CIO, Deborah DeHaas in audit and consulting, Donna Zarcone in Harley-Davidson, Sondra Healy at Turtle Wax, Beth Prichard when she was at Johnson Wax, and even Phyllis Apelbaum at Arrow Messenger Service are all in businesses that traditionally have had a paucity of women in leadership positions. About this, Case said,

> When I started the [financial services] industry was almost entirely male dominated, and we were marketing our services to professional investors and the

investment community that was also entirely male dominated. I can say the first
ten years of my career were exasperating in a lot of respects because as a female I
was discriminated against. Some portfolio managers didn't want to meet with
me and some clients did not want to meet with me because I was a woman. I
found this especially shocking coming from those who had daughters. Again, for
perspective, I am talking about the old boys club of 30 years ago.

The one saving grace of having gone through all this is that it made me very
determined to mentor the people who came after me. Over time I built a team
of brilliant women and men who took the company to new levels. Standing up
for your people and building a respectful environment for both males and
females helped change the course of how women were regarded and rewarded
in our business.

Ellen Carnahan describes her work experience as the financial services
industry was breaking with its reputed male-dominated tradition. At the outset,
many men did not want the women there. But Carnahan soon got very comfortable with being an outsider. She got used to sitting in a room where everyone else was male. Carnahan is clearly comfortable in her own skin. She is
exceedingly self-confident about her talents and capabilities and is something of
an optimist. She doesn't necessarily see these things in her career as obstacles
but as challenges that she must determine how to overcome.

Blackshere had an interesting challenge as the first women to run for the
head of a major union.

As a woman entering this man's world, I became crazy about baseball. It is an
unbelievable icebreaker, so if a woman can talk sensibly about it, it breaks
through things. I ran for the office—a tradition within the labor movement if
you are secretary treasurer. I had won the election for secretary treasurer with no
opponent eleven years ago. The tradition was when the president retired, the
secretary treasurer became president. I expected that to happen. But there was a
challenge for the first time ever—a challenge for the presidency. I ran it like any
other campaign that I've been involved in, and I won. After I was elected a
union man with a beard came up to me and said I had been his kindergarten
teacher.

In our interviews with Zarcone, she never mentioned any issues around
women at HDFS. During her six-year tenure as president, the company's annual operating income grew from $20 million to $168 million, and its managed
loan portfolio increased from $1.1 billion to over $4 billion. Recently HDFS
received the 2004 Catalyst Award, which recognizes companies with strong
initiatives to advance women in business. Twenty-nine percent of HDFS's corporate officers are women compared to the Fortune 500 average of 16 percent—
an amazing statistic considering that the majority of Harley-Davidson customers
are male! Equally impressive, two of the top five earners in the company are
women.

Apelbaum found herself in a man's world when she first tried to get a license to operate her business.

> I decided to take my inheritance, which by the way was $3,500...to get my license and to get started. The truth is I had seven hearings and did not get my license, simply because the Commerce Commission had never given a license to a woman—not for any other reason. Until I met the Chief Hearing Officer for the Commerce Commission. Today he's the Supreme Justice for the state of Illinois, Charles Freeman. I lost. I lost my $3,500; I lost my opportunity to get my license, and at the end of the day I just went barging into his office. He says that I sounded like I sold fish for a living on Maxwell Street. I told Charles the story of what happened, and he corrected it. He saw to it that I got my license and became a mentor and a friend. And thus began the birth of Arrow Messenger Service. I opened up the doors on November 1st [1973] and went to work.

Looking back, when Barbara Provus, principal and founder, Shepherd Bueschel and Provus, started her own career in the late 1970s, very few women were in the executive search industry. She is proud to say that many more women in the field today than thirty years ago. In fact, according to Provus, the real growth has been in the past five to ten years. Not that long ago, Provus was named as one of the top twenty women in search and states that the award should now be for the top 200 women in search because it is a much larger universe.

Provus believes that being female has helped, but she has been careful never to push the "female" agenda. She concluded early on that she would not get many assignments if her potential clients were uncomfortable working with that in mind. They know she does good work and suggests only candidates—particularly female candidates—who are strong in their own right.

TRANSFORMING AND TRANSFORMATIONAL LEADERSHIP

One of the important elements of effective leadership is exemplified in the relationships that develop between a leader and her colleagues, managers, and employees. Motivating managers and employees, particularly in a corporate context where trust, creativity, good decision making, and efficiency are at stake, can make an enormous difference in the firm's long-term effectiveness in highly competitive markets. Engendering trust and loyalty, and most important, retaining the best managers and employees are critical for adding value. As Sneed puts it,

> In corporate America life has been miserable in the last fifteen years. There's been downsizing, there's been outsourcing, mergers, a lot of personal upheaval. This is very different from the twenty-five years before then when companies

were being built. In times like this leaders need to be close to people. They need to be clear about the present and aspirational about the future, and they need to make people want to do their best. I don't know that we always have good leadership in corporate America today. There are a lot of people interested in their own perks but not necessarily interested in the kinds of things that will build companies and allow people to build their own personal futures.

Part of that leadership focus is creating a positive psychological contract between the leader and her employees, and transparency contributes substantially to that positive climate. In the volatile workplace of the twenty-first century, however, where workforce changes due to mergers, acquisitions, outsourcing, and economic exigencies are the norm, creating a positive organizational climate of trust is often difficult. Under the present economic climate, managerial and employee loyalty cannot be counted on. Often, too, in this volatile climate, employee perceptions of what a leader has in mind or what the organization is about can differ significantly from a leader's intentions or the direction of the company. Schein contends that the primary means for changing and maintaining culture are the leader's roles of modeling, coaching, and reacting to critical incidents. Although the structures of organizations and artifacts like the spoken and published mission statements should also be congruent with the primary mechanisms, they are of secondary importance to the leader's role in organizational culture formation and maintenance.[18]

As mentioned in the introduction, in the women leaders we studied, we found consistencies with what the literature calls transforming and transformational leadership. The former, first proposed by James MacGregor Burns, defines transforming leadership as "a relationship of mutual stimulation and elevation that converts followers into leaders and may convert leaders into moral agents. . . . [This] occurs when one or more persons *engage* with others in such a way that leaders and followers raise one another to higher levels of motivation and morality."[19] Examples of this abound. Prichard says of her leadership style,

> You have to get people that really commit to the same strategic direction of the business, so therefore it's doing what's right for the business to grow. Growth businesses are very different to manage than turnarounds, but [managing them] really demands that you clearly communicate . . . the overall goal — the strategy and the vision. But what makes a business successful is the commitment of the people and the understanding of what it really does stand for. Then you can get managers to understand the hard decisions and to participate in the responsibility and the accountability for those decisions.

Apelbaum is convinced that it is essential to be fair and equal to all people regardless of who they are. A sign on her door reads, "Say what you are going to do and do what you say." She treats everyone with respect and courtesy, which provides an environment where nothing short of that is tolerated. Moreover, she is both realistic and humble in her business dealings.

Transformational leadership, a term adopted by Bernard Bass, is slightly different, although the two are often confused. A transformational leader seeks to transform followers, but this is ordinarily a one-way activity rather than an interaction between leader and employee whereby both are changed. The transformational leader seeks to motivate the employee to redirect her self-interests to interests of the firm and to create change in the employee and the organization. The idea in business is to push people to perform beyond their own expectations, thus creating added value for the organization and the employee.[20] Zarcone speaks of that kind of leadership style.

> You look at yourself and the company's goals from the point of view of what you expect from your employees, how you evaluate them, and how you motivate them. We follow a business process where you set overarching goals and then you flow those goals down to the individual on the front line. Everybody knows what it is we're trying to achieve, why it's important, and how each person can make a difference; then you evaluate people on "how did you do?" Did you meet the expectations? Did you deliver on the goals? And if we did that right, do we have satisfied customers? You have to have metrics . . . and . . . a process in place to keep score and if you do that, and it's very much about alignment of the people in the organization to key objectives, people are with you. You have to communicate it; you have to be accountable for it. You have to lead by example, but if you're right there with the power of that unified force, working toward the accomplishment of that goal, [you] can just blow away the target.

In "Ways Women Lead," Judy Rosener suggests that a distinctive and characteristic feature of women in leadership positions is their ability to engage in interactive leadership relationships with their managers and employees and a preoccupation with empowering others. Rosener does not mean to imply that men do not do this, but she suggests that empowerment is almost a mantra for women in leadership positions. As a result, she contends, women are usually not afraid of hiring or working with managers who are smarter or more capable than they are.[21]

Prichard contends,

> It starts with hiring very smart people. If you hire smart people then you need to listen to them and learn from them, so that's the beginning. It's also typified by looking at all the options or issues, not making a decision until you really have asked, "What are my alternatives, what am I trying to sell?" and then finally being willing to make a clear decision. It may be a tough [or] . . . an easy decision, but as a leader you have to have the ability to step up and make that decision and then live with it. Also as a leader you have to be able to admit when it was a wrong decision and very clearly be able to say, "We're changing course; we tried this, made the wrong decision. At the time it might have been right but it's not any more and we're going to change."

Strobel says she strives to give the best of herself every working day—a quality she also expects from her team. Her philosophy is that people who do the very best job they can actually see it as an opportunity to make a contribution. Each day presents new challenges and opportunities when each individual really feels that she can do more. Strobel likes to select people who are growing in their jobs. She looks for intelligence, motivation, a great attitude, and a real willingness to work hard and go the extra mile. In her opinion, with these traits, an individual could work in just about any department and in any position.

Case describes a transactional leadership style that almost none of the women we studied exemplified:

> It was easy in some respects to call yourself a leader a long time ago if you just thought you were a general. Now you have to really work on each individual person whom you need and who is really critical to your operation, and . . . somewhat adapt to that person, and so it's a little trickier. You can't just get up there and give fight speeches because they don't resonate with a multigenerational team. When you look around the room, you need to note what perks up some people and who is shaking their head saying "Yeah, we're just totally lost." You have to adapt your style to different types of people. So I like to think of my leadership as being inclusive.

Crozier has a different style. Her working style is more hands-off. She prefers to be seeking out the next opportunity and predicting what is coming next. She has built a team of people who internally manage the office and take care of her staff. She has a female vice president of operations who has been with the company for ten years and a brother and sister who have been with Computer Services & Consulting (CS&C) since its inception.

Part of being a transforming or transformational leadership is developing buy-in from employees. We were struck with how important that is to most of the leaders in our study. In particular, many took a team-based approach to managing their employees and creating change within the organization. According to the literature, the most effective teams are those that have been given "clear and engaging direction and clear goals, unified commitment, a collaborative climate, an enabling structure, expert coaching, and adequate resources."[22] But the challenge is, as a leader, how do you create and sustain successful teams?

In 2001 Arvia embarked on a massive change initiative within ShoreBank called Building ShoreBank Advantage. Change management was in Arvia's blood—she had already overseen a review of operations with Boston Consulting Group. Because the original four founders of ShoreBank were no longer directly involved, management succession was a key issue. She also wanted to create a whole new environment within the bank and change the culture from one of less consistency to a focus on customer service.

Arvia created a working group known as the Implementation Oversight Committee (IOC)—a cabinet of four people who developed an initiative that implemented a massive culture shift for ShoreBank. The IOC created teams of nine people, across all levels and departments, giving them a recommendation handed out by consultants. Each team was charged with giving ownership of that recommendation to ShoreBank. There was much discussion and changing of the recommendations until every department was satisfied with the final outcome.

> We created a huge process with specific deadlines and timelines, objectives, goals, and created the Change Monster. He became our little mascot and symbol of change because we know people are really afraid of change naturally, but he can also be very cuddly and cute and tame. It was amazing. We rewarded people with these silly little green cuddly monsters. A number of people would call me and ask how they could get their Change Monster across the organization. So I would say, "Well, let's demonstrate behavior that's in support of the change and I'll send you one." It became such that if you didn't have a Change Monster . . . you had to have one.
>
> What was really great about this whole process was that the nine teams did their work, and we thought that they would be done with the initiative in a year. But they all came back and said they wanted to collaborate more across the organization; that's what they thought made sense. They said, "We want to organize around these customer segments that we know we're really good at. Let's get rid of some of these things that we aren't doing so well, but none of it will work unless we raise the quality of service across the bank. And by that we mean both how we treat each other internally and how we treat the customer." One hundred percent of the teams came back and said the same thing. So we responded, "We hear you. Let's create BSA Phase II to address those specific issues." This took another year. And some great stuff—implementation plans, execution plans—came out of all that.

ENTREPRENEURIAL LEADERSHIP

Women have launched entrepreneurial careers in record numbers during the past two decades. The emergence and growth of women-owned businesses have contributed strongly to the global economy and to their surrounding communities. The routes women have followed to take leadership roles in business are varied; but more likely than not, most women business owners have overcome or worked to avoid obstacles and challenges in creating their businesses. The presence of women in the workplace driving small and entrepreneurial organizations has had a tremendous impact on employment and on the culture of the workplace.

As of 2004, there were an estimated 10.6 million privately held, 50 percent or more women-owned firms in the United States, accounting for nearly half (47.7 percent) of all privately held firms in the country.[23] According to the Center for Women's Business Research, between 1997 and 2004, the estimated growth rate in the number of women-owned firms was nearly twice that of all firms (17 percent versus 9 percent); employment expanded at twice the rate of all firms (24 percent versus 12 percent); and estimated revenues kept pace with all firms (39 percent versus 34 percent). Furthermore, women-owned firms employ 19.1 million people and generate $2.5 trillion in sales.[24]

The preferred management styles of women entrepreneurs may be associated with their motives for business ownership. The results of a multicase study on rural small business owners indicated that women entrepreneurs were concerned about relationships with their employees and with creating corporate cultures that minimized interpersonal conflict.[25] These preferences were consistent with their motives for starting their businesses. Researchers have described these relational practices engaged in by women entrepreneurs, which included collaborative decision making.

Founding their own businesses enables women to use, satisfy, and maintain high levels of skill, as perhaps they could not when working for a corporation.[26] Women also cite layoffs, the ability to make one's own decisions, and the need for more flexible working hours to accommodate family demands as reasons for starting their own businesses. Having young children was a strong positive influence on women's self-selection of entrepreneurship.[27] Still, additional motivation comes from the belief that the world can be different and that their businesses can provide a means to change things and make a difference for other women.[28]

One of the primary characteristics of entrepreneurial leaders is the passion that drives them. This passion is demonstrated by their perseverance in the face of adversity, the extraordinary initiative they take to accomplish challenging goals, and their strong need to achieve success accompanied by a low need for status and power.

Apelbaum's aspiration was never power or influence, but she was intent on being independent and self-sufficient.

> Right before my dad's death in June of that year, the company [City Bonded] where I worked was sold. I had new employers, and I wasn't really happy about the change. Whenever there's a massive change like that, people are different, and so the environment is different. I had worked for a couple that were warm and caring and inclusive, and now I was working for somebody who was totally different, and then a month after that my dad dies suddenly.
>
> Coming back on the plane, I thought, "I'm just not going to let this happen to me." [Her father died without fulfilling what he wanted to do with his life.] I decided I would go on and do something else. So I gave my notice and said that I would work until November 1, 1973. What happened during that period of time was my competitors—the people who were my competitors then and today—would call and say, "Oh, have we got a job for you, boy have we got a job for you." And then, one night I was talking to a friend and that person said, "Could you imagine if you're worth that much to them what you could be worth to yourself?" And I said to myself, "That's a possibility."

Nearly twenty years ago, Provus had the opportunity to leave the security of her comfortable salary working for an executive search firm and enter the unknown world of self-employment. Working in an environment where judgment and trust of people was paramount, it was essential that she liked and trusted her fellow workers and could see a great future ahead. Having discussed the idea with her husband, a very successful entrepreneur, Provus decided to press ahead and is now founder and partner of Shepherd Bueschel and Provus, one of the most successful executive search firms in the Chicago area. Provus enjoys recalling the early days when the firm was starting out. In the excitement of setting up their own business, the four entrepreneurs had not really thought through basic business set-up procedures, such as establishing a line of credit. Although they could get phone service, basic telephone equipment was not available to them because they had no credit rating!

Madeleine Ludlow became an entrepreneur after several other careers. For many years she was at Cinergy, the leading energy provider in Cincinnati, as CFO. She left there in 2000 to join Cadence Network, a dot-com company. She worked for one of the original investors who had just raised venture capital. The company had $15 million to spend, and it was going to grow like crazy. The venture capital people recruited her away from Cinergy to Cadence to run it. As Ludlow describes it,

> I had grand plans, make my millions, take the company public, but the year after I got there we had taken the company from 105 people to 35. We had no money; we were on life support, and I spent the next two years after that getting the company to a point where it could survive, and it is now surviving, but there's no growth in it. I realized that I had not left the job I had [at Cinergy] to run a tiny little company that's not going anywhere. I left in January 2004 having agreed to an eight-month consulting assignment when I would come in with strategic stuff. They never called; they paid me, and so I essentially took 2004 off and stayed home with my son.

In 2005 Ludlow began a new job search and after interviewing with several large companies, decided that she would stay in Cincinnati and start her own business.

> I'm starting with a partner an investment banking firm here in Cincinnati to provide capital-raising and mergers and acquisitions advice to middle market private companies, which nobody in Cincinnati does. My partner was doing that with one of the local banks. The bank got bought last year, and the acquirer decided not to continue in that business. He and I began talking about this market, and it fits in with a lot of what I was doing earlier in my career, I have a lot more empathy with a small company than a traditional banker might have. So we started thinking about this last year. We raised capital for our own firm so that we can pay ourselves while we get it up and running.

Her new business, Ludlow Ward Capital Partners, was launched near the end of 2005.

Not all entrepreneurs start or maintain their own businesses. This style of leadership is also found in organizations of all sizes. Today many contend that organizations must be more entrepreneurial to enhance their performance, capacity for adaptation, and long-term survival.[29] Entrepreneurial management emphasizes taking a strategic approach, so that new initiatives can support development of enhanced capabilities for continuously creating and appropriating value in the firm.[30] The basic challenge of entrepreneurial leaders is to envision future possibilities and enable the organization to transform its current transaction set.[31]

Several components of transformational, team-building, and value-based leadership enable powerful individuals to meet this challenge. Entrepreneurial leadership relies on the ability to (1) extract exceptional commitment and effort from organizational stakeholders, (2) convince employees and investors that they can accomplish goals, (3) articulate a compelling organizational vision, (4) promise their effort will lead to extraordinary outcomes, and (5) persevere in the face of environmental change.[32]

Prichard is an entrepreneurial leader. She was, until recently, president and CEO of OrganizedLiving. OrganizedLiving was privately owned by a large equity group focusing on retail concepts. This company had about $110 million in sales with twenty-five very large stores that focused on providing organizational solutions. Prichard was there only a year. Prior to that she spent fifteen years growing and developing Bath & Body Works, which when she started was nine little alcoves of an idea in a store. When she left it was about $2 billion in annual sales, with about 1,600 stores. Before that she spent eighteen years at Johnson Wax and started in the market research department and then in product management. She worked on several of their brands and her last position there was VP of Insect Control.

> Success has changed for me over the years. When I was at Johnson Wax before I had my daughter, success was getting the deal done, being promoted faster. Success was defined in terms of title and salary; that was in my early years. In my mid years success was defined as being in an environment where I could grow personally and professionally. Now success is providing opportunity and growth for many people; that's the thing I get the most joy out of. You can only buy so many toys and . . . so many clothes. Now I can build a business not just because it makes a lot of money but because it is providing careers in general, which is wonderful.

VALUES-BASED LEADERSHIP

At least four leaders we chose for our study are in organizations that have explicit social as well as financial missions. Three of these are in for-profit companies: the Female Health Company, ShoreBank, and CS&C. The fourth, Blackshere, is in the AFL-CIO, a conglomeration of labor unions that organizes workers primarily in the for-profit sector of the economy. Some of each organization's explicit goals are directed to social change and improvement, broadly conceived. Values play an instrumental role in outcomes and their assessment.

Leeper, whom we cited earlier, runs the Female Health Company with the mission to protect women's health, particularly in less developed countries. Yet her organization is a publicly traded company with shareholders who hope for at least a break even performance every year. She was a woman driven by ambition to succeed, but in working with the female condom, what success meant was dramatically transformed into a social mission to help women around the world in HIV prevention. As she says, "For me it's always about what we are doing. It isn't about me as a person. It's about what we are trying to accomplish—bringing the female condom to the developing world."

Crozier is the founder, CEO, and president of CS&C, a technology and education firm based in Chicago. She directs the company's business development and strategic relationships and is recognized as a leading visionary in the field of instructional technology. CS&C provides innovative programs and services to enhance learning in education, business, and government on a local and national level. This firm's aim is to improve education in Chicago and eventually around the country. Yet it is a for-profit operation and supports twenty-five employees, including a number of Crozier's family members.

ShoreBank, long known for its loan program in Chicago's less developed neighborhoods, has a distinctive mission. A success story of the past few years, America's first community development bank was founded in 1973 and is located in what was once one of the poorest neighborhoods in Chicago, the South Shore. Today it has banks in Cleveland and Detroit and partners with international micro lending institutions in some less developed countries. "What we started to do in the beginning was to provide credit to people who didn't have credit," says its CEO, Arvia, with pride. Yet ShoreBank has lower charge-offs of its loans than traditional banks.

These leaders and the institutions they manage are committed to creating added social value as part of their mission and the mission of their organizations. The result is that although these institutions are not unprofitable, with the same investments they could have made more money in a different venue, or their leaders could have been more monetarily successful, if they had stayed in traditional corporate positions or worked in traditional markets. But none of these women would trade what they have created for a high corporate salary or position, because their goals are more socially focused, and their rewards are in satisfaction rather than money or power.

Blackshere is also a values-based leader who is trying to create a new values system for the AFL-CIO. "Our deepest concern is for working families. We can work with everyone that wants to work for working families." These were Blackshere's words as she became Illinois AFL-CIO president in January 2000. Her idea is to change the values base of the union so that it does more than merely represent workers and their wage, pension, and safety rights. Blackshere views labor's agenda as profamily. Under her leadership, the Illinois AFL-CIO has pushed for equal pay legislation in Illinois to prohibit employers from paying women less than men who work for the same employer performing equal work. Although the Equal Pay Act was passed several decades ago, Blackshere maintains that working on the state level to guarantee that the pay gap between men and women is addressed on the local and national union levels is important. Her other priorities include pushing for the passage of living wage legislation for employers that do business with the state and a corporate responsibility bill. She also has obtained family leave benefits for women and men who work for the AFL-CIO and has achieved more diversity in union membership and leadership.

ETHICAL LEADERSHIP AND VALUES INTEGRATION: VALUES "ALL THE WAY THROUGH"

One leadership challenge in today's changing business environment involves integrating one's personal values in a competitive arena where ethical issues seem not to be part of everyday business. An important factor affecting managerial moral judgment is how managers and professionals prioritize personal, client, corporate, and professional responsibilities. The dilemma of which should take precedence and the misalignment of these values are well illustrated in the number of corporate scandals we have witnessed in the past few years. Moreover, in every institutional setting, some practices do not encourage independent decision making or provide avenues for questioning what might be unacceptable activities by standards outside the organization. Sometimes, too, professionals as well as managers become so involved in their roles and clients' or company expectations of them that their judgments become identified with what they perceive to be their responsibilities.

We are enmeshed in a collection of overlapping social, professional, cultural, and religious roles, each of which makes moral demands. This becomes problematic when the demands of a particular role become confused, conflict with another role, or clash with societal norms or commonsense morality.

Role morality can constrain ordinary moral reactions. Sherron Watkins, a former manager at Enron, became an inside whistle-blower. Observing what she believed to be unethical and illegal activities when Enron booked losses to off-book partnerships, she wrote an anonymous letter to Ken Lay, then CEO of Enron, stating her doubts about these activities. She saw herself as a manager with the important role of flagging improprieties. But Watkins did not blow the whistle outside Enron, despite her accumulation of good data to support her suspicions. She was herself first in the role as Enron manager, placing company loyalty above professional, public, or shareholder interests.[33]

In contrast, at WorldCom, whose outside auditors were from Arthur Andersen, the vice president of internal audit, Cynthia Cooper, began to question Andersen's method of financial audits. Following the mandate of WorldCom's CFO, Scott Sullivan, billions of dollars in operating expenses were being booked as capital expenses, thus allowing WorldCom to show a profit instead of a loss for 2001. Both Sullivan and the Andersen auditors violated their professional code as auditors in countenancing these practices. Andersen may have considered the demands of its client, WorldCom, to be more important than its independent professional obligations. Only Cooper and her team of internal auditors, who redid the Andersen audit and eventually went to the board of WorldCom with their findings of fraud, prioritized their personal values of honesty and truth telling and the mandates of the professional auditor (American Institute of Certified Public Accounting) code before their loyalty to WorldCom.[34]

What is to be learned from these episodes is that scenarios such as accounting fraud tend to repeat themselves when individuals lack a perspective on their role and their institution and its demands and fail to integrate personal, social, and professional values into business practice. Unless managers can disengage themselves from the context of a specific problem and evaluate it from their personal and professional values perspective, decisions remain parochially embedded and result in an iteration of the very kind of activities that invite repeated moral failure. An integrative approach to values-based corporate leadership linking personal, professional, and managerial principles can help executives think more carefully about the issues they face in business. The leaders in our study do just that.

What is the difference between ethical leadership and a values-based view? Values-based leaders create or propound values for their instrumental worth to create added social value, and they align employees and shareholders to accept and work for those values. Ethical leadership goes further in several ways. Ethical leaders frame everything they do and stand for in moral terms. They also assume that personal, professional, and organizational values are congruent. Second, the values embedded in the organizational mission and direction are worthwhile not only instrumentally but for their own sake. They are community or global standards that have moral worth even if the company in question fails to achieve them. Leeper's preoccupation with women's health will survive even if the FHC fails because women's health is an intrinsic value. ShoreBank's commitment to community development has become an internationally recognized social value, even for those who have failed at this. Education is always valued, whether or not Crozier's company will succeed in improving it. An ethical leader, under this rubric, not only embodies her personal, professional, and organizational values but expects the same from her employees and managers, shareholders, and the organization. Finally, an ethical leader continually tests these values against societal norms, organizational consistency, and outcomes.[35]

Whether she is consciously aware of it or not, DeHaas clearly models her core values in the workplace and by doing so strengthens the organizational culture at Deloitte. Indeed, this leader's actions are consistent with her values. As DeHaas says, "That is the most important thing I can do—constant, fair, respectful treatment of everybody, whatever [their] title." Her personal values include the need for alignment in her working goals. In any long-term career, there ultimately must be a long-term relationship with the organization that promotes that thinking. Her core values include integrity, quality of client service, quality of people, and a strong commitment to everyone—her clients, staff, family, and community.

Case relied heavily on her personal values and embedded them in her leadership at FRB. She fully supported meritocracy and firmly opposed entitlement; both of these are positions that take constant vigilance to enforce in an organization. She was raised to believe that you earn respect and promotion and are accountable for your destiny.

Maddox's work is diverse, yet it all shares her cardinal rule that "good design addresses problems, promotes business in an ethical climate, creates productive work environments, and is not mere decoration yet is aesthetically believable." Zarcone expressed it this way:

> I believe that it's very important to have high personal integrity. People need to know that what you say is what you believe. I'm also a big believer in fairness and equity to do the right thing. If you do the right thing, it will feel right, people will see it, you'll be able to explain it, and people will follow you because they believe in you. . . . People see that, and they admire that and . . . want to follow it, so that's an important thing for me. You also need to make sure you get your priorities right and value them. I'm married with children, and that's the number one priority in my life, so it's trying to balance that, and balance is hard. But keep your priorities straight, and don't lose sight of what's really important.

Calhoun describes the challenges of this sort of leadership from an organizational perspective.

> The ideal organization respects and listens to its employees, appreciates people's life beyond work and makes that possible, but it also has to be financially sound enough to provide a stable ongoing opportunity for its employees to grow and make money. I think it's a tricky balance; you've got to make money. All that hard work isn't what everything is about, and you have to balance it.

Linking Calhoun's statement to ethical leadership,

> An ethical leader realizes that there is no one set of leadership principles that work in all situations or in all organizations. A leader sees values and ethical principles as being applicable within certain spheres. She challenges herself and her organization to continually step back and rethink the values proposition they embody and operate under. That is, an ethical leader uses moral imagination to make difficult decisions that cross the boundaries of those spheres and frontiers of knowledge.[36]

We argue that all the leaders we studied exemplified that kind of leadership.

Finally, most of the leaders we studied in this small sample seem to care more about the sustained success of their organization than their own legacy. Jim Collins sees that as a trait of what he called level five leadership, where the future of the organization preempts personal glory. Such leaders realize that the best organization is one that can be great without them.[37] "A leader always takes the risk of helping somebody along who is potentially going to supplant [her]. But that is what it is all about. You cannot lead forever, you cannot live forever" (Donni Case).

NOTES

1. Evelyn Murphy and E. J. Graff, "The Wage Gap—Why Women Are Still Paid Less than Men," *Boston Globe*, October 9, 2005, p. C12.

2. "Facts on Women Candidates and Elected Officials," online document available at www.cawp.rutgers.edu/Facts/Officeholders/cawpfs.html (2005).

3. Judith Rosener, "Ways Women Lead." *Harvard Business Review* (November–December 1990).

4. Richard A. Couto, "The Transformation of Transforming Leadership," in J. Thomas Wren, ed., *Leader's Companion* (New York: Free Press, 1994), pp. 102–7.

5. Howard Gardner with Emma Laskin, *Leading Minds* (New York: Basic Books, 1996), chapter 3.

6. Warren G. Bennis and Robert J. Thomas, *Geeks and Geezers* (Boston, MA: Harvard Business School Press, 2002), p. 19.

7. R. E. Freeman, Kirsten Martin, Bidnan Parmar, Margaret P. Cording, and Patricia H. Werhane, "Leading through Values and Ethical Principles," in R. Burke and Cary Cooper, eds., *Inspired Leaders* (London: Routledge Taylor and Francis Group, 2006).

8. Gardner and Laskin, *Leading Minds*, p. 29.

9. Peter Northouse, ed., *Leadership Theory and Practice*, 3rd ed. (Thousand Oaks, CA: Sage, 2004), chapter 6.

10. Ibid., chapter 5.

11. J. M. Kouzes and B. Z. Posner, *The Five Practices of Exemplar Leadership* (San Francisco: Pfeiffer, 2003), p. 8.

12. R. K. Greenleaf, *Servant Leadership: A Journey into the Nature of Legitimate Power and Greatness* (New York: Paulist Press, 1977).

13. G. G. Dess and J. C. Picken, "Changing Roles: Leadership in the 21st Century," *Organizational Dynamics* (Winter 2000): 18–33.

14. Greenleaf, *Servant Leadership*, 1977.

15. Julie Indvik, "Women and Leadership," in Peter Northouse, ed., *Leadership Theory and Practice*, 3rd ed. (Thousand Oaks, CA: Sage, 2004), p. 280.

16. A. Morrison, *The New Leaders* (San Francisco: Jossey-Bass, 1992), quoted in Indvik, "Women and Leadership."

17. Reported by Andrea Hanis in "Morrison's Journey to 'Love'" [Review of a Toni Morrison Book], *Chicago Sun-Times*, November 7, 2003, p. 51.

18. E. Schein, *Organizational Culture and Leadership* (San Francisco: Jossey-Bass, 1985).

19. James MacGregor Burns, *Leadership* (New York: HarperCollins, 1982), pp. 19–20.

20. Bernard M. Bass, *Leadership and Performance beyond Expectations* (New York: Free Press, 1985). See also Richard A. Couto, "The Transformation of Transforming Leadership," in J. Thomas Wren, ed., *Leader's Companion* (New York: Free Press, 1995), pp. 102–7.

21. Rosener, "Ways Women Lead."

22. J. R. Hackman and R. E. Walton, "Leading Groups in Organizations," in P. S. Goodman and Associates, eds., *Designing Effective Work Groups* (San Francisco: Jossey-Bass, 1986), pp. 72–119; C. E. Larson and F. M. J. LaFasto, *Teamwork: What Must Go Right/What Can Go Wrong* (Newbury Park, CA: Sage, 1989), summarized in Northouse, *Leadership Theory and Practice*, p. 211.

23. Center for Women's Business Research, *Privately Held, 50 Percent or More Women-Owned Businesses in the United States, 2004: A Fact Sheet* (Washington, DC: NFWBO, 2004).

24. Center for Women's Business Research, *Top Facts about Women-Owned Businesses* (Washington, DC: Center for Women's Business Research, 2003).

25. S. Robinson, "An Examination of Entrepreneurial Motives and Their Influence on the Way Rural Women Small Business Owners Manage Their Employees," *Journal of Developmental Entrepreneurship* 6(2) (2001): 151–67.

26. S. A. Alvarez and G. D. Meyer, "Why Do Women Become Entrepreneurs?" In *Frontiers of Entrepreneurship Research* (Wellesley, MA: Babson College, 1998).

27. R. Boden, "Gender and Self-Employment Selection. An Empirical Assessment," *Journal of Socio-Economics* 25(6) (1996): 671–82.

28. L. K. Gundry and M. Ben-Yoseph, "Women Entrepreneurs in the New Millennium: Recent Progress and Future Directions for Research, Entrepreneurship Development and Teaching," In H. Welsch, ed., *Entrepreneurship: The Way Ahead* (New York: Routledge, 2003).

29. V. Gupta, I. C. MacMillan, and G. Surie, "Entrepreneurial Leadership: Developing and Measuring a Cross-Cultural Construct." *Journal of Business Venturing* 19 (2004): 241–60.

30. Ibid.

31. R. G. McGrath and I. C. MacMillan, *The Entrepreneurial Mindset* (Boston, MA: Harvard Business School Press, 2000); S. Venkataraman and A. H. Van de Ven, "Hostile Environmental Jolts, Transaction Sets and New Business Development," *Journal of Business Venturing* 13(3) (1998): 231–55.

32. Gupta et al., "Entrepreneurial Leadership."

33. Mimi Swartz and Sherron Watkins, *Power Failure: The Inside Story of the Collapse of Enron* (New York: Doubleday, 2003).

34. Susan Pulliam and Deborah Solomon, "How 3 Unlikely Sleuths Uncooked WorldCom's Books; Company's Own Auditors Sniffed Out Cryptic Clues, Followed Their Hunches," *Wall Street Journal Europe*, October 31, 2002, p. A8; and from personal interviews with Cynthia Cooper in 2005.

35. Freeman et al., "Leading through Values."

36. Quoted from Freeman et al., "Leading through Values."

37. James Collins, "Level 5 Leadership: The Triumph of Humility and Fierce Resolve," *Harvard Business Review* 79(1) (2001): 67–76.

2

Toward an Inclusive Framework for Envisioning Race, Gender, and Leadership

Patricia S. Parker

This chapter calls into question two predominant visions of leadership in the organizational studies literature. One model is based on the notion of masculine instrumentality—aggressive, rugged individualism—and the other is based on the notion of feminine collaboration—nurturing, relationship-oriented behavior. Although these models were formulated almost exclusively from studies of middle-class white women and men in Western societies, they are presented as race-neutral and generalized to all people (Parker & Ogilvie, 1996). The experiences and values of women and men of different races and ethnicities are excluded from these models, as are their potential contributions to the production of leadership knowledge.

I propose an inclusive meaning-centered framework for envisioning race, gender, and leadership that would reclaim the leadership voices that are suppressed by the dichotomous and essentializing notions of "masculine" and "feminine" leadership. Meaning-centered approaches reflect a critical interpretive view of reality and provide the potential for a multifaceted feminist framework that advances new approaches to leadership and new sources of leadership knowledge in the postindustrial era of rapid change, globalization, and diversity. In the first part of the chapter I critique traditional leadership models and advocate for alternative approaches that are more meaning-centered, inclusive, and better suited to the postindustrial age. In the second part, I present an overview of the leadership approach derived from case studies of African American women executives, one group whose traditions of leadership have been suppressed.

An inclusive framework for envisioning race, gender, and leadership necessarily employs intersectionality as a guiding principle for analysis. Intersectionality is "an analysis claiming that systems of race, economic class, gender, sexuality, ethnicity, nation, and age form mutually constructing features of social organization" (Collins, 1998a, p. 278). In this chapter, I focus on gender and race as two influential systems that form mutually constructing features of organizational leadership. Empirical and theoretical work in organizational studies has focused almost exclusively on gendered patterns of organizing (cf. Calas & Smircich,1996). Acker's (1990) theory of gendered organization is one of the most comprehensive models (cf. Kanter, 1977; Marshall, 1993). Acker's framework draws attention to the everyday social processes in which "advantage and disadvantage, exploitation and control, action and emotion, meaning and identity" (p. 167) are patterned through and in terms of gender. The sole focus on gender, however, masks the fundamental influences of race and other systems of domination in women's work experiences (Amott & Matthaei, 1996; Essed, 1991, 1994; Rowe, 2000; Spelman, 1988). Yoder and Aniakudo (1997) pointed out, following Spelman, that "there is no raceless, classless, generic woman" (p. 325). Thus, the focus should be on the ways multiple systems of domination intersect in everyday interactions.

In this study, I use critical communication and feminist theories to advance an inclusive framework for envisioning race, gender, and leadership. Critical communication perspectives direct attention to organization as intersubjective structures of meaning where identity and power relationships are produced, maintained, and reproduced through the ongoing communicative practices of its members (Deetz, 1992; Mumby, 2001). Connections among power, ideology, and hegemony are central to this view of organizational communication. Power is viewed as a dialectical process of domination (control) and resistance that is manifested in everyday organizational life. Hegemonic control functions not simply as ideological domination of one group by another but as "a dynamic conception of the lived relations of social groups and the various struggles that constantly unfold between and among these groups" (Mumby, 2001, p. 598). This directs attention to the tensions between organization as text (e.g., as discursively produced institutional forms) and organizing as conversation (e.g., how women and men struggle to "do difference").

From a critical communication perspective, gender and race are not neutral elements but can be seen as constitutive of organizing and are primary ways of signifying power in social systems (Acker, 1991; Scott, 1986). Power and control are manifested in the hidden micro-processes and micro-practices that produce and reproduce unequal and persistent sex-, race-, and class-based patterns in work situations, such as recruitment, hiring, placement, promotions, and everyday interaction (Parker, 2003). Feminist theories, particularly poststructuralist approaches, enable the deconstruction of raced and gendered organizational leadership contexts, emphasizing the unstable, complex, and ambiguous nature of social reality (Calas & Smircich, 1996). This directs attention to leadership as a process by which organizational members—leaders and followers—struggle to create meaning within such contexts.

Leadership processes and interaction provide a particularly good case for exploring the tensions and paradoxes of contemporary organization. Executive leadership represents an interaction context in which dominant culture norms and values regarding gender and race take on high symbolic importance (Biggart

& Hamilton, 1984). Organizational members come to expect leaders to look, act, and think in ways consistent with the socially constructed meanings of organizational leader and leadership. Traditionally, those meanings have been in conflict with stereotypical assumptions about African American women (Parker, 2001). Thus, exploring the leadership experiences of African American women serves to make salient how race and gender intersect with key organizational leadership issues and processes in twenty-first-century organizations, and it provides insight into an approach to leadership I theorize is borne out of a struggle to balance the tensions and paradoxes of resisting and conforming to discourses of organizing.

The model of leadership presented here is derived from a field study involving fifteen African American women executives, their subordinates, co-workers, and (in four cases) their immediate supervisors (usually the company CEO or equivalent).

VISIONS OF LEADERSHIP COMMUNICATION IN THE INDUSTRIAL PARADIGM: ODE TO THE GREAT (WHITE) MAN

Our mythology refuses to catch up with our reality. We cling to the myth of the Lone Ranger, the romantic idea that great things are usually accomplished by a larger-than-life individual working alone.

—Bennis & Biederman, 1997, p. 2

In the mainstream literature on leadership theory and research, the predominant vision of leadership is the Great Man—the triumphant individual taking charge and directing from a distance—in the tradition of white, middle-class constructions of rugged individualism (Bennis & Biederman, 1997; Manz & Sims, 1989; Rost, 1991). This view epitomizes the industrial vision of leadership, advancing...two problematic ideas about leadership. The fundamental problem is the view of leadership as good management, for it precludes views of leadership as distinct from management and limits an understanding of communication as constitutive of leadership process. It reinforces dualistic thinking about leadership, with an emphasis on individualistic (versus collective), monologic (versus dialogic) and transmission (versus meaning-centered) perspectives (Fairhurst, 2001). Furthermore, it reproduces a mythology grounded in the industrial paradigm that infuses the second problem, a traditionally masculine understanding of leadership that in turn helps normalize a race-neutral feminine-masculine dualism.

Leadership as "Good Management"

In his comprehensive critique, Rost (1991) emphasized that "leadership-as-good-management" is the twentieth century's paradigm and notes that "this understanding of leadership makes perfect sense in an industrial economy"

(p. 94). It is a vision of leadership embedded in the structural functionalism of Western culture that is "rational, management oriented, male, technocratic, quantitative, goal dominated, cost-benefit driven, personalistic, hierarchical, short term, pragmatic, and materialistic" (p. 94). In this view, the collective body of leadership theory and research in the past century, which purports to distinguish among traits, styles, and contingency approaches, can effectively be summed up as, "Great men and women with certain preferred traits influencing followers to do what the leaders wish in order to achieve group/organizational goals that reflect excellence defined as some kind of higher-level effectiveness" (p. 180). Rost added that expressive characteristics, such as consideration and other aspects of humanism "boil down to a therapeutic, expressive individualism . . . [that] help enculturate women into what is essentially a male model of leadership" (p. 94).

The leadership-as-good-management view sets up two problematic issues that have implications for leadership in the complex and ambiguous context of twenty-first-century organization. First, this view emphasizes the preeminence of the profession of management rather than advancing an understanding of the process of leadership as distinct from management. Management processes can be distinguished from leadership in that the former imply maintaining order through the coordinated actions of people in organizationally established authority relationships, whereas the latter implies intending change through mutually negotiated influence relationships (Jacobs, 1970; Katz & Kahn, 1966/ 1978; Rost, 1991). A focus on leadership as distinct from management is critical in the postindustrial era of rapid change and globalization, where identities and relationships are not fixed but must be negotiated (Fairclough, 1992).

The second problem with the leadership-as-good-management view is that it promotes an individualistic, goal-oriented approach to leadership study. Such a view shifts attention away from an understanding of leadership as a negotiated and emergent process. Fairhurst's (2001) critique of the traditional leadership literature reinforces Rost's (1991) claim of an overly individualistic focus and points to important implications for the study of leadership communication. Fairhurst identified the individual-system dichotomy as central among several dualisms in leadership communication research that highlight the paradoxical nature of leadership theory, research, and practice. She noted, as Rost did, that historically the predominant views of leadership have been influenced by a psychological view of the world where "in a figure-ground arrangement the individual is figure and communication is incidental or, at best, intervening" (Fairhurst, 2001, p. 383). Related secondary dualisms exist in the form of transmission versus meaning-centered views of communication and cognitive outcomes versus conversational practices. The focus on message transmission and cognitive outcomes (e.g., individualistic focus on leadership traits, cognitions, acts, and one-way meaning construction) has dominated the leadership literature (Fairhurst, 2001) and contributes to romanticizing the perceived role of the leader (Meindl, Ehrlich, & Dukerich, 1985).

However, increasingly, scholars are emphasizing a systems orientation that reconceptualizes leadership as an emergent property of group interaction (see Fisher, 1985, 1986), exchanges between leaders and group members (Dansereau, 1995a, 1995b; Jablin, Miller, & Keller, 1999), a dialogue (Isaacs, 1993, 1999), or as distributed among leaders and followers who are empowered to bring about organizational transformation (Conger, 1989; Kouzes & Posner, 1995; Senge, 1990; Senge et al., 1999; Wheatley, 1992). A systems orientation directs attention to meaning-centered views of leadership communication and the relational and conversational practices associated with doing leadership.

Yet rather than simply shifting from an individualistic to a systems orientation, Fairhurst (2001) advocated using "both/and" thinking about key dualisms and paradoxes in leadership research. Either/or thinking usually causes researchers to favor one view over another, and over time, produces dominant versus marginal perspectives, such as the race-neutral bias mentioned earlier, and the individualistic orientation of the leadership communication literature. A both/and approach allows researchers to see the wider systems concerns and individual concerns and to view communication more complexly, as transmission and meaning-centered, and studied as both cognitive outcomes and conversational practices.

Normalizing the Feminine-Masculine Dichotomy: Leadership Communication as Traditionally Masculine

Focusing on leadership as good management ultimately reinforces a masculine model of leadership communication, inasmuch as management processes have been defined in traditionally masculine terms, such as authority, structure, and instrumentality. As conceptualized in the leadership literature, the masculine model emphasizes a hierarchical approach in which leaders initiate structure while demonstrating autonomy, strength, self-efficacy, and control (Bem,1974; Eagly, 1987; Loden, 1985). This model is representative of male values (Marshall, 1993) and is most associated with traditional understandings of men's socialized communication patterns (Tannen, 1990; Wood, 1998). According to this perspective, men use more instrumental communication—unilateral, directive, and aimed at controlling others—that is consistent with their learned view of talk as a way to assert self and achieve status (Eagly & Karau,1991). Distance and detachment are common communication themes associated with male values (Marshall, 1993). Common symbolic representations of the masculine leadership model include such characteristics as aggressiveness, independence, risk taking, rationality, and intelligence (Collins, 1998b; Connell, 1995).

A traditionally masculine model of leadership communication pervades the mainstream leadership literature (Alvesson & Billing, 1997; Buzzanell, Ellingson, Silvio, Pasch, Dale, Mauro, Smith, Weir, & Martin, 2002; Fine & Buzzanell, 2000; Parker, 2001; Rost, 1991). Rost provided one of the most comprehensive critiques of this literature and, among other things, observes that this literature reinforces a male model of life. Fine and Buzzanell reviewed main-stream approaches to leadership that focusing on serving, including adaptive leadership (Heifetz, 1994; Heifetz & Laurie, 1997), transformational leadership (Burns, 1978), and self and superleadership (Sims & Manz, 1996). They concluded that these approaches are essentially " 'manstories' (Gergen,1990; Marshall, 1989) [for] they involve often solitary searches for fulfillment and use service to others as a m1pns of developing followers who can assist in achieving organizational or societal goals" (p. 143).

Even so-called alternative approaches, such as servant leadership (Greenleaf, 1977) and some feminine perspectives, are either primarily male-centered or implicitly reinforce traditional understandings of men's socialized communication patterns and worldview (Fine & Buzzannell, 2001, p. 143). For example, Fine and Buzzanell noted that in describing servant leadership as an alternative to traditional approaches, Greenleaf "universalizes the experience of seeker, maintains organizational structures, and never questions the ways in which gender relations may make servant leadership a very different process for women and for men" (Fine & Buzzanell, p. 143).

Furthermore, some feminist perspectives implicitly reinforce a traditionally masculine view and, some would argue, are being co-opted by masculinist aims (Ashcraft, 2005). Feminist critiques of the structural-functionalism of the industrial paradigm expose an alternative vision of leadership communication aimed at valorizing "feminine" leadership as having a relationship rather than an instrumental orientation (Helgesen, 1990; Lunneborg, 1990; Rosener, 1990). However, even in feminine leadership, instrumental outcomes primarily determine the effectiveness and usefulness of the leadership style (Calas, 1993; Fine & Buzzanell, 2001; Fletcher, 1994). Moreover, some scholars have argued persuasively that contemporary organizations standardize feminization while maintaining a gender-neutral stance (Ashcraft, in press; Fondas,1997; May, 1997).

Notwithstanding the view that feminist leadership approaches implicitly reinforce a masculine view as the ultimate measure of effectiveness, the claims of valorizing feminine leadership as an alternative to masculine leadership explicitly reinforce a feminine-masculine dualism. That is, they portray feminine leadership as being in opposition to masculine leadership. However, these approaches do not acknowledge the diversity among women's (or men's) experiences that shape leadership knowledge, and the possibilities of feminine-masculine duality (e.g., a both/and approach). Though not grounded in the implicit image of the great white man, as is the industrial model, the predominant vision of feminine leadership is implicitly based on an ideal white woman.

(WHITE) FEMININE VISIONS OF LEADERSHIP

Feminist perspectives critique the persistence of male dominance in social arrangements and advocate some form of change to the status quo (Calas &

Smirich, 1996). However, despite the common focus on critique and change, there are a range of feminist approaches—liberal, radical, psychoanalytic, Marxist, socialist, poststructuralist and postmodern, and postcolonial—that vary in their ontology, epistemological positions, and degree of political critique and therefore vary in the type of influence on leadership theory. Feminist visions of change range from "'reforming' organizations; to 'transforming' organizations *and* society; to transforming our prior understandings of what constitutes knowledge/theory/practice" (Calas & Smirich, 1996, p. 219).

Overview of Feminist Approaches

Feminist approaches to leadership communication are part of the voluminous literature on women in management that began to accumulate in the late 1960s and early 1970s when the number of white middle-class women in management (and to a lesser extent women and men of color) began to increase. These approaches range from the liberal feminist views of the 1960s and 1970s that advocated women emulate the masculine language of management to the more recent radical, psychoanalytic, and socialist views that advance alternative feminist leadership approaches (albeit from different epistemological stances), to poststructuralist and postmodern feminisms that deconstruct essentialist views of leadership as feminine and masculine.

Universalizing the "Feminine"

As will be discussed later, when combined in productive ways, feminist perspectives provide promise for informing a more inclusive and sufficiently complex framework for envisioning leadership in twenty-first-century organizations. However, I argue that the prevailing vision of feminist leadership is one that reinforces symbolic images of white, middle-class American women, which in effect silences women of different ethnicities, races, and class statuses. The so-called female advantage approach to leadership emerging from radical and psychoanalytic feminisms argues that a "distinctly feminine" style of leadership makes women better leaders than men (Helgesen, 1990; Lunneborg, 1990; Rosener, 1990). According to this view, feminine leadership is an outcome of girls' and women's sex role socialization that produces passive, nurturing, relationship-oriented leaders. This view is in stark contrast to men's socialized leadership—aggressive, rational, strong, independent leaders (Helgesen, 1990; Loden, 1985; Rosener, 1990). The central argument, however, is that the feminine style, grounded in female values such as relationship building, interdependence, and being other-focused, is better suited than the male hierarchical approach to leading contemporary complex organizing contexts, but it is stifled by current male-dominated structuring that values hierarchy, independence, and self-efficacy processes (Grossman & Chester, 1990; Helgesen, 1990; Lunneborg, 1990).

The view of feminine leadership as distinct from a masculine approach is advanced in organizational studies as well as in the popular literature on leadership—books and articles written by management consultants and organizational development specialists—contributing to its reification in the popular consciousness. Helgesen's (1990) best-selling volume, *The Feminine Advantage*, is exemplary. In it, she described what she called the "feminine principles of management," which are characterized as principles of caring, making intuitive decisions, and viewing leadership from a nonhierarchical perspective. Helgesen argued that whereas male-dominated organizations are almost always hierarchical, women tend to think of organization in terms of a network or web of relationships, with leadership at the center of the web, not at the top of a pyramid.

The female advantage argument provides an important critique of the patriarchal discourses that exclude women's experiences. However, it is problematic because it is presented as a race-neutral, universal representation of all women, based on the socialized experiences of middle-class white women (Parker & Ogilvie, 1996). Most importantly, it fails to acknowledge that notions of feminine and masculine are social, cultural, and historical products, constructed according to racial and sexual ideologies that conscript women's and men's embodied identities (Trethewey, 2000). This oversight is significant for the study of African American women leaders given that socially constructed images of white women historically have been used in the systematic oppression of black women (Morton, 1991). To advance a model of feminine leadership based on white women's gender identity essentially excludes black women's experiences in constructing gender identity and therefore excludes black women's voices in theorizing about leadership.

Thus, in an attempt to raise the voices of women in leadership, the feminine advantage model contributes to the silencing of marginalized groups, including (but not limited to) black women. The feminine advantage model does not critique the controlling images of woman as the enabling helpmate and man as the assertive status seeker. Instead, in many ways, it works to reify patriarchal authority and perpetuate distortions of women and men as "feminine" or "masculine." In leadership theory, these images usually form around the dichotomized notions of men as masculine leaders—aggressive, rational, strong, independent leaders—and women as feminine leaders—passive, nurturing, relationship-oriented leaders (Helgesen, 1990; Loden, 1985; Rosener, 1990).

GENDERED LEADERSHIP COMMUNICATION AND THE PROBLEMS OF RACE-NEUTRAL THEORIZING

Both the feminine advantage model and the leadership-as-good-management model of the industrial paradigm reinforce three problems of race-neutral theorizing—domination, exclusion, and containment. It reinforces Western (white middle and upper class) gendered identities as the ideal, and in upholding that ideal, it at once excludes the experiences of other groups and renders them nonlegitimate or peripheral. For example, because race-neutral descriptions of feminine and masculine leadership are treated as universal gender symbols and are often within dominant culture institutions (Collins, 1998b), African American women's experiences are excluded or distorted, as are the experiences of other women of color, men of color, and non-middle-class white women and men. Patricia Hill Collins (1998b) made this point when she said that:

> Aggressive Black and Hispanic men are seen as dangerous, not powerful, and are often penalized when they exhibit any of the allegedly "masculine" characteristics. Working class and poor White men fare slightly better and are also denied the allegedly "masculine" symbols of leadership, intellectual competence, and human rationality. Women of color and working class and poor White women are also not represented [by universal gender symbolism], for they have never had the luxury of being "ladies." (pp. 217–18)

Warren and Bourque (1991) made a similar point in their critique of approaches to "feminizing" technology and strategies for intervention in developing countries. As summarized by Calas and Smircich (1996), these researchers warn against a universal "natural woman(ness)" that is a product of the Western ideal of the egalitarian, nonviolent, and nurturing woman:

> This perspective dangerously romanticizes women's values, the family, the separation of "domestic" and "public" spheres, and the nature of Third World societies, the negotiation of gender identities as they are realized in practice, and the interplay of family dynamics and legal systems to challenge these images of male and female. (Warren & Borque, 1991, p. 287, quoted in Calas & Smircich, 1996, p. 241)

The silencing of some groups of women and men while privileging others in the study of organizational leadership is a product of the theoretical perspectives that frame our understanding of gender, discourse, and organization.

The leadership-as-good management view that has dominated the study of leadership communication is too limited for envisioning leadership in the postindustrial era, for it places an emphasis on goals and outcomes, which assumes we can objectively characterize persons (e.g., as masculine and feminine) and situations (as functionally ordered) to achieve those goals and outcomes (Cheney, Christensen, Zorn, & Ganesh, 2004). Although this view may have been effective for doing leadership in the industrial economy, it is too limiting for the rapid change and ambiguity of the postindustrial global economy (Rost, 1991). More fundamentally, it is not well suited for the multicultural, racialized, often contradictory viewpoints and paradoxical situational challenges of twenty-first-century organization (Parker, 2001).

Here, I use the critical feminist framework to advance a meaning-centered view of leadership communication that would theoretically accommodate the complexity of postindustrial organization. I begin with a discussion of communication and postindustrial organizational cultures, as characterized by fragmentation, ambiguity, and difference; highlighting the centrality of race and gender in everyday organizing; and emphasizing the usefulness of critical feminist perspectives for conceptualizing leadership communication. Next is a meaning-centered definition of leadership that emphasizes a localized, negotiated process of mutual influence and change that occurs in dynamic tension with larger cultural texts.

COMMUNICATION AND POSTINDUSTRIAL ORGANIZATION: CONFRONTING ISSUES OF FRAGMENTATION, AMBIGUITY, AND DIFFERENCE

A common way of envisioning contemporary, postindustrial societies is that in which identities and relationships are not fixed but must be negotiated (Fairclough, 1992). This condition emerges in part from globalization in a market economy that is increasingly diverse and multicultural (Cheney et al., 2004). People of both sexes and of different gender identities, ethnicities, races, classes, sexual orientations, and so on are interacting in ways that help them find meaning and connection in a social world that is increasingly fragmented and disconnected (Giddens, 1991). This view directs attention to postindustrial organizations as fragmented cultures. Cheney and colleagues (2004) define culture as "a system of meaning that guides the construction of reality in a social community" (p. 76). In organizations, cultural meaning systems are constituted in the members' assumptions (e.g., core beliefs), values, (e.g., expressed in behavioral norms), and physical and performative artifacts (e.g., dress and logos, rituals, ceremonies, traditions, and stories [Schein, 1992]).

The fragmentation perspective characterizes organizational cultures as diverse (not unitary or integrated) meaning systems suffused with ambiguity, where consensus and dissensus (e.g., the degree that reality makes sense) are issue-specific and constantly fluctuating (Martin, 1992). Communication takes on a particular negotiated character in a fragmented and ambiguous social world in which identities and relationships are not fixed. Fairclough (1995) identified several characteristics of communication in postindustrial societies that underscore the negotiated character of communication in this context. Some of these include an increased demand for highly developed dialogical capacities; social interaction that is more conversational, informal, and democratic; an increase in self-promotional discourse; and more technologically based communication.

A larger cultural text that reproduces and institutionalizes racism and sexism poses particular challenges for developing and facilitating dialogic, conversational, self-promotional, and technologically based communication capacities. Following Essed (1991), I argue that the fundamental social relations of postindustrial society are racialized relations. This suggests that identities, including gendered identities, are negotiated as part of a larger cultural text that reproduces race relations. Essed used the term *subtle gendered racism* to characterize certain types of subtle discrimination that target African American women, and her theory of everyday racism exemplifies this. Using cross-cultural empirical data, Essed (1991) developed a theory of everyday racism, which she defined as

> a process in which (a) socialized racist notions are integrated into meanings that make practices immediately definable and manageable, (b) practices with racist implications become in themselves familiar and repetitive, and (c) underlying racial and ethnic relations are actualized and reinforced through these routine or familiar practices in everyday situations. (p. 52)

Similarly, critical race theorists point out that racism is "normal, not aberrant, in American society" (Delgado, 1995, p. xiv), and "because it is so enmeshed in the fabric of the U.S. social order, it appears both normal and natural to people in this society" (Ladson-Billings, 2000, p. 264).

In the study of organizational communication, this calls for a shift away from race-neutral understandings of organization and the myopic focus on gender as distinct from a larger cultural text of race relations. Specifically, there should be a move toward reconceptualizing race not as a simple property of individuals but as an integral dynamic of organizations (Nkomo, 1992). As Nkomo aptly noted, this implies a move toward phenomenological and historical research methods that would contribute toward building theories and knowledge about how race is produced and how it is a core feature of organizations. Relevant to the present study, if organizations were viewed as fundamentally raced, then organizational leadership would have to take into account how race relations fundamentally impact everyday interactions within organizations.

Ashcraft and Allen (2003) advocated foregrounding race as central to organizational life. Through their analysis of the racial subtext of organizational communication texts, they demonstrated how the process of reinforcing a particular way of viewing racial relations occurs through theory development in organizational communication, which informs organizational communication practice. They revealed five disciplined messages that "function to sustain raced organization, for they support and obscure the tacit Whiteness of much organizational communication theory" (Ashcraft & Allen, 2003, p. 28).

Conceptualizing postindustrial communication contexts as multicultural and fundamentally raced reinforces the importance of a both/and approach to understanding leadership in terms of individual and systems phenomena. From a critical feminist perspective, leadership can be understood as a socially constructed process of negotiating difference, taking into account the inter-locking oppressions of race, gender, and class that structure organizational life. Grounded in this perspective, I advance a meaning-centered leadership approach that takes into account tensions emerging from the individual-systems dualism and that shifts the focus to leadership as a process of change and emancipation.

FOREGROUNDING MEANING-CENTERED APPROACHES TO LEADERSHIP

Meaning-centered approaches reveal leadership as an ongoing process of social construction (Bensen, 1977; Berger & Luckmann, 1966). These approaches reflect a critical interpretive view of reality, wherein "the individual takes an active, constructive role in creating knowledge through language and communication" (Fairhurst, 2001, p. 385). Grounded in the symbolic inter-action perspective (Blumer, 1969; Mead, 1934), meaning-centered approaches reveal leadership as a symbolic, interactive process through which meaning is created, sustained, and changed (Avolio & Bass, 2002; Deetz, 2000; Fairhurst & Sarr, 1996; Parker, 2001; Rost 1991; Smircich & Morgan, 1982). Cheney et al. (2004) favored a socially constructed view of leaders and leadership situations "as being open to multiple meanings, readings, or interpretations" (p. 192).

Much of this research centers on charismatic and visionary leadership. This literature takes a monologic view, focusing on the leader as the creator and manager of symbolic communication (e.g., myths, legends, stories, and rituals) (see Fairhurst, 2001).

Another line of research shifts to a more systems interactive view. A number of theorists in this line advocate studying alternative approaches to leadership and organizing (Ashcraft, 2000, 2001; Buzzanell et al., 1994; Putnam & Kolb, 2000). For example, Buzzanell and her colleagues summarized this literature in terms of three alternative rationales for organizing. First are contrabureaucratic structures that resist organization that promotes "the employer viewpoint," such as universalism. Second are contrainstrumental relationship approaches that resist the devaluation of noninstrumental and non–goal-oriented activities. Third are value-rational or ideologically focused organization approaches that resist societal values that privilege individual, corporate, and competitive ethics. These approaches are exemplary in illuminating the processes that constrain the development of participatory practices in leadership. However, they do so by emphasizing the either/or thinking in leadership theory that often suppresses other important elements in the process (Fairhurst, 2001).

This chapter adds to the literature advocating alternative leadership approaches. However, in concert with other communication scholars and orga-nizational development theorists (Baxter & Montgomery, 1996; Stohl & Cheney, 2001; Fairhurst, 2001; Senge, 1990), I advocate shifting attention toward more dialogic both/and views of leadership and organizing. This shifts the focus toward understanding the mutual influence of both structure and process. It captures more completely the relationship of leaders and followers in a flow of contested and negotiated meaning production. More specifically, I advance a meaning-centered leadership approach as seen through a critical feminist lens of emancipation and change.

DEFENDING LEADERSHIP IN THE POSTINDUSTRIAL ERA

I combine two meaning-centered views that capture the process of leadership and change and that are exemplified in the approach to leadership derived from my study of African American women executives. First is the view that focuses on leadership as the management of meaning. Second is the view that focuses on leadership as socially critical and focused on emancipation and change.

Smircich and Morgan (1982) advanced a view of leadership as the management of meaning. They defined leadership as "the process whereby one or more individuals succeeds in attempting to frame and define the reality of others" (p. 258). Standing alone, this definition, not surprisingly, leads some to conclude that Smircich and Morgan advocated a monologic view of leadership (see Fairhurst, 2001). However, when viewed within their larger theoretical framework, it is clear that Smircich and Morgan intended a more dialogic, coconstruction focus. Fundamental to their definition is an understanding of leadership as a process of social construction:

> Leadership, like other social phenomena, is socially constructed through interaction (Berger & Luckmann, 1966), emerging as a result of the constructions and actions of both leaders and led. It involves a complicity or process of negotiation through which certain individuals, implicitly or explicitly, surrender their power to define the nature of their experience to others. (Smircich & Morgan, 1982, p. 258)

They further emphasized this negotiated and coconstructed view when they stated "the phenomenon of leadership in being interactive is by nature dialectical. It is shaped through the interaction of at least two points of reference, i.e., of leaders and of led" (pp. 258–59). They added to this view of leadership as coconstruction in noting the power-based construction of organizational leadership. They asserted, "Although leaders draw their power from their [hierarchically legitimated] ability to define the reality of others, their inability to control completely provides the seeds of disorganization in the organization of meaning" (Smircich & Morgan, 1982, p. 259). Thus, from a monologic view, people in formal organizational leadership positions may have the opportunity to attempt to define and manage the reality of others. Yet a dialogic frame directs attention to the ability and willingness of leaders and followers to recognize the contested context within which that opportunity to manage meaning arises.

Weick's (1978) view of leader as medium is very similar to Smircich's and Morgan's (1982) approach in emphasizing the negotiated nature of leadership. Focusing on the group level of analysis, Weick argued that leadership is a process of mediating between the group's organizing process (how things should be done) and their informational environment (the varied plausible interpretations of how things should be done, emanating from inside and outside the group). Morgan (1986) also acknowledged the negotiated character of leadership when he argued that leaders do not have to lead by placing themselves in the forefront of action. Instead, he asserted, leaders can play a background role, shaping the stage of action and the general direction that events will take but leaving choice about the details to those responsible for their implementation. However, the desire to implement the leader's directives depends on whether others see fit to do so.

These views of leadership as the management of meaning conceptualize leadership as a communication accomplishment (Fairhurst, 2001; Garfinkel, 1967). Smircich and Morgan's (1983) definition is especially effective at emphasizing the individual-systems tensions that must be negotiated in everyday leadership situations, for they highlighted the unequal relationship that exists (either explicitly or implicitly) in the leader–follower relationship. However, their definition does not address the notion of change and emancipation.

A critical feminist lens captures the elements of intended social change and emancipation that are crucial in postindustrial views of leadership and are not emphasized in the Smircich and Morgan definition. More fundamentally, a critical feminist meaning-centered approach to leadership shifts the focus away from structural-functionalist, management-oriented, and traditionally masculine views of leadership and toward the process of leadership and how it can facilitate social change. This positions leadership as a socially critical phenomenon, that is "fundamentally addressed to social change and human emancipation, that it is basically a display of social critique, and that its ultimate goal is the achievement and refinement of human community" (Foster, 1989, p. 46–48). This portrays leadership as a localized, negotiated process of mutual influence that would theoretically accommodate the multiple, often contradictory viewpoints and paradoxical situational challenges of twenty-first-century organizations (Parker, 2001).

The notion of transformational leadership (Bass, 1985; Bennis & Nanus, 1985; Burns, 1978; Tichy & Devanna, 1986; Rost, 1991) provides a basis for linking the ideas of leadership as the management of meaning and leadership as a process of social change and emancipation. The notion of transformational leadership was first articulated by Burns (1978) as a process of evolving interrelationships in which leaders influence followers and are in turn influenced to modify their behavior as they meet responsiveness or resistance. According to Burns (1978), transformational leaders seek to raise the consciousness of followers by appealing to higher ideals and moral values, such as liberty, justice, equality, peace, and humanitarianism, not to baser emotions, such as fear, greed, jealousy, or hatred. As Yukl (2002) observed, transformational leadership is viewed as both a micro-level influence process between individuals and as a macro-level process of mobilizing power to change social systems and reform institutions.

Here, I use Rost's (1991) reinterpretation of Burns's (1978) notion of transformational leadership but with a critical eye toward postindustrial assumptions and values that Burns's definition does not address. More importantly, Rost's (1991) definition builds on the strengths of Smircich and Morgan's (1982) definition (e.g., he implicitly acknowledged the creation of meaning through interaction), but he placed a critical emphasis on social change through dialogic interaction: "Leadership is [a multidirectional, noncoercive, but unequal] influence relationship among leaders and followers [in which the followers are active, and there is typically more than one leader in the relationship, and] who intend real changes that reflect their mutual purposes" (Rost, 1991, p. 102).

Rost's definition emphasizes social change and emancipation, as understood from critical/feminist perspectives. He positioned his work as a critique of structural functionalism in leadership studies that has been advanced in feminist scholarship (Buckley & Steffy, 1986; Calas & Smircich, 1988; Kellerman, 1984), and emphasized the development of mutual purposes as a way of working toward emancipation from the oppression of women, ethnic domination, and racial oppression. Mutual purposes, according to Rost, are "common purposes developed over time as leaders and followers interact in a noncoercive relationship about the changes they intend" (p. 151). For leaders and followers steeped in the ambiguous, corporatized, sexualized, and racialized contexts of twenty-first-century organizations, one can envision intended changes emerging from such an arrangement might include progressive activities, such as transformation and emancipation from oppressive and exploitative work processes.

Taken together, Smircich and Morgan (1982) and Rost's (1991) definitions conceptualize leadership in this way: Leadership is an influence relationship among leaders and followers who intend real changes that reflect their mutual purposes; these mutual purposes are negotiated through a process whereby one or more individuals (leaders and followers) succeeds in attempting to frame and define the reality of others.

In summary, this view of leadership emphasizes a localized, negotiated process of mutual influence that would theoretically accommodate the multicultural, racialized, often contradictory viewpoints and paradoxical situational challenges of twenty-first-century organizations (Parker, 2001).

Reenvisioning Instrumentality as Collaboration

This chapter presents an overview of the leadership approach derived from case studies of fifteen African American women executives and their co-workers.

In total, the leadership communication themes revealed in this study challenge the dichotomous notions of instrumentality and collaboration advanced in the gender and leadership literature. This section provides a brief overview of each of the themes and how they inform an approach to leadership that disrupts traditional masculine and feminine models. Later, I discuss the themes in more detail, including the voices of the executives and their co-workers. I show how the women's leadership communication represents a meaning-centered approach that emphasizes both individual and relational (systems) concerns (Fairhurst, 2001).

As mentioned earlier, two competing leadership models are advanced—masculine instrumentality versus feminine collaboration—based almost exclusively on studies of white women and men but presented as racially and culturally neutral (Parker & Ogilvie, 1996). The masculine model of leadership is theorized as representative of *male values*, such as distance and detachment (Marshall, 1993), and men are said to be socialized to use instrumental communication—unilateral, directive, and aimed at controlling others—which is consistent with their learned view of talk as a way to assert self and achieve status (Eagly & Karau, 1991).

The feminine model of leadership is associated with *female values*, such as nurturance and support (Marshall, 1993), thought to be a reflection of traditionally defined white middle-class women's socialized patterns of collaborative communication (Helgesen, 1990; Lunneborg, 1990; Rosener, 1990). Common symbolic representations of this model include characteristics such as nurturance, compassion, sensitivity to others' needs, and caring (Collins, 1998b; Grant, 1988).

Universalizing masculine and feminine models of leadership based on Western (white middle and upper class) gendered identities excludes the experiences of other groups and renders them nonlegitimate or peripheral in the production of knowledge. More generally, these competing models unnecessarily reinforce dualistic thinking about leadership, obscuring the meanings, tensions, and paradoxes of leadership as it is realized in practice (Fairhurst, 2001). The findings of this study challenge these trends by deconstructing and presenting a revision of traditional notions of instrumentality and collaboration.

OVERVIEW OF AFRICAN AMERICAN WOMEN EXECUTIVES' LEADERSHIP APPROACHES

Five themes related to leadership communication were revealed in the interviews and observations of the African American women executives and their co-workers who participated in this study. The themes are (a) interactive communication; (b) empowerment through the challenge to produce results; (c) openness in communication; (d) participative decision making through

TABLE 2.1. African American Women Executive Study Participants

	Executive Title	Industry	Public/Private
1	Vice President, Administrative Services	Insurance	Private
2	Vice President, Marketing	Computer	Private
3	Vice President, Operations	Communications	Private
4	General Manager	Communications	Private
5	Area Manager	Communications	Private
6	Vice President, Marketing	Insurance	Private
7	Area Manager	Communciations	Private
8	Financial Officer	Communications	Private
9	Director	State Government	Public
10	Officer	Federal Government	Public
11	Vice Chair Mayor	Political Party	Public
		City Government	Public
12	Associate Superintendent	Education	Public
13	Director	City Government	Public
14	Officer/Director	Federal Government	Public
		State Government	Public
15	Director	State Government	Public

collaborative debate, autonomy, and information gathering; and (e) leadership through boundary spanning (see Table 2.1).

Interactive Communication

This theme represents the central dimension of the African American women executives' leadership because it forms the basis of their overall approach to communicating leadership. The women's leadership can be characterized as interactive in both a theoretical and relational sense. In the theoretical sense, the women's leadership emphasizes interaction of both individual and systems concerns. They are very much involved in negotiating the space between employees' needs and values and organizational needs and values. The women's leadership is also interactive in the relational sense. That is, all the executives placed a high premium on oral communication for creating and sustaining relationships. Their leadership is practiced primarily through face-to-face interaction.

However, none of the executives are micromanagers who insist on having tight control over employee activities. Instead, the data revealed an interactive leadership approach reminiscent of the traditions supporting self-definition and self-determination in African American women's history. Three themes elaborate the interactive approach as facilitating both personal and organizational growth and learning: (1) knowing the business, its mission, and its goals and being able to communicate that knowledge clearly, directly, and consistently; (2) being accessible to staff and customers; and (3) modeling effective behavior. The women and their co-workers presented an image of the executives as a kind of conduit through which organizational members could determine courses of action, hash out concerns, identify their own successes, and help bring about needed changes.

Empowerment of Employees through the Challenge to Produce Results

From the perspective of these executives, a key tool for motivating employees is expecting high performance, based on the executive's confidence in the person's ability to deliver and then setting specific goals for producing high-quality results. This approach informs a strategy for empowerment that is simultaneously directive (e.g., transmission-centered) and nondirective (e.g., emergent or meaning-centered). It is directive in the sense that there is a clearly initiated structure; it is nondirective in that the employees are encouraged to exercise a great deal of freedom within the initiated structure and indeed to change the structure if they see fit. Employee descriptions of this approach as a form of empowerment provide persuasive evidence of its value.

Openness in Communication

The third leadership theme emerged from descriptions of the executives as direct communicators. *Directness* is a label that is often associated with African American women's communication (McGoldrick, Garcia-Preto, Hines, & Lee, 1988). In the larger historical cultural context that devalues African American women, having a direct communication style is seen as negative, reflecting stereotypes of the black matriarch or Sapphire. Contemporary studies show that whites' generalized perceptions of African American women's communication style are negative (Kochman, 1981; Weitz & Gordon, 1993). However, as revealed in this study, perceptions of African American women's communication in actual interaction reveal a more positive view of directness. From the standpoint of the women and their co-workers, directness as a form of leadership communication style was interpreted positively. Here, directness means (a) bringing important issues into the open, (b) making sure voices (including their own) that need to be heard on a certain issue get that opportunity, and (c) having no hidden agendas. The data revealed that this directness through openness is accomplished not only at the interpersonal level but also at the group and organizational levels.

Participative Decision Making through Collaborative Debate, Autonomy, and Information Gathering

The fourth theme emphasizes employee empowerment and community building through participative decision-making practices. The data revealed that all the executives used some form of participative decision making. Similar to the emphases on building community in historical traditions of African American women's leadership, the women used personal involvement and attention as a medium for initiating structure, identifying places of struggle or conflicting viewpoints, and encouraging autonomy and self-definition. Specifically, the women used a combination of three tactics to facilitate participative decision making: collaborative debate, autonomy, and information gathering. The term *collaborative debate* is used to refer to the process of dialectic inquiry in which employees who are likely to disagree with prevailing opinions are invited to give input via one-to-one argument and explicit agreement and refutation (Kennedy, 1980) for the purpose of collaboratively reaching decisions. This might involve bringing together diverse or conflicting groups or simply pulling together the groups necessary to move forward on a project that had been stifled by indecision and disagreement.

Decision autonomy is another decision participation tactic revealed in the data. Employee accounts showed evidence that the executives encouraged departments to be autonomous in making decisions, for example, "bringing the executive in the loop," as one employee phrased it, "only when they needed to."

The third tactic for inviting participation is information gathering, with emphasis placed on assembling experiences and knowledge dispersed throughout the organizational unit. The women saw themselves as a conduit through which the diversity of viewpoints could be brought together, negotiated, and enacted, and their employees confirmed this viewpoint.

Leadership through Boundary Spanning

The women's leadership communication revealed a reenvisioning of fixed organizational boundaries as permeable and fluid enactments of conversation and community building. According to the executives' supervisors interviewed, women were effective in articulating the organization's mission and purpose and connecting the organization to the community in positive ways. These connections reveal an approach to leadership, reminiscent of the kind of community building in African American women's history, where it is possible to redefine a community based on a pressing need.

DECONSTRUCTING "TRADITIONAL" NOTIONS OF INSTRUMENTALITY AND COLLABORATION

Taken together, these themes challenge traditional notions of instrumental leadership as *directive and controlling* and collaborative leadership as *nurturing and caring*. This study revealed an approach to leadership where collaboration is worked out at the intersections of control and empowerment. *Control* is (re)defined as interactive and personal, rather than competitive and distant, and becomes a means for empowerment. The leader's focus is on the other, not as a means of affirming the other person per se—although that may be a likely outcome—but as a way of assessing points of view and levels of (others' as well as their own) readiness to perform.

Redefining Instrumentality

Instrumentality as a leadership strategy is often characterized as direct—unilateral, competitive, and aimed at controlling others—consistent with traditional views of white, middle-class masculine communication patterns (Eagly, 1987; Itosener, 1990). In this study, African American women executives' communication is described as direct, but the interpretations are positive and proactive. Grounded in the experiences of the executives and the people with whom they interact, the notion of directness is (re)defined as a type of openness in communication designed to invite dialogue and personal growth.

This view reconceptualizes instrumentality as both direct and relational (Fairhurst, 2001). It is direct, in terms of the strategic framing and transmission of messages (Fairhurst & Saar, 1996), and relational in terms of the emphasis on dialogue and meaning construction. This view broadens the concept of instrumentality to include processes associated with transformational leadership—charisma, inspiration, providing intellectual stimulation, and showing individualized consideration (Avolio & Bass, 1988; Bass, 1985). Additionally, with the dual emphasis on strategic message transmission and dialogue, this expanded view of instrumentality casts both leaders and followers as active agents in the creation of organizational meaning.

Redefining Collaboration

In this study, collaboration is revealed as a negotiated and dynamic process that combines redefined elements of instrumentality, control, and empowerment. As a leadership strategy, this view of collaboration emphasizes the paradoxical practice of direct engagement (i.e., constraint/structure) that creates routes for individual empowerment and community building (i.e., creativity/process). It contradicts the either/or thinking of traditional notions of collaboration and instrumentality and more accurately captures the both/and nature of organizational leadership (Fairhurst, 2000; Marshall, 1993). African American women executives' interactive approach to leadership provides a way for leaders in an increasingly diverse workplace to serve as conduits through which a diversity of viewpoints can be brought together, negotiated, and enacted.

Disrupting Traditional Views of "Feminine" and "Masculine" Leadership

This view challenges the symbolic images of women as master collaborators who shun attempts to control others (Helgesen, 1990; Loden, 1985). Rather than viewing collaboration as an alternative to control, where control is defined in terms of traditionally masculine values such as distance, detachment, and inviting competition (Marshall, 1993), *directness* and *control* are a means for collaboration. *Control* is redefined as personal and interactive. The focus is on the other, as a way of assessing points of view and levels of readiness to perform.

The (re)conceptualized notions of collaboration and instrumentality reported here counter the hegemonic discourses that have suppressed black women's ideas and expands traditional views of organizational leadership. By placing black women at the center of analysis, we can begin to see the both/and quality of black women's voices (Collins, 1990). Behavior deemed as controlling, conflictual, or acquiescent through a larger cultural text that devalues African American women is understood here as the capacity for these women to see the infinite possibilities of individual characteristics through a lens of constructing a solution. Emerging from a social location at the intersection of race, gender, and class oppression within dominant culture society, African American women's voices are simultaneously confrontational (in response to different interests) and collaborative (in response to shared interests, Collins, 1998a). The result is a process of leadership that produces what Collins called "contextualized truth." Based on Mae Henderson's (1989) metaphor of speaking in tongues, "contextualized truth emerges through the interaction of logic, creativity, and accessibility" (Collins, 1998a, p. 239). Implicit in the process of producing contextualized truth is the willingness and ability to construe knowledge and values from multiple perspectives without loss of commitment to one's own values (Bruner, 1990, p. 30).

CONCLUSION

One of the greatest challenges in postindustrial organizing is creating communicative environments in which people find meaning and connection in a social world that is increasingly fragmented and disconnected. In the study reported here, I used a critical feminist perspective to examine African American women executives' leadership communication within majority white male-dominated organizations in the United States. By placing African American women at the center of analysis, this research challenged the hegemonic discourses that limit African American women's access to the meaning-making process in leadership theory. As a result, this study revealed new ways of thinking about instrumental and collaborative leadership.

In the twenty-first century, leadership theorizing should reflect the interplay and struggle of the multiple discourses that characterize postindustrial society. An important role of leadership is certainly to animate (i.e., bring to the foreground) and then facilitate the negotiation of this interplay. In the present study, this process is revealed in an interactive approach to leadership in which the executives see themselves as a conduit through which a diversity of viewpoints could be brought together, negotiated, and enacted. We should continue to explicate theories of leadership that acknowledge the facilitation of multi-vocality as a central process.

The themes that summarize African American women's traditions of leadership as an exemplar of best leadership practices are not intended as a final vocabulary on African American women's approaches to leadership and organizing. Rather, they are put forth as a beginning—a positioning of cultural experience into the center of the study of organizational leadership. For too long, African American women's strength as leaders has gone unacknowledged, devalued, and otherwise marginalized. My hope is that future studies of African American women leaders will broaden and enrich the leadership themes presented here.

NOTE

Adapted and used with permission of Lawrence Erlbaum Associates, Inc. from Patricia S. Parker, *Race, Gender, and Leadership: Re-Envisioning Organizational Leadership from the Perspectives of African American Women Executives* (Mahwah, NJ: Lawrence Erlbaum Associates, 2004). © 2004 by Lawrence Erlbaum Associates, Inc.

REFERENCES

Acker, J. (1991). Hierarchies, jobs, bodies: A theory of gendered organizations. In J. Lorber & S. A. Farrell (Eds.), *The social construction of gender* (pp. 162–179). Newbury Park, CA: Sage.

Allen, B. J. (1995). "Diversity" and organizational communication. *Journal of Applied Communication Research, 23,* 143–155.

Allen, B. J. (1996). Feminist standpoint theory: A black woman's (re)view of organizational socialization. *Communication Studies, 47* (Winter), 257–271.

Allen, B. J. (1998). Black womanhood and feminist standpoints. *Management Communication Quarterly, 11*(4), 575–586.

Allen, B. J. (2000). "Learning the ropes": A black feminist standpoint analysis. In P. M. Buzzanell (Ed.), *Rethinking organizational and managerial communication from feminist perspectives.* Thousand Oaks, CA: Sage.

Allen, B. J. (2004). *Difference matters: Communicating social identity.* Long Grove, IL: Waveland Press.

Alvesson, M., & Billing, Y. D. (1997). *Understanding gender and organizations.* London: Sage.

Amott, T., & Matthaei, J. (Eds). (1996). *Race, gender, and work: A multicultural economic history of women in the United States* (2nd ed.). Boston: South End Press.

Andersen, H. C. (1968). *Forty-two stories.* (M. R. James, Trans.). London: Faber & Faber.

Andersen, M. L., & Collins, P. H. (1992). *Race, class, and gender: An anthology.* Belmont, CA: Wadsworth Publishing Company.

Aptheker, B. (1982). *Woman's legacy: Essays on race, sex, and class in American history.* Amherst: The University of Massachusetts Press.

Arnold, R. (1994). Black women in prison: The price of resistance. In M. Baca Zinn & B. T. Dill (Eds.), *Women of color in U.S. society* (pp. 171–184). Philadelphia: Temple University Press.

Ashcraft, K. (2000). Empowering "professional" relationships: Organizational communication meets feminist practice. *Management Communication Quarterly, 13,* 347–392.

Ashcraft, K. (2001). Organized dissonance: Feminist bureaucracy as hybrid form. *Academy of Management Journal, 44,* 1301–1322.

Ashcraft, K. (2005). Gender, discourse, and organization: Framing a shifting relationship. In D. Grant, C. Hardy, C. Oswick, N. Phillips, & L. Putnam (Eds.), *The Sage handbook of organization discourse.* Thousand Oaks, CA: Sage.

Ashcraft, K., & Allen, B. J. (2003). The racial foundation of organizational communication. *Communication Theory, 31,* 5–38.

Avolio, B., & Bass, B. M. (2002). *Developing potential across a full range of leadership: Cases on transactional and transformational leadership.* Mahwah, NJ: Lawrence Erlbaum Associates.

Barge, J. K. (1994). *Leadership communication: Skills for organizations and groups.* New York: St. Martin's Press.

Bass, B. M. (1985). *Leadership and performance beyond expectations.* New York: Free Press.

Bass, B. M. (1990). *Bass & Stogdill's handbook of leadership: Theory, research, & managerial applications.* New York: Free Press.

Baxter, L. A., & Montgomery, B. M. (1996). *Relating: Dialogue and dialectics.* New York: Guilford.

Bederman, G. (1995). *Manliness & civilization: A cultural history of gender and race in the United States, 1880–1917.* Chicago: University of Chicago Press.

Bell, E. L., & Nkomo, S. (1992). *The glass ceiling vs. the concrete wall: Career perceptions of white and African-American women managers* (working paper no. 3470-92). Massachusetts Institute of Technology.

Bell, E. L., & Nkomo, S. (2001). *Our separate ways: Black and white women and the struggle for professional identity.* Boston: Harvard Business School Press.

Bellow, A. (2003). *In praise of nepotism: A natural history.* New York: Doubleday.

Bem, S. (1974). The measurement of psychological androgyny. *Journal of Consulting and Clinical Psychology, 42,* 155–162.

Bennis, W., & Biederman, P. W. (1997). *Organizing genius: The secrets of creative collaboration.* Reading, MA: Addison-Wesley.

Bennis, W., & Nanus, B. (1985). *The strategies for taking charge.* New York: Harper & Row.

Bennis, W. G., & Thomas, R. T. (2002). *Geeks and geezers: How era, values, and defining moments shape leaders.* Boston: Harvard Business School Press.

Bensen, J. K. (1977). Organizations: A dialectical view. *Administrative Science Quarterly, 22,* 1–20.

Berger, P., & Luckmann, T. (1966). *The social construction of reality.* Garden City, NY: Anchor.

Biggart, N. W., & Hamilton, G. G. (1984). The power of obedience. *Administrative Science Quarterly, 29*(4), 540–549.

Blassingame, J. (Ed.). (1979). *New perspectives on black studies*. Urbana: University of Illinois Press.

Blumer, H. (1969). *Symbolic interactionism: Perspective and method*. Englewood Cliffs, NJ: Prentice Hall.

Browne, I. (1999a). Introduction: Latinas and African American women in the U.S. labor market. In I. Browne (Ed.), *Latinas and African American women at work: Race, gender, and economic inequality* (pp. 1–31). New York: Russell Sage Foundation.

Browne, I. (Ed.). (1999b). *Latinas and African American women at work: Race, gender, and economic inequality*. New York: Russell Sage Foundation.

Bruner, J. (1990). *Acts of meaning*. Cambridge, MA: Harvard University Press.

Buckley, K. W., & Steffy, J. (1986). The invisible side of leadership. In J. A. Adams (Ed.), *Transforming leadership* (pp. 233–243). Alexandria, VA: Miles River Press.

Bullis, C. (1993). At least it's a start. In S. Deetz (Ed.), *Communication Yearbook 16* (pp. 144–154). Newbury Park, CA: Sage.

Bullis, C., & Stout, K. R. (2001). Organizational socialization: A feminist standpoint approach. In P. Buzzanell (Ed.), *Rethinking organizational & managerial communication from feminist perspectives* (pp. 47–75). Thousand Oaks, CA: Sage.

Burgess, N., & Horton, H. D. (1993). African American women and work: A sociohistorical perspective. *Journal of Family History, 18*(1), 53–63.

Burns, J. M. (1978). *Leadership*. New York: Harper and Row.

Buzzanell, P. M. (1994). Gaining a voice: Feminist perspectives in organizational communication. *Management Communication Quarterly, 7*, 339–383.

Buzzanell, P. M. (Ed.). (2000). *Rethinking organizational and managerial communication from feminist perspectives*. Thousand Oaks, CA: Sage.

Buzzanell, P., Ellingson, L., Silvio, C., Pasch, V., Dale, B., Mauro, G., Smith, E., Weir, N., & Martin, C. (2002). Leadership processes in alternative organizations: Invitational and dramaturgical leadership. *Communication Studies, 48*, 285–310.

Calas, M. (1987). *Organization science/fiction: The postmodern in the management disciplines*. Unpublished doctoral dissertation, Amherst: University of Massachusetts.

Calas, M. (1993). Deconstructing charismatic leadership: Re-reading Weber from the darker side. *Leadership Quarterly, 4*, 305–328.

Calas, M. B., & Smircich, L. (1988). Reading leadership as a form of cultural analysis. In J. G. Hunt, B. R. Baliga, H. P. Dachler, & C. A. Schriescheim (Eds.), *Emerging leadership vistas* (pp. 201–226). Lexington, MA: Lexington Books.

Calas, M., & Smircich, L. (1991). Voicing seduction to silence leadership. *Organization Studies, 12*, 567–602.

Calas, M. B., & Smircich, L. (1993, March/April). Dangerous liaisons: The "feminine-in-management" meets "globalization." *Business Horizons*, 71–81.

Calas, M. B., & Smircich, L. (1996). From the "Woman's" point of view: Feminist approaches to organization studies. In S. Clegg, C. Hardy, & W. R. Nord (Eds.), *Handbook of organization studies* (pp. 218–257). London: Sage.

Cavanaugh, J. M. (1997). (In)corporating the Other? Managing the politics of workplace difference. In P. Prasad, A. J. Mills, M. Elmes, & A. Prasad. (Eds.) *Managing the organizational melting pot: Dilemmas of workplace diversity* (pp. 31–53). Thousand Oaks, CA: Sage.

Chambers, V. (2003). *Black women and success: Having it all?* New York: Doubleday.

Cheney, G., Christensen, L., Zorn, T., & Ganesh, S. (2004). *Organizational communication in an age of globalization: Issues, reflections, practices.* Prospect Heights, IL: Waveland Press.

Christian, B. (1976). *Black women novelists: The development of a tradition, 1892–1976.* Westport, CT: Greenwood Press.

Clinton, C. (1982). *The plantation mistress: Woman's world in the Old South.* New York: Pantheon Books.

Collins, P. H. (1986). Learning from the outsider within: The sociological significance of Black feminist thought. *Social Problems, 33*(6), 14–32.

Collins, P. H. (1990). *Black feminist thought: Knowledge, consciousness, and the politics of empowerment.* Boston: Unwin Hyman.

Collins, P. H. (1998a). *Fighting words: Black women and the search for justice.* Minneapolis: University of Minnesota Press.

Collins, P. H. (1998b). Toward a new vision: Race, class, and gender as categories of analysis and connection. In M. L. Anderson, & P. H. Collins (Eds.), *Race, class, and gender: An anthology* (pp. 213–223). Belmont, CA: Wadsworth.

Collins, P. H. (2002). Symposium on West and Fenstermaker's "Doing Difference." In S. Fenstermaker, & C. West (Eds.), *Doing gender, doing difference: Inequality, power, and institutional change* (pp. 8–84). New York: Routledge.

Conger, J. A. (1989). Inspiring others: The language of leadership. *The Executive, 5,* 31–45.

Connell, R. (1995). *Masculinities.* Cambridge: Polity Press.

Cooper, A. J. (1988). *A voice from the South.* Xenia, OH: Aldine Printing House.

Cotton, J. L. (1993). *Employee involvement: Methods for improving performance and work attitudes.* Newbury Park, CA: Sage.

Dansereau, F. (1995a). Leadership: The multiple-level approaches, Part I. *Leadership Quarterly, 6,* 97–247.

Dansereau, F. (1995b). Leadership: The multiple-level approaches, Part 2. *Leadership Quarterly, 6,* 249–450.

Davis, A. Y. (1981). *Women, race, and class.* New York: Random House.

Davis, M. (Ed.) (1982). *Contributions of black women to America* (vol. 1). Columbia, SC: Kenday Press.

Deetz, S. A. (1992). *Democracy in an age of corporate colonization.* Albany, NY: SUNY Press.

Deetz, S. A. (1995). *Transforming communication.* Albany, NY: SUNY Press.

Deetz, S. A. (2003). Corporate governance, communication, and getting social values into the decisional chain. *Management Communication Quarterly, 16,* 606–611.

Deetz, S. A., Tracy, S., & Simpson, J. L. (2000). *Leading organizations through transitions: Communication and cultural change.* Thousand Oaks, CA: Sage.

Dill, B. T. (1979). *Across the barriers of race and class: An exploration of the relationship between work and family among black female domestic servants.* Ph.D. dissertation, New York University.

Dill, B. T. (1983). Race, class, and gender: Prospects for an all-inclusive sisterhood. *Feminist Studies, 9*(1), 131–150.

Dougherty, D., & Krone, K. (2000). Overcoming the dichotomy: Cultivating standpoints in organizations through research. *Women's Studies in Communication, 23*(1), 16–40.

Dugger, K. (1991). Social location and gender role attitudes: A comparison of black and white women. In B. Lorber, & S. Farrell, *The social construction of gender* (pp. 38–55). Newbury Park, CA: Sage.

Dyson, M. E. (2003). *Why I love black women*. New York: Basic Civitas Books.

Eagly, A. H. (1987). *Sex differences in social behavior: A social-role interpretation*. Hillsdale, NJ: Lawrence Erlbaum Associates.

Eagly, A. H., & Karu, S. S. (1991). Gender and the emergence of leaders: A meta-analysis. *Journal of Personality and Social Psychology, 60*, 685–710.

Ely, R. (1991). Gender difference: What difference does it make? *Academy of Management best paper proceedings*, 363–367.

Essed, P. (1991). *Understanding everyday racism*. Newbury Park, CA: Sage.

Essed, P. (1994). Contradictory positions, ambivalent perceptions: A case study of a black woman entrepreneur. In K. Bhavnani, & A. Phoenix (Eds.), *Shifting identities, shifting racisms: A feminism & psychology reader* (pp. 99–118). London: Sage.

Etter-Lewis, G. (1993). *My soul is my own: Oral narratives of African American women in the professions*. New York: Routledge.

Fairclough, N. (1992). *Discourse and social change*. Cambridge, UK: Polity Press.

Fairclough, N. (1995). *Critical discourse analysis: The critical study of language*. London: Longman Publishers.

Fairhurst, G. T. (2001). Dualisms in leadership research. In F. M. Jablin, & L. L. Putnam (Eds.), *The new handbook of organizational communication* (pp. 379–439). Thousand Oaks, CA: Sage.

Fairhurst, G. T., & Saar, R. A. (1996). *The art of framing: Managing the language of leadership*. San Francisco: Jossey-Bass.

Fine, M. (1995). *Building successful multicultural organizations*. Westport, CT: Quorum Books.

Fine, M., & Buzzanell, P. (2000). Walking the high wire: Leadership theorizing, daily acts, and tensions. In P. Buzzanell (Ed.), *Rethinking organizational and managerial communication from feminist perspectives* (pp. 128–156). Thousand Oaks, CA: Sage.

Finet, D. (2001). Sociopolitical environments and issues. In F. M. Jablin, & L. L. Putnam (Eds.), *The new handbook of organizational communication: Advances in theory, research, and methods* (pp. 270–290). Newbury Park, CA: Sage.

Fisher, B. A. (1985). Leadership as medium: Treating complexity in group communication research. *Small Group Behavior, 16*, 167–196.

Fisher, B. A. (1986). Leadership: When does the difference make a difference? In R. Hirokawa, & M. S. Poole (Eds.), *Communication and group decision-making* (pp. 197–215). Beverly Hills, CA: Sage.

Fletcher, J. (1994). Castrating the female advantage: Feminist standpoint research and management science. *Journal of Management Inquiry, 3*, 74–82.

Flores, L. A., & Moon, D. G. (2002). Race traitor. *Western Journal of Communication, 66*, 181–207.

Fondas, N. (1997). Feminization unveiled: Management qualities in contemporary writings. *Academy of Management Review, 22*, 257–282.

Fordham, S. (1993). "Those loud black girls": Black women, silence, and gender, "passing" in the academy. *Anthropology and Education Quarterly, 24*(1), 3–32.

Forman, J. (1985). *The making of black revolutionaries*. Washington, DC: Open Hand.

Foster, W. F. (1989). Toward a critical practice of leadership. In J. Smyth (Ed.), *Critical perspectives on educational leadership* (pp. 39–62). London: Falmer.

Fra-Molinero, B. (1995). The condition of black women in Spain during the renaissance. In K. M. Vaz (Ed.), *Black women in America* (pp. 159–178). Thousand Oaks, CA: Sage.

Garfinkel, H. (1967). *Studies in ethnomethodology*. Englewood Cliffs, NJ: Prentice Hall.

Gergen, M. (1990). Baskets of reed and arrows of steel: Stories of chaos and continuity. In S. Srivastva (Ed.), *Symposium: Executive and organizational continuity*. Cleveland, OH: Case Western Reserve University, Weatherhead School of Management, Department of Organizational Behavior.

Giddens, A. (1991). *Modernity and self-identity: Self and society in the late modern age*. Cambridge: Polity Press.

Giddings, P. (1984). *When and where I enter: The impact of black women on race and sex in America*. New York: William Morrow.

Gilkes, C. T. (1980). Holding back the ocean with a broom: Black women and community work. In L. Rogers-Rose (Ed.), *The black woman* (pp. 217–232). Beverly Hills, CA: Sage.

Gittell, M., Ortega-Bustamante, I., & Steffy, T. (1999). *Women creating social capital and social change: A study of women-led community development organizations*. Howard Samuels State Management and Policy Center, The Graduate School and University Center, CUNY.

Goffman, E. (1976). Gender display. *Studies in the Anthropology of Visual Communication, 3*, 69–77.

Goffman, E. (1977). The arrangement between the sexes. *Theory & Society, 4*, 301–331.

Gonzalez, A., Houston, M., & Chen, V. (Eds.). (1997). *Our voices: Essays in culture, ethnicity, and communication* (2nd ed.). Los Angeles: Roxbury.

Grant, J. (1998). *Ella Baker: Freedom bound*. New York: John Wiley & Sons.

Greenleaf, R. K. (1977). *Servant leadership: A journey into the nature of legitimate power and greatness*. New York: Paulist Press.

Grimes, D. S. (2002). Challenging the status quo? Whiteness in the diversity management literature. *Management Communication Quarterly, 15*(3), 381–409.

Grossman, H., & Chester, N. (1990). *The experience and meaning of work in women's lives*. Hillsdale, NJ: Lawrence Erlbaum Associates.

Guinier, L., & Torres, G. (2002). *The miner's canary: Enlisting race, resisting power, transforming democracy*. Cambridge, MA: Harvard University Press.

Gyant, L. (1990). Contributions of African American women to nonformal education during the Civil Rights Movement, 1955–1966. Unpublished doctoral dissertation, The Pennsylvania State University.

Haraway, D. J. (1997). *Modest witness@second_millenium: Femaleman meets Oncomouse*. New York: Routledge.

Harding, S. (1987). Introduction: Is there a feminist method? In S. Harding (Ed.). *Feminism & methodology*. Milton Keynes: Open University Press.

Harding, S. (1991). *Whose science? Whose knowledge?* Ithaca, NY: Cornell University Press.

Harding, S. (1996). Gendered ways of knowing and the "epistemological crisis" of the West. In N. Goldberger, J. Tarule, B. Clinchy, & M. Belenky (Eds.), *Knowledge, difference, and power: Essays inspired by women's ways of knowing* (pp. 431–454). New York: Basic Books.

Hardwick Humanities in Management Institute (2003). *Hardwick classic leadership cases*. Oneonta, NY: Hartwick College.

Hartsock, N. (1987). The feminist standpoint: Developing the ground for a specifically feminist historical materialism. In S. Harding (Ed.), *Feminism and methodology*. Milton Keynes: Open University Press.

Harley, S. (1997). Speaking up: The politics of black women's labor history. In E. Higginbotham, & M. Romero (Eds.), *Women and work: Exploring race, ethnicity, and class* (pp. 28–51). Thousand Oaks, CA: Sage.

Hecht, M., Ribeau, S., & Roberts, J. K. (1989). An Afro-American perspective on interethnic communication. *Communication Monographs, 56*(4), 385–410.

Heifetz, R. A. (1994). *Leadership without easy answers*. Cambridge, MA: Belknap.

Heifetz, R. A., & Laurie, D. L. (1997). The work of leadership. *Harvard Business Review, 75*(1), 124–134.

Helgesen, S. (1990). *The female advantage: Women's ways of leadership*. New York: Doubleday.

Henderson, M. G. (1989). Speaking in tongues: Dialogics, dialects, and the black woman writer's literary tradition. In C. A. Wall (Ed.), *Changing our own words: Essays on criticism, theory, and writing by black women*. New Brunswick, NJ: Rutgers University Press.

Henri, F. (1975). *Black migration: Movement north, 1900–1920, the road from myth to man*. New York: Anchor Press.

Hine, D. C. (Ed.). (1993). *Black women in America* (Vols. 1–2). Brooklyn, NY: Carlson.

Hine, D. C., & Thompson, K. (1998). *A shining thread of hope: The history of black women in America*. New York: Broadway Books.

Hirschmann, N. J. (1997). Feminist standpoint as postmodern strategy. In S. J. Kenney, & H. Kinsella (Eds.), *Politics and feminist standpoint theories* (pp. 73–92). New York: Haworth.

Holcomb-McCoy, C. C., & Moore-Thomas, C. (2001, October). Empowering African-American adolescent females. *Professional School Counseling, 5*, 19–27.

hooks, b. (1981). *Ain't I a woman: Black women and feminism*. Boston: South End Press.

hooks, b. (1984). *Feminist theory from margin to center*. Boston: South End Press.

hooks, b. (1990). *Yearning: Race, gender, and cultural politics*. Boston: South End Press.

Horne, G. (2000). *Race woman: The lives of Shirley Graham Du Bois*. New York: New York University Press.

Hull, G. T., Scott, P. B., & Smith, B. (Eds.). (1982). *All the women are white, all the men are black, but some of us are brave: Black women's studies*. Old Westbury, NY: Feminist Press.

Isaacs, W. N. (1993). Taking flight: Dialogue, collective thinking, and organizational learning. *Organizational Dynamics, 22*, 24–39.

Isaacs, W. N. (1999). *Dialogue: The art of thinking together*. New York: Currency.

Jacobs, T. O. (1970). *Leadership and exchange in formal organizations*. Alexandria, VA: Human Resources Research Organization.

Johnston, W. B., & Packer, A. H. (1987). *Workforce 2000: Work and workers for the 21st century*. Indianapolis, IN: Hudson Institute.

Jones, J. (1985). *Labor of love, labor of sorrow: Black women, work, and the family from slavery to the present*. New York: Basic Books.

Kanter, R. M. (1977). *Men and women of the corporation*. New York: Basic Books.

Katz, D., & Kahn, R. L. (1966/1978). *The social psychology of organizations* (2nd ed.). New York: Wiley.

Kellerman, B. (1984). Leadership as a political act. In B. Kellerman (Ed.), *Leadership: Multidisciplinary perspectives* (pp. 63–89). Englewood Cliffs, NJ: Prentice-Hall.

Kennedy, G. A. (1980). *Classical rhetoric.* Chapel Hill, NC: University of North Carolina Press.

Keto, C. T. (1989). *The Africa centered perspective of history.* Blackwood, NJ: KA Publications.

King, D. K. (1988). Multiple jeopardy, multiple consciousness: The context of a black feminist ideology. *Signs, 14*(1), 42–72.

King, M. (1973). The politics of sexual stereotypes. *Black Scholar, 4,* 12–23.

Kochman, T. (1981). *Black and white styles in conflict.* Chicago, IL: University of Chicago Press.

Kotter, J. P. (1982). *The general managers.* New York: Free Press.

Kouzes, J. M., & Posner, B. Z. (1995). *The leadership challenge.* San Francisco: Jossey-Bass.

Ladson-Billings, G. (2000). Racialized discourses and ethnic epistemologies. In N. K. Denzin, & Y. S. Lincoln (Eds.), *Handbook of qualitative research* (2nd ed., pp. 257–278). Thousand Oaks, CA: Sage.

Lerner, G. (1972). *Black women in white America: A documentary history.* New York: Vintage.

Loden, M. (1985). *Feminine leadership or: How to succeed in business without being one of the boys.* New York: Times Books.

Logan, S. W. (1999). *We are coming: The persuasive discourse of nineteenth-century black women.* Carbondale, IL: Southern Illinois University Press.

Lorde, A. (1984). *Sister outsider.* Trumansburg, NY: The Crossing Press.

Lubiano, W. (1992). Black ladies, welfare queens and state minstrels: Ideological war by narrative means. In T. Morrison (Ed.), *Race-ing justice, En-gendering power* (pp. 321–361). New York: Pantheon.

Lunneborg, P. (1990). *Women changing work.* Westport, CT: Greenwood Press.

Mainiero, L. (1994). Getting anointed for advancement: The case of executive women. *The Academy of Management Executive, 8*(2), 53–68.

Manz, C. C., & Sims, H. (1989). *Super-leadership.* New York: Prentice-Hall.

Marshall, J. (1993). Viewing organizational communication from a feminist perspective: A critique and some offerings. In S. Deetz (Ed.), *Communication Yearbook 16* (pp. 122–143). Newbury Park, CA: Sage.

Martin, J. (1992). *Cultures in organizations: Three perspectives.* New York: Oxford University Press.

Mathis, D. (2002). *Yet a stranger: Why black Americans still don't feel at home.* New York: Warner Books.

May, S. K. (1997). Silencing the feminine in managerial discourse. Paper presented at the annual meeting of the National Communication Association, Chicago, IL.

McCluskey, A. T. (1997). "We specialize in the wholly impossible": Black women school founders and their mission. *Signs: Journal of Women in Culture and Society, 22,* 403–426.

McGoldrick, M., Garcia-Preto, N., Hines, P. M., & Lee, E. (1988). Ethnicity and women. In M. McGoldrick, C. Anderson, & F. Walsh (Eds.), *Women in families* (pp. 169–199). New York: Norton.

Mead, G. H. (1934). *Mind, self, and society*. Chicago: University of Chicago Press.

Meindl, J. R., Ehrlich, S. B., & Dukerich, J. M. (1985). The romance of leadership. *Administrative Science Quarterly, 30*, 78–102.

Minnich, E. K. (1990). *Transforming knowledge*. Philadelphia: Temple University Press.

Mintzberg, H. (1973). *The nature of managerial work*. New York: Harper and Row.

Morgan, G. (1986). *Images of organization*. Beverly Hills, CA: Sage.

Morton, P. (1991). *Disfigured images: The historical assault on Afro-American women*. New York: Greenwood Press.

Mouffe, C. (1995). Feminism, citizenship, and radical democratic politics. In L. Nicholson, & S. Seidman (Eds.), *Social postmodernism* (pp. 315–331). Cambridge, UK: Cambridge University Press.

Mumby, D. (1993). Feminism and the critique of organizational communication studies. In S. Deetz (Ed.), *Communication Yearbook 16* (pp. 155–166). Newbury Park, CA: Sage.

Mumby, D. K. (2001). Power and politics. In F. M. Jablin, & L. L. Putnam (Eds.), *The new handbook of organizational communication: Advances in theory, research, and methods* (pp. 585–623). Newbury Park, CA: Sage.

Mumby, D. K., & Putnam, L. L. (1992). The politics of emotion: A feminist reading of bounded rationality. *Academy of Management Review, 17*, 465–486.

Nkomo, S. M. (1988). Race and sex: The forgotten case of the black female manager. In S. Rose, & L. Larwood (Eds.), *Women's careers: Pathways and pitfalls* (pp. 133–150). New York: Praeger.

Nkomo, S. M. (1992). The emperor has no clothes: Rewriting "race in organizations." *Academy of Management Review, 17*(3), 487–513.

O'Brien Hallstein, D. L. (1997). A postmodern caring: Feminist standpoint theories, revisioned caring and communication ethics. *Western Journal of Communication, 63*(1), 32–56.

O'Brien Hallstein, D. L. (2000). Where standpoint stands now: An introduction and commentary. *Women's Studies in Communication, 23*(1), 1–15.

Omi, M., & Winant, H. (1986). *Racial formation in the United States: From the 1960s to the 1980s*. New York: Routledge.

Omolade, B. (1994). *The rising song of African American women*. New York: Routledge.

Palmer, P. M. (1983). White women/black women: The dualism of female identity and experience in the United States. *Feminist Studies, 9*, 153–155.

Parker, P. S. (1997). African American women executives within dominant culture organizations: An examination of leadership socialization, communication strategies, and leadership behavior. Doctoral Dissertation, The University of Texas at Austin. (UMI No. 9802988).

Parker, P. S. (2001). African American women executives within dominant culture organizations: (Re)conceptualizing notions of instrumentality and collaboration. *Management Communication Quarterly, 15*(1), 42–82.

Parker, P. S. (2002). Negotiating identity in raced and gendered workplace interactions: The use of strategic communication by African American Women senior executives within dominant culture organizations. *Communication Quarterly 3*, 251–268.

Parker, P. S. (2003). Control, resistance, and empowerment in raced, gendered, and classed work contexts. *Communication Yearbook 27* (pp. 257–301). Mahwah, NJ: Erlbaum.

Parker, P. S., & Ogilvie, D. T. (1996). Gender, culture, and leadership: Toward a culturally distinct model of African-American women executives' leadership strategies. *Leadership Quarterly*, 7(2), 189–214.

Payne, C. M. (1995). *I've got the light of freedom: The organizing tradition and the Mississippi freedom struggle*. Berkeley, CA: University of California Press.

Prasad, P. (1997). The Protestent ethic and the myths of the fontier: Cultural imprints, organizational structuring, and workplace diversity. In P. Prasad, A. J. Mills, M. Elmes, & A. Prasad, A. (Eds.), *Managing the organizational melting pot: Dilemmas of workplace diversity* (pp. 129–147). Thousand Oaks, CA: Sage.

Prasad, P., Mills, A. J., Elmes, M., & Prasad, A. (Eds.). (1997). *Managing the organizational melting pot: Dilemmas of workplace diversity*. Thousand Oaks, CA: Sage.

Putnam, L. L., & Kolb, D. M. (2000). Rethinking exchange: Feminist views of communication and exchange. In P. Buzzanell (Ed.), *Rethinking organizational and managerial communication from feminist perspectives* (pp. 76–104). Thousand Oaks, CA: Sage.

Quint, C. I. (1970). The role of American Negro women in the growth of the common school. Unpublished doctoral dissertation, Brown University.

Radford-Hill, S. (2002). Keepin' it real: A generational commentary on Kimberly Springer's "Third wave black feminism?" *Signs: A Journal of Women in Culture and Society*, 27(4), 1083–1090.

Rogers-Rose, L. (Ed.). (1980). *The black woman* (pp. 217–232). Beverly Hills, CA: Sage.

Rosener, J. B. (1990). Ways women lead. *Harvard Business Review*, 68(6), 11–12.

Rost, J. C. (1991). *Leadership for the twenty-first century*. Westport, CT: Praeger.

Rowe, A. (2000). Locating feminism's subject: The paradox of white femininity and the struggle to forge feminist alliances. *Communication Theory*, 10(1), 64–80.

Schein, E. H. (1992). *Organizational culture and leadership* (2nd ed.). San Franciso: Jossey-Bass.

Scott, J. (1986). Gender: A useful category of historical analysis. *American Historical Review*, 91, 1053–1075.

Seibold, D., & Shea, C. (2001). Participation and decision making. In F. M. Jablin, & L. L. Putnam (Eds.), *The new handbook of organizational communication: Advances in theory, research, and methods* (pp. 664–703). Newbury Park, CA: Sage.

Senge, P. (1990). *The fifth discipline*. New York: Doubleday.

Senge, P., Kleiner, A., Roberts, C., Ross, R., Roth, G., & Smith, B. (1999). *The dance of change: The challenge to sustaining momentum in learning organizations*. New York: Doubleday.

Shuter, R., & Turner, L. H. (1997). African American and European American women in the workplace: Perceptions of workplace communication. *Management Communication Quarterly*, 11(1), 74–96.

Sims, H. P. Jr., & Manz, C. C. (1996). *Company of heroes: Unleashing the power of self-leadership*. New York: John Wiley.

Smircich, L., & Morgan, G. (1982). Leadership and the management of meaning. *Journal of Applied Behavioral Science*, 18, 257–273.

Smircich, L., & Stubbart, C. (1985). Strategic management in an enacted world. *Academy of Management Review*, 10, 724–736.

Spelman, E. (1988). *Inessential woman: Problems of exclusion in feminist thought*. Boston: Beacon Press.

Springer, K. (1999). *Still lifting, still climbing: African American women's contemporary activism.* New York: New York University Press.

Stack, C. B. (2000). Different voices, different visions: Gender, culture, and moral reasoning. In M. B. Zinn, P. Hondagneu-Sotelo, & M. Messner (Eds.), *Gender through the prism of difference* (2nd ed., pp. 42–48). Boston: Allyn and Bacon.

Stall, S., & Stoecker, R. (1998). Community organizing or organizing community? Gender and the crafts of empowerment. *Gender & Society, 12*(6), 729–756.

Stinchcombe, A. L. (1965). Social structure and organizations. In J. G, March (Ed.), *Handbook of organizations* (pp. 142–193). Chicago: Rand McNally.

Stohl, C., & Cheney, G. (2001). Participatory processes/paradoxical practices. Communication and the dilemmas of organizational democracy. *Management Communication Quarterly, 14,* 349–407.

Strauss, A., & Corbin, J. (1990). *Basics of qualitative research: Grounded theory procedures and techniques.* Newbury Park, CA: Sage.

Tannen, D. (1990). *You just don't understand: Women and men in conversation.* New York: William Morrow.

Taylor, B. C., & Trujillo, N. (2001). Qualitative research methods. In F. M. Jablin, & L. L. Putnam (Eds.), *The new handbook of organizational communication: Advances in theory, research, and methods* (pp. 161–194). Thousand Oaks, CA: Sage.

Thomas, D., & Gabarro, J. J. (1999). *Breaking through: The making of minority executives in corporate America.* Boston: Harvard Business School Press.

Tichy, N., & DeVanna, M. (1986). *The transformational leader.* New York: John Wiley.

Ting-Toomey, S. (1986). Conflict communication styles in black and white subjective cultures. In W. Gudykunst, & Y. Kim (Eds.), *Interethnic communication* (pp. 7–88). Newbury Park, CA: Sage.

Trethewey, A. (1997). Resistance, identity, and empowerment: A postmodern feminist analysis of clients in a human service organization. *Communication Monographs, 64,* 281–301.

Trethewey, A. (2000). Revisioning control: A feminist critique of disciplined bodies. In P. Buzzanell (Ed.), *Rethinking organizational and managerial communication from feminist perspectives* (pp. 107–127). Thousand Oaks, CA: Sage.

Twine, F. W. (2000). Feminist fairy tales for black and American Indian girls: A working-class vision. *Signs: Journal of Women in Culture and Society, 25*(4), 1227–1230.

Vaz, K. M. (Ed.). (1995). *Black women in America* (pp. 159–178).Thousand Oaks, CA: Sage.

Walker, A. (1983). *In search of our mothers' gardens.* New York: Harcourt Brace Jovanovich.

Warren, K. B., & Bourque, S. C. (1991). Women, technology, and development ideologies: Analyzing feminist voices, In M. di Leonardo (Ed.), *Gender at the crossroads of knowledge: Feminist anthropology in the postmodern era* (pp. 278–311). Berkeley, CA: University of California.

Weedon, C. (1987). *Feminist practice and poststructuralist theory.* Oxford: Basil Blackwell.

Weick, K. (1978). The spines of leaders. In M. W. McCall, & M. Lombardo (Eds.), *Leadership, where else can we go?* (pp. 37–61). Durham, NC: Duke University Press.

Weitz, R., & Gordon, L. (1993). Images of black women among Anglo college students. *Sex Roles, 28,* 19–34.

Welter, B. (1966). The cult of true womanhood, 1820–60. *American Quarterly, 18,* 151–174.

Welton, K. (1997). Nancy Hartsock's standpoint theory: From content to "concrete multiplicity." *Women & Politics, 18*(3), 7–24.

Wheatley, M. (1992). *Leadership and the new science.* San Francisco: Berrett-Koehler.

White, D. G. (1985). *Ar'n't I a woman? Female slaves in the plantation south.* New York: W. W. Norton.

Williams, J., & Dixie, Q. (2003). *This far by faith: Stories from the African American religious experience.* New York: William Morrow.

Williams, L. E. (1996). *Servants of the people: The 1960s legacy of African American leadership.* New York: St. Martin's Press.

Witherspoon, P. D. (1997). *Communicating leadership: An organizational perspective.* Boston, MA: Allyn & Bacon.

Wood, J. T. (1994). *Who cares: Women, care, and culture.* Carbondale, IL: Southern Illinois University Press.

Wood, J. T. (1998). *Gendered lives: Communication, gender and culture* (2nd ed.). Belmont: Wadsworth.

Yoder, J. D., & Aniakudo, P. (June, 1997). "Outsider within" the firehouse: Subordination and difference in the social interactions of African American women firefighters. *Gender & Society, 11*(3), 324–341.

Yukl, G. (2002). *Leadership in organizations* (5th ed.). Upper Saddle River, NJ: Prentice-Hall.

3

Leadership Journeys: The Courage to Enrich the World

Nancy J. Adler

Do not forget, you are here to enrich the world. You impoverish yourself if you ever forget that errand.

—Woodrow Wilson

This chapter focuses on the global aspects of business in the twenty-first century and the need for good leaders who have a global perspective. It is a review of the history of research on women in international management and global leadership, including studies on women as expatriate managers. I frame my understanding of the increasing role that women are playing both in terms of women's need to gain international experience and in terms of the world's need for a new type of leadership that can simultaneously bring fiscal and societal success. This chapter was originally drawn from a keynote address on women's contributions to global leadership that was given at the Hofburg Palace in Vienna, Austria, to the executive leadership of the United Nations.

VIENNA, 2003

Vienna symbolizes the height of human civilization, having given the world great architecture, art, music, philosophy, psychology, and so much more. The Hofburg Palace stands in the center of Vienna as elegant testament to Austrian leaders and power, past and present. As executives from the twenty-three major United Nations' organizations and their international-development and private-sector colleagues enter the palace, they cannot help but feel awed by the grandeur of the sculptural facades elevating each building beyond the majesty of its neighbor, beyond mere practicality and everyday ordinariness.

Vienna also symbolizes the nadir of civilization, and both the heights and the nadir are present with me this morning as I walk toward the palace along Vienna's grand boulevards, meandering at random through her beautifully manicured gardens. "Was this the park where my mother played as a young girl? Is this the street where Nazi thugs kicked yet another Jew until he fell to the ground and then continued kicking while they forced him to scrub the boulevard with a toothbrush?"

I enter the Hofburg Palace. My invitation is to deliver the keynote address on women's contributions to global leadership to the assembled conferees, all of whom care equally passionately about the performance of their organizations and the quality of civilization on this planet.

As I move toward the podium, I am aware of the necklace my grandmother smuggled out of Austria more than sixty years ago lying gently around my neck. Encircling my words is the strength, love, and support of multiple generations of my family, with its lineage of strong women, each of whom was a leader in her own time in history. Although my voice comes from inside me, it also comes from these strong and beautiful women. They died so I might be born; their voices cannot be denied, "Speak your truth Nancy, for if not, we died in vain."

Even moments before I begin to speak, I am still unclear as to exactly what I want to say. Yet as I begin, the words flow without hesitation.

> Nobody in this room chose their profession randomly. Nobody chooses to confront society's inequities because a help-wanted ad happened to appear on the day they were looking for a job. Nobody makes this kind of commitment to contribute to the world unless they have the courage to see reality for what it is— complete with all its devastating imperfections—while simultaneously maintaining the hope needed to try to do better.

In poetry and paintings, the collage of wisdom I had created for the executives appears—an aesthetic reflection supporting profound and courageous leadership. The collage invites the audience of leaders to return to the deeper reasons they remain so committed to the world and its inherent possibilities, even in the face of terrorism and unimaginable inequities. As Hewlett-Packard's former CEO, Carly Fiorina described it, the collage invites each executive into a "world of dreams expressed in art; [a world] . . . freed from the laws of every day."[1]

> All of us chose our profession—our calling—because we know that the world is in trouble. All of us know we must do better than we have done historically. I too did not choose my profession randomly. I did not choose to focus on global leadership without reason. The reasons for my choice are embedded right here, in Vienna. As I remember my Viennese great-grandmothers, grandmother, and mother, all of whom lived in this city, I understand my choice, and I understand, at the deepest levels, why we must do much, much better.
>
> My mother was born in Vienna less than ten minutes from the Hofburg Palace. My mother's first thirteen years were filled with all the splendor that has

given Vienna its worldwide reputation for high culture. Then 1938 arrived and my mother's world, along with that of all her neighbors, descended from cultured heaven into unadulterated hell. If it had not been for an Austrian family from a completely different religious and cultural background than that of my mother—a family who, unlike the vast majority of Viennese, chose not to deny the new horrifying and inhumane reality—my mother would not have lived. If it had not been for a family with extraordinary courage, that risked the life of every member of their household to hide a little girl, my mother would never have escaped, and I, needless to say, would never have been born. Good transcends evil; even as evil eclipses good.

"...the unimaginable is now possible. The survival of the human species can no longer be taken for granted. The human species is now an endangered species." Joseph Rotblat

Artist "Marc Chagall gave this nihilist century a worthy concept—hope."

"We are all born with the potential to become human. How we choose to live [and to lead] will be the measure of our humanness. Civilization does not assure our civility. Nor does being born into the human species assure our humanity. We must each find our own path to becoming human." David Krieger

Carman Moore, "When I feel what it feels like to be really human, I hear music."

Ramon Munoz Soler: "At school we are programmed to give science and technology the last word, but in the maelstrom of our civilization we long to hear the first word."

"What we cannot comprehend by analysis, we become aware of in awe." Abraham Joshua Heschel

Donella Meadows, "We do, with astonishing frequency, produce moments of nobility. Our culture just doesn't choose to feature them on the nightly news."

Nobel Peace Prize Laureate Elie Wiesel reminds us that it is human to have hope; that hope is not an empirical conclusion based on the evidence at hand, but rather an individual choice to assert our humanity.[2] Former U.S. President Woodrow Wilson insisted that our job, as leaders and as human beings, is to enrich the world. Our job is to confront reality with hope—not with a trite, superficial hope, but with a strong, robust hope founded on all our collective wisdom and experience. Fundamentally, leadership is about committing ourselves to things far greater than ourselves.[3] It's about returning reality to possibility.

There is no possibility we can return the world to a civilization we are proud of without including the voices, wisdom, talents, and experience of people from all continents and countries. We need the very best of what women and men worldwide can contribute. Yet, up until now, the world has rarely listened to most people, including ignoring the voices of most women. The message from those, like my great-grandmothers, grandmother, and mother, who walked these streets and witnessed the apex of civilization dissolve overnight into its nadir, is that global leadership is too important to attempt alone. It is too important for us not to draw on the wisest among us, whether male or female, Buddhist or Christian, Jew, Jain, or Muslim; whether European or Asian, African or American. As poet David Whyte reminds us:

> [T]he journey begins right here.
> In the middle of the road.
> Right beneath your feet.
> This is the place.
> There is no other place…
> [There is] no other time.[4]

COMPETITIVE FRONTIERS: WOMEN MANAGERS IN A GLOBAL ECONOMY

At this point in history, what does it mean to be a woman and a global leader? I have known for years that a global perspective was essential for twenty-first-century leadership and have conducted research on both male and female leaders for more than a quarter century. In the late 1970s, however, as I finished my doctorate at the University of California at Los Angeles (UCLA) and began looking for an academic home, I found few management schools at major U.S. universities interested in taking a global perspective. In interview after interview, I was told that international management constituted too narrow a focus. "Strange," I thought, "They view domestic studies as appropriately broad, and yet global studies as too narrow." At one top-ranked university, I was even told that they would offer me a professorship if I promised never to teach "that stuff" (referring to international management) to their MBAs. I declined their offer and accepted a faculty position in Canada at McGill University. In Montreal's multilingual and multicultural setting, I found a management school where the overall perspective was so cosmopolitan that no seminar needed to be explicitly labeled international—for what would the other seminars be labeled? Parochial? Offering managers a choice between the international and parochial (domestic) versions of a particular curriculum—be it marketing, finance, or strategy—seemed clearly absurd to me as well as to my new McGill colleagues.

My research in the early 1980s focused on a broad range of cross-cultural management issues facing companies, including the complexities of strategic international human resource management. Given that I, along with many other observers of the rapidly shifting geopolitical landscape, was already convinced that successful businesses could no longer remain local, the paucity of women gaining international experience concerned me. No matter how much emphasis North Americans placed on employment equity, especially for the increasing number of women managers, it seemed highly unlikely that anyone would be promoted into the senior leadership of the next generation of global companies if he or she had not had the opportunity to work abroad. The results from my research on women expatriate managers confirmed my fears: whereas more than 40 percent of domestic North American managers by that time were women, less than 3 percent of the people being sent abroad by major multinationals on expatriate assignments were women.[5] With this preponderance of men defining the universe of future corporate leaders, the situation did not bode well for either the women or the companies as they entered the most competitive economic era that business had ever faced.

Why were multinational companies continuing to limit their competitiveness by restricting their choices to men? At that time, most multinational companies believed three "myths" and used them to explain the dearth of women managers being sent abroad. The truth of none of the three myths, however, had ever been tested:

- Myth 1: Women do not want to become international managers;
- Myth 2: Companies refuse to send women abroad; and
- Myth 3: Foreigners' prejudice against women renders them ineffective, even when they are interested in going abroad and succeed in having their companies send them.

We researched each of the three myths to assess whether they were, in fact, true. Myth #1, we discovered, was blatantly false. Whereas women from prior generations may have hesitated to take foreign assignments, by the 1980s women and men had become equally interested in seeking opportunities to work abroad.[6]

Myth #2, on the other hand, proved true. The majority of multinational companies did hesitate, if not altogether resist, in providing their women professionals with opportunities for international experience.

Myth #3 was more difficult to assess, but ultimately proved false. For years, companies had assumed that the level of resistance to expatriate managers varied according to the cultural traditions of host countries. To our surprise, however, we discovered that 97 percent of the women who were sent abroad succeeded, irregardless of country; a much higher success rate than that of their male counterparts.[7] Indeed, almost half the women (42 percent) reported that being a woman offered them more advantages than disadvantages to their professional success.[8] Only 20 percent reported that being a woman was a net disadvantage.[9] Such evidence proved that the belief that host-country discrimination acts as a barrier against foreign women managers' success was, in most cases, a myth. Host nationals, in most cases, treat foreign women managers with the respect they need to succeed.

In the 1970s and 1980s, the women who worked as expatriate managers were very much pioneers. Typically, they were the first women their companies had ever sent abroad. Because international positions were rarely forthcoming, many had to persistently encourage their companies to send them, and often had to strategically position themselves within the company to seize international opportunities when they arose. Because, in most cases, there was no woman predecessor to act as a role model, their deliberate choices to seek positions abroad required courage, resolve, and resiliency—qualities other women, including my great-grandmothers, had displayed in other historic settings. The major barrier to women's international success was rarely the women themselves, nor a falsely assumed discrimination by local host cultures around the world. Rather, the major barrier remained the resistance put forth by the women's own companies as the decision makers continued to believe in Myths #1 and #3, and therefore chose, with few exceptions, not to offer international assignments to even their highest potential female managers.

Given the increasingly competitive nature of the global economy in the 1980s and 1990s, companies needed to change their assumptions and provide more opportunities for both their high-potential women and men to gain expatriate experience. Summarized most succinctly by Harvard Business School Professor Rosabeth Moss Kanter:

> Meritocracy—letting talent rise to the top regardless of where it is found and whether it is male or female—is essential to business success in free-market economies. Within this context, the equality of women in the work force is no longer a political luxury. It has become a competitive necessity.[10]

To dispel the erroneous myths that were hindering companies from selecting their best candidates for international assignments, without regard to gender, our recommendations included: Don't assume foreigners will treat expatriate women the same way they treat their local women; they won't. Similarly, just because the prior era's male expatriates often blamed failed assignments and early return on their wives, don't assume that women in general have trouble adjusting abroad. The role of the spouse provides very different, noncomparable challenges to those faced by expatriate managers. Similarly, don't assume that married women will not accept international assignments. If companies want women to accept assignments abroad and to succeed once there, they need to offer them flexible benefits packages and an infrastructure of support. Today, many companies offer packages that include executive-search facilities to help the trailing spouse find a job, airline tickets to allow commuting couples to stay connected, and other benefits designed for dual-career couples and single women expatriates. The era of simply offering a nice home and membership in the international club is over. Leading companies have discovered that they have much more control over women's worldwide success—and therefore their own competitive success—than most had ever initially imagined. They have learned that exercising initiative leads to success for both the companies and the women.

GLOBAL LEADERS: NO LONGER MEN ALONE

By the early 1990s, as my research shifted from focusing on expatriate managers to global leaders, I increasingly questioned the "pipeline myth"—the belief that women just needed more time in their companies' career-path pipeline before they would naturally be promoted into top positions. As I began examining the career paths of women who had actually achieved the number one leadership position in their country or company, it became clear that the women's routes to power differed significantly from those taken by most men.[11] Rather than working their way up through the corporate hierarchy—up through the pipeline—most women laterally transferred into their leadership positions.

In the political realm, for example, most women presidents and prime ministers did not progress up through the political-party hierarchy. Instead, they laterally transferred into their country's number one leadership position from other careers. Tansu Ciller, for example, taught economics at Turkey's prestigious Bogazici University until shortly before she was elected Turkey's first woman prime minister. Gro Harlem Brundtland, after having begun her career as a medical doctor, was elected as Norway's first woman prime minister, and subsequently reelected for two additional terms before going on to lead the World Health Organization. In the business realm, a similar pattern holds true for many of the women who become CEOs of major multinational companies. Those who succeed rarely advance through the ranks of their company until they ultimately reach the top. Rather, they gain the number one position by laterally transferring into the CEO position in one company after having built their career in another company. Carly Fiorina is probably the most prominent example of this pattern. Fiorina grew her career at Lucent before being recruited to take over as CEO at Hewlett-Packard, a Fortune top thirty company.

Certainly, the pattern of laterally transferring into senior positions of power calls into question the belief that a "glass ceiling" stops women from reaching the top. It appears that many women who become CEOs find it more expeditious to go around the glass ceiling than to try to break through it. Whereas it is true that within-organization hierarchical power structures in the political and corporate realms generally fail to support women as candidates for senior leadership, such lack of support does not stop the women from gaining power. Politically, for example, women often draw their support directly from the people rather than primarily from existing political-party hierarchies. Former president of Ireland Mary Robinson and former prime minister of Pakistan Benazir Bhutto provide good examples. Neither gained her support from a narrow political elite, but rather each campaigned in more small communities than any politician in her country had before her. Women business leaders often exhibit similarly "democratic" approaches, drawing their power directly from the marketplace rather than primarily from the hierarchical power structure within their own company. Successful entrepreneurs, of whom an increasing proportion worldwide are women, dramatically reflect this pattern. As Mary Robinson observed in her presidential acceptance speech:

> I was elected by men and women of all parties and none, by many with great moral courage who stepped out from the faded flags of Civil War and voted for a new Ireland. And above all by the women of Ireland . . . who instead of rocking the cradle, rocked the system, and who came out massively to make their mark on the ballot paper, and on a new Ireland.[12]

The nontraditional approach used by such women as Mary Robinson to obtain power and to reach the most senior positions offers an interesting model for twenty-first-century leadership that contrasts sharply with that used by most twentieth-century male leaders.

Also contrasting the twentieth-century leadership dynamics surrounding most male leaders, women bring powerful public symbolism when they assume senior leadership roles that differs quite distinctly from the symbolism surrounding their male colleagues. In particular, because of their newness to such powerful positions, women are frequently viewed as symbols of hope, unity, and the possibility of change.[13] When a woman is chosen to lead her company or country, especially in circumstances in which no woman has held that office before, people begin to believe that other more substantive and significant changes are possible.

Similarly due primarily to their newness as senior leaders, women enjoy higher visibility than most of their male contemporaries. Carly Fiorina, for example, after being selected as the first woman and first outsider to lead Hewlett-Packard, received more press coverage in her first three months as CEO than Lew Platt, her predecessor, received in his entire eighteen years as CEO.

Although the pattern is not yet clear at senior leadership levels, many suggest that women also use more democratic, inclusive, and unifying strategies than do their male counterparts.[14] In the political realm, for example, it was a woman, Agatha Uwilingiyimana, former prime minister of Rwanda, who was willing to sign the peace treaty between the warring Hutu and Tutsis in an attempt to end the war in that genocide-ravaged country. Her predecessor, a man, refused to engage in a peace process that included representatives of all factions for fear he would be seen as disloyal by his own party and tribe. Demonstrating huge courage, Uwilingiyimana accepted the position of prime minister and signed the peace treaty at a time when no man was willing to do so. In one more tragedy in that already unimaginably tragic country, Uwilingiyimana was murdered for her leadership, not by the opposition, but sadly, by members of her own political party and tribe who resisted her attempts to reunify the country by creating an inclusive peace.

Change, whether societal or organizational, whether sweeping or subtle, requires tremendous courage. The challenges facing today's world leaders require a global perspective and extremely broad commitments. As former Body Shop CEO Anita Roddick recognized: "Leaders in the business world should aspire to be true planetary citizens. They have global responsibilities since their decisions affect not just the world of business, but world problems of poverty, national security and the environment. Many, sad to say, duck these responsibilities, because their vision is material rather than moral."[15]

Twenty-first-century leaders, whether women or men, derive their power from broadly based networks. They must be vision-driven, globally inclusive, and multiculturally persuasive, while simultaneously exhibiting courage and humility. As global leaders they are charged with taking ideas, people, organizations, and societies on a journey. The power to shape history means that a leader's most critical task is to seek to enrich the world, rather than diminish it; to promote good and dispel evil; to propel civilization to its heights, while saving it from descending to its nadir. Economic viability and competitive success, while critically important parts of the equation, remain far from sufficient to define a leader's most significant contributions.

THE ART OF LEADERSHIP: GIVING OURSELVES FOR THINGS FAR GREATER THAN OURSELVES[16]

Do women offer a greater possibility for significant leadership than do men?[17] Symbolically, perhaps, but there is no gender-based entitlement to virtue or efficacy. Many predicted that women would demonstrate new, more inclusive and humanistic approaches. Examples of corrupt and damaging leadership, however, can be found among women as well as among men. As we have always known, but perhaps conveniently forgotten in other eras, our task is to seek out and to grow the types of leaders our time in history requires, not to inequitably prejudge either men or women as the ready-made, guaranteed solution.

Today, to create the needed shift in our leadership approaches and vocabulary, I find myself turning away from most traditional leadership models and increasingly embracing the arts and artistic processes.[18] The move from successful to significant leadership, as former CEO and president Frances Hesselbein describes it, cannot take place within the limitations of our current dehydrated leadership vocabulary.[19] Significance relies upon traditional organizational efficiency and effectiveness. However, it is neither defined nor limited by these traditional management pursuits. Achieving significance demands new concepts, new imagery, and a new language; it demands that leaders reengage with the possibility of enriching the world. World-renowned corporate architect, recognized by *Time Magazine* as the 1999 Hero of the Planet,

William McDonough reminds us, and our corporations, that being "less bad" does not make us good.[20] And being good—being a contribution—demands new approaches.

A global leadership seminar I conducted in the late 1990s for women business executives from around the world demonstrated the power of artistic processes to open new and needed perspectives. At the beginning of the seminar, I invited each of the participants to introduce herself by describing one time in which she had been particularly powerful at work. The discussion that ensued quickly turned overwhelmingly negative. The women saw power as primarily manipulative, coercive, military-based, hierarchical, and dominantly masculine. Indeed, these business leaders seemed on the verge of rejecting the notion of power altogether until one of the most senior women challenged the others by saying: "Unless you can tell me that the world is perfect, your country is perfect, your company is perfect, your community is perfect, and your family is perfect, don't tell me that you're not interested in power." Everyone understood her message.

As a professor and consultant, it is my goal to help executives access and use power for worthwhile ends; it is not my role to encourage them to reject power. In the seminar, my challenge was to find a way to reunite the women executives with their power without referencing the traditional, constricted, hierarchical modes that most had grown up with. My challenge was to reunite them with a contrasting approach to power that could support the possibility of enriching their companies and the world, rather than the probability of diminishing either or both. Such a conception of power, of course, demands courage, including:

- the courage to see reality as it actually is—to "collude against illusion" even when society and colleagues reject your perceptions;[21]
- the courage to imagine a better world—to imagine possibility even when society and colleagues consider such possibilities naive, unattainable, or foolish; and
- the courage to communicate reality and possibility so powerfully that others can't help but move forward toward a better future.

After my failure to engage the women executives in a productive discussion of power, I switched from words to an artistic process—in this case, to visual imagery. The following day, I offered the participants a pile of art supplies and invited them to create their own image of power. Without speaking or using any words in their artwork, each executive visually explored what power meant to her. After signing and posting their power-art, the executives interpreted the power images of their colleagues. What emerged was the most robust, positive, and owned definition of power I have ever witnessed. By shifting their vocabulary from words to images—from the commonplace to the novel, and from linear to holistic associations—each participant broadened her conception of power along with her relationship to its uses. After having viewed the gallery of power-art, everyone could again see the possibility of using power to simultaneously achieve positive personal, organizational, and societal outcomes.

In the years that followed that initial experiment, other exciting programs for women who are global leaders have been successfully designed. One of the most exciting, the Judy Project, was launched this year as a living legacy to Judy Elder, an outstanding woman executive who died long before her full contribution as a mother, wife, and corporate leader could be fully achieved.[22] To initiate the inaugural program, we invited Ben Zander, conductor of the Boston Philharmonic, to use music and artistic metaphors to open the realm of possibility. Similarly, Smith College and Dartmouth's Tuck School of Business teamed up to launch the world's first completely global program for women leaders.[23] Did we use traditional approaches or leadership vocabulary in either program? Of course not. It was neither what we aspired to nor what would have worked.

LEADER AS ARTIST: ARTIST AS LEADER

As an artist, my own paintings have involved similar, ongoing explorations. Artists, like leaders, constantly face the challenge of seeing reality as it is, even as they shift that reality into the realm of possibility, and communicate it powerfully and courageously. Perhaps the era has arrived when we can no longer be leaders of the economy and society without also reclaiming our birthright as artists and citizens. Success and significance cannot be achieved within the traditional language and models of twentieth-century leadership. As I described in my artist statement for the most recent exhibit of my paintings:[24]

> For me, allowing a painting to be born is to stand in awe of one of life's most beautiful mysteries. Invited by the blank paper, the best of my intentions and experience enter into a dance with uncontrollable coincidence. Neither the process nor the resulting art are ever completely defined. Which way will the colors run? What surprises will the ink reveal as it, ever so gently, touches the paint? I purposely use water-based media that don't stay put where I place them on the paper. There's never any illusion that I control the process. I only enter the dance; paintings emerge out of the dance. For me, being an artist is about giving birth to the possibilities inherent in mystery. Creation—whether on a canvas of words, visual images, or action—is, in fact, about relearning to dance with God.

VIENNA 2003: MUSIC SCAPES

> At the close of the United Nations conference, I walk onto the stage once again. This time, I am not preparing to speak but to paint—to visually accompany

world-renowned violinist Miha Pogacik as he plays Bach.[25] As soon as the music starts, the entire audience seems to disappear and I seemingly disappear with it, slipping into the music and the moment. The music surrounds me and becomes me. It is as though the music is choreographing me; I become a puppet following its motions. The paint gives birth to images; the music scape is born. The audience applauds; they, Miha, and I are engulfed in the magic. "Painting is not a performing art!" "Who cares! Leadership is a performing art." I am in Vienna, where the apex and nadir of civilization have met. We are all in Vienna to engage in a new conversation about global leadership, and the role that both women and men are being invited to play. No one can erase the nightmare memories of past atrocities. Each of us, however, can and will shape future history. The choice is ours, today, to enter into a new conversation. The world needs us. The world is depending on us. For without our courage and compassion, there will be no future. By creating and entering into a new conversation, the world's children will remember our contributions, and our leadership, with pride.

NOTES

Reprinted with permission of John Wiley & Sons, Inc., from Linda Coughlin, Ellen Wingard, and Keith Hollihan, eds., *Enlightened Power: How Women Are Transforming the Practice of Leadership* (San Francisco: Jossey-Bass, 2005), copyright © 2005 by Linkage, Inc.

1. Carly Fiorina's commencement address at the Massachusetts Institute of Technology (MIT) on June 2, 2000, available online at www.hp.com/ghp/ceo/speeches/mit.html.
2. Based on Mary Rourke's article on Elie Wiesel titled, "His Faith in Peace Endures," *Los Angeles Times*, fall 2002.
3. Based on Joan Chittister's "To be human is to give yourself for things far greater than yourself," as cited in Frederick Franck, Janis Roze, and Richard Connolly, eds., *What Does It Mean to be Human?* (Nyack, NY: Circumstantial Productions Publishing, 1998), p. 194.
4. David Whyte, *The Heart Aroused* (New York: Currency Doubleday, 1994), p. 27.
5. See Nancy J. Adler, "Competitive Frontiers: Women Managing across Borders," in Nancy J. Adler and Dafna N. Izraeli, eds., from *Competitive Frontiers: Women Managers in a Global Economy* (Cambridge, MA: Blackwell, 1994), pp. 22–40. Also see Nancy J. Adler, "Women in International Management: Where Are They?" *California Management Review*, 26(4) (1984): 78–89.
6. Nancy J. Adler, "Women Do Not Want International Careers: And Other Myths about International Management," *Organizational Dynamics*, 13(2) (1984): 66–79.
7. See Nancy J. Adler, "Pacific Basin Managers: A Gaijin, Not a Woman," *Human Resource Management*, 26(2) (1987): 169–92.
8. Ibid.
9. Ibid.
10. Rosabeth Moss Kanter's comment on Nancy A. Nichols's *Reach for the Top: Women and the Changing Facts of Work Life* (Boston: Harvard University Business School Press, 1994), as cited in the book review by John R. Hook in *Academy of Management Executive*, 8(2) (1994): 87–89 (cited on p. 89).

11. Nancy J. Adler, "Did You Hear? Global Leadership in Charity's World," *Journal of Management Inquiry*, 7(21) (1998): 135–43.

12. Mary Robinson's presidential acceptance speech, RDS, Dublin, 9 November 1990 as reported by Fergus Finlay in *Mary Robinson: A President with a Purpose* (Dublin, Ireland: The O'Brien Press, 1990), p. 1.

13. Nancy J. Adler, "Shaping History: Global Leadership in the Twenty-First Century," in Hugh Scullion and Margaret Linehan, eds., *International Human Resource Management* (London: Palgrave/Macmillan, 2003).

14. Alice H. Eagley and Blair T. Johnson, "Gender and Leadership Style: A Meta-Analysis," *Psychological Bulletin*, 8(2) (1990): 233–56, cited in Susan Vinnicombe and Nina Colwill, *The Essence of Women in Management* (London: Prentice Hall, 1995), p. 32.

15. Anita Roddick, *Body and Soul* (New York: Crown, 1991), p. 226.

16. For a broader discussion of the ideas in this section, see Nancy J. Adler, "Leading Globally: Giving Oneself for Things Far Greater than Oneself," *Insights: Journal of the Academy of International Business*, 1(2) (2001): 13–15.

17. For a discussion of predicted differences between women's and men's leadership, see Adler, "Shaping History."

18. Nancy J. Adler, "The Art of Leadership: Coaching in the 21st Century," in Howard Morgan, Phil Harkins, and Marshall Goldsmith, eds., *Profiles in Coaching* (Burlington: Linkage Press, 2003). Also see Nancy J. Adler's seminar description at McGill University, "Leadership, Power, and Influence: The Art of Leadership," Montreal, Canada, 2003.

19. Private conversation with Frances Hesselbein, former CEO of the Girl Scouts and president of the Drucker Foundation, at the Learning Network, Del Mar, California, January 2000. The phrase "dehydrated management vocabulary" comes from poet David Whyte.

20. From "The Next Industrial Revolution: William McDonough, Michael Braungart and the Birth of the Sustainable Economy" video program. See William McDonough, "William McDonough on Designing the Next Industrial Revolution," *Timeline*, July/August 2001, pp. 12–16.

21. See Parker J. Palmer, *The Active Life: A Spirituality of Work, Creativity, and Caring* (New York: Harper and Row, 1990) for a discussion of "collusion against illusion."

22. The Judy Project, sponsored by a consortium of major Canadian companies, was launched in April 2003. Without the vision and support of Frank Clegg, CEO of Microsoft Canada, where Judy Elder had last contributed as a corporate leader, and Colleen Moorehead, president of E*TRADE Canada, this innovative program would not have been born. The author was a co-designer of the program.

23. The Smith-Tuck Program for Global Women Leaders was launched in 2003. The author was a co-designer and faculty member for the program.

24. Nancy Adler's paintings were exhibited at the Aquatreize show, which opened on June 11, 2003, at Galerie Espace in Montreal.

25. Pogacik regularly combines his music with profound leadership messages for executive audiences worldwide.

4

Corporate Culture and Leadership: Traditional, Legal, and Charismatic Authority

Deborah A. Woo and Gillian P. S. Khoo

The accounting practices that rocked Wall Street in late 2001 prompted much of the country to question the leadership of several major firms. Since then, large institutional investors have sued, and elements of government have attempted to rein in wayward corporations, calling for a whole new level of financial accountability from corporate leaders.[1] Had such corporate corruption been associated exclusively with women or persons of African, Asian, or Latino descent, media interpretations and explanations almost certainly would have speculated about how ethnicity and upbringing might have factored in. In sharp contrast, the subject of gender or race never arose when the alleged perpetrators of this unprecedented crime wave continually fell within a particular demographic profile. Although biographical details were not omitted as scandal after scandal identified the CEO at the helm,[2] the sociological imagination of most reporters simply did not entertain the idea that race or gender were factors that might account for the patterns observed. We are not necessarily suggesting it should have, but the lack of symmetry illustrates a certain ubiquitous mindset pervading corporate cultures (i.e., the white male CEO as normal) such that minorities and women always have been more closely scrutinized and subjected to higher or different standards.[3] This chapter focuses on the defining nature of leadership cultures—specifically the implications of traditional, legal, and charismatic authority for those who are culturally marginal.

This chapter begins with a story of rebellion against a particular mold of corporate leadership, that is, the "tough" boss CEO. The high-profile drama involved consummate insiders within the business elite, that is, white males who were Morgan Stanley executives. The turmoil inside the organization marginalized those who self-identified with a more give-and-take subculture and who tried to distance themselves from the more autocratic leadership style. According to sociologist Max Weber, traditional authority implies status derived from personal allegiances, traditional customs, or age-old practices. This typically patriarchal authority commands personal loyalty and obedience that stem from sharing a common background rather than from specific rules for behavior. Its modern-day corporate equivalent similarly recruits advisors, associates, board members, and fellow officers from an informal network of favorites, already known or related to one another in some way. Not surprisingly, this form of recruitment excludes many women and minorities who are not part of this inner circle.

By contrast, "legal authority" is anchored in an impersonal order, emphasizing objective rules and norms, whereby hierarchy reflects different levels or spheres of competence or specialized training.[4] For minorities and women, the legal or rational bureaucratic order offers specific rights and protections otherwise denied those who are not part of the key social networks: "It may be true that the law cannot make a man love me, but it can keep him from lynching me and I think that's pretty important" (Martin Luther King Jr.).[5] The research in the second section of this chapter illustrates how within a given corporate culture traditional and legal authority can represent competing orientations and how in turn the traditional leadership culture erects a glass ceiling for Asian Americans. Ironically, although ensconced in a scientific workplace environment that celebrates the impersonal ideal of rational authority (science), these professionals became the quintessential representatives of the scientific ethos.

In contrast to traditional and legal authority, Weber's concept of charismatic authority captures the visionary perspective demonstrated by most high-performing executives. In Weber's view, charisma is a rare personal quality or trait, that is, one that is not so much acquired or achieved via individual effort, coaching, or training but a quality with which one is gifted. However, we believe this quality can be inculcated under the right circumstances. In the third and final section, "Managing and Leading in the Twenty-First Century," Khoo's experience as an executive coach provides a case study that illustrates how strategic leadership can be actively fostered. Woo's emphasis, however, is on how effective leadership inheres not simply in *individual* qualities but also in a set of *relationships.* If so, there are theoretically diverse ways in which a strategic, visionary, or charismatic leadership might be cultivated, depending on the social or cultural nexus in which such a person is expected to lead.

"IN BUSINESS, TOUGH GUYS FINISH LAST"

With the merger of Dean Witter and Morgan Stanley in 1997, a crisis in management ensued that eventually brought the authoritarian style of corporate leadership under scrutiny. The above title to a *New York Times* column might seem a strange observation to most.[6] Whether one believes the playing field in corporate America is level or not, the image of alpha males falling behind the pack is incongruous. The *Times* story, however, was about a clash between two different corporate cultures at Morgan Stanley Dean Witter. The former head of

Dean Witter, Philip J. Purcell, would run Morgan Stanley with the same autocratic style to which he had been accustomed for almost two decades. This was consistent with a kind of leadership that emerged during the 1980s—one that emphasized a certain brand of toughness, rule by fear, unapologetic ruthlessness, and brutal self-expression that took the form of fist-pounding, tough talk, abusive language, and explosive tempers. Purcell's undemocratic and isolationist tendencies antagonized many who valued Morgan Stanley's "culture of give and take and constructive disagreement."

> Back in the 1980's, Fortune published a feature called "America's Toughest Bosses."... If Fortune were compiling such lists today, Mr. Purcell might rank near the top. He wasn't a screamer... Nor is he the sort to bang his fists on the table.
>
> But during his nearly two decades running first Dean Witter and then Morgan Stanley, where he became chief executive when the companies merged in 1997, he was ruthless, autocratic and remote. He had no tolerance for dissent or even argument. He pushed away strong executives and surrounded himself with yes men and women. He demanded loyalty to himself over the organization. He played power games. He had little contact with rank and file.[7]

Disaffection and defection were legion until eight former Morgan Stanley executives reemerged from retirement to organize Purcell's ouster.[8]

Purcell's tendency to insulate himself from detractors and surround himself with only loyals is a form of traditional authority," which sociologists have long associated with feudal, highly exclusive patriarchal cultures that manifest themselves today in the old boy network. Aspects of Morgan Stanley culture, too, shared these problematic elements.

In July 2004, the securities firm was found guilty of sex discrimination involving 340 women. The $54 million settlement was the second largest reached by the Equal Employment Opportunity Commission (EEOC) with a company it has sued—a "watershed in safeguarding and promoting the rights of women on Wall Street," according to federal judge Richard Berman.[9] At least $12 million would be paid to Allison Schieffelin, a key plaintiff and bond salesperson who sued on the grounds she had been denied a promotion to managing director because of her sex. Her complaints also included inappropriate behavior witnessed or endured on the trading floor, lascivious male behavior, and retaliatory firing. Elizabeth Gross, the lead trial lawyer for the EEOC, saw Morgan Stanley as merely the tip of the iceberg: "discrimination is very much a problem.... I expect that we will hear more from women on Wall Street and from racial minorities on Wall Street." Given that the $54 million was but a fraction of the $1 billion Morgan Stanley had earned the previous quarter, Purcell was likely pleased with the settlement: "We are proud of our commitment to diversity and would like to thank the E.E.O.C. staff for working with us to conclude this matter in such a positive way."[10] Outside of the settlement costs, the company agreed to earmark $2 million to diversity programs, monitored by an independent agency to improve occupational opportunities for its women employees.

If the seismic rumblings within Morgan Stanley represent two different movements within the corporate culture, the rebels challenging Purcell's regime represent one fault line. The female employees challenging sexism represent another. Whether they are precursors to other, more fundamental changes in the corporate culture remains to be seen. When Carly Fiorina stepped up to the helm of Hewlett-Packard (HP), she believed (and may still believe) there is no glass ceiling for women made of the "right stuff." Her departure, however, may have received more scrutiny because she was female.[11] But her removal is also noteworthy not for reasons of gender bias but because she did challenge the HP culture while failing to establish strategic alliances with people within HP.[12]

Although corporations have moved toward more diffuse or decentralized forms of governance, and away from command-and-control models of management,[13] this shift has not necessarily translated into mobility for women or minorities. Thus, despite growing appreciation for leadership qualities commonly associated with women, some organizations simply turned to training men in these skills, no longer seeing these traits as distinctly female.

> As doubts about the effectiveness of the command-and-control model made their way into the executive suite, these same behaviors began to appear in a positive light and were no longer considered female. They were now simply good leadership traits.... Similarly, when the attributes associated with the interactive leadership style are considered organizationally effective, they are often presented as gender-neutral. Ironically, in some organizations men are now being trained to be interactive leaders while women are still hitting the glass ceiling because they *are* interactive leaders.[14]

It has been speculated, moreover, that a glass ceiling for women derives from the fact that bosses and peers continue to use traditional sex role criteria in evaluating performance. For example, women who seek and value others' opinions are seen as more effective by their peers than women who don't; by contrast, this quality is irrelevant to men, who are seen by their bosses as more effective when they are adopt a "forceful, assertive, and competitive approach."[15] At the most senior levels, these gender-specific styles persist, and although both men and women are seen as equally effective in their general leadership, women are at a certain disadvantage because they are more results-oriented rather than strategically oriented. One theory is that they experience a greater need to prove their worth, perceiving strategic thinking as a luxury and a riskier endeavor.[16]

In attempting to arrive at core criteria for senior executive service (SES), the Office of Personnel Management conducted research that ultimately identified five core qualifications which would define the "SES corporate culture"—leading both change and people, building coalitions/communications, being results-driven, and having business acumen.[17] However, attempts to hire or promote from underrepresented groups matter little if, as the research in the next section points out, an implicit organizational preference exists for a narrow range of leadership skills.

CANARIES IN THE COAL MINE

The phrase "glass ceiling" was coined in the mid-1980s as a metaphor for the artificial barriers preventing white women in corporate America from rising into the executive ranks. Documented complaints of such a ceiling had appeared at least a decade earlier—among Asian Americans. As "canaries in the coal mine," however, they did not form the critical mass that white women did. White women, by contrast, were much better positioned as a cohort not only to be heard but to provide the major inspiration for alternative theories of leadership. Until the 1980s, these were primarily of three types—trait, behavioral, and situational.[18] The theory that a stable set of core traits ensures the makings of a good leader with the right stuff has since been discredited. Yet a dominant type of personality continues to be selected and groomed for management. It is one, moreover, that continues to constitute a major glass ceiling barrier for Asian Americans.

As a diverse population in the United States that comprises more than fifty subethnic groups, speaking over thirty different languages, Asian Pacific Americans (or more accurately, a specific subgroup of Asian Americans) have become highly visible in the professional occupations yet are disproportionately underrepresented as executives, faring worse than other minorities, with Asian American women doing even less well than their male counterparts.

In 2002, their professional-managerial representation in private industry was a lopsided ratio of three to one, with things only slightly better in the federal workforce.[19] By contrast, white males were overrepresented in management compared to their numbers in the professional workforce. Other studies have reported lower returns on education despite similar levels of education or work experience.[20]

This section focuses on how both the organizational culture and structure constituted serious impediments. The research site in question, referred to as XYZ Aerospace, is a government research center with a large concentration of scientists and engineers, accounting for almost 60 percent of XYZ's workforce in 2000. From its inception, it was a highly prestigious organization with a culture that emphasized technical competence and an "ivory-tower" approach to research. The projects themselves had a certain glamour, and working in such an organizational enterprise bestowed the status of being affiliated with the best and the brightest." The work situation alone was highly attractive—decentralized, flexible, providing a great deal of individual autonomy and control as well as abundant opportunities for hands-on experience that was intrinsically satisfying. Thus, although the salaries of scientists and engineers were not as competitive as in the private sector, recruitment of talented scientists and engineers was never a problem. Finally, the overall culture and politics of the workplace was described as a "liberal" atmosphere, which included leadership support for diversity.

The description of the organization provided by Asian American employees is congruent with the organization's public face. A 1991 survey of Asian American employees indicated they still saw XYZ as a place that gave one the opportunity to use one's "talents and expertise" to reach one's "maximum potential." At the time of the study, downsizing and outsourcing, however, had already created a more bureaucratic and centralized agency, dampening the original élan and transforming managerial work into administrative burden. Thus one employee explained:

> I'm not too happy about the direction the whole agency is going.... Our budgets are being cut... the agency is suffering somewhat from administrative burdens, whereas in the beginning, I think, the agency had a "can-do" attitude, and they were able to do a lot of things.... There seems to be just ever-increasing administrative burden—more reports, generating more reports. And it's difficult to understand why these reports are needed.... And when you have reports and response to headquarters [it] takes the time away from your real management job. (Asian American male)

In an entity where scientists and engineers are the heartbeat of the organization, Asian Americans formed a critical mass at 13 percent of the science and engineering workforce, compared with 4 percent for Hispanics, 2 percent for blacks, and 1 percent for Native Americans. Their technical competence was unquestioned. However, for most of their history at XYZ, they have been largely absent in the executive ranks. Complaints about the glass ceiling formally surfaced in the early 1970s, when the Asian American Employee Association assumed the task of representing the career development concerns of more than 200 Asian American employees at the research center, approximately half of whom were scientists and engineers. According to one person, studies of their managerial representation were initiated at the request of the center director, whose explicit aim was to show that Asian professionals at the center were a "model" for other minorities, who were more vocal and aggressive about problems at XYZ. According to another view, the studies were launched only when the center faced a race discrimination suit from Asian professionals themselves. Whatever the motivating factor, the statistical findings proved surprising. Instead of being a model of mobility, Asian American employees were one grade lower than expected, and the critical comparison group was not other minorities but white males.

Despite such documented disparity, for almost fifteen years there continued to be no high-ranking Asian American managers—not until the intervention of former Congressman Norm Mineta, which led to the appointment in 1986 of XYZ's first Asian American senior executive. Since then, the pipeline has continued to be constricted, with repeated surveys eliciting similar concerns about racial discrimination, "preselected" candidates and disparities at the highest levels, the need to work harder than others, and the failure to realize substantial reform.[21] In 2005, there were no Asian Americans at the senior executive level. The remainder of this paper discusses how the organizational culture and structure effectively screen out Asian American candidates.[22] Although racial stratification is the outward and most visible manifestation of mobility barriers, the glass ceiling at XYZ in many ways was experienced not so much as a racial issue but expressly as a cultural issue.

Culture Conflicts, Corporate and Ethnic

The culture at XYZ, premised as it is on scientific pursuits, reinforces the impersonal rules for advancement that inhere in a legal/bureaucratic rationality, specifically merit-based criteria. Still, the corporate culture was perceived as problematic in many ways. First and foremost, the lightning rod for much criticism was the dominance of an authoritarian style that inhibited the full participation of all employees and represented a negative model for Asian Americans aspiring to be managers. Second, this corporate culture included a subculture and social network that converged to preselect candidates, while bypassing eligible and qualified individuals who were outside this traditional old boy network. One major form of culture conflict, therefore, was rooted in a clash between the traditional, authoritarian model, on one hand, and the more impersonal model based on scientific or legal/bureaucratic procedures on the other hand. Third, another form of culture conflict was rooted in ethnic differences in values and behavioral styles and a certain racial/ethnic consciousness.

In terms of everyday interaction, race or ethnicity were not salient parts of consciousness, and work relations were seldom said to be characterized by overt or covert racial prejudice. However, the aggressive behavioral style of white males was identified as a major factor responsible for the glass ceiling experienced by not only Asians but women:

> The glass ceiling occurs because we're still operating under the cultural values of white males, ... not all that compatible with Asian American culture or ... [the] culture represented by women. ... If you're not aggressive, self-promoting, direct and articulate and ... viewed as a risk-taker—if you don't have those traits—it's hard to climb the ladder of management, unless, of course, the whole culture of the organization changes. (Asian American male)

Because Asian Americans were not aggressively assertive or outspoken, they were not perceived as having the required leadership skills.

> I think if you sit in on several meetings at Aerospace, you'll see that there's a general style of communication, of how a decision is made.... The most vocal people will just get their opinions out there on the table, and try to drive them forward. That will be a small subset of the people represented there and typically the Asians ... aren't going to be the first ones to get their opinions out there, and sometimes they won't get their opinions voiced at all because they don't want to vocalize what they're thinking for many different reasons ... people who are more assertive and I think in some ways more aggressive will get their voices heard, will get perceived to be the more active-thinking, more involved people, and then so there's kind of a mindset set up by the superiors, the higher-level managers—"Well, Jim, he speaks up at all the meetings. He's got leadership, whereas Ted, you know, he's not voicing his opinions. He's a good engineer, but I don't see him as management material." (Asian American male)

At its worst, the corporate culture favored those who adopted a "bullying" approach, where the prerequisite mentality was "to be willing to step on other people's toes," "think of only yourself, and not for the collective group," "to beat other people down for their ideas, because your ideas are better." Not surprisingly, such individualistic behavior stifled opinion and exchange, creating an atmosphere of intimidation. Yet as another researcher has noted, expert cultures reaffirm this authoritarian style by valuing the conspicuous display of expertise, a style that also happens to be consonant with the style of majority males.

> In the expert sector, with its majority of men and minority of women, one of the most salient aspects of the workplace culture is the emphasis on expertise and the need to prove oneself and one's expertise; "conspicuous expertise," a constant fear of "not being the expert," and the common response of doing a "snow job" to impress others have been found to be characteristic of expert-sector micropolitics.... Conspicuous expertise is more consistent with traditional male gender, giving men some advantages in the new types of micropoliticking. Masculinity has traditionally been associated with proving one's expertise, particularly in technical matters.[23]

The act of transforming one's self to fit this mold is experienced as "a very artificial and very uncomfortable choice" (Asian American female). Adjustment seemed to pivot around whether they possessed a "killer instinct." The lone Asian American executive at XYZ at the time traced his own abilities in this regard to having attended a Jesuit high school, where students were socialized to develop this instinct, to see themselves as among "the best," and to display their talents so that they were positioned to lead. This included the ability to take a "controversial stand," to "do battle," to choose direct confrontation over negotiation. By contrast, "the Asian personality tends to be low-key, quiet. We'll talk when there is a requirement to talk. White males will pound the table" (Asian American male).

Asian styles of participation, by contrast, revolved around cultural norms of modesty, self-effacement, deference and respect toward others, collective decision making, and consensus building. For many, the implicit bias in XYZ's organizational culture transformed deeply held personal values into negative attributes.

> I was brought up by my grandparents who were very devout Buddhists, and you don't, in Japan, for example, you don't promote yourself. That's a real "no-no," you know. So I was brought up with that, so it's very difficult for me, for example, in an interview process to say a lot of good things about [myself] . . . that's a detriment, and I think Asian Americans suffer from that, a lot of them. . . . I think it's more ingrained than people realize, that trait.

Cultural modesty not only failed to earn one recognition at XYZ but was a serious liability. As a young, aspiring manager pointed out, bluffing and expressions of bravado are necessary for demonstrating one's worth to others: "Most of them [Asian Americans] . . . do not know how to boast." Even where Asian American employees are not actively self-disparaging (one way cultural modesty gets manifested), they still unwittingly undercut evaluations of their own job performance by failing to "toot their own horn" and by assuming the objective merits of their work are obvious.

In sum, on the surface, "communication skills" or "leadership skills" are neutral criteria or standards, but given the relational dimension to these qualities, there are culturally diverse ways in which these might be displayed. At XYZ Aerospace, however, there was a deeply entrenched subculture that impeded the recognition of other managerial styles.

When asked if there were any special Asian American managerial traits, respondents mentioned the following: (1) listening and consensus-building skills, (2) "thoroughness and follow-through," (3) an ability to effectively coordinate a team, and (4) skill in assessing the *individual* rather than seeing the individual simply as part of a group.

Listening skills lent themselves to organizational goals in different ways. They were associated with greater efficiency, especially given the competition for "air time" in compressed and hurried meetings. As one manager observed, a "quiet" person is likely to "make a very thoughtful decision, and you don't have to hear a whole long, drawn-out dissertation before they reach that decision." Similarly, another person noted that the same quality might facilitate the ability to quickly achieve consensus through the ability to hear and absorb different viewpoints. The etiquette involved in being "considerate" almost required a certain amount of mind-reading—being "considerate in the sense that you consider everybody's needs and what they're really saying or asking, with some thought about what they need." In this way, good listeners were transformed into "consensus builders," managers who are "not autocratic, not dictatorial," departing markedly from the "real cutthroat kind of style."

A cultural concern about efficiency attends not only how things get communicated but how they actually get done. Thus, one person underscored "thoroughness and follow-through" as a trait Asian Americans are likely to bring to administrative tasks, which may explain their overrepresentation as low- and middle-level managers, as well as their criticism of managers with little follow-through: "I've seen a lot of other managers who jump from project to project and never finish their work, and it's frustrating working with them." The following middle manager echoed this view, noting that Asian Americans displayed a "get-it-done attitude." When asked about artificial barriers, she responded:

> Some of what I perceive to be the barriers are just the differences in management styles. I've noticed a lot of non-Asian managers having a difficult time making decisions or at least expressing their stand on a subject area. Whereas most of the Asian American managers I've seen want to discuss a subject and come to a conclusion at the same meeting ("get it done" attitude) and it becomes frustrating always waiting for things to happen. (Asian American female)

The very appeal of middle and upper managerial work was linked with the desire to achieve visible results, to have a direct influence on organizational decisions or policy. The opportunity to influence the direction of the organization through the grooming of successors was a second, key factor. As an interview with the sole Asian American senior executive explained:

> It [senior management] allows you to define, create, and implement a vision of where you want to go and where you want the organization to go, and how it fits within the overall [XYZ Aerospace] vision. And second is, it helps you groom and train your successors or your "fast track" people. (Asian American male)

Finally, the fourth self-ascribed trait that Asian Americans see themselves as bringing to managerial work are their sensibilities when it comes to assessing the *individual*. This may seem incongruent with a collective orientation, but the two issues are closely interconnected. Thus, an administrative manager in human resources reported that Asian Americans would "trust and believe in individual abilities," "look at what a person can do," elaborating, "They don't look at a person as part of a group but as an individual." At the same time, their cultural expectations about mentoring assume that supervisors will take a more active, paternalistic role in monitoring their careers. By contrast, the corporate culture at XYZ was that each person was individually responsible for managing his or her own career. The following person described how the culture clash worked against Asian Americans who focused simply on doing a job well.

> It's easy to come into an organization, especially a large government organization, and say, "They're going to take care of me. As long as I do my work, I'll get recognized. I'll get my promotions." That would be fine, but that's not always the case, and things aren't going to work as smoothly as that at times . . . I think that this is a cultural value that Asians have. . . .
>
> But American culture focuses on the individual, and so you really need to take care of yourself, and XYZ is pretty clear in career development. They say career development is the individual employee's responsibility, so even though there are certain mechanisms to help the employee—there's the performance plan, and career development plans—your manager may not have the time to come to you and say, "I'd like to sit down with you . . . and work out where you'll be in the next few years, so you'll get what you need to get your job done, and get to your fifteen or twenty-year career goal." . . . If the individual doesn't take the initiative to go to his or her manager and say, "I want to sit down and spend some time with you and talk about the work I'm doing and the areas I need to improve," that type of discussion isn't going to happen, and they're going to fall behind on their career. (Asian American male)

The individual cannot be entirely blamed for failing to take charge of his or her career. Long-range career planning was also thwarted by a "chaotic management structure" that was at odds with the "traditional Asian preference for clear lines of authority." As a chair of the employee association explained:

> It's a rather chaotic management structure where there are no clear levels of responsibility. It opens up opportunities to those who are aggressive. This is a cultural environment which is contrary to the traditional Asian preference for clear lines of authority. For example, I have two different bosses—a supervisor who is responsible for my performance evaluation and appraisal and a project manager who determines my assignments. They may not speak to one another, and I would have to get the project manager, who knows my work better, to lobby on my behalf. This kind of structure repeats itself all the way, with each person having two or three bosses.

For this reason, it is not simply mentorship in the form of periodic feedback that is essential but sustained mentorship over the long haul, for example, sponsorship in critical developmental assignments, ensuring that the individual maintains high visibility and exposure to wider networks. This kind of mentoring, moreover, was not simply there for the asking, and Asian Americans were rarely identified for fast-tracking.

Ironically, though disinclined toward self-promotion, the very fact that Asian Americans were not part of the old boy network ultimately impelled many to exert greater initiative on their own behalf. Thus, the following GS-15 level manager described how his progress up the ladder had been arduous, the result of sheer perseverance and aggressiveness in applying for vacancies.[24] He did not have the endorsement or sponsorship of his immediate supervisor, who resented these individual career moves and worked against him at every turn.

> The training office does say that "these positions are open and anybody can apply, and please come and take at look at what is applicable for you." But if you're not chosen by somebody or sponsored by somebody, it's tough to get in.... I wasn't appointed to high-visibility assignments. I actually went for them and aggressively asked for them. There were no role mentors. I had no individual career plan written. I had a goal and I didn't have any feedback worthwhile from the supervisors.

Dual Ladders and Dual Standards

If the corporate culture was implicitly skewed toward rewarding the behavioral styles of white males, this was not the only artificial barrier. The dual ladder and dual standards represented two quite different forms of internal structural barriers.

The Dual Ladder

The dual ladder is comprised of an administrative and a technical ladder. The promotional criteria for each ladder differ. The technical ladder was created to accommodate professionals who wanted to pursue their research careers rather than be forced into management, originating out of a sincere attempt by organization to "make alternative goals viable" to valued professionals.[25] At XYZ, Asian Americans were concentrated on the technical ladder. Although senior executive positions are theoretically available to employees on either ladder and technical proficiency continues to be a formal requirement, in practice crossing over to the administrative ladder is difficult. For one, at the point of midcareer, when managerial aspirations are likely to develop,[26] the window of opportunity for making the transition to the administrative ladder is exceedingly narrow. As one respondent explained, there might only be "two or three chances" in the course of one's entire career. Personally, he was given few such opportunities in his formative years.

> My complaint in the past was if you were not given an opportunity to manage . . . when you are in the thirties and early forties, as a first-line manager, you would never reach a middle manager by the time you are fifty. And then you will never reach the top manager. And one person, any person, can have only two or three chances in his or her career to move from one area to the other . . . and if they don't let you to do it, you will forever will be bounded in terms of the lower management, which is the most difficult part of the management. In the earlier part of my career, when I was in the forties and

I aspired to choose a managerial career because I thought it will be a faster way of promotions, and whenever the chances arrived, I applied [on] a number of occasions. It was just a dead-end. (Asian American male)

Second, highly specialized training is now reputed to be a liability when senior management calls for broad-based organizational and communication skills necessary for participating in a global environment encompassing a wider range of publics, organizational units, or domains.

In general, the dominant perception was that Asian Americans were neither interested nor qualified to assume such leadership positions. The head of the Diversity Leadership Consortium called attention to the pervasiveness of this stereotype as follows:

I think the perception at XYZ and maybe a lot of organizations is that Asians don't want to be in charge. They're not meant to be in charge of anything. They're good workers, they're good analysts, they're good engineers, they're good accountants, because they really get in and learn it and do well, but they're not meant to be in charge ... [of a project] or an organization. Not just the people part, but the whole thing. Setting the tone, being accountable, being the one whom everybody comes to when something goes wrong. . . . That they're not good business managers. Meaning actually managing the business of the organization.

The employee survey data, however, have repeatedly indicated significant managerial interest (53 percent) among Asian Americans at XYZ. Upper management, in fact, was described as complicit in creating the perception that Asians were "not interested" in management—for example, by soliciting applications from those already committed to research activities. As one person explained, "The game is being played that they don't ask those, except those they know aren't interested. . . . It's a way to keep the pipeline dried up and empty."

Increasing seniority has been associated with increasing perceptions of a glass ceiling.[27] Jayjia Hsia thus observed: "Across all fields, Asian Americans with less than 15 years of experience earned comparatively higher salaries than those with more experience. Overall, Asian Americans with 15 years or more of experience earned on the average up to 4% less than whites with similar experience."[28] At XYZ, older employers were more likely to perceive artificial barriers than younger recruits.

Age may be correlated with career mobility for three reasons: (1) cultural, (2) relative competitiveness on the labor market, and (3) location on the ladder. The cultural explanation suggests that older and less acculturated Asian Americans will have greater communication problems as well as greater social or cultural constraints preventing them from venturing outside certain networks or niches. Younger, more acculturated Asian Americans, by contrast, have the

cultural currency for making themselves more visible, being less culturally reserved, more outspoken, "savvy," or outgoing.

A second possible reason for the greater barriers experienced by more senior
scientists and engineers is related to institutional efforts to retain "young, promis-
ing" recruits who are competitively sought by other employers. According to one
senior scientist, this practice occurs at the expense of "older, productive" members.

Third, perceptions of a glass ceiling obviously vary by age because of one's
location on the ladder. At XYZ, opportunities to apply for managerial jobs with
important decision-making responsibilities do not arise until one has already
passed through certain grade levels. GS-13 is, strictly speaking, a "nonmanagerial" position and was considered the cut-off point or dividing line between
nonmanagerial and managerial jobs. Younger employees, those below level
GS-13, were said to be more optimistic about their career prospects. The following twenty-five-year-old male was thus "highly satisfied," with the "exposure"
already given him in terms of visible job assignments. Informally, he socialized with his supervisors and other superiors after hours, playing on a softball
team. Overall, he was confident that his hard work will continue to pay off in
the years ahead.

> I think I am on track. So at twenty-seven, you should be [at grade level] 13. At
> thirty, you should be at 14. If by thirty I am not on 14, that means I am slow....
> There is "no unequal opportunity."... I haven't encountered any problems
> with promotion.... If you work hard, well, and are reliable, you will get pro-
> moted. You might have a problem communicating with your supervisors—as
> long as they know and that you don't slack off. I do know interpersonal barriers
> exist, but I have not experienced it personally. If you are good, sooner or later you
> will get promoted. (Asian American male)

Despite the optimism of such young recruits, several of their senior
counterparts pointed out that it is only with increasing seniority that one presses
against the upper levels of the corporate structure. A chief engineer thus predicted: "The younger (Asian Americans)...don't feel that strongly about the
glass ceiling. And that's because they haven't bumped up against it yet. They're
not old enough, but it's going to hit them sooner or later." Another engineer,
close to retirement, confirmed this, stating that his younger colleagues were now
coming around to this view: "Some of the younger colleagues...Asian Americans didn't see it [the problem of a glass ceiling] because they were in their
twenties. Now they're in their thirties. They recognize that I spoke with a voice
of experience instead of a voice of dissatisfaction only."

Double Standards

Depending on which side of the dual ladder one is on, there are different
promotional criteria. A more sinister kind of double standard involves the

arbitrary application of evaluative criteria and the numerous, shifting rationales invoked to justify a particular appointment or denial.

Both middle-level and senior managers, for example, saw lack of management training as mere pretext for exclusion given that much of their work had been learned on the job—not as a result of prior training. As one person explained, it was a catch-22 situation to require management training beforehand, when eligibility for that very training tended to be available only *after* promotion to certain grade levels. Reflecting on her own experience, a thirty-six-year-old middle manager stated: "I believe a lot of these skills (communication skills, interpersonal skills, supervisory, and leadership skills) must be *developed while in a management position* and cannot be learned and possessed before being in a management position" (Asian American female).

Other managers minimized the value of in-house training precisely because it lacked this experiential component. A forty-five-year-old contracting officer with an MBA thus explained:

> The courses are designed to familiarize the specialist with the regulations, the processes, but it doesn't teach him how to make a decision. So that kind of comes from the school of hard knocks. You make some good decisions and some bad, and hopefully you learn from the bad decisions, and the good decisions. (Asian American male)

A sixty-eight-year-old engineer with a thirty-nine-year history at XYZ similarly noted that managerial experience was primarily acquired on the job, humorously adding that in the past there was no pretense to these appointments being anything other than fairly informal and casual. "They give you a two- or three-week course at the training facility back east, but they don't really teach you how to be a manager. I think you really have to learn it on the job. What they used to do is they used to pick the best researchers.... They'd say, 'Hey, we're promoting you to a manager.'" A fifty-seven-year-old administrator with a doctorate in electrical engineering commented that on-the-job training was more important than the degree he had in hand.

> I have a Ph.D. in electrical engineering, and that background helps me to understand the research environment of our organization, R&D activities that go on in my organization. But I don't use that training per se. I don't have to have a Ph.D. to do my job. So it's sort of like on-the-job training along the way, so to speak, which got me here.
>
> I think I'm a good manager, and I've learned various skills on the job and also through training. You just acquire lots of experience when you're in management over the years, and you're using all those experiences, background to manage this organization. So it's pretty broad.

In keeping with the legal/scientific mentality that framed their organizational experience as scientists, Asian Americans took seriously the emphasis on the government's professed concern for objective qualifications like educational and work experience. To be bypassed by less qualified candidates was the source of many grievances.

The following account by a senior scientist with a doctorate is discussed at length because it best illustrates how various rationales were invoked to disqualify—lack of management training, lack of certain degree requirements, and concern over possibly losing a person's valuable contributions as a researcher. He recounted how upper management repeatedly ignored his superior degree qualifications. Initially denied the opportunity to move into management because he lacked management training, he was subsequently denied training on the grounds that he was not management material. Refused the privilege of receiving training at the XYZ Aerospace's own facilities, he relied on his own resources to pursue an MBA.

> So finally I said, "If I have to do it, I have to do it myself." And to go to evening school . . . is one of the least desirable avenues for any XYZ employee because usually you get paid full-time to go . . . for training in the XYZ facilities. . . . Working full-time and holding an evening job is not desirable for most of the XYZ employees. [I wanted] to prove the point that management is not that difficult, or that it should be limited to a particular race or particular age group. That's why I went for the MBA training.

Like management training, the MBA was seen as largely irrelevant— except as a screening device. As a chair of the Diversity Leadership Council frankly stated: "I'd be surprised if there were two MBAs at XYZ in managerial positions."

Eventually appointed as branch chief at the GS-15 level, this same manager was again bypassed on two subsequent occasions when he sought to move to the level of assistant division chief. As he related this, in the first instance the center hired someone from outside the division, who lacked his experience and superior degree qualifications. When confronted on the contradictions here, management offered a new rationale for its decision—alleged concern that his own technical project might suffer if he were to be promoted.

> I was told, "He [the other candidate] is an excellent candidate. He has excellent qualifications." So I asked what was his qualification. They said, "Oh, he has a master's degree in electrical engineering from Stanford." "Oh," I said "I have a master's and a Ph.D. degree from the same university." Then I was told he has an MBA degree from [name of university], which is a correspondence course. I said, "I have an MBA from [name of university], which is a much better university. Besides I've been in the division and know the things, and I've been at headquarters for a year." But then the argument was, "You are so valuable as a member of the technical staff. We cannot afford to lose you. If you move up in the managerial ladder, your technical project will flounder." I didn't buy that argument at all. I could have trained and nurtured the project half time, and carried the managerial duties [as well] . . . that's the first time I began to realize

> there is a subconscious—I'm not saying there is conscious discrimination—but there is a very inbred discrimination—they prefer white males over Asian Americans.

Later on, when the position of assistant division chief again became open, he once again applied and again was passed over, this time by someone with even lower qualifications.

> I was encouraged to apply and I did. I was not even considered, and the whole process was totally ludicrous to me because I was told they selected somebody who has better scientific qualifications. But in the end it's somebody who has only a bachelor's degree with no publications or records.... The rating is very subjective.

In sum, the decision-making process was perceived as overly subjective and arbitrary in the manner it removed certain candidates from managerial consideration and continually adjusted the rationale for exclusion. As one person succinctly stated, "If they want to promote you, they don't need a reason. If they don't want to hire you, they'll come up with a thousand reasons why not." Perfunctory interviews of minority and women candidates reinforced this view. One person thus recalled not being taken seriously in his own interview:

> I remember one time there was an opening for this technical assistant, and I applied for the job. And then he invited me in for an interview. And I remember sitting upstairs in his office, and he had a set of questions that he had prepared. So he'd read off a question, and I'd start to expand—you know, give him my answers. And I looked at him, and he was kind of looking out the window ... he wasn't really paying attention. All he was doing was going through the motions, so he could say, "I interviewed an Asian."

In sum, although the popular mindset is accustomed to thinking of preferential treatment in terms of unfair advantages given to minorities and women, the strong opinion among Asian American professionals was that preferential treatment has been disproportionately accorded to white males. Reflecting on his history with the organization over the past several decades, another manager singled out the buddy system as the major reason for the glass ceiling.

> Promotion is not on merit but through social circles.... The criterion is not ability but friendship. I don't think people are out to "get" Asians. I just think that Asians aren't in these social circles. You can quote me on that.... It's my perception that what had happened in the old days was that the old white boy network reserved the managerial jobs for themselves. That was their preserve; they didn't want to let any minorities in.

In the context of his immediate work sphere, he had observed his supervisor promoting only a small coterie of individuals: "all his white male friends . . . got to be deputy directors, directors, branch chiefs, division chiefs, despite some of them being very, very poor administrators and very poor researchers." That these individuals turned out to be inferior or mediocre in both research and management is perhaps the most objective evidence that the standards were vulnerable to inappropriate subjective bias.

Bad appointments not only impeded those working under such administrators but produced periodic crises for the organization as a whole.

> I know I'm a very good manager. I've been told by my subordinates as well as my superiors that I was very good manager, in terms of administrative ability as well as personnel judgment. . . . The disappointment was that the people who were chosen above me were not as competent. . . . I mean, it's not only one occasion, there are a couple of occasions. Their lack of performance [indicates] . . . that system is not choosing the best person available.

According to an employee survey conducted during a widespread organizational crisis in the 1970s, one division head had garnered more than 200 complaints. Suboptimal performance among white male administrators, however, rarely evoked sanction. In this instance, the division head was not fired but moved "upstairs." Moreover, poor leadership was more likely to be framed by center management as an individual problem rather than as a problem generalizable to other white males.

Tolerance of mediocrity and failure by white males was a luxury not granted others. By contrast, minorities and women who experienced difficulties as administrators often became lightning rods for backlash against minorities, women, and all those labeled "affirmative action" hires. One respondent described this dual standard as follows:

> I am appalled by the quality of individual that gets promoted here very often, who gets put at the level of responsibility that I think they have no qualification for or no right to be there. . . . I'm amazed by the incompetence that's rewarded and promoted here. . . . There's a tolerance for white males to get promoted even though they're totally incompetent, whereas there's not tolerance for an Asian, or other type of minority, or woman to get promoted, if they're incompetent. So I think in one way that the glass ceiling is manifested in the lower tolerance that people feel towards Asians specifically and minorities in general. . . . Poor leadership has been a problem since the late 1970s and X [Asian administrator] was merely the lightning rod for people to focus their dissatisfactions with the center and the future onto him. The same thing with other Asians who get promoted. . . . So in a nutshell, I think women and minorities are scrutinized much more closely than white men. (Asian American male)

MANAGING AND LEADING IN THE TWENTY-FIRST CENTURY

Ideas such as diversity and excellence, the diversity advantage, and diversity management emerged in the 1980s and were publicly embraced by leaders in government, corporations, and universities alike. However, concern or uncertainty continues about how this diversity is achieved and the extent to which the selection process is optimally designed to recognize diverse criteria for excellence and thereby broaden the pool of eligible leaders.

The preceding section echoed what many social analysts have already pointed out in other contexts—that employer evaluations are highly subjective, vulnerable to subtle biases that implicitly favor certain candidates over others.[29] At XYZ Aerospace, glass ceiling barriers indicated a playing field tilted to favor a narrow group of individuals and an authoritarian style of leadership. Weber's concept of traditional authority is an ideal type that captures many elements of this leadership style—a command-and-control form of management exercised through a patriarchal structure and revolving around individuals linked through personal loyalties and shared backgrounds. Asian Americans were quick to note that this leadership culture was antagonistic to their own culturally preferred modes of social interaction. Interviewees repeatedly observed, moreover, that while promotions were cloaked in the language of merit and universalistic criteria,[30] so, too, was discrimination. Their grievances drew legitimacy from a government bureaucracy that is publicly committed to providing standardized, bureaucratic guidelines related to job assignment, evaluation, and promotions. In short, all of this occurred, moreover, in a liberal workplace environment that has claimed to pride itself on diversity.

More than two decades ago, Rosabeth Moss Kanter observed that the authoritarian model is becoming increasingly outmoded:

> In the new environment . . . the unquestioned authority of managers in the corporation of the past has been replaced by the need for negotiations and relationships outside the immediate managerial domain, by the need for managers to *persuade* rather than *order*, and by the need to acknowledge the expertise of those below.[31]

Other writers subsequently echoed this theme, acknowledging that more innovative organizations call for more flexible, nonhierarchical relations that give employees greater initiative and discretion in problem solving.[32]

This dynamic operating environment now characterizes a number of working environments where micromanaging—being in full control—can actually cripple one's capacity to lead. At XYZ, Asian Americans were perceived as being perfectionists, unwilling to delegate for fear that another's mistakes would negatively affect their own performance: "They try to control everything. And that's *disaster* for them because when you get to be a division head, there's no way you're going to be able to control all this stuff" (Asian American male, senior executive). Jean Otte, founder and CEO of WOMEN Unlimited Inc. (WUI), made this similar observation when discussing this tendency as the most troublesome of the top five issues facing women executives at Fortune 1000 companies: (1) trying to do it all, (2) lack of confidence in the position ("impostor syndrome"), (3) lack of strategic alliances (no old girls network), (4) not feeling valued by their organization, and (5) the tension between women in the workplace.[33]

In her coaching work, Gillian Khoo is often called by the board of directors of a company where a CEO's performance is undermined by some character flaw. A typical profile is someone who is "charismatic, results-oriented, technically brilliant but whose abusive style is causing high turnover and low morale." Thus one executive was capable of being "extremely charming" but could transform into an abusive boss when his orders were not carried out to the letter. In short, Weber's three types of authority, though historically based, are analytically distinct as ideal types. In practice, today's CEOs can embody elements from one or more ideal types.

The following case study illustrates how certain obstacles to advancement can evaporate with the strategic intervention of an executive coach. As described by Khoo, the case illustrates how coaching was effective in broadening and deepening the skills of an Asian American female manager who was thereafter able to cultivate a strategic orientation that enabled her to move into the senior ranks. Khoo's client's challenges are not unique but are faced by many (male and female, from different industries and racial and cultural backgrounds) at both the managerial and executive ranks with whom she has worked over the past fourteen years.

CASE STUDY: FAZ FINANCIAL SERVICES

Mavis works at a Fortune 100 company, FAZ (pseudonym), a financial services firm that has cornered the market on credit cards, auto loans, and home mortgages. The culture at FAZ is young, aggressive, and fast paced. The majority of associates, a handful of whom are already VPs, are in their twenties. It is common for associates to have four different bosses in one year as FAZ aggressively reorganizes and restructures to keep ahead of business trends and challenges. FAZ values intellectual exchanges for what they might generate in terms of new ideas or solutions.

Mavis joined FAZ five years ago and was viewed as an interpersonally skilled manager with excellent project management skills. A single Indian female who grew up in Asia, she was in her early forties at the time of her coaching experience, and had been a U.S. resident for about eighteen years. She enjoyed a strong reputation for delivering superior results on time and under budget. Yet despite her qualifications and exceptional record of achievement she was viewed as a "subject matter" expert, that is, one who was not capable of leading a larger organization with multiple jobs and functions. She therefore hired Khoo as her executive coach to help her overcome the barriers to the next level of promotion. Khoo conducted a series of 360-degree qualitative interviews with Mavis's key stakeholders, after which she worked explicitly on broadening Mavis's leadership skills. Specifically, this included strengthening her strategic thinking and alignment as well as her self-confidence and influencing skills. Mavis was successfully promoted within six months.

Strategic thinking refers to a leader's ability to recognize relationships and complexities, understand the broad implications of issues from multiple perspectives, and visualize what might or could be, all the while tying day-to-day operations to broader organizational goals. Strategic planning is an event, whereas strategic thinking is an approach. Many mid-level managers experience difficulty thinking strategically because the requirements of management focus the individual elsewhere, namely, on executing tasks and delivering short-term results. So it is not surprising that Mavis was perceived by her peers, superiors, and internal customers as having a narrow bandwidth when it came to leading an organization with multiple functions. Specifically, her challenge with thinking strategically had less to do with an absence of skills per se than with an overemphasis on details that prevented her from integrating the business challenges she was working on with the complexities FAZ was facing. This misplaced emphasis prevented her from focusing on the broader context and in turn created a perception of her as a leader who was not capable of thinking strategically. One of her superiors thus suggested the following:

> She still has a greater opportunity from where she is now from an analytical perspective to a strategic perspective. She will dive into the details, which is fantastic, but she has a tendency to go to the details versus solving a broader problem. What I have seen others do is you have the person on the ground who will take care of the tactics so you don't have to concentrate on that. It is a delegation issue. It frees you up to build up the longer-term strategy.

Her internal customers, in turn, offered the following insights:

> The most critical thing that Mavis needs to do is engage in integrative thinking and specifically define what are the big opportunities. Organize the opportunities, define the problems, and effectively govern her team through producing results that come out from a really well-thought-through strategy.
>
> She knows what is going on strategically, but she does not put in into context. How is she aligning herself against those strategic priorities and how is what we are doing aligned with those priorities? How is she explaining it, representing her and her team against that strategic vision?

A second barrier for many mid-level managers pertains to the lack of *strategic alliances* across their organizations. Strategic alignment involves networking and building relationships throughout the organization, cultivating deep pockets of support, and influencing key stakeholders who are willing to back up and expand one's visibility. About the importance of strategic alliance, Otte succinctly observed, "It's not what you know. It's who knows you know."[34]

Mavis's visibility was narrowly confined to her areas of responsibility, and she lacked visibility with her boss's boss and the rest of the senior executives. Her boss's boss commented:

> Content wise, she has yet to create a story for her business or herself. What is the elevator speech on Mavis? I don't know. To date, that five-minute story, what she has done and where she has proven her competencies has been single dimensional. She has that opportunity now, which she didn't before, to . . . influence, help shape the strategy, and contribute. Mavis needs to put a stake in the ground and say, "Here is what I am doing. Here is what I can do for you. Here is what we can do together." Otherwise, how will I know what she can do? How can I sell her to my peers (the rest of the senior management team) if I don't know what her story is?

The quote illustrates that strategic alignment involves more than just building key relationships; it requires framing one's value proposition ("this is what I am about") and inspiring followership ("this is what we can do together"), establishing one's identity as a leader ("this is what I stand for").

Incorporating these perspectives, Khoo adopted the following steps to put Mavis on track. The two worked together to modify not simply Mavis's behavior but her overall cognitive orientation toward her work, so that her objectives encompassed larger outcomes.

Strategic Thinking

1. We started by having Mavis envision the many possibilities and opportunities in her line of business and for the overall company. She was encouraged to generate as many possibilities as she could from a variety of perspectives: In her current role as a group manager, in her desired role as a senior director, and as the CEO. These exercises freed her from artificial constraints, helped her extrapolate different business opportunities across the organization, and then ground her goals and vision by building the business case for it.
2. Recognizing her tendency to dive into the details and tactics, Khoo had Mavis concentrate instead on organizing opportunities and defining problems. This enabled her to become more proactive and less reactive. Some of the key questions Khoo had Mavis ask herself were: "What are my business goals and how am I aligning myself against my strategic priorities? How will success be measured? What are the implicit and explicit conditions of satisfaction? What is the 180-degree view of what

I want to do and what is the impact of that? Where can I focus my energies to yield maximum impact? To what extent am I managing that change and impact?"

3. In addition, Mavis started holding regular sessions with her team whereby they shifted their focus from activity (tasks, details, what needs to be done) to impact ("What do we want to achieve at the end of the day? In what ways will it support the broader strategy?"). The distinction between impact and activity was an important one and assisted Mavis in governing her team toward producing results from a well-thought-out strategy.

4. To counter the perception that Mavis was not capable of leading a larger organization with multiple jobs and functions because of her perceived (narrow) subject matter expertise, we leveraged her strong interpersonal skills to help her use the expertise of others. Whereas in the past Mavis might have felt compelled to become a subject matter expert, she now had to learn how to use her relationships to get the work done. Mavis began to meet with experts in and out of her areas of responsibility, and was careful to listen to their challenges and input. As a result, she was able to paint a picture of the business and political landscape that captured the web of relationships essential to success.

Building Strategic Alliances

5. Mavis was willing to acknowledge that her deep expertise and strong record of achievement did not automatically qualify her for a promotion, and that it was necessary for her to develop more effective influencing and political savvy skills (strategic alignment). Though she was initially frustrated, she did not allow her frustration to turn into resentment. This paved the way for her to have conversations with those above and around her as to how she was perceived and what she could do to address their concerns about her perceived lack of leadership and strategic thinking skills. These conversations, along with her genuine willingness in addressing their concerns, had the added benefit of helping Mavis establish closer relationships and garner support for her promotion.

6. With the assistance of Mavis's boss, Khoo and Mavis mapped out an action plan that redirected Mavis's efforts into projects that would yield the biggest payoff and alignment to FAZ's most pressing business challenges. They also included a stakeholder analysis and incorporated opportunities for Mavis to interface and influence these stakeholders in their action plan. Her boss was very willing to discuss her achievements with his boss and his peers and was conscious about including Mavis in these meetings, where appropriate.

7. They focused on strengthening and fine-tuning Mavis's communicating and influencing skills and used a variety of mediums (role-plays, observing, and/or video-taping Mavis at meetings and presentations) to reinforce these learnings.
8. Mavis was accountable for having follow-up conversations with key stakeholders about her progress in addressing their concerns. This gave her the opportunity to share her ongoing accomplishments with them and allowed her to better manage their perceptions.
9. Mavis and Khoo administered a mini-survey after three months and again at six months to measure the extent to which Mavis was being perceived as being more effective on the skills she was cultivating. For example, "On a scale from 1 (ineffective) to 5 (very effective), to what extent has this person become more (or less) effective at the following behaviors?"

The executive coaching engagement was concluded on Mavis's successful promotion six months later.

Coaching is more effective than formalized mentorship programs because the latter does not enforce accountability. If an individual's company does not have the resources to provide coaching, Khoo offers the following recommendations:

1. Let go of the thinking and expectation that great work and stronger qualifications will automatically lead to greater promotions. Although this may be true at the lower and more technical levels, it stops being so at the upper levels of management.
2. Take full responsibility for your own career advancement. Have regular and candid discussions about what it takes to be successful. For example, what are the behaviors that are rewarded? Punished?
3. Cultivate a deep understanding of your own strengths and opportunities. For Asian Americans, make sure the list of developmental opportunities is not greater than your strengths.
4. Learn how to seek and give feedback (at least monthly) without being defensive.
5. Have the courage to ask your boss, peers, internal customers, and direct reports about what they see as your key areas of strengths and opportunities for development. Thank them for their feedback, and act on their suggestions where appropriate.
6. Become a student of organizational politics. Who has the most influence, and how do they exert and use it? Do you know who your key stakeholders are and what matters most to them? Which relationships are most important to cultivate? How are decisions made in your organizations? Whose decisions matter most? What can you control or influence? What can't you?

7. Create a network of support as you work to address areas for development and strengthen your strengths. People love to help if asked, . . . and asking for help is not a sign of weakness but a sign of strength.
8. Have quarterly meetings with your bosses to discuss current business goals and critical priorities. If you don't, you will waste your time working on the least important thing instead of refocusing your energies on that which will lead to the biggest payoff.
9. At the end of the day, practice gratitude for all that you are and for all that surrounds you.[35]

FINAL THOUGHTS

Although corporate cultures have changed over the years, two competing models of authority—traditional versus legal/rational—still play themselves out as crosscurrents in many organizations. The subjective interpretation of objective standards is one major example of how these crosscurrents converged. As contradictory subcultures, they together erect artificial barriers for women and minorities. One reason is that newcomers to the scene fervently want to believe in the legal/rational ideal of merit-based promotion—that they will be judged based on their qualities, not by some ascribed attribute like race or gender. At the same time, these individuals are excluded from those professional networks that are tied into higher levels of decision making. Their objective achievements mean little, in other words, without the strategic alliances that make these accomplishments visible to upper management.

For both Woo and Khoo, an important aspect of leadership is to provide opportunities for employees to grow. The tough boss model is highly problematic in diverse workplace environments where a heterogeneous workforce manifests different cultural sensibilities and behavioral styles. Environments of fear suppress the free expression of ideas. The directive style is more common among older managers and leaders (i.e., in their fifties or older) and more prevalent in stable organizations (e.g., government) than, say, in fast-paced and leaner companies on the cutting edge. Although a directive style is associated with Asian and Asian American leadership styles, other valued traits include humility and self-knowledge.[36] By contrast, the aggressive domineering style evident among white males at XYZ Aerospace allowed no room for more collective styles of expression and persuasion. The closed nature of the old boy network, in turn, denied outsiders access to strategic alliances.

Although FAZ did not revolve around an autocratic culture like that at XYZ, it nevertheless favored a certain group of employees (i.e., young males in their twenties). Specifically, the company espoused competitive, "in your face" business debates to generate new ideas and solutions. Young, aggressive males, however, are more willing to "stick their neck out" in situations of conflict and engage more forcefully than are females, who, for the most part, are more inclined to adopt an accommodating or collaborative negotiating style. Khoo's intervention enabled her client to redirect her existing skills in other ways that were self-transformative. In doing so, she demonstrated that executive skills are not simply inborn qualities often associated with charismatic leaders. Rather, they can be cultivated, acquired, and fine-tuned with systematic mentoring or coaching.

Woo and Khoo differ in their orientation toward legal/rational authority as well as in their interpretation of the glass ceiling and what should be done about it. For Woo, legal/rational authority provides women and minorities a modicum of official protection against the arbitrary abuse, and therefore glass ceiling complaints that are framed in these terms need to be taken seriously. For Khoo, however, the very notion of objective standards and neutral criteria is extremely misleading, belying what actually counts in the upper levels of the organizational world. Hence, she downplays the paper résumé in her coaching work because résumés focus mostly on activities and not impact. She is not surprised that technical expertise has served Asian Americans well as an indispensable qualification for middle management or that they are blocked from further advancement. Rather she perceives this as a direct result of their naive belief in bureaucratic rationality and their unrealistic expectation that superior qualifications will guarantee promotions. The barriers they face are not so much artificial but real. Asian Americans may complain about a glass ceiling when in fact they overestimate their abilities because they lack the broader organizational perspective of what is required for executive success. Hence, her earlier advice to Asian Americans to "make sure the list of developmental opportunities is not greater than your strengths." There is no glass ceiling, no artificial barriers but rather individuals who mistakenly believe they are qualified and ignore the political and organizational realities of what it takes to be successful.

Woo, on the other hand, believes that there continue to be many factors that artificially prevent otherwise qualified individuals from advancing, including the fact that the magnifying glass of scrutiny is overly applied to minorities and women. As project managers, Asian Americans at XYZ were skilled at managing problems associated with teamwork and employee participation. Their marginality to important social networks constituted an artificial barrier that excluded them from further developmental opportunities. The epitome of disregard for legal authority was the promotion of those who failed to meet what Woo would call even the basic procedural qualifications in the bureaucratic selection process (e.g., a high school diploma being acceptable in the case of white males but not other applicants). Both authors agree that an individual's résumé may imperfectly mirror a person's actual qualifications, that the selection process can become very subjective, and that the qualification standards themselves may not be reliably linked to ability to do the job. For both Woo and Khoo, this has consequences for the organization. Khoo is optimistic about helping clients individually transcend these barriers, whereas Woo is concerned about the need for greater organizational commitment toward addressing inequities that arise from the differential application of standards and the differential distribution of resources, whether they are personal connections or career development opportunities.[37]

When Woo revisited the situation at XYZ in 2005, she learned that the proportion of Asian Pacific Americans in the workforce had risen to 18.8 percent, and a higher percentage than ever before had now reached the GS-14 and GS-15 levels, poised for an SES appointment.[38] However, none were in the SES ranks, and there were now new organizational requirements as to what was required for promotion into the SES ranks, specifically, greater emphasis on "outside" management experience and the requirement to take an SES Candidate Development Program, which stipulates a minimum of two assignments outside of XYZ. "For some strange reason, there are no SESers," remarked one employee, who went on to point to an Asian American candidate who was exceptionally well qualified.[39]

> It's been two years since A went through the SES Candidate Development program. . . . I'm baffled why he's not an SESer. You usually get an appointment within twelve months usually. . . . He's done very well. People respect him, think he has leadership qualities. He has all the desirable traits. Excellent communicator, good strategic thinking, tech savvy, knows how to play the networking game. Very good about getting new business. Has done his time in Washington.

No reason has yet been offered for why this person has not been promoted. A glass ceiling, however, cannot be ruled out. Congressional testimony given by the Asian American Government Executives Network in October 2003 drew on two major reports from the Government Accountability Office, pointing to "the pervasive and pernicious existence of glass ceilings for Asian Pacific Americans throughout the federal government."[40]

Another difference between Woo and Khoo relates to their perspectives on intervention. As an organizational psychologist, Khoo tends to see solutions in more individualistic and actionable terms, for example, coaching the high-potential individual to better meet the requirements of a designated position within the company. FAZ, for example, is described by Khoo as among the best companies in terms of its willingness to invest heavily in various forms of employee and leadership training, which is highly effective when combined with executive coaching for their high-potential candidates. The fact that FAZ has been able to capture and demonstrate a positive and significant correlation between the impact of executive coaching and performance evaluations and business results reinforces the value of micro interventions.

Woo applauds such efforts but believes that grooming a select few for success leaves intact those undesirable aspects of the closed corporate culture that cause many to leave. Even enlightened leaders at XYZ and FAZ largely emphasize mentoring and assimilating individuals into the workplace rather than challenging the dominant corporate culture, or optimally realigning organizational structures and cultures so that the potential of all employees can be maximized. Most large companies in the financial industry, for example, have lagged in providing the kind of flexibility that women often need if they are to pursue both family and career.[41] Had Mavis not been single and childless, she might have encountered an impenetrable glass ceiling, regardless of the coaching she received.

Finally, Woo and Khoo agree that the talent or training required at any particular level of XYZ or FAZ does not smoothly convert into skills needed at the next level. All employees thereby have a steep learning curve when it comes to cultivating those interpersonal skills and strategic alliances that would enable them to perform more effectively in a more encompassing context. Mid-level managers, for example, have great difficulty with the transition to upper management because their work requires micromanagement as opposed to developing a more long-range vision for company goals. This tends to handicap Asian Americans as well as women in general, who are also inclined toward a perfectionism that leads them to overlook the broader implications of the business in favor of the details. About the negative effects of such perfectionism on individuals, Otte states, "They spend an enormous amount of time collecting information on which they will base their decision. Unfortunately, the quest for perfection can lead to missed deadlines and lost opportunities."[42]

For Khoo, perfectionism is more a personality trait—an "inner glass ceiling"—that one has to unlearn. For Woo, perfectionism is organizationally structured into the position of middle managers. Organizations, in other words, create these very transition problems by narrowly circumscribing the nature of tasks at this level. Like the doctor who is rushing to save people who are drowning at the bottom of the river, the organization needs to be more alert to how dangers upstream are propelling individuals into the river. How organizations structure middle management positions may be shortsighted, causing them to lose some of their best employees. Again this is not to suggest that individual rescue measures, such as coaching and mentoring, are for naught. As another anecdote elucidates, a person standing along the shoreline desperately sought to save individual fish that somehow got washed ashore. A passerby commented on the futility of saving them all: "What difference does this make?" To which the other smilingly replied as she tossed one fish back into the sea, "To that one, all the difference in the world!"

On the issue of the glass ceiling, the crux of the difference between the authors' perspectives is an important conceptual one that has to do with how the glass ceiling has been defined. Officially, the glass ceiling has been defined as "artificial" barriers impeding otherwise qualified individuals from advancing. "Real" barriers by extension imply that an individual lacks the necessary qualifications.[43] Although the federal Glass Ceiling Commission did not explicitly draw this contrast, the distinction was implicit and deserves closer examination because of the fine line that exists here. Importantly, it has implications for the degree of responsibility to be borne, respectively, by employer and employee.

Even if one takes the bottom-line view that all hiring and promotion decisions should be based simply and solely on qualifications, the dividing line between real and artificial barriers is blurry. The commission explicitly designated lack of mentoring and lack of management training as artificial barriers. Yet these artificial barriers have a direct bearing on real barriers, preparedness, and the very issue of who is—or is not—qualified. If women are unprepared to enter managerial work because they have been poorly mentored compared to men or provided with fewer developmental opportunities, what is to be done? If their lack of required skills is the main consideration, then they may be seen as held back by barriers so fundamental that little can be done. If, on the other hand, it is recognized that mentoring and management opportunities have gone disproportionately to white males, then employers are better positioned to remove such artificial constraints. In short, despite commonly held assumptions of a level playing field, the issue of where one draws the line between artificial and real barriers is ultimately a political decision, one that has less to do with the capabilities of the candidates than with the judgments of decision makers.

In sum, leadership in the twenty-first century needs to be agile and responsive to the situational demands of a heterogeneous environment. The diversity of the workforce and the rich and varied possibilities that can constitute excellence here have yet to be fully appreciated. Minorities and women can provide a radical critique of the organizational culture, to which astute managers would be well advised to heed. Rather than suffer these employees to be canaries in the coal mine, it would be better to explore the gold mine that they represent as unique and complex individuals as well as social markers for equally unique and complex collective experiences. Potential, moreover, should not be narrowly construed as merely innate. In the case of leadership, it is precisely the intrinsically *relational* character of the concept to which organizational analysts should turn more of their attention.

NOTES

Modified from Deborah Woo, "Glass Ceiling at XYZ Aerospace," as it appeared in *Glass Ceilings and Asian Americans* (Lanham, MD: Alta Mira Press, 2000). Used with permission of Rowman and Littlefield Publishing Group.

1. Geoffrey Colvin, "CEO Knockdown," *Fortune*, April 4, 2005.
2. Ariana Huffington, *Pigs at the Trough: How Corporate Greed and Political Corruption are Undermining America* (New York: Crown), 2003.
3. Bari-Ellen Roberts and Jack E. White, *Roberts vs. Texaco: A True Story of Race and Corporate America* (New York: Avon Books, 1999); Anthony Stith, *Breaking the Glass Ceiling: Sexism and Racism in Corporate America: The Myths, the Realities and the Solutions* (Los Angeles: Warwick, 1998); Ellis Cose, *The Rage of a Privileged Class: Why Do Prosperous Blacks Still Have the Blues* (New York: Perennial, 1995).
4. Guenter Roth and Claus Wittich, eds., *Max Weber: Economy and Society*, vol. 1 (Berkeley: University of California Press, 1978), pp. 217–41.
5. Stith, *Breaking the Glass Ceiling*, p. 136.

6. Joseph Nocera, "In Business, Tough Guys Finish Last," *New York Times*, June 18, 2005.

7. Ibid.

8. Bethany McLean and Andy Serwer, "Brahmins at the Gate," *Fortune*, May 2, 2005.

9. Patrick McGeehan, "Morgan Stanley Settles Bias Suit with $54 Million," *New York Times*, July 13, 2004.

10. Ibid.

11. Amy Joyce, "If a Man Falls in the Firm, Does Anybody Notice?" *Washington Post*, February 20, 2005.

12. "She was the poster child of a leader who didn't realize you have to have followers. There was no alignment with people in her corner who could speak for her" (Jean Otte, "Special Executive Forum: Workplace Issues and Success Strategies for Women," Brisbane, CA, July 21, 2005).

13. Judy B. Rosener, *America's Competitive Secret* (New York: Oxford University Press, 1995), pp. 26–44.

14. Rosener, *America's Competitive Secret*, pp. 12–13.

15. Helen Peters and Rob Kabacoff, "A New Look at the Glass Ceiling: The Perspective from the Top," Management Research Group, Portland, ME, 2002.

16. Robert I. Kabacoff, "Gender and Leadership in the Corporate Boardroom," Management Research Group, Portland, ME, 2000; Robert I. Kabacoff, "Gender Differences in Organizational Leadership," Management Research Group, Portland, ME, 1998.

17. U.S. Office of Personnel Management, *Executive Core Qualifications*, July 1, 1998; U.S. Office of Personnel Management, *Guide to Senior Executive Service Qualifications*, February 24, 1998.

18. Margaret Karsten, *Gender, and Race in the 21st Century* (Lanham, MD: University Press of America, 2006), chapter 1.

19. Presentation by Nancy Chen, Career Advancement for APA Women—Breaking the Glass Ceiling, FAPAC Conference, 2004.

20. Deborah Woo, *Glass Ceilings and Asian Americans* (Lanham, MD: Alta Mira Press, 2000), chapter 2.

21. Woo, *Glass Ceilings and Asian Americans*, chapter 5.

22. The major goal of the interviews was to identify barriers as well as obtain a perspective on how diversity is officially managed within the organization. Thus, the interviews included middle-level managers facing barriers to their own mobility as well as senior executives who could provide a rare glimpse into these same issues from their own perspective. To provide some insight into the organizational culture and structure, I also contacted former chairs or cochairs of the Asian American employee association, two EEO officers, two members of the EEO Council, two members of the Diversity Leadership Council, and two human resources personal. In total, nineteen individuals were interviewed, fifteen of whom were Asian American. Nine were chairs or cochairs of the employee association, and ten were managers, two of whom were senior executives. The majority of Asian interviewees were male (eleven out of fifteen), with some diversity here in terms of age (from twenty-five to sixty-eight) and length of employment at Aerospace (from four to thirty-nine years), both of which influenced perceptions of the glass ceiling, as well as attitudes toward how aggressive the employee association should be in advocating for social change.

23. Beverly H. Burris, *Technocracy at Work* (New York: SUNY Press, 1993), p. 100.

24. Federal government positions have been designated by wage grades referred to as GS (general schedule) or GM (general management) levels. At XYZ Aerospace, the GS levels ranged from GS-4 to GS-16, and the GM levels ranged from GM-13 to GM-15. (The GM category was in the process of being phased out, a response to downsizing efforts.) GS-14 is the minimum pay grade for senior engineers, scientists, and managers. The highest grade is SES, and the glass ceiling is seen as resting at around the GS-12 or GS-13 levels.

25. Fred H. Golder and R. R. Ritti, "Professionalization as Career Immobility," *American Journal of Sociology* 72 (1967): 489–502.

26. In *Striking the Mother Lode in Science* (New York: Oxford University Press, 1992), Paula Stephan and Sharon Levin offer several theories about the relevance of age for researchers in scientific fields. In a chapter titled, "Why Age May Matter," the authors discuss how age is related to "the will to do science," or the willingness to continue along this career path. Even though they do not directly explore age in relationship to managerial aspirations or rewards, what they do indicate is of relevance to the glass ceiling in that at the midcareer point researchers begin to personally review and assess their career accomplishments and weigh these against other life goals. These scientists were academic scientists, primarily doctorates in the physical, earth, and life sciences (as opposed to mathematics or engineering). The "puzzle, ribbon, or gold" are the three motivating forces behind the will to do science. These undergo a reassessment or reevaluation as one approaches one's middle years (around age forty) or midcareer (associate or full professorship). From this developmental point of view, scientists are like other human beings who begin to recognize their own mortality. They begin to weigh their work aspirations against other sources of rewards in their lives as well as against the possibility of achieving or satisfying the goals that originally motivated them in their early years. For scientists, this means taking stock of their present status in the scientific community, their productivity or contributions (ability to solve "the puzzle"), and the degree to which this has won them social recognition among their colleagues or peers ("the ribbon"). The "gold" factor takes the form of determining whether there is sufficient material incentive for placing work issues above nonwork issues. Increasing age makes it increasingly apparent that financial rewards will decline with each additional year simply because there are fewer years left in one's career to collect. As a result, one may make rational calculations as to whether the costs of doing research and the further investments in time required are worth the effort. Because the remaining years in which one can cash in on one's investments are limited, the kind of financial rewards a scientist is receiving from publications, royalties, consulting fees, and speaking engagements may be important factors determining whether he or she continues along this path. In this accounting process, material factors can also affect whether the puzzle aspect of science continues to be intrinsically satisfying or whether the funding pressures for doing this work become too onerous. Alternative professional opportunities, moreover, may present themselves as viable, competing alternatives to research at this time, including a detour into administration.

27. Asian Americans for Community Involvement (AACI), *Qualified But . . . : A Report on Glass Ceiling Issues Facing Asian Americans in Silicon Valley* (San Jose: Asian Americans for Community Involvement of Santa Clara County, 1993), pp. 18–19.

28. Jayjia Hsia, *Asian Americans in Higher Education and at Work* (Hillsdale, NJ: Lawrence Erlbaum Associates, 1988), p. 199.

29. Barbara F. Reskin, *The Realities of Affirmative Action in Employment* (Washington, DC: American Sociological Association, 1998); Avery Gordon, "The Work of Corporate Culture Diversity Management," *Social Text* 44 13(3) (fall/winter 1995): 3–30, pp. 4, 7; Gertrude Ezorsky, *Racism and Justice: The Case for Affirmative Action* (Ithaca, NY: Cornell University Press, 1991).

30. For a discussion of how the discourse around merit and universalistic criteria has been permeated with arbitrary rationalizations for exclusion, which serve mainly to perpetuate the existing structure of privilege, see Troy Duster, "The Structure of Privilege and Its Universe of Discourse," *American Sociologist* 11(2) (May 1976): 73–78.

31. Rosabeth Moss Kanter, *The Change Masters: Innovation and Entrepreneurship in the American Corporation* (New York: Touchstone, 1983), p. 48.

32. Taylor H. Cox Jr. and Joycelyn A. Finley, "An Analysis of Work Specialization and Organization Level as Dimensions of Workforce Diversity," in Martin Chemers, Stuart Oskamp, and Mark A. Costanzo, eds., *Diversity in Organizations: New Perspectives for a Changing Workplace* (Thousand Oaks: Sage, 1995), pp. 62–88; Roosevelt Thomas Jr., *Redefining Diversity* (New York: Amacom, 1996), pp. 57–78; Annalee Saxenian, *Regional Advantage: Culture and Competition in Silicon Valley and Route 128* (Cambridge, MA: Harvard University Press, 1998).

33. On this last point, Otte sadly remarked that women were more inclined to take conflicts personally, whereas men engaged in fierce debate or angry exchange understood that such joustings were part of the "game." Nevertheless, women must still walk a tightrope so that they don't appear overly aggressive or domineering, on the one hand, or else unassertive or unsure. A few, like Carly Fiorina, are able to get away with a competitive negotiating style if it is part of their nature. "Special Executive Forum: Workplace Issues and Success Strategies for Women," Brisbane, CA, July 21, 2005. Jean Otte writes about the impostor syndrome in chapter 3 of her book, *Changing the Corporate Landscape: A Woman's Guide to Cultivating Leadership Excellence* (Atlanta, GA: Longstreet Press, 2004). The impostor syndrome, she says, is a experienced by successful individuals who are so driven by perfectionism that they have an unrealistic assessment of their own abilities because they typically exaggerate their shortcomings, while failing to appreciate their strengths.

34. "Special Executive Forum: Workplace Issues and Success Strategies for Women," Brisbane, CA, July 21, 2005. See also Otte, *Changing the Corporate Landscape: A Woman's Guide to Cultivating Leadership Excellence*, p. 179.

35. Because many clients focus on the negative, on what's wrong and what's missing in their careers, having them practice gratitude helps shift their attention and energy away from being the victim toward being more their own advocate.

36. D. Quinn Mills, "Asian and American Leadership Styles: How Are They Unique," Harvard Business School Working Knowledge, June 27, 2005.

37. Neutral procedures such as personal connections and qualification standards have been found to have "the greatest racist impact within employment" (Ezorsky, *Racism and Justice*, p. 24).

38. FAPAC Conference, May 31, 2005.

39. Interview with Asian American male manager, September 2, 2005.

40. Jeremy Wu and Carson Eoyang, "Asian Pacific American Senior Executives in Federal Government," in Deborah Woo, Guest Editor, special issue of AAPI Nexus, "Glass Ceiling?" Winter/Spring 2006.

41. Kathleen Pender, "The Glass Ceiling Is Still Intact," *San Francisco Chronicle*, August 4, 2005.

42. Otte, *Changing the Corporate Landscape*, p. 239.

43. This distinction is discussed in Woo, *Glass Ceilings and Asian Americans*, chapter 6. Given a certain discursive slippage in the English language, there is likely to be confusion over what is an artificial barrier and what is a "real" barrier, for lack of a better term. Woo is by no means suggesting that "artificial" barriers (e.g., discrimination) are not "real." Although the claim that one is being discriminated against might need to be established, once this is established, discrimination clearly has an objective reality or substantive consequences. What she means by "real barriers" are those having to do with the individual prerequisites for promotion, for example, education, work experience, and the like. Those who lack these bottom-line qualifications—legal, rational, bureaucratic criteria—can be perceived as in the pool of eligible candidates who are otherwise qualified to advance.

5

American Indian Women: Ways of Knowing, Ways of Leading

Linda Sue Warner

THE HEART OF THE EXPLORATION

American Indian women's interests in sovereignty and self-determination have solidified radically in recent decades.[1] The results include a transformation of roles—roles that now more readily exemplify tribal autonomy and cultural preservation. The role of American Indian women in leadership is not investigated enough. Johnson points out that native women's leadership experiences in both historic and contemporary times have been largely overlooked.[2] As a result, the research literature describes this role in terms such as "invisible" or "hidden" and references of "mystical" behaviors often are attributed to American Indian women. Studies on the double bind of minority women,[3] including American Indian women, appear as well. Fitzgerald characterizes the silence surrounding indigenous women and leadership as "deafening."[4] Her characterization of the research of leadership behaviors of indigenous women represents efforts which invite mainstream researchers to consider different views. This essay seeks to illuminate the complexities of the relationships in Indian communities, putting the leadership role of American Indian women in formal organizations at the heart of the exploration.

The analysis of the material introduces perspectives from the pedagogy of native ways of knowing. It raises questions about the nature of gendered identities and power relations in tribal communities and how they might relate to wider discourses on social and economic reform. Some of the existing literature conceptualizes American Indian women as marginalized, yet the evidence from narratives and experiences presented in this chapter suggests that gender relations are not so simply and universally determined unless we apply just one lens. Indeed, it points to alternative discourses and practices and to the evidence of clear resistance to stereotypes of princesses or squaws.

After a general review of writings about and by American Indian women, I propose a theoretical model for indigenous leadership that will enable a more focused research approach. The model is designed to characterize indigenous leadership as contextualized within a tribal community and maintained through persuasion. It is important to stress the persuasive use of words in the exercise of leadership and how that differs from corporate leadership. In contrast to corporate leadership, which is linked to a hierarchical set of specialized job performance requirements, indigenous leadership, based in native ways of knowing, has fewer boundaries.

For example, tribal governments often operate many business ventures and function as successful mainstream corporations. As such, they require job descriptions and personnel performance evaluation consistent with standard business practices. Is it possible to use these business tools in a tribal context? In a Wisconsin Indian corporation, the use of such standardized business operations was modified to incorporate American Indian core values so that budget and job performance were linked directly to the business mission. In 2003, Susan Applegate Krouse and Heather Howard-Bobiwash traced this company's history in an article titled "Keeping the Campfires Going: Urban American Indian Women's Community Work and Activism."[5] They note that "native women have adapted traditional approaches and concepts to the contemporary contexts." American Indian women formed the initial corporation, negotiating precedent-setting agreements to obtain trust status and secure the organization's financial status. The leadership continues to be provided by American Indian women when new controversies and challenges emerge.

I begin this discussion first with a disavowal of the white Eurocentric notions of leadership and propose that the historical lens that included patriarchal language is ill-equipped to provide an understanding of the roles of American Indian women in societies that are not always patriarchal. Although many factors affect the process of role construction in any culture, I propose that it is not enough to reframe these roles in contemporary social constructions with comparisons to other minority women's roles. Although that process reflects a stage in a continuum of understanding these roles, we may also inquire into the more basic adaptations of role construction using native ways of knowing. Am I suggesting that one cannot understand American Indian women's roles in leadership contexts without first understanding the fundamentals of traditional languages and cultures? Perhaps. But that would take a lifetime of experiences; the nuances of culture get reduced to the individual within it eventually. I am suggesting that ways of viewing the world and one's role in it are decidedly different for American Indian women who honor their traditions and cultures by navigating issues of success in community terms. And I am further suggesting that the lessons of this leadership style have value for disparate cultures, including those found in corporations.

For these suggestions to be valid, dealing with the range of cultures found in Indian country is critical.[6] Currently over 500 federally recognized tribes exist; this figure contrasts with the nearly 1,000 tribes and bands estimated to have occupied what is now the contiguous United States at the time of European contact.[7] The decline in the number of tribes is the result of many factors; however, contemporary American Indian communities are not simply surviving remnants of precontact societies. These communities survived the combined results of (1) political policies and practices enacted by the U.S. federal government in their sovereign-to-sovereign history and (2) American Indian efforts to shape, accommodate, or resist those policies and practices. American Indian women's leadership role exemplifies the latter through this traditional Cheyenne saying: "A nation is not conquered until the hearts of its women are on the ground. Then it is done, no matter how brave its warriors nor how strong their weapons." White Eurocentric male descriptions shaped the literature and public perceptions of American Indian women through an identity controlled by forces of capitalist patriarchy and theology. It is tempting to dismantle these conceptual frameworks as a reassuringly critical stance in relation to those found in the academic literatures of feminism and the world of work; however, the connections among identity, power, and gender in American Indian communities are more complex than the collective and deterministic descriptions provided to date.

GENDER, RACE, IDENTITY: A RESEARCH EVOLUTION

So although I propose to rethink role acquisition and its connection to leadership from an indigenous perspective, I did not start this inquiry at that point. The inquiry began with the same quantitative lens designed by mathematicians for hypothesis testing, moved to a more holistic perspective (still bound by conventional design), and evolved (is evolving) as a process to bridge naturalistic inquiry with native ways of knowing, teasing out the similarities and highlighting the rigor in language usage.

In the late 1980s, a quantitative correlation study of American Indian women supervisors was designed to test the relationship of gender, race, and job satisfaction.[8] This study, "Stereotyping and Job Satisfaction among American Indian Female Supervisors," was a correlational study of ethnic stereotypes, gender stereotypes, and job satisfaction based on Festinger's hypotheses on dissonance avoidance.[9] I found that the interaction of gender and race created contradictory roles, especially when compared to similar research on women of color. The dissatisfaction with stereotypes was higher in gender-specific roles than with stereotypes of ethnicity; yet overall, the 144 women who participated in the study did not indicate high levels of dissatisfaction as supervisors in positions in education, law, health care, governmental services, and social services—at least not statistically significant results. In fact, compared to the literature on other minority women at the time, it appeared as if American Indian women supervisors fared well in terms of job performance and salary.

The substance and strength of stereotypes shape the identities of American Indian women outside tribal communities, yet within their own tribal and intertribal interactions, specific roles are acknowledged and accepted.

A later ethnographic study, "A Study of American Indian Females in Higher Education Administration," describes six American Indian women living and working in Lawrence, Kansas, at a federal boarding school.[10] The analysis provides theoretical insights into notions of self and the construction of identities within the context of the federal workplace. The study finds that identities of gender, race, and leadership intersect and often produce dissonance within the workplace. Role-modeling emerged as a theme throughout the interviews. These American Indian women valued their contributions to the community in terms of their ability to affect other American Indian women's career choices. In this study, conclusions mirrored previous results that minimized or negated the double bind for American Indian women.

These perspectives on gender, race, and identity combine to represent strong connections with narrative examples provided by participants on identity construction. However, what is particularly relevant about this work is that the discussion is framed through standard, traditional contexts for academic research. The federal context and the nature of the conclusions make this work an important predecessor to the next examination. The 1995 study generated questions about

a. the nature of work identities in federal context;
b. how those identities relate to wider discourses; and
c. what aspects of race and issues of gender might manifest themselves across the tribal communities.

The dissonance these women described was produced when the requirements of work conflicted with the constructs of tribal community traditions. For example, an American Indian female supervising an elder American Indian male resisted using organizational sanctions for poor performance because of his status as an elder in the community. The roles within the community constrained her corporate, bureaucratic behavior.

The last study is even more narrowly focused. It is a longitudinal, comparative case study of school leadership with female and male American Indians as subjects.[11] Observation, shadowing, and interviews over a period of four years found that gender and race were linked inextricably to leadership in a fundamental community process. For both, spirituality and the sense of tribal connectedness was key to the leadership function. Leadership in indigenous communities reflects situations within traditional practices inherent in daily interactions of both the leader and the community of followers. Indigenous leadership may be constrained by gendered identities but within tribal communities is both complex and unambiguous.

INSIGHTS FROM INTERTRIBAL NARRATIVES

A discussion of intertribal issues, such as the one focusing on leadership, necessitates the conventions of comparison and this discussion on the role of American Indian women is no different. In spite of assertions and personal beliefs about differences among tribes, I have moved this discussion to one of similarities across tribes with which I am familiar through experience or scholarship.

Despite the range of environments and narrative myths surrounding indigenous women, they have made and continue to make essential contributions within their communities. The United Nations Platform for Action Committee's (UNPAC) essay on aboriginal women and the economy provides a compelling narrative of indigenous perspectives on women's work; discrimination based on gender, race, and tradition; and the resiliency of indigenous women in today's market economy.[12] The report includes efforts to develop alternatives to exploitive economics. Clearly situated in native ways of knowing, UNPAC advocates economic models based on sustainability acknowledging indigenous women's place in the informal economy.

Another essay describing misrepresentation of female roles in Lakota cultures and traditions gives evidence linking American Indian women's role in tribal communities to activism. The nine American Indian women who co-authored this article on misappropriation of cultural roles note that "men and women have different roles in Lakota society; they [women] are not subordinate, they are just different."[13] Based on their direct knowledge of the Lakota tribe's traditions and oral histories, the coauthors critique a children's book that misrepresents American Indian women's role in that tribe. The act of writing the article acknowledges a leadership role and situates this leadership in a context of community activism.

To describe the relationship among leadership and gender, race, and identity in indigenous communities, I rely on perspectives from several fields to better understand the leadership role of American Indian women. Beatrice Medicine, a cultural anthropologist, provides a basic understanding of the shifting, negotiated, and relational nature of identities and the subtle deployments of leadership in matriarchal and patriarchal communities.[14] The body of work that Medicine contributed precedes the feminist narratives of Paula Gunn Allen, Leslie Marmon Silko, Winona LaDuke, and Wilma Mankiller in exploration of conditions of leadership in contemporary tribal communities.

Medicine's career is a hallmark for scholarship that describes indigenous relationships and the role of women in American Indian societies. Trained as an anthropologist at the University of Wisconsin-Madison, Medicine's advocacy continues to influence native and nonnative scholarship, including that of scholars mentioned in the previous paragraph.

For example, an essay by Paula Gunn Allen, a Laguna Pueblo/Sioux, titled "The Sacred Hoop Perspective,"[15] links traditions and practices through feminists' relationships to provide indigenous perspectives on women's roles. Silko's (Laguna) fiction and poetry portray the relationships between traditions and practices in contemporary lives of American Indian women who attempt to negotiate these relationships daily. Silko's *Almanac of the Dead* converges around the lives of two American Indian women and seeks to define the search for balance.[16] Winona LaDuke is an Anishinaabeg (Ojibwe) and founder of White Earth Land Recovery Project. In both 1996 and 2000, LaDuke ran for vice president on the Green Party ticket. Her activism on behalf of American Indian and environmental issues can be seen in *Last Standing Woman*,[17] which is fiction, and in a nonfiction work titled *All Our Relations*.[18]

Wilma Mankiller, former principal chief of the Cherokee Nation in Oklahoma, attributes her own community activism to her understanding of her people's history, including her own family's forced removal to California and her subsequent participation as a student in the occupation of Alcatraz Island.[19] Thus, the nature of American Indian women's roles as represented in oral histories, biographies, fiction, and poetry reinforces social science scholarship on these same leadership roles.

A more extended argument made recently by Mihesuah in *Indigenous American Women: Decolonization, Empowerment, Activism* is that the concept of leadership negates the separation of individual identity and tribal community, as the individual American Indian woman and her role in the tribal community are inextricably intertwined.[20] This suggests that a different conceptualization in the study of leadership for indigenous people exists placing community at the center of future inquiry.

Mihesuah's work quotes Katsi Cook, a Mohawk activist, describing leadership by traditional women from a matrilineal clan through "relationships, not roles, within the universe and within society."[21] Mihesuah's scholarship on feminists, tribalists, and activists mirrors this theme and grounds the discussion of leadership in relationships within native communities. In contrast, Jaimes and Halsey premise their discussions on individual authority and authentic voice, equating American Indian female leadership with individual activism.[22] For their discussion, the American Indian woman in the leadership role must be Indian or feminist enough on some personal scale of these variables. Their scholarship appears to exclude the lives and work of the majority of contemporary American Indian women.

The role of American Indian women is not only underresearched, but existing readings such as the ones noted often focus on individual identity. Native ways of knowing can refocus the study of leadership roles, bringing new perspectives to bear on attempts to answer such questions as the following: What sort of leadership is this? What is the relationship among gender, race, and identity roles in indigenous leadership within tribal communities?

To answer these questions, we consider narratives within intertribal cultures and find traditions, cultures, and values (native ways of knowing) at the essence of the separate and varied answers. We move away from a linear research model into a holistic model that embraces observation (regardless of its method). We can, and sometimes do, use indigenous mathematics and science to explain the world, and such frameworks allow us to consider native ways of knowing in the social sciences, as well.

Native Ways of Knowing

Indigenous mathematics relies on other disciplines, for example, anthropology, archeology, and linguistics.[23] The diversity of number systems includes different levels of maturity, variety in their bases, and simultaneous or contemporaneous existence prior to white contact.[24] Mainstream mathematics relies on a base ten number system; indigenous mathematics may use other bases, for example, the Yup'ik use a base twenty. Denny makes a compelling case that the ability for abstract thought is equally well developed in subsistence hunting cultures and industrial societies.[25] Indigenous science has a theoretical and philosophical basis in relationships. Cajete describes indigenous science as the "cornerstone of tribal community" and the "foundation of tribal identity." Indigenous peoples relate their self-identity to a "communal soul" of their people.[26]

Leadership is therefore based on service to one's community, and indigenous communities perceive it as a role earned in the commitment to a tribal community's well-being. Cajete's assertion that our "physical and biological survival is intimately interwoven with the communities we create" and reciprocally with those communities that "create us" provides a succinct explanation for indigenous science in complex physical, social, and psychological relationships today. Indigenous society further acknowledges a "deep and abiding relationship to place" orienting discussion of leadership, particularly women's leadership, to geography, that is, to their traditional home and community.

The result is that the opportunity for inquiry expands, as we acknowledge the rigor of indigenous methods and use them to complement more familiar ones. This understanding of inquiry allows—perhaps requires—that we include narratives, such as oral traditions, in analyses for answers to our questions.

WARNER/TAHDOOAHNIPPAH LEADERSHIP MODEL

For purposes of comparison, the Warner/Tahdooahnippah Leadership Model (WTLM) begins with familiar linear expressions of variables and research methods. The descriptions are then migrated into a model that reflects native ways of knowing and begins to contextualize leadership holistically. The type of leader, determined by the extent to which the variable occurs, merges finally into the Tekwanipapu, literally "one who speaks for us all." The definition/s of leadership variables for the proposed WTLM, particularly those describing American Indian roles advance from the following:

1. perspectives of quantitative and qualitative research methods, including specific studies;
2. related narratives and oral traditions; including fiction, poetry, and creative nonfiction; and
3. experiences.

The combination, or intersection, of these three combines variables that create the beginning of a conceptualization of a leadership model for Indian country using native ways of knowing. The proposed model is the next iteration in the study of American Indian leadership and builds on the original descriptions and model.[27]

The WTLM is aligned philosophically with Smith's argument that indigenous peoples must become active participants in the research act if the goals of indigenous self-determination are to be realized by including input from colleagues and peers.[28] This model mirrors other indigenous scholars' efforts, such as Karen Gayton Swisher's initial article, "Authentic Research: Interview on the Way to the Ponderosa." Gayton Swisher continued to encourage indigenous scholarship with her 1996 publication of "Why Indian People Should Be the Ones to Write about Indian Education."[29]

In a special topics issue of *Harvard Educational Review* published in spring 2000, Lomawaima discussed issues such as access to subjects and analysis and interpretation of data, including issues of intellectual property rights.[30] In the same year, Brian Brayboy added to this scholarship in his essay on reflections of current practices.[31] Recently, Carolyn Kenny linked native ways of knowing to aboriginal research in a study of First Nations to consider a culturally appropriate research method to encourage the development of indigenous peoples as researchers.[32]

This is not a claim that the WTLM is a universally appropriate and applicable leadership model for all tribes or for American Indian women specifically; rather, it demonstrates through one case just how American Indian models allow us to include native ways of knowing in our own research perspectives. The WTLM allows us to contextualize American Indian female leadership roles in an indigenous design. The design of this leadership model was conceived as a circular, interconnecting model (see figure 5.1a). As Black Elk suggested, "Everything an Indian does is in a circle, and that is because the power of the world always works in circles, and everything tries to be found. In the old days, when we were strong and happy people, all our power came to us from the sacred hoop of the nation, and so long as the hoop was unbroken the people flourished."[33]

Traditional American Indian leadership is based on a core of spirituality tied to the community. Each of the leadership styles in this model is derived from a spiritual core that connects it to an indigenous community; in other words, though American Indian communities are spiritual communities, they are not all alike. This particular model's characteristics describe a time and

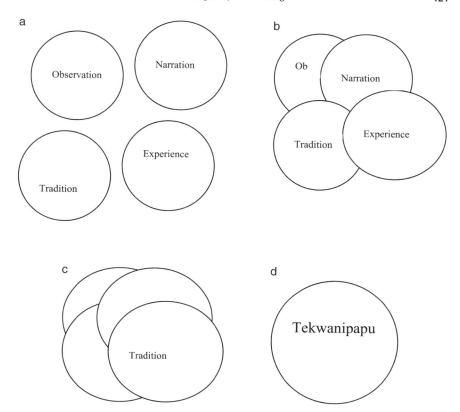

FIGURE 5.1. Warner/Tahdooahnippah leadership model.

place of leadership using four primary leadership skills, derived from the use of language, specifically the concept of persuasion. Leadership by persuasion is similar in effect to that which Alfred describes in *Peace, Power, Righteousness: An Indigenous Manifesto*. Alfred defines leadership as persuading individuals to pool their self-power in the interest of the collective good. His essay draws on Russell Barsh's concept of the "primacy of conscience," where there is no central or coercive authority and decision making is collective. "Leaders rely on their persuasive abilities to achieve a consensus that respects the autonomy of individuals."[34] Leadership is conceptualized as distributed within a community based on the skills and experience an individual accumulates.

Figure 5.1a is a graphic representation of the four primary modes of persuasion that facilitate leadership, namely, observation, experience, tradition, and narration. These four modes are descriptive of the use of persuasion, whether written or spoken. The model intersects with and overlays each of the other types of persuasion. This allows us to conceptualize, in the series of Figure 5.1a–d, the dynamic of leadership as exactly that—moving and shifting with the circumstance or situation. This model embraces inclusion of the variables in differing degrees for various situations. Its dynamic, temporal nature is difficult to represent on a grid or page. No numerical, hierarchical scores are associated with each because no predetermined best rank exists; instead diagrams in Figure 5.1 are merely heuristics to facilitate understanding. In Figure 5.1a, I represent each of the four variables as separate to describe them and their connection to persuasion. In reality, none of the variables would exist as discretely as a Western model likely would propose in a grid or even as these four discrete circles.

DEFINITIONS

The modes of persuasion (variables) are proposed as anchors to begin the discussion of American Indian leadership and are defined as follows: *Narration* is the objective, first-person retelling of events. *Observation* includes objective, third-person witnessing and data collection as a participant observer. The ability to contextualize data from an experience base is *experience*, which is defined as subjective and in the first person. Finally, *tradition* is defined as subjective collective wisdom or understanding of a community and is best contextualized by those participants most closely affiliated with the community.

Each variable is situated in words or actions that allow an individual to persuade other individuals (plural). I did not include the singular because that would appear to warrant a different type of discussion of leadership and is not central to this one. These definitions are specific to the description of this model.

Figure 5.1a presents an incomplete model using persuasion to form the framework for determining four variables (observation, narration, experience, tradition). Persuasion is linked to the use of written and spoken words and actions, that is, a leader may persuade followers through observation, narration, experience, or tradition.

A social scientist may persuade followers by presenting the logic found in data collection or observation. American Indian social scientists, scholars who study American Indians from an insider perspective or as participant observers, are more frequently found in academic scholarship. Before the end of the twentieth century, the number of American Indian scholars in academe had increased greatly.

An author persuades through the use of written words; however, the types of writing vary. Authors may include leaders who write fiction or nonfiction, curriculum designers, Web masters, and professional development trainers in any field who use technical expertise to provide knowledge, skills, or abilities to others. They may use creative nonfiction to persuade.

An elder relies on community traditions and expectations to persuade. Each community, urban or reservation, defines an elder. Most of these leaders use the spoken word to persuade. Elder status is frequently linked to age by outsiders; however, many communities define an elder as a leader whose traditional knowledge and experience is an important link to community decision making.

The role model persuades followers using actions as examples. The role model's experiences provide community credibility for followership, and this individual bases decisions on tribal cultural traditions.

Table 5.1 lists each of the four variables for each leadership style. The order of the variable represents its strength for each characteristic. For example, for the social scientist persuasive rendition of observation is the primary means of leadership enactment, followed by narration, experience, and, least of all, tradition. Each leadership role uses each of the variables to differing degrees. For this model, the type of leadership exhibited is based on the primary use of the four variables. The author would use narration, writing fiction, creative nonfiction, poetry, news articles—essentially any venue for written expression— as the primary locus for leadership. The elder would use oral traditions to complement traditional experiences as the primary locus for leadership. The role model would use experience, and persuasion would be linked to actions.[35]

As the variables related to persuasion (words and actions) move closer together, the proposed leadership model is more accurately pictured in Figure 5.1b. Figure 5.1b in this representation exhibits each of the circles, now intersecting, to indicate that the styles often merge. In this specific representation, Figure 5.1b shows narration visually to the forefront; it would represent the author as the primary leadership style. From this representation, we see observation, tradition, and experience in the same space, yet ordered in the same manner as in Figure 5.1a. Each of the leadership styles could be represented in the same manner, with the variables in similar fashion.

As the leadership model moves to represent Tekwanipapu, shown in Figure 5.1d, the next iteration would be something similar to Figure 5.1c. In Figure 5.1c, the leadership styles begin to merge into one; so that by Figure 5.1d, we have all circles combined to create one circle. In this model, I continue to merge the circles that represent the strength of the variables because in

TABLE 5.1. WTL Model

Warner/Tahdooahnippah Leadership Variables			
Social Scientist	Author	Elder	Role Model
1 Observation	Narration	Tradition	Experience
2 Narration	Observation	Experience	Tradition
3 Experience	Tradition	Narration	Observation
4 Tradition	Experience	Observation	Narration

American Indian communities a leadership role is linked by the tribal community to the use of persuasion from words and actions so completely that the strongest leaders will exhibit abilities to move from through these four roles as the situation requires. The strength of their abilities to merge the four roles results in the designation illustrated in Figure 5.1d.

Figure 5.1d shows the complete fusion of each of the four leadership styles; Tekwanipapu translates to "one who speaks for us all."[36] This designation is gender-free. This model, then, visually represents the ability of American Indians, and for this discussion, American Indian women, to assume leadership roles in several tribally specific community contexts. The leader, designated Tekwanipapu, can move into various situations and use different forms of persuasion to Indian communities.

American Indian women who use persuasion by words or actions can be found in traditionally matrilineal and patrilineal tribes. The leadership role, as identified by these variables, is not specific to a tribal culture and was designed to describe behaviors that are more easily seen as cross-cultural or intertribal. The variables are not specific to tribe, gender, class, or culture.

In summer 2003, the Institute of American Indian Arts in Santa Fe, New Mexico, invited 100 scholars to the Convocation of Scholars to begin planning for Achein: A Lifelong Learning Center. This convocation mirrored those of the 1970s, first at Princeton University and then at the Aspen Institute for Humanistic Studies.[37] Some participants in the 2003 convocation, including Pulitzer Prize winner N. Scott Momaday, had attended the first two meetings. The 2003 convocation was patterned after the earlier meetings held by the American Indian Historical Society and attracted participation from each of the four leadership styles in the proposed WTLM. Examples are:

- Social scientist: Janine Pease Windy Boy (Oglala) founder and former president of the Little Big Horn College and recipient of the MacArthur Fellows . Pease is the author of several articles on native ways of knowing and indigenous pedagogy.
- Author: Rayna Green (Cherokee), chair , Division of Cultural History and Director of the American Indian Program at the Smithsonian Institution's National Museum of American History. Green writes on the politics of culture in contemporary American Indian art and music and American Indian women.[38]
- Elder: Henrietta V. Whiteman (Southern Cheyenne) is a professor of Native American Studies at the University of Montana. Whiteman worked to draft legislation that created the American Indian Religious Freedom Act.[39]
- Role model: Della Warrior (Otoe/Missouria) is the former president of the Institute of American Indian Arts in Santa Fe. Warrior is the first and only woman elected as chairperson of the Otoe-Missouria Tribe.

The leadership styles represented here are embedded in a tribal or multitribal organization. Is it possible, then, that these abilities, the variables of persuasion identified as key in tribal communities, do not allow American Indian women to successfully work in nontribal, corporate management?

RED WHITE-COLLAR WOMEN

Corporate managers in the United States come in all colors. Initially the Industrial Revolution produced a metaphor of white- and blue-collar workers; in 1977 Louise Kapp Howe coined the term "pink collar" to describe the female equivalent of the blue-collar worker. In 1985, Robert E. Kelley used the term "gold-collar" worker to describe corporate, highly skilled individuals. None of these phrases describes American Indian women in corporate management; unless the corporation is tribal-owned and -operated, it is unlikely that we can find a group of such women. American Indian women in leadership roles are found in tribal services, government services, and education. They are more often found in leadership roles in service organizations that provide support to tribal communities. Johnson characterizes this in her research as "life and leadership are woven into one."[40]

Krouse and Howard-Bobiwash describe urban Indian women's community work and activism. They make the case that Indian women adapt traditional approaches and concepts to solve problem in urban Indian communities, specifically in the shaping of identity and community membership.[41] The corporation they describe is a multimillion-dollar enterprise that operates an educational facility in tandem with other social and health services. In their article describing an urban Indian initiative in Milwaukee, they note that women moved a home school program into a multimillion-dollar nonprofit corporation. Indian women's activism sustained the change; yet like other initiatives where American Indian women lead in social change, their efforts are targeted to schools and health care—in other words, to issues of community.

Castle's work centers on American Indian women activists, documenting the history of the Red Power Movement, Women of All Red Nations, the Black Hills Alliance, and others.[42] For most of the corporate world in the United States, American Indian women are on the other side of the fence—activists against corporate irresponsibility, environmental racism, and consumerism.

Miller's overview of gender roles in tribal politics begins with an overview of feminist perspectives and concludes that American Indian women's participation can be seen in family networks and community well-being.[43] He found that American Indian female tribal leaders began their political careers at an early age, influenced largely by leadership roles within their immediate families. American Indian women in politics within the majority culture face different constraints; the gender gap is more evident in mainstream politics.

Theresa D. LaFromboise and others explored traditional and contemporary roles of Indian women and their resilience despite continuous role readjustment, value conflict, and economic pressure.[44] They found the continued use of traditional coping mechanism was affirmed through tribal diversity and predominantly egalitarian structural similarities in roles of leadership, particularly as transmitters of cultural knowledge.

Celene Krauss's work on race, class, and gender examines activism and American Indian female leadership as basic to tribal communities where their traditional roles as mothers create a resource for their resistance activities in such broad issues as the inequality underlying environmental hazards. Krauss's study underscores that leadership in tribal communities, particularly by females, is secured in social issues that affect the community.[45]

At the federal level, specifically regarding Indian education and health, American Indian women are found in such positions as Assistant Deputy Secretary in the Office of Indian Education within the Department of Education (Victoria Vasquez) and U.S. Department of Health and Human Services (Eugenia Tyner-Dawson).[46] Ada Deer, former Menominee chairwoman, was the first Assistant Secretary for Indian Affairs, the highest federally appointed position held by an American Indian in the U.S. government. Cynthia Linquist-Mala, president of Cankdeska Cikana Community College (aka Little Hoop Community College) in Fort Totten, is the current chairwoman of the National Advisory Council on Indian Education, appointed by President George W. Bush in 2002. I find evidence of scholarship and role modeling in each of these examples.

INDIGENOUS LEADERSHIP THEORY

The disquieting feature of Western leadership theories is the limited and traditional way in which the work of corporate leaders and managers continues to be conceptualized, structured, and researched. Western thinking suggests that a normative leadership theory is possible and assumes that leadership is a fixed and rational activity that can be affected in culturally specific ways. We need to explore, in various forms, the relevance of this discussion of leadership in a global society.

Russell Barsh's "Nature and Spirit of North American Political Systems" describes the characteristics of a native leader and transformative leadership which he situates in four general traits:[47] Such leaders draw on their own personal resources as sources of power, set an example, are modest and funny, and serve as role models.

Alfred builds on these characteristics in his *Indigenous Manifesto* by describing native leadership as a demand for mutual respect between leaders and the community.[48] This link to community helps us begin to understand indigenous leadership and the role of women within native communities, giving insight into the function they play. The leadership role and influence of women in American Indian communities is hard to ignore. They are seldom presented as leaders, and their roles are underresearched in academic scholarship. Their particular invisibility can be reexamined using indigenous pedagogy. But this exploration suggests that ultimately instances of subtle deployments of leadership require us to question any view that indigenous women are powerless or ignored within their own cultures. It further suggests the difficulty of interacting in non-Indian communities where separate cultural dynamics inform the practice of leadership roles. Identity and one's relationship within a culture are inextricably linked to roles of leadership and followership.

Leadership is long established as a fundamentally social rather than individual process because it requires followership. American Indian leadership may be constrained by gendered identities, but situated in tribal communities, it is multifaceted or ambiguous to outsiders. Male patriarchal identity, as a construct in tribal communities, can be recognized in matrilineal and patrilineal tribes, the women at times collaborating in its production and maintenance. The complexity of gendered identities in tribal communities necessitates the use of native ways of knowing to reveal multiple, shifting forms of leadership that are constantly negotiated and renegotiated in separate tribal communities. How does this conceptualization, the WTLM, of leadership intersect with leadership roles for American Indian women? In an effort to describe a culturally specific phenomenon, the cultures become less specific in the model. For the reader, then, the question is whether this adds to the understanding or muddies the waters.

NOTES

1. I use American Indian, Alaska Native, or Native Hawaiian when referring to indigenous people in the United States in my scholarship. When other authors use native, Native American, or First Nations, I cite those as found. In citing individual membership, I defer to the individual, for example, Linda Sue Warner (Comanche) rather than Linda Sue Warner (Nunumuh).

2. Valorie J. Johnson, "Weavers of Change: Portraits of Native American Women Educational Leaders" (PhD diss., Michigan State University, 1997), p. 60.

3. *Double bind* is that set of conflicting expectations that may be created when an individual is considered to have membership in two distinct groups, including references to dual discrimination of race and gender; also, referred to as double jeopardy. This term was coined in 1972 by Frances Beale and referenced in the literature as interactive discrimination.

4. Tanya Fitzgerald, "Locating Indigenous Voices in Educational Leadership," paper presented to the New Zealand Education Administration and Leadership Conference, Rotorua, 2002. Cited with permission, August 14, 2005.

5. Susan Applegate Krouse, "Keeping the Campfires Going: Urban American Indian Women's Community Work and Activism," *American Indian Quarterly* 27(3&4) (Summer and Fall 2003): 489–90.

6. Indian country is defined sociologically to include urban regions, border towns, and checkerboard regions. It is not limited to the legal definition found in *Arizona v. Blaze Construction Company* (1998) codified in 18 U.S.C. § 1151 as including (1) federal reservations, whether created by statute or Executive Order, see *Donnelly v. United States*, 228 U.S. 243 (1913), including fee land.

7. John Reed Swaton, *The Indian Tribes of North America* (Washington, DC: Smithsonian Institution Press, 1971).

8. Linda Sue Warner, "Stereotyping and Job Satisfaction among American Indian Women Supervisors" (PhD diss., University of Oklahoma, 1989).

9. Leon Festinger, *A Theory of Cognitive Dissonance* (Evanston, IL: Row, Peterson, 1957). Festinger's hypothesis of dissonance avoidance proposed that pressure to reduce dissonance appeared as soon as the dissonance was manifested.

10. Linda Sue Warner, "A Study of American Indian Females in Higher Education Administration," *Initiatives: Journal of NAWE* 56(4) (1993): 11–18 (ERIC Document Reproduction Services No. EJ: 504-687).

11. Linda Sue Warner, "The Double Bind for American Indian Women: Two Decades of Inquiry," *International Studies in Education Administration*, CCEAM (forthcoming).

12. UNPAC, "Women and the Economy: Aboriginal Women and the Economy," online document available at unpac.ca/economy/awe.html (accessed August 8, 2005).

13. Ann Rinaldi and others, review of *My Heart Is on the Ground: The Diary of Nannie Little Rose, A Sioux Girl Carlisle Indian School, Pennsylvania, 1880*, Dear America Series (New York: Scholastic, 1999). Online document available at www.oyate.org/book-toavoid/myHeart.html, p. 15 (accessed August 8, 2005).

14. Beatrice Medicine, *The Native American Woman: A Perspective* (Las Cruces, NM: National Education Laboratory Publications, 1978), p. 334.

15. Paula Gunn Allen, *The Sacred Hoop: Recovering the Feminine in American Indian Traditions* (Boston, MA: Beacon Press, 1975, 1986, 1992).

16. Leslie Marmon Silko, *Almanac of the Dead* (East Rutherford, NJ: Penguin Press, 1991).

17. Winona LaDuke, *Last Standing Woman* (Stillwater, MN: Voyageur Press, 1999).

18. Winona LaDuke, *All Our Relations: Native Struggles for Land and Life* (Cambridge, MA: South End Press, 1999).

19. Activities associated with American Indian activists, particularly AIM (American Indian Movement) in the 1960s and 1970s include the occupation of Alcatraz, the Trail of Broken Treaties, Wounded Knee, and the Longest Walk. AIM began in Minneapolis when urban Indians organized to assert rights and reclaim their heritage.

20. Devon Abbott Mihesuah, *Indigenous American Women: Decolonization, Empowerment, Activism* (Lincoln: University of Nebraska Press, 2003), p. 43.

21. Cook, "Seeking the Balance: A Native Women's Dialogue," *Akwe: won Journal* 10 (summer 1993): 16–29.

22. M. Annette Jaimes and Theresa Halsey, "American Indian Women: At the Center of Indigenous Resistance in North America," in M. Annette Jaimes, ed., *The State of Native America* (Cambridge, MA: South End Press, 1989), pp. 311–44.

23. Michael P. Closs, ed., *Native American Mathematics* (Austin: University of Texas Press, 1997), p. 2.

24. Ibid., p. 24.

25. J. Peter Denny, "Cultural Ecology of Mathematics: Ojibway and Inuit Hunters," in Michael P. Closs, ed., *Native American Mathematics* (Austin: University of Texas Press, 1986), p. 131.

26. Gregory Cajete, *Native Science: Natural Laws of Interdependence* (Santa Fe, NM: Clear Light), p. 86.

27. Linda Sue Warner and Keith Grint, "Native Ways of Knowing: American Indian Leadership and Culture," paper presented at the 3rd International Studying Leadership Conference, December 15–16, 2004, University of Exeter, UK.

28. Linda Tuhiwai Smith, *Decolonizing Methodologies: Research and Indigenous Peoples* (London: Zed Books, 1999), p. 125.

29. Karen Gayton Swisher, "Authentic Research: Interview on the Way to the Ponderosa," *Anthropology and Education Quarterly* 17(3) (1986): 188; "Why Indian People Should Be the Ones to Write about Indian Education," *American Indian Quarterly* 20(1) (spring 1996): 83–90.

30. K. Tsianina Lomawaima, "Tribal Sovereigns: Reframing Research in American Indian Education," *Harvard Education Review* 70(1) (spring 2000): 1–21.

31. Brian M. Brayboy, "The Indian and the Researchers: Tales from the Field," *Qualitative Studies in Education* 13(4) (2000): 415–26.

32. Carolyn Kenny, *A Holistic Framework for Aboriginal Policy Research*. Research study funded by Status of Women Canada's Policy Research Fund (October 2004).

33. Black Elk and J. G. Niehardt, *Black Elk Speaks* (Lincoln: University of Nebraska Press, 1961).

34. Gerald Taiaiake Alfred, *Peace, Power, Righteousness: An Indigenous Manifesto* (Ontario: Oxford University Press, 1999), p. 25.

35. Originally published in a slightly different form in Linda Sue Warner and Keith Grint, "American Indian Leadership: A Model for Research," in Peter Chase, ed., *Leadership* (Lancaster, UK: Sage, 2006).

36. Linda Sue Warner and Keith Grint, "Native Ways of Knowing: American Indian Leadership and Culture," paper presented at the 3rd International Studying Leadership Conference, December 15–16, 2004, University of Exeter, UK.

37. Princeton University convened the first Convocation of American Indian Scholars in March 1970 with 200 participants; in September 1971, the Aspen Institute for Humanistic Studies hosted the second Convocation of American Indian Scholars; and the third Convocation of American Indian Scholars was hosted by the Institute of American Indian Arts in Santa Fe, New Mexico, in June 2003.

38. Rayna Green. For a more complete list of research projects, honors, and publications, see National Museum of American History, online document available at americanhistory.si.edu/about/staff.cmf?key+12&staffkey=166 (accessed August 17, 2005).

39. American Indian Religious Freedom Act of 1978. P.L. No. 45 U.S.C. chapter 21. Subchapter I, later amended as P.L. No 103-344 in 1994.

40. Johnson, "Weavers of Change," p. 291.

41. Susan Applegate Krouse and Heather Howard-Bobiwash, "Keeping the Campfires Going: Urban American Indian Women's Community Work and Activism," *American Indian Quarterly* 27(3&4) (2003): 489.

42. Elizabeth A. Castle, "Keeping One Foot in the Community: Intergenerational Indigenous Women's Activism from the Local to the Global (and Back Again)," *American Indian Quarterly* 27(3&4) (2003): 840.

43. Bruce G. Miller, "Women and Tribal Politics: Is There a Gender Gap in Indian Elections?" *American Indian Quarterly* 18(1) (winter, 1994): 25–41.

44. Theresa D. LaFromboise, Anneliese M. Heyle, and Emily J. Ozer, "Changing and Diverse Roles of Women in American Indian Cultures," *Sex Roles: A Journal of Research* 22(7–8) (April 1990): 455–76.

45. Celene Krauss, "Women and Toxic Waste Protests: Race, Class, and Gender as Resources of Resistance," *Qualitative Sociological* 16(3) (September 1993): 247–62.

46. Victoria Vasques, Assistant Deputy Secretary, Office of Indian Education is Diegueno of the San Pasqual Band of Mission Indians, California. See: http://222.ed.gov/print/about/offices/list/ods/oie/vasques.html (Accessed August 22, 2005). Eugenia Tyner-Dawson (Sac and Fox Nation) is Senior Advisor for Tribal Affairs, Office of Inter-governmental Affairs, Immediate Office of the Secretary, U.S. Department of Health and Human Services. See: http://www.hhs.gov/ofta/Bio_Tyner_Dawson.html (Accessed August 22, 2005).

47. Russell Barsh, "The Nature and Spirit of North American Political Systems," *American Indian Quarterly* 10(3) (summer 1986): 181–98.

48. Alfred, *Peace, Power, Righteousness*, p. 90.

6

This Is How We Do It:
Black Women Entrepreneurs'
Management Strategies and Styles

Cheryl A. Smith

Management is . . . planning, organizing, coordinating, controlling, thinking. Managers efficiently control resources, financial, human, and social. Management also has "softer" elements, such as leadership, followership, spirituality, respect, process, and flow. Most of all, management is about awareness; good managers are aware of themselves, their employees, their vendors, customers, and markets. Many entrepreneurs in particular have a holistic view of their businesses, understanding the social, cultural, economic, and political contexts that impact how they manage. Small business owners are usually also aware of their style of managing, having made a choice about how they will run their businesses and the company culture they will create.

This chapter presents the management strategies and styles of nineteen black women entrepreneurs identified as successful business owners and by extension good managers. The business experiences of these women entrepreneurs from New York state provide a glimpse into their lives, culture, and history as they relate their strategies for starting and managing their small businesses. In-depth interviews provided the rich data that contribute to their stories, most often unknown, untold, and unrecognized in traditional management literature.[1] Types of capital accumulation will be discussed as illustrations of how they affect the management approaches of these black women business owners. I will show how their human capital or the skills, abilities, and knowledge accumulated, coupled with their personal characteristics, contributed to their management abilities and styles and how their cultural traditions, especially their social capital networks of support, including black women and extending beyond them, guided their holistic approach to operating their businesses. In addition, I will explain how human and social capital formation strategies, in turn, contributed to the growth of their financial capital, usually identified as the main goal of a business and job of a manager. Finally, I will discuss the impact of race, culture, and gender on this group of women's management styles and strategies, recognizing that other factors such as class and ethnicity should also be considered. While understanding that black women (defined here as women of African descent) are not a monolithic group, that this small sample of women do not represent all black women entrepreneurs, and that these strategies are not used by only black women, I present their stories as a beginning discussion of the way in which the intersection of their many unique realities reflect the way they manage, the goals they set for their businesses, and the way they measure success.[2]

As a black woman entrepreneur, scholar, and educator, I know that we as a group are rarely identified as skilled managers, hitting concrete ceilings in the corporate world, having more difficulties obtaining financing than other groups of entrepreneurs, and being essentially ignored in the world of entrepreneurship as presented by traditional business schools and organizations. It is not surprising that non–business school models of management, encompassing some of the softer elements mentioned earlier, are ignored or trivialized. A more inclusive and expanded look at management is therefore warranted to understand the significance of these black women entrepreneurs' approach to business.

DEFINITIONS OF MANAGEMENT

Merriam-Webster: *man-age-ment*. Function: noun. "1. The act or art of managing: the conducting or supervising of something (as a business). 2. The *judicious* use of means to accomplish an end."[3]

Management is a broad term, often used without thought, to describe how people, businesses, and institutions are governed. Management is a usually thought of as a business term, regulated by hard-and-fast rules for what makes it good and what makes it work. Those rules come out of corporate America, which has created a discipline, a field of practice, and a market. The history of the American Management Association has its roots in the corporate world; it was founded in 1913 as the National Association of Corporate Schools. Since its founding it has merged with a number of similar organizations, including many dedicated to management education, culminating in its recognition as an educational institution by the state of New York.[4] This corporate paradigm, taught almost exclusively in business schools, is grounded in a white, male-dominated perception of what constitutes good business and success. In entrepreneurship education, also as taught in traditional business school, the Schumpterian model of business creation and management is the model, based on a goal of cornering a market while crushing the competition.[5] Strategies to achieve those ends, defined as success for individual gain, are taught to would-be managers and entrepreneurs. As we know from the recent spate of corporate scandals, *judicious* means to achieve their ends are sadly lacking in many corporations and financial institutions.

However, management and similarly entrepreneurship have interdisciplinary roots, including economics, history, education, psychology, and sociology.

A paradigm precludes open, inclusive, and holistic approaches that can be more effective on many levels, including ethical, respectful, and collaborative practices that can result in excellent profitability. Additionally, these strategies are often antithetical to many groups, including people of color and women, as well individuals from countries and cultures in which collaboration, concern with, and connection to community and outcomes that benefit the common good rather than individuals alone are their exemplars. An increasing number of challenges of this dominant worldview are being seen as people, often those marginalized by the dominant group, reject the traditional ways of doing business and create their own based on their own value systems, goals, and motivations. Those creations often come from entrepreneurs.

Entrepreneurs are the ultimate business managers, for they usually do it all, especially in the start-up phase of their business development. For the purposes of this work I use the terms *entrepreneur* and *small business manager* interchangeably while recognizing the differences: Entrepreneurship involves the creation of new enterprises for the purpose of making a profit, whereas small business management is for the purpose of growing and sustaining businesses. Entrepreneurship involves creativity, and small business management involves assessment. The women business owners whose stories will be told are both creators and sustainers. Their small businesses, or more accurately micro-enterprises, are constantly being monitored, reviewed, and changed as needed, usually by one person, the business owner. Their people and processes have to be understood holistically. To sustain and grow the businesses, they need to know key individuals as they relate to a social order in a given community. They need to understand the economic and political forces in the broader society that impact their businesses and how they manage them.[6]

BACKGROUND AND CONTEXT

Black women entrepreneurs have a history and tradition of thousands of years of entrepreneurial activity and success beginning with the powerful market women of ancient Africa. But their stories remain largely untold in entrepreneurship, management, or history yet "in their business activities, black women have sustained a commercial cultural tradition of self-help that has distinguished the economic lives of black women in America for almost 400 years."[7] The tradition of excellence in entrepreneurship, management, and economic development has continued over time and place and is visible in the present-day economic activities of black women entrepreneurs.

> Their views of the world, their ways of acting in and on it, while displaying many commonalities with entrepreneurs in general, possess some unique aspects resulting from the intersection of race, gender, and class in their lives. These include their spirituality, their concern for balance, their integrity, their will,

their coping mechanisms and their connections with others, notably their mothers and their "sisters," their communities, and the larger society. For them, Black women's history and culture have positively impacted their business activities. Their ways of doing business, anchored by centuries-old cultural traditions, offer alternative models of business development and expanded definitions of success, wealth and power.[8]

The literature in management, business, and economics is replete with references to small business management and entrepreneurship in general. The literature base on women in management and entrepreneurship has grown exponentially in the past two decades. In contrast, there is a paucity of literature focused on black women entrepreneurs. Most research has focused on how women manage differently than men, how women manage men, how women should or should not try to be more like men to succeed in business, how female entrepreneurs do business, what their management style is, and the like. When black women are studied as businesswomen and entrepreneurs, they are usually peripheral to the research and counted twice, either as a woman or a "minority"; they are two-fers. Happily, literature and research by, for, and about black women entrepreneurs is growing, though still sparse. Graduate schools of management, such as Simmons, in Boston, are gradually beginning to notice the value of studying and surfacing the stories and strategies of this group of women.

The Center for Women's Business Research, formerly the National Foundation of Women Business Owners, is the premier organization conducting research and disseminating information on women's business ownership. It is a standout organization because it is one of the few (if not the only) broad-based entities that produces studies placing women of color in the center of their research rather than "integrated" into studies of mainstream women. The center has conducted two recent studies that pertain to the progress and status of black women, a term I prefer because African American does not apply to all black women in the United States. It excludes Caribbean, African, Latina, and Native American women who identify as black. The broader based term is more accurate and inclusive, providing a global perspective on the lives of women of the African diaspora.

Statistical and comparative data that situate black women entrepreneurs in the wider context in which they operate is instructional in understanding how they compare to other groups of female entrepreneurs and to entrepreneurs in general. The groups studied are African American, Latina, Asian, and Native American. The center's 2002 report, "Women Business Owners of Color: New Accomplishments, Continuing Challenges," updates the 1998 study, "Women Business Owners of Color: Challenges and Accomplishments." The key finding was that "Growth Is the Key Focus for All Women Entrepreneurs, Regardless of Ethnic Background." The critical issue in this finding, however, is that how and how fast growth is achieved differs for women of various ethnic and racial groups. For example, there are many commonalities among all groups, including regarding their primary goal, business growth, the fact that most started their businesses from scratch, capitalize their businesses primarily through business proceeds, and face the challenges of being taken seriously by the men in their own or other ethnic groups. However, the striking difference is that although approximately 25 percent of three ethnic groups reported problems when seeking financing, almost twice as many or 47 percent of black women reported obstacles. They were also the most likely to need additional financing in the following year.[9] These findings point out that gender is not unifying, that the playing field for women entrepreneurs is not even, and that business growth is impacted by factors associated with discrimination, racism, and sexism, those that go beyond merit, ability, and accomplishments.

It is likely that the outcomes of these differences will result in slower growth rates and smaller profits in these businesses, rendering them "unsuccessful, uninteresting, and nonimportant" in the eyes of economists, entrepreneurship and business educators, bankers, policy makers, and the general public. The myth of black women not being good business managers and owners is thus perpetuated. The reasons for these discrepancies need to be examined in the light of differential life and business chances of black women, whose unique standpoint in U.S. society is a result of the 400-year-old ongoing legacy of discrimination based on racism and sexism. As Lynn Burbridge, who fashioned the theory of time poverty, believes, "in order to challenge the dominant economic paradigm of researchers, scholars and educators, we need to examine the totality of factors and life challenges of Black women entrepreneurs."[10]

The center's most recent findings on the state of black women's businesses in the United States are, however, encouraging. Its 2004 fact sheet presents the most up-to-date data on African American women's majority-owned, privately held businesses in the United States. The most cogent findings:

- African American women–owned businesses exceed 414,000, employ nearly 254,000, and generate $19.5 billion in sales nationwide.
- 29 percent of firms owned by women of color are owned by African Americans; they own 6 percent of all majority women-owned firms in the United States.
- African American–owned businesses are in all industries, with the majority (78.3 percent) in the service sector, where there was the greatest growth between 1997 to 2002.[11]

These most recent findings exceed those reported in the 2002 Fact Sheet and attest to the fact that in spite of barriers and obstacles to obtaining financing and not being taken seriously as efficient and excellent business owners, black women continue to open, build, and manage profitable businesses. They are a force to be reckoned with on the economic landscape. Business start-up and growth are accomplished by good management. To understand the significant and continued growth of black women–owned firms, looking at the way *they* started and manage their businesses is useful. One way to begin this analysis is to understand what managers do. A self-study seminar of the American Management Association titled "What Managers Do" breaks the job down into its components: "planning, organizing, staffing, directing, and controlling."[12] Recognition of the stylistic differences in management is a hopeful sign that even in the most traditional management education, there is variation, fluidity, and recognition of personality, styles, and values that speak to how the content is delivered. Similarly, the style or way a business is managed is as important to its success as what, or the content, that is managed. The softer components of management stated in the beginning of this chapter account for style or how the businesses are managed, and the traditional, linear view is related to what is managed. Black women are known for their style and the way they manage their businesses. Though not all the same, they share some common styles and concrete substance that contribute to their success. The discussion is especially important considering the rapidly increasing diversity of businesses, managers, and employees in the global marketplace.

Manfred Davidmann has written extensively on management, management behaviors, and style. He identifies two styles of management: authoritarian and participative. The authoritarian style is a top-down, military-type hierarchy where decisions are made at the top and orders given to those below; people are assumed to hate work and fear motivation. In contrast, participative styles delegate work, use teams, co-lead, invite participation in decision making, assume people want to work well, and reward motivation and creativity.[13] A more recent and entertaining take on management and business styles is offered in the popular literature that says the same thing while addressing the differences between men and women.

A book by Ronna Lichtenberg takes on the gender stereotypes of women versus men by identifying pink and blue management and business styles. According to Lichtenberg, pink style people put their emphasis on connection and relationships, whereas blue style people focus on the task at hand, the activity of the business. Pink can be aligned with the participative style of Davidmann and the blue with the authoritarian. She proposes that pink is usually true for a woman and blue for a man, but not necessarily so. Blues see themselves as independent of relationships in the workplace and view their success, defined as being well paid, as a result of their individual efforts.[14] Lichtenberg's position is that men and women alike should use both styles to achieve business success.

In relation to business success, management styles and perceptions are literally also colored by race and gender. Two Simmons management professors, Stacy Blake-Beard and Laura Morgan Roberts, have examined another popular medium, television, for examples of how styles are perceived and responded to when taking into race into account. They examine the stereotypes that prevail in the workplace that drive assessment and success as illustrated by the popular reality show *The Apprentice*, in which contestants compete to win a place as Donald Trump's apprentice, running one of his businesses for a year. The only African American contestants in the first season were Omarosa Manigault-Stallworth and Kwame Jackson. Highly credentialed, these two provided much of the excitement and tension apparent in the competition. However, given the interest the show has generated among the general population, in water cooler discussions in offices around the country, and even in schools of business and management as a teaching tool, Blake-Beard and Morgan felt compelled to raise the "more challenging conversations around the underlying issues of race, gender, and class that scripted the group dynamics and created the true drama in this show."[15] As black women and professors of management, they felt duty-bound to look at the unique standpoint of those two would-be apprentices, the outcomes of the contest, and the lessons learned from their experiences that can inform our ideas about the impact of race, gender and class on business success.

The overarching issue people of color, particularly black people, face in dominant-controlled organizations, businesses, the academy, and many aspects of everyday life is that of invisibility and hypervisibility.[16] Used as a frame of analysis of Omarosa's and Kwame's strategies on the show, Blake-Beard and Morgan identify two methods each employed: Omarosa's approach was to make herself visible by standing out from the crowd, Kwame's was to blend in and slip under the radar. Omarosa was "fired" after nine weeks of competition, and Kwame remained in contention until the final cut was made. He did not win. In Omarosa's quest to win by becoming hypervisible to succeed, she employed tactics taught in business schools to stand out from the crowd to become winners and leaders. They included displaying traits such as intelligence, autonomy, aggressiveness, and self-confidence.[17] Of course, these behaviors work for white men but are problematic for women, especially assertive black women who are perceived as being arrogant, abrasive, and confrontational; "uppity" black women do not know their places. Omarosa was ostensibly fired because she was perceived to be in constant conflict with her team. It can be argued that Omarosa displayed a blue style of management.

Perhaps she was more memorable than the winner, a white male, as Blake-Beard and Morgan argue that maybe "Omarosa has become a caricature, holding all the negative stereotypes, anger, and fear that this culture has of Black women."[18] She may embody one of the most pernicious and persistent stereotypes, that of Sapphire—a loud, emasculating woman; this and many other deeply ingrained negative stereotypes about black women had their origins in the times of chattel slavery and post–Civil War U.S. society. According to Leith Mullings, a scholar and researcher in black studies and black feminist theory, "women of color, and particularly African American Women, are the focus of well-elaborated, strongly held, highly contested ideologies concerning race and gender."[19] History, therefore, as well as race and gender, impacts how black women in management and business are perceived and regarded.

Kwame, on the other hand, took the other road. A Harvard Business School graduate, he chose to slip under the radar, becoming invisible at times rather than standing out from the crowd as he may have been taught. A *Harvard Business Review* article reveals the prevailing views of success strategies in business: "Winners in our society are still defined as those who step forward and 'employ killer strategies' for trouncing the competition."[20] This approach enabled him to stay in the game until the last round. Kwame may have taken this approach because he recognized the visceral reactions of whites to black men, especially assertive, aggressive ones who often are perceived as threatening, dangerous, violent, and criminal. Interestingly, his management style with his team was pink and participative, focusing on relationships, cooperation, and collaboration. This softer approach ultimately cost him the contest.

Similar to Lichtenberg's suggestion for the use of a combined pink and blue style, either alternatively or even simultaneously, Blake-Beard and Morgan suggest that "tokens" or "onlys" in majority-dominated organizations blend the visibility strategies to achieve what they call tempered visibility." Omarosa and Kwame might have done well to take a page from each other's books and employ cooperation and collaborative tactics so that at least one of them could win.

These insights from the corporate workplace can be extrapolated to provide a theoretical frame of analysis of the management styles and strategies of black women entrepreneurs whose history, culture, race, and gender are also critical to how they create, grow, and manage their businesses. One must be careful, however, of cultural determinism. Societal issues and strictures such as racism, sexism, and classism affect black women entrepreneurs in particular ways given their unique standpoint in history yet by no means determine how every black woman does business. Black women doing business in the hegemonic white male–dominated economic system, however, face unique challenges. These challenges also impact other groups, as seen in the case of Kwame, as well as white women, nonelite whites, and immigrants who have been marginalized in the existing economic systems. The differences may be more in degree than in kind. Nonetheless, black women entrepreneurs, operating under the double yoke of racism and sexism in an economic system that has ignored or trivialized their accomplishments, have fascinating and instructional stories to tell that will benefit all regardless of race, ethnicity, or gender.

THE STORIES

Women of the African diaspora in the United States are unique. As I pointed out in *Market Women: Black Women Entrepreneurs Past, Present and Future,* black women's uniqueness is related to the fact that they "share with White women a similar experience of what it means to be female in a sexist society and with Black men what it means to be Black in a racist society."[21] In addition, black women have been historically viewed as an "inferior" sex of an "inferior" race.

African American women also share the experience of being women of color in a white male–dominated society but are different even from other women in that many of their ancestors were brought here in chains from Africa and suffered under chattel slavery for centuries.

More importantly, black women are barely noticed in history because until relatively recently, history was written by white men, and black history by black men. Absent from standard histories of business, economics, and entrepreneurship, I discovered the extensive history of women of African descent who have a long tradition of entrepreneurial activity, skill, and success by reading across disciplines. This tradition provided for the retention and adaptation of entrepreneurial marketing skills over time and place and advanced the success of several black women entrepreneurs in both the slave and free communities in the colonial and antebellum eras of American history, throughout the eighteenth and nineteenth centuries to the present day.[22]

Any discussion of black women entrepreneurs' management skills and styles would be incomplete without presenting the stories of women whose accomplishments provide the foundation for the economic activities, values, and strategies that underlie current methods of achieving business success. The women's histories were presented in detailed chronological order in *Market Women*, establishing a sense of time, place, and historical context, so here I will only share a few of the stories of women of the past who can serve as unknown mentors and sources of inspiration to market women of the present. I will then present some market women of the present, using narratives that illustrate in their own words the management strategies, skills, and attitudes they used that enabled them to manage their businesses successfully and effectively.

MARKET WOMEN OF THE PAST

According to Melville Herskovits in his groundbreaking work *The Myth of the Negro Past*, the genius of ancient African women in the economic sphere had many facets, including their management strategies and abilities:

> In the field of production, this discipline takes the form of *cooperative labor* under responsible direction and such mutual self-help is found not only in agricultural work but in the craft guilds, characteristically *organized on the basis of kinship. This genius for organization* also manifests itself in the distributive processes. Here the women play an important part. Women, who are for the most part sellers in the market, *retain their gains* often becoming independently wealthy. *With their high economic status, they have likewise perfected disciplined organizations to protect their interests in the markets.* These organizations comprise one of the primary price-fixing agencies, prices being set on the basis of supply and demand, with due consideration for the transportation of goods.[23]

Far back in history, black women displayed excellent management skills they used to control not only individual businesses but also cooperative guilds and empires. I begin the historical journey with one of the most famous of the ancient African queens and pharaohs, Hatshepsut, who lived and ruled in the 1400s B.C.E.

> The Queen Hatshepsut is the direct descendant of Ahmose-Nofretari through royal incest. She is notable because, as the daughter of a god, she chose not to rule as a regent but declared herself Pharaoh. When she did so, she shed her feminine exterior, appearing with a symbolic beard and loincloth. Her achievements included a rule of peace that was an oasis between wars. *She focused on the prosperity of the Kingdom, managing its wealth skillfully,* exercising her strength and desire for peace such that no war occurred during her reign. Trade was established with people of the East and with the Greeks. Turquoise mines were opened in the Sinai and *rather than use slaves cruelly, she requested and obtained Egyptian volunteers and Bedouins to harvest the stones.* She also sent caravans deep into Asia and the land of Punt around 1495 B.C.E.[24]

This queen behaved in such a way that her kingdom prospered without cruelty or war. She was a leader who used cooperation rather than competition and coercion to rule and manage, providing a tradition that endured after her reign. As we can see from Hatshepsut's story, issues of gender, power, and control were evident in her time. Refusing to bend to the prevailing gender stereotypes of the day, she took control over her kingdom, as was her birthright, and continued to use her power with rather than over people. However, like many of the female rulers in the ancient world, she acceded to the conditions of the times by donning a beard as a symbol of masculinity when wielding her power in recognition of the patriarchal nature of her culture. She managed her kingdom and its economic systems using a combination of pink and blue styles for the benefit of her people. Her success was measured in a kingdom that prospered without conflict, establishing an ongoing tradition of peace, cooperation, and collaboration for the greater good.

As we move along the continuum of history, I will tell a bit of the story of Elleanor Eldridge, an entrepreneur of note in New England in what was then the colony of Rhode Island. There was also a great deal of entrepreneurial activity in the New England colonies, known for its "female economies" of the eighteenth and nineteenth centuries. According to Angel Kwolek-Folland, a white woman historian, 10–25 percent of the female population in preindustrial America was engaged in entrepreneurship, primarily in the retail trade in urban areas.[25] Although she talked about the business activity of New England women in those "female economies," Kwolek-Folland did not mention Eldridge, a figure whose activities were well documented in New England history.

> Eldridge (1784–1845) was from Rhode Island and was an entrepreneur and amateur lawyer who started a series of businesses in her lifetime, based on the skills she developed as an apprentice in several places in which she was

employed. She was born free on March 27, 1784 in Warwick, RI. At 14, she was a full-fledged master weaver skilled in "double and ornamental" weaving and made carpets, tapestries, and the like. After leaving the weaving business at age 16, she worked at a dairy owned by a Captain Benjamin Greene, soon becoming a cheese-maker, said to have been the best "premium quality" cheese maker in Warwick.

After the death of her father and Greene, she and her sister Lettise went into business together, weaving, making soap, and providing nursing services. With the money earned from that business Elleanor began to buy real estate, buying a lot, building a house and renting it out for $40/year. Upon the request of another sister, she moved to Providence where she opened other businesses, including a wallpapering and painting business that were so successful she was able to expand her real estate holdings. She continued making significant profits in all her areas of endeavors, continuing to buy and build houses. Having accumulated $600, she bought a lot that cost $100, for which she paid for "all in silver dollars." She then built a house for $1,700, one side of which she lived in adding an addition on several years later, she rented the addition at a rate of $150/year.[26]

While Elleanor was recovering from typhoid fever, one of her white male neighbors tried to steal her property from her. She went to court in 1837, sued, and won; her case was made in part from the testimony of one of her white women friends.

One of the reasons we know Elleanor's story is because of the court case, which was documented and the fact that in 1838 she wrote *The Memoirs of Elleanor Eldridge*, one of the few such accounts written and published by a free black woman.[27] The fact that her story was left out of Kwolek-Folland's history of women in business in the United States is evidence that black women continue to be peripheral in the academic business literature. On the other hand, black and white women historians such as Darlene Clark Hine, Katherine Thompson, and Dorothy Sterling have told Eldridge's story in several of their histories of black women in the United States.

Elleanor's story illuminates the stresses and triumphs of black women trying to do business in colonial America. Her management strengths indicate true entrepreneurial skills, including opportunity recognition, vision, persistence and perseverance, and use of her family social capital resources as well as her networks of support outside her immediate family and community. She increased her profits in each business, skillfully managing her cash flow and using those profits to create new businesses, succeeding in tough times.

One of the most fascinating figures in history is Mary Ellen "Mammy" Pleasant, (1814–1904), a black female entrepreneur and activist in San Francisco whose life spanned the late eighteenth and early nineteenth centuries. One of a number of eminent black women of the Old West, she was best known for her participation in the financing of John Brown's raid on Harper's Ferry. Her biographer, Lynn Hudson, has provided a detailed account of her life and, importantly to this piece, her entrepreneurial history. Through Hudson's excellent work, we learn the details about how she made the money she used for social and political activism.

> Everything about her life was contested. Called a madam, a voodoo priestess, an ex-slave, a mammy, Pleasant manipulated the press and the media at the time so that she told her own story, rather than having her identity and personhood defined by others. Possibly born and definitely raised in New England, including Nantucket Island in Massachusetts, Mary Ellen learned business skills from being employed by Quaker women business owners on Petticoat Row. She also learned about "entrepreneurship and institution building: public spaces and institutions that black people controlled" from the Black business community in New Guinea, the Black neighborhood on Nantucket. Leaving Nantucket, she went to Boston, becoming involved in that city's "female economy" further honing her skills, accumulating capital, both financial and social, that would enable her to go West during the Gold Rush.
>
> Like many other Black people, Pleasant went West somewhere between 1849 and 1852 where ... the climate for business and living was [considered] more hospitable for Black people than any other area in the country. Using her domestic skills and taking advantage of the prevailing stereotypes about Black women and mammies, she worked as a cook, picking up investment tips from her wealthy clients, buying laundries, purchasing real estate, trading commodities and stocks. She chose her businesses well, watching and analyzing the needs of the mostly male population in Gold Rush California, for example purchasing and running an exclusive brothel where she picked up even more investment tips.[28]

According to Hudson, Pleasant's varied business activities in San Francisco consisted of men's businesses, such as investments in mines and land as well as those based on women's work such as laundering and running boarding houses. What is fascinating about Pleasant's story is how she used her gender-based skills to achieve success in her business ventures. Then, having attained economic self-sufficiency, she used observation of white men's ways of doing business and obtaining information in less than judicious ways to further her business growth. Then, in the tradition of black women entrepreneurs, she used the profits from those businesses for activities and activism for the purposes of betterment of her community of black people. However, because she used tactics that were not considered to be genteel or even legal, she is not seen in the same light as many other social reformers of the time. The silence she kept about the details of her own life enabled her to control how and what people said about her. Silence was used for self-definition, and as with many black people, especially women, as a means of resistance and survival.

Finally, the last unknown mentors and role models from history I will discuss are the Walkers: Maggie Lena and Madame C.J. I discuss them briefly because they are the most well-known black women entrepreneurs of the past.

Maggie Lena Walker (1867–1934) was the first woman of any color in the United States to found, own, and operate her own bank, the St. Luke's Penny Savings Bank. In addition to the bank, she created many other businesses from her base, the Order of St. Luke's in Richmond, including a printing business and a department store. The bank still exists, although it is now called the Consolidated Bank and Trust Company of Richmond; her home and businesses are now preserved as part of the National Park Service in that city.[29]

Madame C.J. (Sarah Breedlove) Walker is best known as the first self-made black woman millionaire in the United States. Her business was the creation and manufacture of hair care products and processes for black women. She created a vast empire, including her own factory, a cadre of sales agents and trainers who crossed the country teaching people the "Walker method" of hair care, a chain of beauty parlors, and a training center for her agents.[30]

Born in the same year, Maggie Lena and Madame C.J. Walker each came to create their businesses in different ways and yet each had as their primary motivation the economic empowerment of black women and social and political justice for black people. Their own words describe their management strategies, motivations and goals best:

> I see as my first work to draw around me the women...to put their mites together, put their hands and their brains together and make work and business for themselves. (Maggie Lena Walker)[31]
>
> The girls and women of our race must not be afraid to take hold of business endeavor and, by patient industry, close economy, determined effort, and close application to business, wring success out of a number of business opportunities that lie at their very door.[32]

MARKET WOMEN OF THE PRESENT

Juliet E. K. Walker, the premier black business historian, believes "...that reviewing the economic activities of African women in America from the Colonial period to the development of the new nation provides a basis on which to establish the foundation of business activities of African American women."[33] As can be seen from the narratives, the skills, strategies, values, and motivations of market women of the past are interconnected, consistent, and viable. Their descendants, the present market women, display similar skills, strategies, and styles, grounded in part in the Afro-centric humanistic worldview that lies at the heart of black culture and tradition. In the vignettes that follow, we will see evidence of participative management styles, based on the cooperative economic system of African communities; we will hear how the women learned to do business and from whom, how the use of profits connects them to the ongoing battle for social justice and equality, and how tried-and-true as well as innovative approaches to doing business their own way work for them. First,

I will provide a short description of the research methodology used and summary of the demographic profile of the nineteen study participants and their businesses.

The research methodology employed here was qualitative or naturalistic. I used several qualitative data collection methods to gather information, including interviewing to obtain life and business experience information, critical incident to obtain and confirm participants' perceptions of business success and learning experiences, and document review or analysis to gather demographic and statistical information. The study population consisted of nineteen black women entrepreneurs who are successful graduates of the New York State Entrepreneurial Assistance Program (EAP), a training and technical assistance program. They all self-identified as being black; several were of Hispanic ethnicity and two were Caribbean-born. A majority of the study group participants were between thirty-one and forty years old; one participant was over sixty. The group was composed of a highly educated group of individuals, several with postgraduate and doctoral degrees. They also brought years of work experience and both business and communication skills, and thus had a high degree of human capital accumulations, which they brought to bear on their businesses. In terms of family configuration, over half were married with children; the remaining were single, divorced, or separated, some with and some without children. Most had supportive family members, spouses, and partners.

The businesses they owned clustered in the service industries; one also had a manufacturing component. The average age of the businesses was three years because the EAP program focused primarily on start-up, however, two of the businesses were over ten years old. Over half the women engaged in what is called income patching, that is, working full- or part-time while running their businesses. A majority of the businesses had revenue ranging from $50,000 to $100,000 per year,[34] a level that traditional business researchers and educators consider unimportant and uninteresting. Owners of such businesses definitely would not be considered successful. However, these women constructed their own definitions of success, much as they employed management approaches that would not make them winners in the white male business climate. They present worldviews, business acumen, management strategies, and contributions to success that offer alternative ways of doing business that may be more comfortable and livable for groups not privileged by race, gender, or class.

The black women's themes that emerged from their stories have been affirmed in many of the recent studies that place black women at the center of their research; they relate directly to capital formation methods. I will discuss those aspects of the black women entrepreneurs' human capital accumulations as they bear directly on their management skills. The overarching finding of my study was the breadth and depth of social capital possessed by these women, so I will highlight a few whose business approaches are representative of how social capital enhances business success and ways in which social capital activities were

---

Black Women's Themes

Sisterhood: having, feeling, and acting on a sense of connection with other black women and women of color.

- Mother–daughter bond: bond with mothers and with daughters.
- Spirituality: sense of faith, belief in higher being, use of prayer, values.
- Community: concern for and involvement with community.
- Will: determination, strength, and force of will.
- Trust: Ability to trust others and being trustworthy.
- Time poverty: social, familial, economic factors that are more compelling for black women than other women.

---

interwoven with the women's financial capital growth. Because time management is a component of traditional management education, I will share how the issue of time poverty has been dealt with by these time-poor women so that they can run their businesses.

HUMAN CAPITAL

When asked to describe the personal characteristics they felt most influenced their business success, all participants in the research described the business skills they had accumulated, in other words, what they knew and what they could do, their human capital. The skills reported included marketing, pricing, purchasing, negotiating, strategic planning, budgeting, cash flow management, human resource management, and time management—all core skills involved in managing a small business successfully. How they learned is also part of who they are. Outstanding findings about educational experiences of this group related to their levels of education, use of both formal and informal learning strategies, and their continual learning to improve and expand their businesses. They are a group of lifelong learners.[35] Table 6.1 exhibits their own descriptions of the acquired business skills they brought to bear on the management of their businesses.

The women accumulated those skills through work experience, education, and training. According to the Center for Women's Business Research, black women are more likely to obtain training and seek advice than other groups of women entrepreneurs. There may be several reasons for this phenomenon; one might be that the tradition of using education to achieve self-sufficiency and to advance the race is embedded in black history and culture. Education has always been viewed as a route to freedom, both literally and figuratively. Second, cooperative learning rather than competition is the rule rather than the

TABLE 6.1. Business Skills

They have to be segmented. So that's why you have not masses but only X number
of people who can hear it. That's why targeting the market is so important because
that's what I'm doing with the various markets.

So I know that you double what you make and that's what I assumed. So what that
will do is make me a master at the one thing or master at my particular style
of development. It's not about just kicking out a bunch of stuff and getting a
million customers anymore . . . organize, plan, project, visualize . . .

I would say, um, it became apparent when you, when I needed to order more
inventory for shows and stuff because I had to create a, credit line. And
sometimes it's tough when you first start off because they don't give you much
credit.

So we went back and I had to negotiate with the fabric people to get them to
come down on their minimum.

The longer I can hold my money the better it is for me.

By having so many parties, I know how much food you're going to need, okay.
And then for my reference material, it's. it's X number of dollars for adults . . .
da, da, da.

My cash flow is better. I think I can keep track in terms of knowing whether or
not I have been taken for a ride. Oh yeah, I manage it . . . that has increased my
business 15 percent.

In business, you know, I can negotiate well.

I'm trying to grow it very slowly. And in a developmental way, field test and market
to find out that whether or not people are interested in this, if this is a demand.

I made constant lists. And I have a book for everything I spent. I had to make a
list of now of what I do I need. I live by my lists.

I plan for one whole year already. Because I know that it's important in order
to get the business off the ground. And plus it's helping me to look at future things.

And it turned out the company would give me fifteen days terms.

Then I said by my first year I wanted to make, $ . . . K Next year, $ . . . K. Go up
and up. And pretty much I'm on track.

I negotiate, I try to get the barest minimum as much as possible.

I have an ad in the Yellow Pages and I've gotten a lot of big jobs.

I mean literally, I had so many phone calls I could not believe it, off that one ad.

I'll establish a fee schedule for them to be able to book it. I mean that's the plan.

I have good computer skills

We'll do it for ourselves. We have some designers but we will also be using
the CAD system.

---

exception in the black community and is closely connected with the practice of
cooperative economics. Therefore, black women in particular actively seek and
use advice from peers, friends, and family mentors, known and unknown. Using
and seeking advice is also a social capital formation strategy that intersects with
the human capital aspect of doing business. In their own words, they describe

how and what they learned in informal learning settings outside of the class-room. For black women in particular, much of the learning is in the informal sector as well as in formal learning settings. This type of learning is powerful and effective. The women of the group speak clearly about how that learning enhanced their business management.

Devya is a mediation mentor who has been operating her business for over fifteen years. She provides mediation training workshops and seminars as well as mediation products. She was over sixty years old when she entered the EAP program and felt her whole life and work experiences have been a preparation for this business, which she identifies as her life's purpose: "I also realized that everything I've ever done in my entire life was training me or developing me or moving me to this life . . . building me up . . . and I think that's what moved me into the life's purpose."

Efua owns a janitorial and maintenance company serving individuals and commercial clients. She discussed the fact that she learned a good deal of her business management techniques from experience: "I think the everyday run-ning of the business is the best learning experience. You don't know until you do it. I mean anybody can tell you what they want to tell you but it's nothing like that actual every day dealing with payroll, dealing with taxes, dealing with the bank."

Deborah is a forty-something woman, a divorced mother of two, who owns and operates a floral arranging business using fresh and artificial flowers; she uses Afrocentric fabric in her arrangements. She initially talked about how she first learned to make them form her former business partner:

> And my partner D. said "Ah, I know how to do that." And I said "You do? Well I want to learn how to do it." So she said "I'll show you how to do it." And . . . she showed me how to make a bud and we started making them up. I also had an individual study with ah floral, a flower, a teacher from Japan who made actual flowers.

Collaborative learning and cooperative economics, seeking and using advice are all approaches Deborah continues to use as she readily gives advice to others interested in going into business for themselves.

One factor to which business success is attributed is the presence of an entrepreneur in the family. Three women recalled working or being appren-ticed in a family business from an early age. They told stories about working in their family business from a very young age and learning about the value of business ownership not only in developing general skills but also in cultivating specific business skills—accounting, stocking and doing inventory, purchasing, marketing and selling, and customer relations. More interesting, they learned the value of honoring relationships in business from observing their family members.

Helen, a Caribbean-born woman, is also a Buddhist nun whose business was a community-based retail store operated as a not-for-profit service to her local community. She recalls:

> I was, I probably went down there [grandmother's store] from six years old until I left.... Because my grandmother ran a boutique. It wasn't even really a store. What it was, was it was when the ships came from the harbor. It started out as racks. Clothing racks ... and they would make all these dashiki things for the tourists and real cool shirts. So it was in my heart. [Selling] was kind of in my blood.

Relationship and connectivity, a subtheme in social capital accumulation, were also prominent in the incidental, self-directed management education of these black women. Recognition of their true support systems—that is, who their real friends were—enhanced knowledge and affirmed their need to maintain positive relationships with vendors, customers, colleagues, and employees. This was an essential part of their learning about how to do business successfully. Most of the women reported that they learned the value of social capital and its accumulation, the significance of relationship in business, the importance of commitment to the work contract, and concern for quality and efficiency of operations from a variety of sources. Some of their own words follow:

> *Jackie K.* a high-end hat designer and manufacturer: It's taught me about having your stuff in order. Keep your stuff in order. And I've been on the train and how people give me lessons like that [laughter] just talking to you about things ... listening to older people say things ... there are also young people, you know, you can just learn from everyone ... even on TV. [laughter].
>
> *Ava*, a single woman from Brooklyn who owns a health food store: And so I'm very proud of—what I've learned about business, is building relationships. That's the key. I try to help people in the community and I try to work with people in the community. But I learned that you have to give the job to the person that can do it best.
>
> *Sandy*, the owner and founder of a family-owned apparel retail and manufacturing business: I've learned that ... if you want to keep your business successful always involve your customers and your community.

These women exhibit management approaches that are not based on crushing or killing the competition but on "raising all boats" in the community, a purpose long honored in the black tradition.

One aspect of social capital is the use of mentors and role models. Using the assistance of mentors and role models as well as serving as both was a contributor to and a measure of success for this group of black women entrepreneurs. The prevailing notion in the management literature is that black women have few (if any) role models and mentors, which often preclude their ascent up the corporate ladder. Because most research conducted in this area focuses on wage-earning workers in corporations, access to other types of role models known and unknown is often unrecognized in the corporate sector.[36] Sharon, who holds a doctorate in education, owns a tea gallery and conducts workshops and seminars for women of color intended to help them maintain a balance in their busy lives. She reported meditating before she begins her day, when she calls on her mentors and models. During the meditation, she thinks about a host of historical figures and identifies the attributes she admires and seeks to emulate in her daily life and business. Her historical role models include:

- Bessie Coleman—at a time when you could not even conceive of a woman flying, this was a black woman who flew. She went to France to get skills to do this and didn't settle for keeping her dreams grounded. She became airborne.
- Nat King Cole—his elegance, his sophistication, his command of his God-given gifts.
- Hattie McDaniel—her personal power and love of people.
- Zora Neale Hurston—her writing ability and insight into people, customs, and cultures.
- Josephine Baker—her worldliness, humor, sophistication, and ability to speak a foreign language .
- Mother Hale—her ability to work with children.
- Adam Clayton Powell—his charisma, confidence, competence, oratorical skill, innovation, and originality.

Ella Bell and Stella Nkomo, in their definitive study of the different ways of black and white women managers in corporate life, also found that many of the black women in their participant group used images, photos, and paintings of their cultural ancestors in their offices to remind them of those who came before them, ground them in their cultural traditions, and remind their majority colleagues that they were proud black women.[37] They, too, used them as sources of inspiration and models for how to conduct themselves in hostile environments or difficult situations, affirming the methods of my market women for seeking inspiration, support, and guidance.

The market women of this study identified three elements of black women's lives that contributed to their success: sisterhood, the mother–daughter bond, and spirituality. Those elements are not surprising because they are integral parts of African traditions and survival strategies that shaped life for Africans in America. They are reflected in the black women's themes and have also been found to be elemental in black women's lives by many researchers, including Bell and Nkomo, Blockson, Johnson and Johnson, Woodward, and

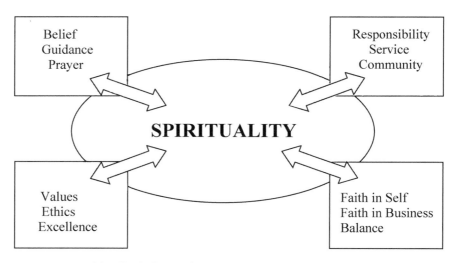

FIGURE 6.1. Spirituality indicators in entrepreneurship.

Ehrhardt-Morrison.[38] Figure 6.1 displays the elements of spirituality as found in these women's lives and how it serves to support, inspire, and guide their business management decisions.

FINANCIAL CAPITAL

If a business does not make money, it is not a business. Financial capital growth is one of the tasks of an owner of business, and the main task is cash flow management. The market women speak briefly about how they raised and retained capital so their businesses would grow and prosper. Paulette's story is especially illustrative of the way in which human, social, and financial capital intersections are critical to the growth if these businesses.

Paulette, the Scarf Lady, is the owner of a very successful accessories retail business. We enter her narrative as she discussed how she needed to raise capital to move her business from a home-based one in which she sold her products in various venues. She has an opportunity to move into retail space in an excellent location with very short notice. Because her margins were relatively thin and she had not yet obtained outside financing, she was in danger of losing the opportunity to move. She tells her story:

> And when I walked in, all my girlfriends were there. And they all had $100 bills on the floor. Twelve of them. I had $1,200. Because they all said "We knew what was happening. None of us really had any money that we could give you or

loan you, but we figured we could do this together. You know you could do something with it." So I had $1,200 the week coming in. It was so unexpected . . . and it was a gift. I cried like a baby. Because I know that they're single mothers, most of them, and I know that $100 means a lot.

Paulette was able to move into her retail space, and her business is now thriving. The nurturing social capital bonds of her sisters enabled her to raise the funds she needed to take her business to another level.

Once seed capital is raised, the next step in financing a business is usually to leverage the seed capital into financing from outside sources. Paulette was able to leverage her start-up capital, the funds she raised and received from friends, to obtain an expansion loan from a traditional lending source. Similarly, other women reported they had obtained or were in the process of obtaining financing from outside sources, which included local loan funds, traditional SBA bank-based loans, loan funds specifically for women-owned businesses, and in one case, a special grant for businesses started by women living or doing business in low-income areas. As we know from recent studies, black women continue to have the most difficulty obtaining outside capital compared to other women, yet they continue to do so in creative ways, including using nonmonetary sources of financial capital from their support network. Those sources include bartering of services, "free" labor, space, time, and goods from friends, family, and even vendors and potential customers.[39]

Another aspect of financial capital that is important to these black women is the use of profits. Similar to black women throughout history, these women are concerned with their families and communities and so have as goals and measures of success the extent to which they can help their families and communities. A few representative words from Jackie L., the hat designer who wanted to achieve a level of financial success to ensure independence and security for herself and her family: "As a Black person, it is so important to have your own, to own your own, and I just [wanted] to make sure there would be something there I would have that you know, my friends and I would see my family, many times they got laid off and want a job; this was a place where they could come and get a job." Figure 6.2 provides a visual image of how the intersection of human, financial, and social capital enhances business growth.

TIME POVERTY

It takes time and energy to meet the challenges of entrepreneurship and to make things work well. Burbridge defined time poverty as occurring when women who do double duty of working and raising families become increasing time poor, which directly affects the income data used as measures of economic

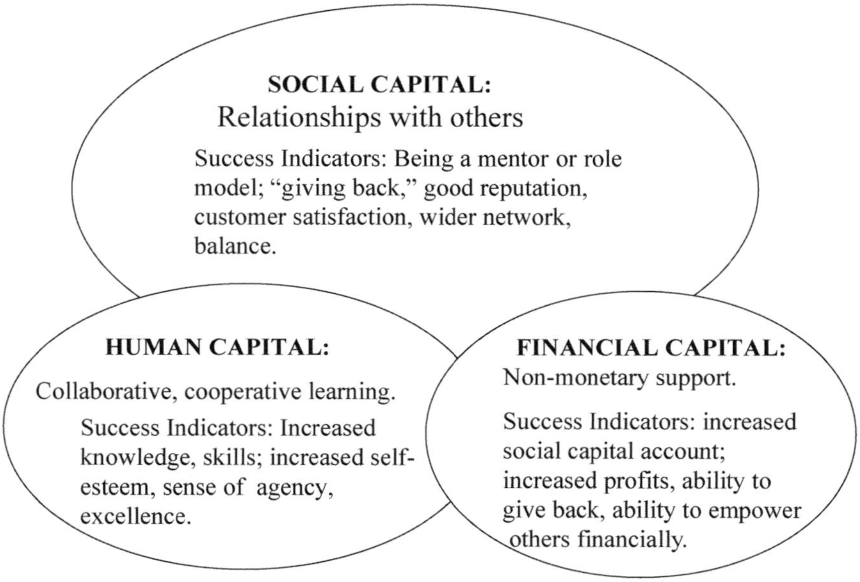

SOCIAL CAPITAL:
Relationships with others

Success Indicators: Being a mentor or role
model; "giving back," good reputation,
customer satisfaction, wider network,
balance.

HUMAN CAPITAL:

Collaborative, cooperative learning.

Success Indicators: Increased
knowledge, skills; increased self-
esteem, sense of agency,
excellence.

FINANCIAL CAPITAL:
Non-monetary support.

Success Indicators: increased
social capital account;
increased profits, ability to
give back, ability to empower
others financially.

FIGURE 6.2.   Capital accumulations.

success.[40] This concept can be applied to entrepreneurship, when women, especially black women, do triple duty, starting businesses, working for wages, and raising families while fighting racism and sexism along the way. As reported earlier, black women, possibly more often than other women, including other women of color, are likely to own and operate businesses without partners and run them part-time while working full-time. These responsibilities constitute a very heavy load. The market women of my study were very clear about their time poverty issues and the steps they took and price they paid to manage their business and families.

Their words best describe their experiences. Jackie L. says: "I'm one person. One person pretty much runs this business.... Me, I'm the only one."

Some women made reference to the fact that they had too little time to go to networking events they knew would help them grow their businesses. Nancy, the owner of a music production company, says: "It's through no fault of the association [professional trade], I need to put more energy, but right now as I said my time ... is somewhat limited as I'm sure you know, everyone else's is." Networking, a way to build social capital and contribute to business success, presents many opportunities but as can be seen from these statements, is not always accessible because of time. These issues often impact women entrepreneurs of varying ethnicities but do not have the same impact on women of upper socioeconomic classes.

These issues are especially pressing for women with families and children: The most pervasive and powerful reported indicators of time poverty involved family and business balance. They were especially true for those women who were single parents, most of whom were in very labor- and time-intensive businesses. Cheryl H., a single mother of a school-age son, describes herself as a cake and balloon artist who serves individuals, churches, and organizations and often feels frustrated because

> I kept on saying I can't have a business because I just didn't think I could, you know, I was just a single parent, how am I going to have a business? But then I didn't know how to work out the situation with my son. Like who's going to take care of him . . . because I'm a real single parent. I've got to do everything with him. So I had to think of all these things.

She did and planned for them, managing her time by putting into place supports from her extensive nurturing network and having her son help her in the business.

Burbridge's concept of being time poor also involved not having enough leisure time or time for oneself. Several women specifically mentioned lack of time for themselves and the effect on them mentally, physically, and socially. Sharon, who started the tea gallery and consulting business, said she wanted to provide a way to help women achieve balance in their lives: "a time out that women generally don't take for themselves. Somewhere down the line you'll get a chance to do this. But then that's when I started to take care of me a little bit and do a few things for me. Things I had never done." Other women talked about the personal price they paid in trying to do everything. Cheryl O. is an artist with a thriving arts and craft business. She is married with a grown son and a very supportive husband, and yet to run her business she admits, "I don't do vacations, and I don't spend a lot of money, and my house is in shambles" (laughter).

These market women are time poor for a variety of reasons. They have all made the choice to do business, delaying immediate and personal gratification. Many hope the financial success of the business will enable them to have a better lifestyle that is more balanced and includes leisure, relaxation, and time for themselves. The irony is that the time poverty they experience also precludes their businesses as being seen as successful and interesting. They are judged as being small, inefficient, and unsuccessful, resulting in a lack of equitable access to capital and markets and perpetuating the stereotype that black women are lacking in business skills. The matrix of factors that impact women's business activities is complex and interconnected. Only by truly appreciating their experiences within their unique contexts and using multiple measures of success can statements be accurately made about their business acumen.

Burbridge, who developed the theory of time poverty, believes that to challenge the dominant economic paradigm of researchers, scholars, and educators, we need to examine the totality of factors and life challenges of black women entrepreneurs. As we have heard many times, what doesn't kill you will make you stronger. The challenges, coping strategies, and triumphs have enabled women of the African diaspora, past and present, develop a strong sense of self. We need to recognize "the importance of kinship networks, time poverty, and the valuation of unpaid labor and support received from extended family networks in conducting holistic research on Black women's economic lives."[41]

LESSON LEARNED

The market women of my study learned many lessons about how to start, grow, and manage their businesses and have provided insights they share with those who are coming behind them. They are role models and unknown mentors to many who seek success in businesses and other endeavors. Their personal characteristics—strength, will, determination, perseverance, creativity, vision, honesty—are those associated with success in entrepreneurship; however, they have their own style and grace in the way they do business. Grounded in their traditions, they consciously or unconsciously base their ways of doing business on their historical and cultural mores and values. They are all pink, understanding and valuing the use of relationships in their businesses, however they are blue when needed. And, as affirmed by the preliminary findings of a long-term study being conducted by Blockson, Johnson, and Johnson, they employ "a low-key, laid-back approach in operating their businesses."[42] Additionally, as recommended by Bell and Nkomo and Blake-Beard and Morgan, they employ the tactic of tempered visibility when dealing with vendors and lenders, create strategic alliances with bridging social capital networks, and strengthen the ties with their nurturing networks, including their sisters, mothers, and communities. The role of spirituality in their lives, both personal and business, is paramount and guides many of their decisions about the way they do business, using judicious means to achieve their ends.

Race and gender had a significant (mainly positive) impact on the way these black women entrepreneurs do business. Those who described negative experiences as a result of their sex and or color stated that those incidents only served to inspire them to work harder and better as they overcame obstacles placed in their way. All felt that race had a greater impact than gender on their business lives, a finding supported by Woodard's similar study of black entrepreneurs, male and female. He found that although black men and women faced barriers in doing business in a white world, black women had more to contend with. To deal with gender-based barriers is an additional burden for black women doing business. To their credit, black women entrepreneurs consider this a moot issue and see any bias, regardless of the source, as just another impediment to navigate before conducting business.[43] He found, as did I, that they were adroit at turning negative situations into positives for the benefit of their businesses. Race, like gender, is thus not always unifying either. The unique standpoint of black women in U.S. society and, in fact, the world accounts for the strength, determination, and willfulness they display in their endeavors.

David McClelland, who has written extensively on achievement and motivation in business, has identified several factors that distinguish outstanding from average entrepreneurs.[44] Those factors are displayed in Table 6.2, juxtaposed with the advice given by my market women for those seeking success.

These black women entrepreneurs are vibrant, funny, feisty, caring, concerned, connected, skillful, and successful by their own measures. They manage their businesses well and in their own ways. By redefining success in their own terms, they empower themselves and others. They are sources of hope, inspiration, and guidance. They say it best: "I am phenomenal . . . charming . . . smart . . . strong . . . stubborn . . . blessed."

TABLE 6.2. Business Strategies Associated with Entrepreneurial Success

McClelland	*Market Women*
Proactivity • Increase verbal and written communication skills, become assertive • Ask for what you want, need • Reach out to others	Human Capital • Learn your business, get training, train your employees • Be clear about what you want to do, make lists • Know your business and be committed to it 24/7, 100 percent • Take calculated risks • Have a vision, dream big, do it
Efficiency Orientation • Recognize opportunity and act on it • Operate business efficiently and have excellent products/services • Plan your business/write a plan	Financial Capital • Make a personal investment of money • Develop a cash flow, put savings back into the business, watch your money • Write a business plan
Commitment to Contract • Make a commitment to work respectfully with others—customers, clients, vendors, family • Make commitment to work contract	Social Capital • Surround yourself with professional, knowledgeable people • Network with people who have the same vision • Build relationships in and outside of the industry • Be true to yourself

NOTES

1. C. A. Smith, "Market Women: Learning Strategies of Successful Black Women Entrepreneurs in New York State" (PhD diss., Organization and Leadership, Teachers College, Columbia University, New York City, 1999).

2. Cheryl A. Smith, *Market Women: Black Women Entrepreneurs Past, Present and Future* (Westport, CT: Praeger, 2005).

3. *Merriam-Webster Online Dictionary* [online dictionary] at www.m-w.com. Merriam-Webster, 2005.

4. "Our History," American Management Association, 2005. Online document available at www.amanet.org/history.htm.

5. Smith, *Market Women.*

6. The term *microenterprise* comes from a number of sources and is defined by Women's World Banking, and the term *small business* is defined by the U.S. Small Business Association (SBA) in the following ways: Microenterprise: Revenues of less than $500,000, five or fewer employees, minimal distinction between the business and the principal (owner) (Women's World Banking, "Innovative Banking for Microbusinesses," 1995). Small Business: Fewer than 500 employees and less than $6–12 million in sales depending on the industry (U.S. *SBA Size Standards*. U.S. SBA, 2002; Online document available at www.sba.gov).

7. Juliet K. Walker, "Trade and Markets in Precolonial West and West Central Africa: The Cultural Foundation of the African-American Business Tradition." in T. D. Boston, ed., *A Different Vision: Race and Public Policy* (London and New York: Routledge, 1997).

8. Smith, *Market Women*, p. 12.

9. "Growth Is Key Focus for All Women Entrepreneurs Regardless of Ethnic Background," Center for Women's Business Research, 2002. Available online at www.nfwbo.org/mediacenter/10-22-2002/10-22-2002.htm.

10. Lynn Burbridge, "Black Women in the History of Economic Thought: A Critical Essay," in T. D. Boston, ed., *A Different Vision: African-American Economic Thought* (London and New York: Routledge, 1997).

11. "African-American Women-Owned Businesses in the US: A Fact Sheet," Center for Women's Business Research, 2004. Available online at www.womensbusinessresearch.org.

12. "Managerial Skills," American Management Association, 2005. Online document available at www.amanet.org/self-study/manskills.htm.

13. Manfred Davidmann, "Role of Managers under Different Styles of Management," American Management Association, 1998. Available online at www.solbaram.org/articles/clm/clm2su.html.

14. Ronna Lichtenberg, *Pitch Like a Girl: How a Woman Can Be Herself and Still Succeed* (New York: Rodale, 2005).

15. Stacy Blake-Beard and Laura Morgan Roberts, "Releasing the Double Bind of Visibility for Minorities in the Workplace," *CGO (Center for Gender in Organizations) Commentaries*, 4 (2004): 8, 1.

16. Ella Bell and Stella Nkomo, *Our Separate Ways: Black and White Women and the Struggle for Professional Identity* (Boston: Harvard University Business School Press, 2001); S. Harley, ed., *Sister Circle: Black Women and Work* (New Brunswick, NJ: Rutgers

University Press, 2002); Blake-Beard and Roberts, "Releasing the Double Bind," p. 2; Marjorie Jones and Cheryl A. Smith, "Value-Added: The Impact of Faculty of Color on Students in Higher Education," Proceedings of the 23rd Annual Conference of the Adult Higher Education Alliance, Asheville, NC, October 2003.

17. Blake-Beard and Roberts, "Releasing the Double Bind," p. 3.

18. Ibid.

19. Leith Mullings, "Images, Ideology and Women of Color," in M. Zinn and B. Dill, eds., *Women of Color in U.S. Society* (Philadelphia: Temple University Press, 1994).

20. Blake-Beard and Roberts, "Releasing the Double Bind."

21. Smith, *Market Women.* All references are Chapter 1.

22. Ibid.

23. Melville J. Herskovits, *The Myth of the Negro Past* (Boston: Beacon Press, 1941).

24. S. Schwarz-Bart with A. Schwarz-Bart, *In Praise of Black Women: Ancient African Queens*, trans. R.-M. V. Rejouis (Madison: University of Wisconsin Press, 2001).

25. Angel Kwolek-Folland, *Incorporating Women: A History of Women in Business in the United States* (New York: Palgrave, 2002).

26. Darlene Clark Hine and Katherine Thompson, *A Shining Thread of Hope: The History of Black Women in America* (New York: Broadway Books, 1998); Dorothy Sterling, ed., *We Are Your Sisters: Black Women in the Nineteenth Century* (New York: Norton, 1984).

27. Sterling, *We Are Your Sisters*; D. C. Hine, E. B. Brown, and R. Terborg-Penn, eds., *Black Women in America: An Historical Encyclopedia*, 2 vols. (Bloomington: Indiana University Press, 1993).

28. Lynn M. Hudson, *The Making of Mammy Pleasant: A Black Entrepreneur in Nineteenth-Century San Francisco* (Urbana and Chicago: University if Illinois Press, 2003).

29. Virginia G. Drachman, *Enterprising Women: 250 Years of American Business* (Chapel Hill and London: Schlesinger Library, Radcliffe Institute of Advanced Study, Harvard University, and University of North Carolina Press, 2002); Hine and Thompson, *A Shining Thread of Hope.*

30. A'Lelia Bundles, *On Her Own Ground: The Life and Times of Madame C. J. Walker* (New York: Scribner, 2001); Drachman, *Enterprising Women*; Hine and Thompson, *A Shining Thread of Hope.*

31. Brown in Drachman, *Enterprising Women.*

32. Bundles, *On Her Own Ground.*

33. Walker, "Trade and Markets in Precolonial West and West Central Africa."

34. Smith, "Market Women: Learning Strategies."

35. Ibid., and Smith, *Market Women.* All findings and participant quotes appeared first in the 1999 dissertation and appear in the 2005 book as well.

36. Laurent Parks Daloz, *Mentor: Guiding the Journey of Adult Learners*, 2nd ed. (San Francisco: Jossey-Bass, 1999).

37. Bell and Nkomo, *Our Separate Ways.*

38. Ibid.; D. Ehrhart-Morrison, *No Mountain High Enough: Secrets of Successful African-American Women* (Berkeley, CA: Conari Press, 1997); M. Woodard, *Black Entrepreneurs in America: Stories of Struggle and Success* (New Brunswick, NJ: Rutgers University Press, 1997).

39. Smith, "Market Women: Learning Strategies"; Smith, *Market Women*.

40. Burbridge, "Black Women in the History of Economic Thought."

41. Ibid.

42. L. Blockson, J. Robinson, and S. Robinson. "Doing It Our Way: Economic and Sociological Influences on the Success of African American Women Entrepreneurs." (Paper read at Eastern Academy of Management, Springfield, MA, June 2005).

43. Woodard, *Black Entrepreneurs in America*.

44. David McClelland, "Characteristics of Successful Entrepreneurs," *Journal of Creative Behavior* 21 (3) (1986): 219–33.

7

Blue-Collar Women in Traditionally Male Jobs: Reconsidering the Glass Ceiling

Jeanie Ahearn Greene

In 1991, as part of Title II of the Civil Rights Act of 1991, the U.S. Congress passed the Glass Ceiling Act and created the Glass Ceiling Commission. The commission's purpose was to examine artificial barriers to the advancement of women into corporate management positions. The findings confirmed "the existence of invisible, artificial barriers blocking women and minorities from advancing up the corporate ladder to management and executive level positions."[1]

THE GLASS CEILING COMMISSION AS A NATIONAL POLICY ANCHOR FOR WOMEN'S OPPORTUNITY AND DISCRIMINATION IN MANAGING THE WORKPLACE

The purpose of breaking the glass ceiling is to allow individuals to "achieve their full employment potential" and to develop "a national corporate leadership fully aware that shifting demographics and economic restructuring make diversity at management and decision making levels a prerequisite for the long-term success of the United States in domestic and global market places."[2] The commission endeavored to expose the artificial barriers by examining the component parts, particularly the specific behaviors, practices, and attitudes, that prevent advancement by minorities and women.

Beyond looking at women in top-tier executive positions, the mission of the commission was expanded to include the investigation of "women's advancement in a broader range of occupational groupings, including the skilled trades."

Up to now, the public's principal perception of the Glass Ceiling Commission activities has been the advancement of women into mid- and upper-level white-collar corporate positions. This perception must be changed to include minorities' and women's advancement potential in a broader range of occupational groupings, including the skilled trades. Too often, minorities and women are steered into jobs that limit their career growth, with the a rationale that they have insufficient or inappropriate skills or that they are just not interested. This includes being steered away from blue-collar traditionally male and skilled trade jobs.

The commission stated that the specific discriminatory behaviors, practices, and attitudes that prevent advancement into management also stop minorities and women from "reaching positions where they can even see a glass ceiling." Specifically, the commission's "advancement study" should examine the ways that various forms of sex- and race-based discrimination at every step and level of the work force create the glass ceiling.

Yet the focus of the glass ceiling investigation, and women's advancement in the workplace in general, into decision making, leadership, and management positions has remained on women in executive and top-level corporate positions. But what of the women who are in trades and skilled occupations that are traditionally male? What of the invisible barriers blocking their advancement? What of the career, leadership, decision-making power, and economic growth of individual women (with) in blue-collar traditionally male occupations?

To understand the daily work lives, occupational choices and the "invisible" or "pervasive" barriers to women's advancement in employment, I conducted intensive interviews with seventeen women in traditionally male blue-collar jobs over more than ten years. Although this is not a policy analysis of the glass ceiling, it is a response to the request for identifying the invisible barriers that exist and a consideration of the contribution of women in the skilled trades to management in the workplace and their more general contribution to the economy of the United States.

I propose that the reason that women working in traditionally male blue-collar jobs do not promote into management positions is twofold and is due, first, to informal interpersonal barriers and second, to formal organizational and policy barriers. The combined results are that the personal and occupational costs of moving from a blue-collar or skilled trade job into management positions often outweigh the benefits. What I have found is that women in blue-collar jobs usually do not advance within a workplace or organization into upper-level management positions; however, they perform key management functions and contribute to the success and functioning of the workplace as managers while continuing to perform traditionally male blue-collar jobs. This is in part by choice and in part due to employment discrimination. However, because of the invisible, insidious, and pervasive nature of employment discrimination, drawing a clear line between the interdependent overt and covert nature of the glass ceiling is impossible. In this chapter, I explore the artificial barriers to advancement into leadership and decision-making positions as experienced by women in traditionally male blue-collar jobs. I then consider the advantages and disadvantages to women working in those jobs of accepting traditional management positions versus remaining in the skilled trades or shifting to different careers altogether. Finally, I consider how women who remain in traditionally male blue-collar jobs contribute to the workplace organization by performing management functions, although they are not in management jobs.

WOMEN IN BLUE-COLLAR TRADITIONALLY MALE JOBS

I place women's occupations into three categories: (1) blue-collar, both skilled and unskilled labor-intensive jobs; (2) pink-collar, including secretarial, clerical, and administrative jobs; and (3) white-collar management, decision-making, leadership, and professional positions. As the U.S. economy has changed over the past century, the line between the different employment collars has become increasingly vague and targeted to the culture of the particular workplace or product. For example, in one utility a customer service representative may be a pink-collar clerical job, whereas in another workplace it may be a blue-collar traditionally male job when it means working with contractors monitoring the installation of power lines. In still another, it may be a white-collar management job if it is not union represented and involves supervision and coordination of products and services within the organization and with customers. The same ambiguities exist across workplaces and cultures with regard to whether a job is traditionally male or female.

When we talk about women in management, we usually look to women's advancement into corporate positions. Although they may move from one company to another, for the most part the progression into management is a linear progression up a ladder into positions with increasing pay, decision-making capabilities, and overall power, prestige, and leadership. For women working in blue-collar traditionally male jobs or in the trades, management jobs are clearly differentiated from blue-collar jobs. Moving from blue-collar jobs to management usually means loss of union representation. Thus, representation (or lack thereof) is a clear dividing line. For the purposes of this chapter, management positions are referred to as nonrepresented jobs. Ambiguity exists in this distinction between labor and management, however, because supervisors usually are top-level union-represented jobs before incumbents advance to management. By definition, a supervisor is considered a manager. Though union/nonunion status differentiates labor from management artificially, organizations typically rely on that distinction to define their labor force. Because of the ambiguities about what is traditionally male versus female and what is blue-collar versus management, in my interviews I asked women to self-identify as blue-collar women performing traditionally male jobs.

What is consistent is that women are historically and presently underrepresented statistically in traditionally male occupations of management (white-collar) and labor (blue-collar) job categories. According to the U.S. Equal Employment Opportunity Commission (EEOC), sex-based occupational representation and job segregation are similar for women whether they have crafts and trades, management, or professional positions when looking at the broad occupational job classifications that define the U.S. labor force (see Table 7.1).

Furthermore, within these broad statistical categories women's representation decreases even more when the jobs are higher level, whether in management or the skilled trades, yielding to the need to further probe the intricacies and impact of the glass ceiling.

Women's representation in the higher-paying, higher-status jobs of management and the professions is similar to their representation in traditionally male jobs in the crafts and trades and as laborers. Like management positions, higher-paying blue-collar nontraditional jobs represent a way out of poverty for women.[3] Although the wage gap is narrowing and women's labor force participation has increased, the percent of women in high-paying, traditionally male blue-collar occupations and in upper-level management remains low. Pay equity and occupational representation indicate quantitatively that men and women have unequal employment status and infer that opportunity for women in higher-paying and higher-status blue-collar and white-collar positions is not equal.

The costs of the occupational divide go beyond wages to broadly impact the personal, economic, and social lives of women. Pay inequality and occupational segregation result in economic disadvantages for women and their families. They may live in communities where they have less purchasing power and economic independence than men. The impact spans the life cycle as the disadvantages extend to denial of promotions to highly compensated jobs; this results in lower pensions, social security payments, and other employment benefits, such as health care.

Beyond economic inequality at work is social inequality and "power" in the workplace. Workers gain a sense of self, personal power, and prestige from the work organization.[4] In a bureaucracy, which is characteristic of most work organizations in the United States, including blue-collar workplaces, as individuals are promoted, they attain increasing levels of power and prestige. Though the level of power and prestige attached to positions varies in general and from one workplace to the next, it is the upper-level management jobs that are particularly characterized by power, leadership, and prestige. These are the jobs to which the glass ceiling ultimately denies women access and which the Glass Ceiling Commission seeks to address. Additionally, the commission calls for broad consideration of the glass ceiling as well as barriers to women to all jobs that offer increased power, prestige, and leadership.

Equal employment opportunity policy and practices seek to rectify the tangible problems of sex-based disparate compensation and job segregation and the social inequalities of low-paying unskilled jobs—key indicators of the less tangible artificial barriers and discrimination referred to as the glass ceiling. Labor force indicators show that discrimination continues over time and across workplaces and occupations. They do not explain why or how women are

TABLE 7.1. 2002 EEO Occupational Employment for Private Industry by Sex

Participation Rate

Sex	Total	Officials and Managers	Professionals	Technicians	Sales Workers	Office and Clerical Worker	Craft Workers	Operatives	Laborers	Service Workers
Male	52.5	65.3	47.9	53.2	44.3	20.2	87.0	72.2	65.3	42.6
Female	47.5	34.7	52.1	46.8	55.7	79.8	13.0	27.8	34.7	57.4
Total	100.0	100.0	100.0	100.0	100.0	100.0	100.0	100.0	100.0	100.0

Source: EEOC, 2004, Employer Information Report EEO-1.

discriminated against and denied upper-level management positions. Subsequently, twenty-five years after the passing of Title VII of the Civil Rights Act of 1964, Congress created the Glass Ceiling Commission as part of the Civil Rights Act of 1991 to identify and address the invisible barriers that were continuing to affect the ongoing disparities in occupation status, representation, and pay for women—specifically women's and minorities' advancement into decision-making management positions. However, more than a decade after the Glass Ceiling Commission's report, occupational segregation continues with women disproportionately holding lower-paying, lower-status jobs with less power to direct the workplace and economy.

To better understand the glass ceiling, blue-collar women's experiences are best considered on two levels: (1) their experience working as blue-collar women in traditionally male jobs and (2) their experience in pursuit of management roles. Women in blue-collar jobs have been found to endure the same daily adversity and discrimination as women in management positions.[5] As skilled workers, women in blue-collar jobs receive pay similar to or higher than the management positions for which they are qualified. What differentiates blue-collar traditionally male jobs from management positions, in most cases, is the skills-based nature of job performance, the promotional structure, the compensation system, and the impact of a bargaining agreement, because most blue-collar jobs are associated with union representation and hourly wages. When one considers the glass ceiling from the perspective of women working in traditionally male blue-collar jobs, one can focus on the both the informal and formal barriers and functions of managing that go beyond pay and the quantifiable realms of the glass ceiling. One can consider the interpersonal and organizational constraints and uncover the unrecognized contributions that women working in blue-collar traditionally male blue-collar jobs make to the workplace organization.

INFORMAL BARRIERS TO PROMOTION

Most women in traditionally male blue collar jobs who were interviewed were so consumed and boggled by the constant daily harassment and adversity from co-workers, supervisors, and managers that they did not even think about promotions. Their energy was spent on just surviving and performing the job that they were hired to do. Daily work life was fraught with a continuum of sex-based discriminatory, harassing, and hostile behaviors ranging from devaluing their competency to verbal harassment to interference with job performance to physical and sexual assault.[6] When this harassment persisted, it was a constant reminder that they were unwelcome in their present job and were unlikely to be considered for—or want—promotions.

The first promotion for some women was just moving from their entry-level job to the one for which they had originally applied and been hired. For some, an entry-level job had been created purposely to discourage them from even taking it in the first place and/or designed to make them quit once in the job. The carpenter was hired at a national historic park as a maintenance mechanic, which meant "you had to be able to fix everything" but was "warned" that her job included cleaning the toilets and taking out the trash to discourage her. For a woman who was hired to fill a position on the state highway road crew,

> The supervisor swore he would never hire a woman for the road crew. He had six vacancies and they told him that the next new hire would be a woman. So, he invented a new job position, actually it was on the books but it hadn't been filled in twenty years. He called it the barnsman, basically a janitor. I was going to be hired to scrub the urinals and [was] warned that he couldn't control the men urinating all over the walls. And I would have to make the coffee and keep the lunch room clean. I did some research and found out that he could make me be the barns-man or barns-woman because I was the new hire. But he still had five other vacancies to fill . . . by September and this was March. If he didn't fill those five vacancies by September, then those five positions would be eliminated. If he filled the jobs with men, and they put those men out on the road and left me in the barn, then he'd face a sexual discrimination lawsuit. So, I thought, "You have to grit your teeth and scrub the urinals for a little while but at the most it will be till September." Before September I was on the road.

The frontline manager or supervisor contributed to hostility and adversity both by affecting daily work and by circumventing promotions. The supervisor was in a position to impose interpersonal harassment; to control, interfere with, and sabotage a woman's ability to do her job; and affect promotion opportunities by evaluating her job performance. A meter reader describes her supervisor's interference with her job and impact on her reported performance:

> It started with him not liking the way I did my time sheets and progressed to him not giving me overtime to complete my work, even though he gave it to the guys. As a matter of fact, one day I got off the phone with him, and I was brought to tears. It was just one of these, "You're getting paid good money to do your job, and I don't think you're doing your job." And I said, "Well, name something that I'm not doing. You know, maybe I don't know what I'm supposed to be doing." "Well, I can't think of anything right now but I know. I have a notebook on you. I'm watching you and I think you're not doing your job." And I thought, "Oh, God!" You know it's bad enough if you have to hoof it every day and you're in the snow and you're tired. You just want to come in. You want to do your job. You don't want to be badgered.

This harassment from the supervisor and co-workers made performing the job difficult or impossible. Promoting to management would only mean further entangling themselves in the same hostile workplace.

When asked whether they had considered management positions, and if not, why they hadn't, the answers varied. The nuclear fire watch quickly stated,

"It never occurred to me. I never thought of it. I was just there doing my job." In response to more probing, she said, "I knew it wasn't an option; I wouldn't have been considered. You had to know someone or be related to someone and I wasn't." On the other hand, the customer service representative in the utility said that she aspired to management, but the informal eligibility path was not from her position. She had applied for such jobs repeatedly. "You have no idea how many times I tried to get into management. I always felt my heart . . . [was] more with management, as I felt I was a good worker."

Having a promotional opportunity, to an extent, depended on connecting with and then being "pursued" by the supervisor in the sought-after department. The customer service representative wanted to promote into management but did not apply for a promotion until

> Suddenly, his "assistant." a guy I used to work with, called me and asked if I had put my résumé in. I said no and told him why. I wasn't sure the job was a good fit and I would have to commute forty-five minutes to work. He emphatically told me that John *wanted* me to apply and that this guy had been instructed to call me. So I did, and went up there and interviewed with the assistant.

A security guard considered applying for groundskeeper and, to increase her odds of being selected, connected with workers and supervisors in that department as they passed in front of her guard station each day. The electric planner had started at the utility as a security guard. She was promoted from security guard to meter repair when the head of the meter repair shop asked her to train and apply for a job. From there, she sought the electric planner position, which involved much more training, but the experience with her promotion into meter repair gave her confidence to pursue further promotions in the organization. Yet when asked if she aspired to be in management she reiterated, "No, I have the best job in the company now." This confidence and increased assurance became more important for workers as they aspired to higher-level jobs, which were fewer in number and more competitively sought after by men, who had traditionally held them. As can be shown statistically, this narrowing of opportunity follows whether pursuing upper-level blue-collar traditionally male jobs or management positions.

To qualify for a promotion, a woman had to be liked, respected, and pursued by management, in addition to meeting the qualifications posted on the job opening announcement. Managers did not recruit women who were feminists. Another informal barrier was that the women had to first establish themselves as "one of the guys." Becoming one of the guys included "working twice as hard and being twice as good" as the guys, but it also meant "not causing any trouble." Feminists on the other hand, "fight sexist oppression against women." One woman indicated that she "went from being angry to having the tools to fight," but remained a "closet feminist," perhaps because she feared jeopardizing her chances for promotion if she declared her feminist beliefs openly.

Regardless of how accepted women were and how well they had proved they could perform the job, they still said that being related or connected to the person doing the hiring was essential. Even the police officer who had ranked second on her civil service test had to get a reference and had to have shown exemplary work performance. Because she was a woman, her supervisor had avoided putting her in the dangerous situations that would have set her apart from her co-workers, the men. These informal requirements or invisible barriers typically excluded the women I interviewed from consideration for management jobs.

The women interviewed learned of promotional opportunities within their workplace either formally, through job postings, or informally, through word-of-mouth. Typically, a combined formal and informal notice was necessary before women would consider pursuing a promotion. Many were initially hired at an entry level to meet a minority specification for that position. This made them all too aware that without a similar specification, a promotion was unlikely, if not impossible. When a job of interest was posted, they assessed the likelihood of being hired, which included determining if an affirmative action requirement existed for the desired position and if someone already had been slated for the position. They were less likely to apply for a job that was not earmarked for a woman or minority and/or one for which someone already had been pre-selected. On the other hand, if they learned of a promotion requiring an affirmative action hiring, they might apply for a job they hadn't considered before. The auto assembly worker assessed her odds and applied for an apprenticeship leading to an electrical journeyman position, which would be a significant promotion involving the use of higher-level skills. This is how she describes her decision:

> Every so often they have applications for apprenticeships. I always put it off because although I'm smart enough, the test is real hard; they only take the top third of the test for the interview, and you have to go through the interview, and that's pretty tough. And, in places like auto plants or these big factories, it's a man's world. But I learned that there are fifteen positions, and at least two have to be women or minorities, and no blacks applied and only three women. I am waiting to hear.

The women interviewed cited three primary conditions needed to compete for promotions both within blue-collar trades and in management and professional jobs. They had to (1) be visibly accomplished at their current jobs; (2) complete training, apprenticeships, and education certifying their qualifications for promotion; and (3) know somebody or have a mentor. Although all three involved artificial barriers and sex-based discrimination, the most frustrating and defeating was the third criterion—knowing and being sponsored by someone. For example, although the police officer scored second on the civil service test for captain, she was passed over for a man who was one of the boys.

The security guard took a required screening test and applied for a meter re-pair position due to the department supervisor's prompting. The postal worker considered management only because human resources told her that she was qualified based on a test she had passed and her seniority. Still, human resources encouraged her to stay in the secretarial career path, but she chose the tradition-ally male path. Having promotional standards that included training, education, tests, and seniority seemed to provide a rational basis for selection decisions, but the need to know someone and be visible often took precedence. Such standards at least helped women determine whether they were locked out of promotions due to personal inadequacies or the discriminatory nature of the workplace.

As recognized by the Glass Ceiling Commission, the overriding obstacle to women's advancement is that existing, persistent barriers and discrimination exclude them from positions "where they even see the glass ceiling." At face value it might seem that the women simply did not pursue or want management jobs because they did not apply, thus making it appear to be a personal choice. Not to negate their astute judgment in declining management opportunities and promotions, a more critical look reveals that embedded circumstances and a pervasively hostile environment influenced many of their decisions.

For women in blue-collar traditionally male jobs, this discrimination in-cludes daily sex-based verbal, physical, and sexual harassment and abuse that interfere with their ability and opportunity to perform their jobs. A promotion into management often means exchanging one hostile male-dominated work environment for another. Although many of the women believe that they would bring to management expertise, understanding, and capabilities beyond those of male co-workers, they refuse to pay the personal price of increased hostility and adversity they likely would find in management. As one woman who worked as a longshoreman and in an engineering firm as a grant writer said, the sexual harassment was pervasive in both workplaces, "but the engineers should have known better." These women already knew from their experience as front-line workers that management most often did not support them as female employ-ees. Workplace policies did not protect them from misery at work, and it was understood that this adversity was pervasive at any level, whether front-line worker or manager.

ORGANIZATIONAL BARRIERS TO PROMOTIONS

Choosing to promote from skilled laborer, craftsman, or service worker into blue-collar jobs often means a loss of many of the attributes of the job that attracted women in the first place. Promoting into management meant losing some protections and benefits that had made enduring harassment and hostility tolerable. These changes were apparently neutral but had differentially adverse consequences for women working in traditionally male blue-collar jobs, thus contributing to the glass ceiling.

One cost of promotion into management for women in traditionally male blue-collar jobs who were interviewed is loss of certain union protections. For example, harassment by co-workers, sex-based or otherwise, violates the collective bargaining agreement between the union and management. In nonrepresented jobs, harassment must violate federal civil rights or state human rights laws to be illegal. Thus, it is only prohibited if it is based on sex, race, religion, ethnicity, age, or another designated protected class. Employees in union-represented jobs can grieve harassing behavior and be protected from management and co-worker exploitation without having to play the sex card. Having to identify unwelcome behavior as sex-based further alienates them from male co-workers and increases the risk of being labeled a feminist, which usually diminishes their chances to be promoted.

Another disadvantage of management positions is the expectation that the manager will serve the company without additional compensation, regardless of how many hours it requires. Workers in blue-collar traditionally male jobs, on the other hand, usually are paid an hourly wage. In blue-collar jobs the union and labor law protections require compensation for overtime. Generally overtime is anticipated, and accommodations are made for personal responsibilities and costs (e.g., child care, meals). For some jobs, the blue-collar work schedule has seasonal fluctuations, which, because they can be anticipated, allow for enhanced opportunities to balance family and home. For example, the carpenter worked at a national park, which meant that she could take leave for the academic year while she was attending college. The trucker worked for a construction company and was laid off for the holidays, when she spent time with her family, and in the winter, when she vacationed in the South. The security guard could work second shift so she and her husband could split child care duties and avoid the expenses of paid day care.

One characteristic often ascribed to management is autonomy. Women in nontraditional male occupations who become managers often have reduced autonomy and independence. Moving to management may mean a loss of flexibility to balance jobs with home responsibilities, education, or leisure activities. Most management positions do not allow for such liberal accommodations. The community police officer describes the benefit of her line job over management as:

I have a choice. I don't work any overtime now due to my job of being a mother. I'm exhausted. I don't really have the time. When I was married, I worked more overtime because my husband was home with the kids. Some of the other women are in their forties and fifties, and they choose to do the overtime.

Furthermore, autonomy and independence in their daily work lives allowed women a way to distance themselves from the stress and adversity imposed by co-workers. When the electric planner could not take the harassment in the office, she would do a field inspection. The truck driver spent most of her hours driving the truck alone and only encountered her co-workers at the beginning and end of a day. This relief would be lost if these women moved into management.

One reason to take a promotion is for increased compensation and the potential for future pay raises. For many women, accepting a traditionally male blue-collar skilled trade job involved a promotion and a substantial pay increase compared to their previous, traditionally female jobs as secretaries, clerical, or service workers. For others, skilled trade positions paid more than the low-level business or social service jobs that they qualified for after completing a college degree. In an economy with limited entry jobs in any field, a skilled trade job was the best if not the only option. In other words, the women had already received monetary benefits of promotion by entering a blue-collar traditionally male job; they just had not promoted into management.

Increased pay does not offer an appreciable incentive for women in traditionally male blue-collar jobs to move into management. Blue-collar traditionally male jobs offer high pay for rewarding work, clear seniority and promotion lines, and good benefit packages. Entry-level management jobs do not usually offer any net gain in pay or benefits. The community police officer does the math:

> I make $21,000 base. I'm maxed out on my raises. I can work all the overtime I want. One girl works in my job made $35,000 last year, but all she does is work. Now a cop's base pay is like $26,000. I'm $21,000–$22,000—the extra $5,000 is not worth it to me. I can make it up and then some with overtime.

The cumulative effect of loss of union protections, increased work demands, loss of independence and autonomy, and negligible increased compensation combined with the interpersonal and informal barriers to promotion made it less likely that women would apply for or be promoted to management jobs.

CAREER PATHS FOR BLUE-COLLAR WOMEN IN TRADITIONALLY MALE BLUE-COLLAR JOBS

What was striking about the women interviewed was their degree of excitement and enthusiasm for their jobs. Whether painter, auto assembly line worker, electric planner, meter reader, police officer, longshoreman, or truck driver, they all thought they had the best job in the company. They were proud of their jobs and were committed to doing them well. Any problems involved adversarial relationships with co-workers and company policies and practices, which made work difficult and, at times, unbearable.

All of the women considered and most had taken steps to move to another career, occupation, or job. However, having the best job in the company, or performing a skill or providing a "service they loved" was valuable enough to cause some women to avoid changing jobs and, instead, to remain and endure the (inter-) personal anguish of the workplace.

Most often the women chose promotions within the trades or blue-collar jobs to keep doing the work they loved, continue to receive union pay rates and protections, and avoid either going into management or stagnating. Job choices were not primarily motivated by increased power or prestige but by a desire for increased leadership, challenge, and compensation. The electric planner had worked as a security guard and completed a difficult training regime to be hired in that position, moving from security guard to meter repair shop to electric planner. She described her job as the best in the company. She was still in a union-represented blue-collar position and did not aspire to be promoted further because it would mean moving into management, which was of no interest to her. Although she completed a bachelor's degree in social work while employed at the utility, she decided to continue as a planner because she loved her job, and its pay and benefits exceeded her potential earnings as a social worker.

The painter completed an associate's degree in dental hygiene and worked part-time as a dental assistant to escape the hostility of the male-dominated painting industry. She worked in a dental office but also continued painting as an independent contractor because "I just love to paint. It's too bad it just couldn't have been a better experience." These are two examples of women who could not even see the glass ceiling.

Over time many women accepted the harassment and abuse as business as usual and decided to put up with it to be able to perform the job they loved and receive the pay and benefits. Options for getting out of their current occupations theoretically included promotions into management, but these women did not consider such a move. The most common solution for escaping an unacceptable or unbearable work situation was to retrain in a related skilled job, usually at a higher level within the trades, or return to school and earn an academic degree in a new profession.

Working in a blue-collar traditionally male job usually provided benefits that would pay for education. The women did not pursue education, however, to gain an internal promotion into management. Education was usually in a helping profession, such as teaching, health, or human services. Follow-up interviews found women pursuing or having completed degrees in conflict resolution, nursing, social work, dental hygiene, and sociology. Many were teaching at the college level and were committed to workplace diversity, social justice, and civil rights. Many wanted to become advocates for women's rights, particularly with regard to work. Others combined their educational degree with their traditionally male blue-collar trade. The state highway crew worker completed her master's degree in social work while on leave, but when she graduated, she chose to return to the highway crew because she liked the work, benefits, and job security and could use her social work skills by being the Employee Assistance Program liaison for her co-workers.

An additional consideration for women in blue-collar career paths is the impact of aging and disability. Because these jobs are usually physically demanding, career or job changes are required to accommodate incapacitation. In adapting, the women did not want to give up their passion for their work. Opportunities were pursued that provided either a direct connection to the same trade or replaced the specific trade with a related occupation. When she became disabled, an electrician moved into apprenticeship training. Another electrician promoted to industrial hygienist (electrical inspector) to accommodate her age and disability and stay connected to electrical engineering, which she loved. The truck driver in her fifties completed her certification to teach truck driving so she could share her skills and enthusiasm with other aspiring truck drivers.

Determining whether the reason why some women changed careers was due to aging and the job's physical demands or due to the stress of the hostile workplace is unnecessary and impossible. The result, however, was that after years of performing personally and economically rewarding jobs and enduring physically and psychologically demanding work, they switched careers rather than promote into management within their own trade or company. The longshoreman went to work for an engineering firm while still in her twenties, then returned to school and became the director of a conflict resolution center during her thirties. The police officer became a professor of criminal justice and a playwright; the postal worker, carpenter, and electrician became professors. In addition to teaching at a college, the electrician also became a videographer and activist. The nuclear fire watch opened a computer business and then began working at a technology temporary employment business. After ten years, only two of the twelve women contacted were still performing a traditionally male blue-collar job, and only one had ever promoted into management. The others had all pursued alternative careers or left the workforce.

FUNCTIONAL MANAGEMENT BY BLUE-COLLAR WOMEN

Based on interviews with women in traditionally male blue-collar jobs, focusing on women's promotion on a linear management track is myopic. Doing so falls short of revealing women's impact on the leadership and management of the workplace and, more generally, the U.S. economy, consistent with the ultimate vision of the Glass Ceiling Commission. Regardless of whether women are denied promotions into management or choose not to be promoted, they still seek to perform "management" functions. Redefining or reconsidering management in terms of its functions shows that blue-collar women performing traditionally male blue-collar jobs are not only capable but also creative in fulfilling their desire, need, and ability to work as managers. Managing differs and goes beyond leading to include controlling, planning, and organizing.[7] Blue-collar women in traditionally male jobs provide the opportunity to expand our understanding of the functions of management by example.

Although women in traditionally male blue-collar jobs may not aspire to or be promoted into management positions, they want to contribute to the workplace or their trade as leaders, role models, mentors, and "managers." When we go beyond identifying women as managers by job title and consider their performance of management functions, we see that women in blue-collar traditionally male jobs may have broken through the glass ceiling. They are working in skilled jobs; they have higher pay and more benefits than are typically available in pink- and white-collar jobs for which they are qualified; and, like managers, they provide leadership, decision making, and analytical functions at work and, more globally, for their trade or occupation.

I propose that we step outside the word *management* and look at the functions that define it. This shifts us from a linear construct to a functional approach. Austin, Kettner, and Kruzich conceptualize management functions as a triangular framework organized into three major dimensions—leadership, interactional, and analytic.[8]

Leadership can be conceptualized as the ability to direct, empower, and motivate people toward a common goal. It includes teamwork, strategic planning, organizational development, and boundary spanning. While working in blue-collar jobs, women found both formal and informal opportunities to be leaders. Many were the first or only women to hold such leadership positions.

Unions provided leadership opportunities for many women, but to assume them, they had to be elected by their peers—men. Women were elected union stewards, executive board members, and presidents of the local chapters. These were formal leadership positions in which they had power, strategic planning, and decision-making responsibilities. In many cases, the union leadership roles also allowed the women to move from being perceived as women doing the job to being regarded as respected co-workers.

Other women assumed more informal leadership positions by uniting with females to confront the adversity and hostility that male co-workers and the workplace in general imposed. It could be as simple as choosing not to quit and instead applying for an apprenticeship, guaranteed by a company's affirmative action plan, to serve as a role model for other women or as grand as founding and leading community and national tradeswomen or women's rights organizations. For many, it involved taking courses in feminist studies, labor relations, or employment law and carrying the word back to other women at work and in the community. For one woman, it entailed combing the Internet for strategies to create a more welcoming and productive workplace for all employees.

Reaching beyond the work organization and representing the company or job to the larger community is the leadership role of boundary spanning. Many women assumed this role by becoming active in tradeswomen organizations, promoting women in trades, entering apprenticeships, and policing schools to alleviate employment discrimination. Working with customers and representing the company to them provided an additional opportunity to lead outside the firm or span the organization–community boundary. The painter worked with the employer to negotiate the job and ensure satisfaction, and the electric planner worked with contractors and other utility companies to assure quality, safe, and coordinated service delivery. The police officer negotiated between hostile citizens and also provided guidance and leadership to the courts, community businesses, children, and elected officials.

Interactional roles include communicating, advocating, and facilitating. Many women in traditionally male blue-collar jobs state that one attribute they bring to the workplace is a caring, nurturing component that is not typically present in male co-workers. This they ascribe to sex-role socialization, but nonetheless it is an important part of their contribution to work. They feel that it more than compensates for their limitations in performing some of the mechanical tasks of the jobs that male sex-role socialization typically includes.

Nurturing and caring played out in both leadership and interactional functions. In some workplaces the women set up informal committees and work groups with other females. The electric planner was the only woman in her department when she started her job, but over time, six more were hired. After the number of women increased, the electric planner said that the "girls had an unwritten rule that if they had a problem or didn't know how to do the work" they would first go to each other and then ask a man. When the assembly line worker was sexually assaulted at work, she talked with another female co-worker to see if she had been singled out or if that was how women were treated there. Because the women had proved themselves to be strong emotionally by enduring harassment and adversity, male and female co-workers sought them for advice on handling problems, particularly with management.

Overall, the women had to establish complicated communication lines to navigate the workplace. They had to communicate in a way that was perceived as masculine but that would not stigmatize them. In a nonthreatening way, they had to educate the men, including the managers, about acceptable and harassing behavior. In this way they had to advocate for themselves, for Title VII rights in general, and for other women co-workers. For women working in blue-collar traditionally male workplaces, communicating, advocating, and facilitating were high-level skills that required persistence, diplomacy, and political savvy.

Some women had to pursue interactional opportunities outside the workplace. They found these opportunities in tradeswomen groups, the union hall, academic settings, and informal collectives of their female peers. These associations led them to advocate for women's work rights and define tolerable and unacceptable workplace behavior, thus affecting the way business was done across workplaces and, on a small scale, the way employment discrimination was defined. Such interactional associations resulted in consciousness raising among many of the women, who became more aware that business as usual was not only unacceptable but illegal and intolerable. They transformed their intolerance from being a victim to being a leader by finding ways to connect with other women within and outside of the trades. They became public speakers, writers, activists, and teachers. Unfortunately, the double-bind was that if they stood up for their rights, they often were labeled troublemakers and then not sought after for promotions into management.

Some women were not interested in forming bonds with other females. Instead, they pursued interactional ambitions by becoming active within their male work group. Informally, one step in opening communication and facilitating change was being invited to have lunch with the men or go out "drinking with the guys." Being invited was considered a rite of passage and an accomplishment that signaled progress toward being accepted as co-workers; it was part of joining the brotherhood. One woman said she was "like their mother." Another was "like their sister," and male co-workers felt they could go to her with their problems. In time, some men asked these women for advice about how to deal with the boss, because the women often had to develop more creative, stronger strategies for dealing with adversity than the men had. Male co-workers chose one woman to be the employee assistance representative to advocate for help with their personal problems. This degree of acceptance and camaraderie with co-workers, particularly men, was what had first prompted some women to join the blue-collar traditionally male workplace. Performing interactional functions on behalf of male co-workers was a notable accomplishment.

The women were seen as negotiators, facilitators, and advocates within the workforce, across work groups, and with customers and the community. The police adopted a policy requiring women officers to be considered or used to negotiate hostage and domestic violence incidents. The truck driver was asked to file a lawsuit, and her male co-workers supported her pursuit of a sex-based human rights violation against the employer.

Analytic roles of work include enforcement of policy, increasing efficiency of job production, and evaluation of job performance. Through the union protections and agreement, many women contributed to the analytic dimension of the workplace. Many could quote the bargaining agreement and professed the need for all represented employees to be versed in their rights and protections. Because of a perceived physical vulnerability in a workplace designed for men, they made themselves aware of municipal codes and demanded the enforcement of safety regulations. The painter refused to stand on a snow-covered roof in oversized boots. The industrial hygienist insisted on red-tagging any substandard electrical box. Beyond safety, the women were acutely aware of their employment rights in general and as union employees. They worked hard to be able to differentiate between what was illegal and what was just intolerable. Improved sanitation and the addition of bathroom facilities for all workers was the result of demands by women to provide combined Title VII and Occupational Health and Safety Act protections.

Regarding injuries and physical risk, women were vulnerable to ridicule if they were injured because they were considered "weak women." As a result, when the assembly line worker hurt her back, she was sent to the company doctor and then returned to work. A male co-worker, on the other hand, was placed on medical leave. The women countered this differential treatment by having clear knowledge and understanding of disability and sick leave policies.

Performing their jobs required the ability to protect them by being versed in company and union policies and applicable state and federal laws.

To avoid co-worker ridicule, the women said they had to outperform men doing the same job. This was a twofold task. It often meant determining more efficient ways to perform the job, because the usual way was devised for and by males. It also meant being able to evaluate their job performance compared to the standard and to the performance of the men. For the carpenter, doing the job required ensuring that her tool belt was always ready for any task. For the truck driver, it meant being able to ask for help to change a tire that was too big for any one person to change. The police officer had to combine physical and mental acuity to negotiate hostile and criminal situations. These women took great pride in finding different ways to perform their jobs that replaced their assumed lesser or different strengths than male co-workers with skills and attributes they had, such as caretaking, organizing, negotiating, and teaming.

Analytic functions usually were performed as part of their normal daily job routine. In most cases, however, management did not benefit from the expertise and creativity of the women, who were not valued in blue-collar jobs due to their gender. No one asked for their ideas or gave them the opportunity to share efficiencies or innovations. More often, the women tried to disguise their creativity because doing the job differently than the male way might have been seen as indicating incompetence or weakness, which would leave them open to ridicule.

Although most women in traditionally male jobs do not aspire to management, they want to perform management functions. They provide leadership, interactional skills, advocacy, and innovation. In addition, they facilitate change in the work group, organization, and economy while remaining in blue-collar traditionally male jobs.

RECONSIDERING THE GLASS CEILING

The Glass Ceiling Commission's vision was to promote women's leadership at a national level. When we require use of the words *management* or *corporate managers* in job titles to indicate whether women occupy key decision-making and leadership positions in the workplace, we miss and misunderstand women's potential, role, and impact there. It has been over forty years since Title VII of the Civil Rights Act outlawed sex-based employment discrimination. Although progress has been made, discrimination and hostility continue and are pervasive. One result is the underrepresentation of women in top executive positions. The glass ceiling is the point where sex-based discrimination, harassment, and workplace hostility merge to impose artificial barriers to the advancement of women into management, particularly its upper levels.

The reluctance of blue-collar women in traditionally male blue-collar jobs to enter management is due partly to overt discrimination in promotion and hiring and partly to covert discrimination of interpersonal harassment and hostility. These women are reluctant to accept promotion into positions that may mean reduced protection, benefits, job security, or personal accommodation. They are reluctant to move higher among co-workers whom they have found hostile, adversarial, and even abusive based on their experiences as line workers. The first step in removing the barriers to women's advancement at work and getting women to a place where they can see the glass ceiling is to aggressively enforce Title VII.

Although not in management jobs, women in traditionally male blue-collar jobs perform management functions at work and for their trade in general or among their co-workers. In blue-collar traditionally male jobs they earn wages and benefits, which are high compared to those they could earn in comparable traditionally female jobs. In blue-collar jobs they find camaraderie, job security, the schedule, and their ability to perform a particular job or trade or use certain skills attractive and satisfying. For these reasons many are not advancing and being promoted in the sense described by the Glass Ceiling Commission and tracked by the U.S. Department of Labor. Yet in many cases, these women have attained leadership, status in their occupations, workplace autonomy, and pay usually associated with management positions.

In many cases, a promotion to management would only reduce their compensation, benefits, job satisfaction, and job security. The result is a subtle, obscure form of employment discrimination that falls into the invisible and artificial barriers the Glass Ceiling Commission sought to expose. These women offer suggestions to other women for creating a career path that is fulfilling, family-friendly, highly paid, and secure, but that may or may not be in management.

When we identify the managerial behaviors and contributions of blue-collar women working in traditionally male jobs, we "reconstruct knowledge from the point of view of those that are on the margins."[9] Based on the choices that women in traditionally male blue-collar jobs make, we can identify some invisible barriers to management. Affirmative action is necessary and should be expanded to counter embedded workplace nepotism and favoritism and to give male and female workers notice that women *are encouraged* to apply for jobs and promotions. Employers must offer and pay for training, apprenticeships, and education that lift women's qualifications for promotions to compensate for inequities in skill development both in our culture and when on the job. Additionally, although union membership and influence have plummeted in recent decades, employers must offer the same benefits, protection, and accommodations typical of union jobs to retain productive, qualified employees and encourage them to promote, lead, and manage.

Without assuming management positions, women have taken on workplace, community, and national leadership roles and responsibilities in which they can make decisions, provide supervision, enhance (teach/mentor) the workforce, and increase productivity. Based on interviews with seventeen women employed in traditionally male blue-collar occupations, women excel, promote, and develop as leaders and skilled tradeswomen within the trades and in traditionally male blue-collar jobs. They have careers. They also hit glass ceilings. However, the obstacles they face and the remedies they devise differ markedly from those of white-collar, often upper middle-class women, whose situations the Glass Ceiling Act seemed designed to address.

NOTES

1. U.S. Glass Ceiling Commission, *A Solid Investment: Making Full Use of the Nation's Human Capital* (Final Report of the Commission). Washington, DC: U.S. Government Printing Office, 1995.

2. Glass Ceiling Commission, Vision Statement, available online at www.mith2.umd.edu/WomensStudies/GenderIssues/GlassCeiling/LaborDeptInfo/mission-statement (retrieved July 22, 2005).

3. K. Kissman, "Women in Blue-Collar Occupations: An Exploration of Constraints and Facilitators." *Journal of Sociology and Social Welfare*, 17(3) (1990): 139–49.

4. R. M. Kanter, *Men and Women of the Corporation*, 2nd ed. (New York: McGraw-Hill, 1993).

5. P. K. Mansfield, P. B. Koch, J. Henderson, J. R. Vicary, M. Cohn, and E. W. Young, "The Job Climate for Women in Traditionally Male Blue-Collar Occupations." *Sex Roles*, 25(1/2) (1991): 63–79.

6. J. A. Greene, *Blue Collar Women at Work with Men: Negotiating the Hostile Environment* (Westport, CT: Greenwood, in press).

7. Margaret Foegen Karsten, "Race, Gender, Class and Management: An Introduction," in *Management, Gender, and Race in the 21st Century* (Lanham, MD: University Press of America, 2006), pp. 19–26.

8. M. J. Austin, P. M. Kettner, and J. M. Kruzich. Assessing Recent Textbooks and Casebooks in Human Service Administration: Implications and Future Directions. Paper presented at the *Journal of Administration in Social Work* Editorial Board Meeting, University of South Carolina, Columbia, 2002.

9. M. L. Anderson and P. H. Collins, "Reconstructing Knowledge: Toward Inclusive Thinking," in M. L. Anderson and P. H. Collins, eds., *Race, Class and Gender: An Anthology*, 5th ed. (Belmont, CA: Wadsworth, 2003), pp. 1–5.

_____ 8 _____

The Ties that Bind and Separate Black and White Women

Stacy Blake-Beard, Maureen A. Scully, Suzzette Turnbull,
Laurie Hunt, Karen L. Proudford, Jessica L. Porter,
Gina LaRoche, and Kelly Fanning

Ignoring the differences of race between women and the implications of those differences presents the most serious threat to the mobilization of women's joint power.

—Audre Lorde

INTRODUCTION

Audre Lorde (1984, p. 117) offered these words over two decades ago—and they ring as true today as they did when she wrote them. In the years since Lorde's proclamation, women have both progressed and stalled. Recent statistics support the progress that women have experienced in navigating their careers. In 2001, women earned a growing proportion of educational degrees (57.3 percent of U.S. bachelor's degrees, 58.5 percent of all master's degrees, and 44.9 percent of all doctorates) and increased their presence in the workforce (in 2002, women made up 46.5 percent of the U.S. labor force and 50.5 percent of management and professional specialty positions) (Catalyst, 2004).

Yet despite the growing numbers of women in the professions, they still hold a small number of the top positions in organizations (Catalyst, 2004). Women make up only 15.7 percent of corporate officers and 13.6 percent of board directors; ten are Fortune 500 CEOs. If we look at the situation facing women of color, those statistics become even more dismal. Several factors are offered as barriers preventing women from reaching the tops of organizations in proportion to their presence in the workforce. These obstacles are exclusion from informal networks, challenge in accessing mentoring relationships, stereotyping and misconceptions about women's roles and abilities, and failure of senior leadership to be accountable for women's advancement (Catalyst, 2004).

In this endeavor, we wanted to look beyond these organizational and societal factors to focus on how women can help each other.

How can women help each other? Two decades later, Holvino (2005, p. 1) echoes Lorde's sentiment. She firmly maintains that "the best way for women to achieve power, support each other and make our organizations better is by engaging with our differences as women within and across racial-ethnic groups." In this effort, we focus specifically on the discourse between black and white women in the workforce. From an organizational context, black and white women are often the two largest groups of women represented (U.S. EEOC, 2003). As such, it is particularly important to understand how these two groups might be allies; it is equally important to understand what gets in their way. We do not see the challenges between black and white women as totally encompassing or illustrative of struggles that other women of color have with white women, or with black women for that matter. As Lorde (1984, pp. 127–28) so eloquently notes "The Woman of Color who is not Black and who charges me with rendering her invisible by assuming that her struggles with racism are identical with my own has something to tell me that I had better learn from, lest we both waste ourselves fighting the truths between us." Holvino (2005) purposefully centers on the experiences of Latinas to give voice to their often ignored perspectives. All of our stories are important; other scholars have devoted energy and time to illuminating the experiences and stories of women of color (Anzaldúa & Keating, 2002; Eng, 1999; Hurtado, 2003; Moraga & Anzaldúa, 1983).

The scope of this chapter is focused on the unique conversation between black and white women. It is based on a structured conversation among four black and four white women about their past experiences with women across the racial divide. We specifically asked one another a series of structured questions; the overarching guide to our research was to explore the ties that bind and separate us in our efforts to work together. We offer an exploration into the sociohistorical tale between black and white women as it is with us now—the ways that we connect and disconnect from one another. Furthermore, we recommend actions that black and white women can take to support one another.

UNEASY HISTORY: THE DIFFICULTY AND PROMISE OF OUR SEGREGATED SISTERHOOD

As we began this project, we had ample evidence (Bell & Nkomo, 2001; Blake, 1999; Connolly & Noumair, 1997; Granger, 2002; Lorde, 1984; Thomas, 1989; Thompson, 2001) that our sociohistorical pasts should be considered. Thomas (1989) writes about the impact of historical race relations, particularly the legacy of slavery, on the development and maintenance of relationships between blacks and whites formed in an organizational context.

Delving into works that documented black women's participation in the feminist and civil rights movements (Giddings, 1984; hooks, 1989; Hurtado, 1989), we found a historical bias undergirding the challenging relationships between black and white women. Although not widely acknowledged, several black female activists were ardent advocates of black women's participation in the women's rights struggle (Breines, 1996; Wallace, 1979). Yet black women faced virulent racism from their white counterparts as they worked "together" in the feminist movement.

The differences that emerged in the suffrage movement continue to affect contemporary relationships between white and black women. Bell, Meyerson, Nkomo, and Scully (2003)—two black and two white female academics working together on a research project—describe the impact of traditional race relations on their interactions. One of the black women claimed that due to her assumptions, which were based on past experiences, she had low expectations of white women's willingness to speak out on her behalf. One of the white women replied that such assumptions made it quite challenging to enter their partnership with a nondefensive stance and contribute her critical perspective, particularly if she disagreed with her black colleagues. In her dialogue with a white female colleague, Connolly confesses that "I do approach White women with skepticism until I get to know them as individuals and we work through our historical relationship. If there is no opportunity to work through our troubled collective past, there is no hope for a real personal relationship in the present" (Connolly & Noumair, 1997, p. 324). This legacy of anger, mistrust, and fear of betrayal has important implications for relationships in which black and white women can engage. They are not starting with a clean slate; so understanding the dynamics of their relationships, both the difficulty and the promise, is necessary to overcome this legacy.

OUR PROCESS

Our effort started with a set of questions that Blake-Beard (a black woman) wanted to answer—what allows black women and white women to support one another? What enables these relationships? What gets in their way? She extended an invitation to three black and four white women colleagues (see Table 8.1 for a description of coauthors). Several examples exist of researchers who have entered this dialogue of understanding relationships between and among black and white women in a similar way (Ayvazian & Tatum, 1994; Connolly & Noumair, 1997; Granger, 2002). Granger's (2002) research on black and white women's friendships offers an example of Blake-Beard's recruitment strategy to enlist her fellow contributors. For her study, Granger selected black and white female acquaintances who were involved in cross-race friendships. Rather than using purposeful sampling, Granger specifically wanted to connect with and study women who were committed to working against injustice and had a certain degree of sophistication and savvy in understanding and dealing with issues of race and racism. Connolly and Noumair (1997, p. 323) describe their collaboration as "a political act. It is a dialogue between two women, one Black

TABLE 8.1.   Coauthors of Study

Stacy Blake-Beard	Black	Professor, Simmons School of Management	• PhD in Organizational Psychology
			• Two step-children
			• Married
			• Oldest of four siblings
			• Born in Washington, DC
			• Grew up in Maryland
			• Research is on mentoring and diversity
			• Three Important Things:
			  ○ Authentic Interactions
			  ○ Empathy
			  ○ Community

Maureen Scully	White	Professor, University of Massachusetts, Boston	• PhD in Organizational Behavior
			• One child
			• Married
			• Oldest of four siblings
			• Born and grew up in Massachusetts
			• Research is on employee grassroots efforts and meritocracy
			• Three Important Things:
			  ○ Purposefully teaching in social responsibility in business school
			  ○ Teaching and writing to address social inequality and change
			  ○ Enjoying being mom to 4-year-old

Suzzette Turnbull	Black	Associate Director of MBA Program, Simmons School of Management	• MBA
			• No children
			• Single
			• Born in Jamaica
			• Grew up in Jamaica, New York, and Florida
			• Second of three siblings
			• Expertise in staff and volunteer management and fundraising
			• Three Important Things:
			  ○ Tactile and detail oriented
			  ○ Goal to think and talk more provocatively
			  ○ First time engaging in an intimate discussion and analysis of race relations

TABLE 8.1. (Continued)

Laurie Hunt	White	Consultant and Coach, Laurie Hunt & Associates	• MA in Gender Studies
			• No children
			• Married
			• Born in western Canada
			• Grew up in Ontario
			• Third of five siblings
			• 20+ years in high-tech industry
			• Three Important Things:
			  ○ Values are important—integrity, courage, respect, health,
			  ○ Formerly was a white woman who didn't "get it"
			  ○ Challenge is to control Canadian arrogance

Karen Proudford	Black	Professor, Morgan State University	• PhD in Management
			• No children
			• Single
			• Born in Germany
			• Grew up in Delaware
			• Youngest of four siblings
			• Research is on intergroup dynamics, leadership, and diversity
			• Three Important Things:
			  ○ Loves doing conceptual/theoretical work
			  ○ Loves doing applied work with practical implications for change
			  ○ Very "in tune" and up-front about race dynamics

Kelly Fanning	White	Internal Consultant, Blue Cross Blue Shield	• MBA
			• No children
			• Committed long-term relationship
			• Grew up in Massachusetts
			• Youngest of two siblings
			• Background in youth and social services
			• Three Important Things:
			  ○ Very honest
			  ○ Greatest strength and weakness is works hard and has high standards
			  ○ Traveled abroad to counter upbringing in racially homogenous town

(continued)

TABLE 8.1.   (Continued)

| Gina LaRoche | Black | Managing Director, INSPIRITAS | <ul><li>MBA</li><li>Two children</li><li>Married</li><li>Grew up in New York and Massachusetts</li><li>Oldest of three siblings</li><li>18+ years in sales and training in high-tech</li><li>Three Important Things:<ul><li>○ Athletic—training to do first marathon</li><li>○ Fled corporate America and started two companies, one with husband</li><li>○ Love to help people grow</li></ul></li></ul> |
| Jessica Porter | White | Research Associate, Harvard Business School | <ul><li>MBA</li><li>Two children</li><li>Married</li><li>Grew up in Michigan</li><li>Oldest of two siblings</li><li>Founder and past Executive Director of Association of Labor Assistants and Childbirth Educators (ALACE)</li><li>Three Important Things:<ul><li>○ Like to have fun while working</li><li>○ Gestates ideas, so silence should not be mistaken for indifference</li><li>○ Appreciates feedback from people with whom she works</li></ul></li></ul> |

Data for this table were compiled from coauthors' bios and their responses to one of the invitation questions: As we are jumping into this work, what are three important things that we should know about you?

and one White. It is a deeply personal account of both our thoughts and feelings about race, gender, and sexuality and a description of the processes involved in exploring them within ourselves and with each other." Much like our predecessors, we wanted to create a space to do a deep dive into our similarities and differences. In her initial invitation, Blake-Beard suggested, "I wanted to assemble a multicultural community of scholars whom I trust to really mull over this topic. I see this chapter as an invitation to actually do what we are writing about—draw from our past experiences to illuminate how black and white women can effectively and authentically work together."

We are alike and different from one another in interesting and important ways. Our group represents different disciplines and professions; our varied backgrounds add to the depth of our effort. We all hold advanced degrees. Half of us have children. Some are married; some are in committed relationships; others are single. We hail from several states in the United States, as well as

Jamaica and Canada. Most of us reside and work in the Boston metropolitan area; only one lives in another state. The common denominator was that Blake-Beard knew and trusted each of the invitees; she believed that each would be able to enter this collaboration open to authentic sharing and learning.

Bell and colleagues (2003) also provide a model for our work—their research evolved from an investigation of black and white women's efforts to address workplace inequality to include a focus on their process as black and white women engaged in change. They acknowledged that for their work, the act of writing became a microcosm of their topic of inquiry. Bell et al. (2003) suggest that work done in this manner represents a "spirit of reflexive ethnography," which they describe as "an ongoing conversation about experience while one is simultaneously living in the moment. By extension, the reflexive ethnographer does not simply report the 'facts' or 'truths' but actively constructs interpretations of his or her own experiences in the field and then questions how those interpretations came about." Like Bell et al. (2003), we were writing about our own interaction as black and white women; our discourse with one another was the subject of our research effort. Unlike Bell and her colleagues, our entire team never met face to face. All of our research was conducted using a series of email messages, dissemination of shared documents, and conference calls (see Figure 8.1 for a timetable and description of our process).

In addition to the structured conversations and analysis of these conversations, Turnbull also conducted a literature search to uncover historic themes characterizing the challenges and opportunities facing white and black women working together. We juxtaposed the themes identified in the literature with the issues emerging from our own discourse.

Our next step was to break the team into four cross-race dyads. Each of the four pairs was charged with documenting the learning on one of several themes that we identified as critical in our work together. Each pair used the documents that we had produced as a team and the literature on black and white women to understand the dynamics we saw emerging in our group. The four pairs directed their documents to Blake-Beard, who synthesized our separate pieces into one cohesive document. Each coauthor was then given an opportunity to respond to Blake-Beard's synthesis, correct any glaring misperceptions, and ensure that the words in this chapter accurately reflected her experience of our interactions.

THEMES

Through the process of our structured conversations, e-mail compilations, conference calls, and dyadic work teams, several themes emerged. We focus on three in particular to deepen our understanding of factors that both get in the way and support collaborative action between black and white women. These three themes, which we found were interrelated, are intragroup and intergroup connections, fear and silence, and making friends and building allies.

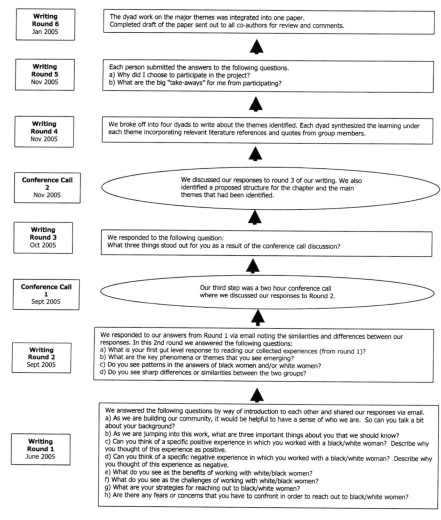

FIGURE 8.1.   Research process.

Connections: Intragroup and Intergroup Dynamics among Black and White Women

> Women must recognize that power circulates in many directions, and because we all have the experiences of advantage and disadvantage, this knowledge allows for the possibility of connection that breaks the cycle [of denial, accusation, confession and disconnect in women's groups].

> —Holvino (2005, p. 5)

As we discussed our reactions to our personal histories, we recognized interesting patterns. For example, we noted that the black women seemed to connect to each other's experiences. The social psychological processes of similarity and attraction (Byrne, 1971) were operative as the black women recognized and were drawn to one another. LaRoche said, "I felt an immediate collegiality with the black women on the call. I only personally know about a handful of powerful black women (outside my family), so I think this group has grown to a place of special meaning for me." Proudford indicated,

> What was most striking to me about our conversation was what seemed like an instant affinity among the black women and the lack thereof among the white women. As a black woman, I think I listened for points of connection with the experiences of other black women—because it is so (or has been) so rare to be in situations with my black female peers. As soon as I hear one, I feel a rush of excitement and want to say, "Yes! That's just how I saw it!" or "That's just what it was like for me!

Blake-Beard described these feelings as associated with being wrapped in a warm, comforting, perhaps healing blanket.

The reaction of the black women may have been tied to also being one of few, or holding token status in their career journeys. Kanter (1977, p. 207) described tokens as "the few of a different type in an organization with a numerically dominant type." Many professional black women are still one of few in their work settings. Rarely do they have an opportunity to see and interact with other women of color—so when the opportunity is offered to connect with other black women, the interactions are valued and treasured. As Turnbull indicated, "When you're in the minority and you see a peer, those feelings rise within you, and you gravitate to that person. Sometimes, just knowing you're in the same room or in the same organization can provide that sense of relief."

The warm blanket metaphor seemed to resonate with white women as well. Hunt noted, "I was envious. There were three other white women 'dissidents' on the call…and yet we did not feel that sense of community so evident among the black women." One described a recent experience at a conference attended by women of color:

> the white women sat at two tables individually and the black women immediately created a community in a large circle. I looked across the room in envy that time as well. What do white women need to create that type of community?… What is it that keeps us at a distance and prevents us from getting close to keep each other warm as black women do?

This striking contrast between bonding among black women and the experiences of white women was echoed by other white women. As Scully indicated, "White women have seen this quick way in which black women are relieved and delighted to meet another sister who 'gets it.' I think white women are a little envious of this fast bonding and know that we don't have this quick connection at work in general, except in some very male-dominated environments." Hunt added,

> White women do not come from the same place or level of "getting it." Although we have a common underpinning, our experiences are not immediately unifying. The competitiveness between white women and the resulting lack of solidarity means I can't totally rely on my fellow white women to be supportive even knowing they are fellow dissidents. There are various levels of "getting it" for white people and seemingly a more absolute level of "getting it" for black women because it is their lived experience—their warm blanket of common experience.

Turnbull was not surprised at the differences in how the two groups formed at this conference. "I've taken that dynamic for granted, because it's the way we've always interacted as a race. For the same reason, I've never noticed that white women don't gravitate the same way to one another."

It may be that white women were engaged in an internal (intragroup), perhaps even intrapsychic dialogue about race. Porter said, "I see how race has shaped me in the form of privilege, but when I examine my identity I don't feel a tremendous bond or affinity with other white people. In fact, I am more likely to feel alienated and embarrassed by them." Porter's experience is illustrated in Bell and Nkomo's (2001) exploration of white and black professional women. They found that the black women were very vocal in stating what they cherish about their racial identity. In contrast, the white women expressed ambivalence, confusion, and frustration when asked to describe what they cherished about being white women.

As we grappled to understand the differences we saw between the black and white women in our group, we suggested potential explanations for the lack of connection that the white women in our group felt. Scully offered this explanation: "In our own dynamics on the phone, it seemed like the white women were not so much directly connecting with each other as simultaneously engaged in the activity of working on understanding the black women's perspective." Although there is a problem with white women and trust (intragroup), Hunt suggests that the dynamic on our first conference call was the white women trying to find the balance between respectfully listening to what the black women had to say—letting their voices be heard—while at the same time contributing to the conversation.

Scully suggested that the need to bond may not be as urgent for white women because they are now present in larger (though not large) numbers. Scully's suppositions are supported by Ely's (1995) research on proportional representation and gender. In her research on female lawyers, Ely found that in firms with a greater number of women in high-status positions, women throughout those organizations experienced several benefits. Women in sex-integrated firms were more easily able to integrate aspects of masculinity and femininity and regarded feminine attributes as a source of strength, in stark contrast to women in male-dominated firms. As more women enter and advance in the workplace, and token status diffuses, women draw strength from their numbers and the presence of alternative models of successful women. Drawing on her past experiences as a woman in a predominantly male organization, Scully speculated:

> Here's what I think may be going on for white women: White women have now infiltrated many work places in great enough numbers such that we aren't in solo positions and starved for connection with someone in similar shoes, but not in such great numbers that there is gender equity and no need for bonding. I remember at [a leading business school], the faculty women talked about how when there were 6 women on a faculty of 100, they met regularly and gave each other a lot of sustenance. By the time I was there and there were 17 women out of 100, there were too many of us to find a time and fit at any one person's dining room table for dinner, but we were still few enough that there were plenty of gender issues.

The presence of those remaining "issues" and challenges ensures that connection will remain a priority. As Hunt indicates:

> I think white women do come together for bonding. More and more in organizations women's networking groups are appearing with a focus on addressing gender issues and for connection.... I think white women are starved for connection. I know I was for most of my corporate marketing career in a male-dominated industry (high tech). When I became involved in women's leadership and diversity, I can still remember the overwhelming sense of "I am not alone" once I started to realize how many other women felt the same isolation — regardless of race or ethnicity or job or level in the organization. When it comes to race, however, I think white women just don't know what it means to consider race; they don't understand the significance of race to them as white women. So ... in conversations like the one we're having in this group, for race-conscious white women, I think we're just trying really hard to get it right.

Hunt's comments make it clear that it can be quite difficult for white women to engage in a discussion *with each other* about race. So intragroup connection among white women is complicated, making intergroup connection with black women more complicated.

We are tentative about reaching conclusions about the dynamic we have noted, however. On closer inspection, the intragroup dynamics among black women and among white women do not fall neatly into a solidarity/lack of solidarity dichotomy. There are, for example, ways in which white women act in concert. Dumas (1985, p. 330) gives an account of the backlash encountered when a black woman assumed a position as dean in a large university:

When she took the position her faculty, all White women seemed very happy to have her, and wanted to get to know her better. She spent a great deal of time with them in social gatherings and orientation meetings.

However, when the time came to turn her attention to work, she began to have problems. The faculty that seemed so eager to work with her and who appeared from the academic and professional credentials to be well qualified for their jobs began to appear more and more insecure and immature.

The dean's efforts to have faculty members take more responsibility for their work were met with stiff resistance. Dumas indicates that faculty complained when the dean was away, seemed unable to keep small disagreements from escalating into major conflicts, and reported being less satisfied with their jobs. The lone faculty member who did accept the dean's challenge and on whom the dean had come to rely, received an Afro wig in the mail. Though no evidence exists that white women knowingly engaged in a concerted effort to oust the dean, the actions of at least several white women—and presumably, the silence of white women who may not have been so inclined—resulted in overtly racist behavior. Such examples raise the question of what being "connected" looks like for white women—or of what the possible consequences of disconnection may be.

Nor are the dynamics among black women easily codified. Black women also disagree intensely about a range of issues including age, skin color, and socioeconomic status, which challenges their ability to sustain relationships with one another. As Connolly and Noumair (1997, p. 325) note, "Internalized racism and sexism are felt most profoundly in the contempt that Black women feel for each other. Sisterhood works conceptually but does not begin to touch how angry, judgmental, and vicious we can be with each other." Black women are not immune to the "queen bee syndrome," the competitive and even destructive behavior senior women visit on more junior women whom they are not willing to help (Poe & Courter, 1994; Rindfleish, 2000). Black women also may struggle with competitiveness if they are in an environment that signals that only one spot is available at the top. Connolly indicates that she is "most in touch with my feelings of competition and envy when I am around smart, high-achieving, successful Black women" (Connolly & Noumair, 1997, p. 325). A lack of connection among black women may not look the same—may not be as visible—as it is among white women. But it still exists. Lorde (1984, p. 160) names black women's pain in not being in connection with one another, "In order to withstand the weather, we had to become stone, and now we bruise ourselves upon the other who is closest."

The perception about who is or is not connecting can affect the level of trust between the groups—both whether or not each group sees itself as trustworthy and trusts the other. As Porter pointed out, "It seems that we have this critical question in front of us, which is: how do we help black women to trust that white women are capable of being loyal and antiracist and how do we assist white women to step forward into a relationship where they feel disempowered and likely to be rejected?" The complexities of intragroup and intergroup dynamics affect how we perceive trustworthiness within and between groups. Our perceptions often turn into self-fulfilling prophecies. We tend to look for and focus on information that confirms our prior perceptions about a person's trustworthiness and ignore or minimize information that disconfirms them. If we don't trust a person we will look for, find, and remember incidents of breach of trust. If we trust a person, we are more likely to overlook or forget a breach of trust if it does happen.

We must become adept at navigating both intra- and intergroup dynamics. Reaching conclusions about who is more and less connected is difficult, though we certainly have impressions that drive our behavior (in ways that may further highlight and reinforce only the differences). The intragroup dynamics among white and black women have a similar ring. However, when juxtaposed against the larger organizational and societal dynamics, these distinctions may be over-shadowed by the intergroup power dynamics. Acknowledging the intragroup dynamics reminds us of the similarities, whereas recognizing the intergroup dynamic reminds us we are not identical. The interplay of both sets of dynamics may erect barriers, particularly fear and silence that preclude black and white women from fully seeing and experiencing each other.

Fear and Her Sister: Silence

I have come to believe over and over again that what is most important to me must be spoken, made verbal and shared, even at the risk of having it bruised or misunderstood.

—Lorde (1984, p. 40)

Our group realized that this task that Lorde discusses in her germinal book *Sister Outsider* is at the heart of the work that we must do together to realistically and effectively answer the question of how black and white women can work together. In fact, to connect with one another across dimensions of race and other dimensions of difference, we need to be visible and present. How is it that we each bring our authentic voice, including the questions and doubts, the concerns and the insecurities, to understanding our common and unique destinies? The concept and presence of voice, the distinctive expression of an individual (hooks, 1989), is critical.

Through our work together, we also learned that bringing our authentic voice to our endeavor is no easy feat—in fact, there are many ways that we can be fearful as we engage with one another across dimensions of difference. Proudford said, "probably the biggest fear is that my contributions will be discounted, ignored—or worse, reformulated and presented as someone else's. I am always concerned about 'getting lost.'" Lorde's work is a powerful source of understanding for us; her writings are relevant and salient because she has lived the very phenomenon we are trying to describe and live through our group experience.

A challenge we faced as were doing our work was the fear of self-revelation in such a way that might lead our colleagues to reevaluate our worth. Lorde (1984, p. 42) talks about fear as emerging from the act of self-revelation, "And of course I am afraid, because the transformation of silence into language and action is an act of self-revelation, and that always seems fraught with danger." For some of us, it felt that opening up and sharing might put our relationships at risk, so we remained silent. Hunt remained silent "because whiteness and privilege are a part of me in ways that are not apparent to me, I'm afraid sometimes to speak because my privilege and racism will surface unknowingly." As we thought about our interactions, the symbol of a mask emerged. We drew from Dunbar's (1913) imagery of a mask that we wear, a mask that "grins and lies, it shades our cheeks and hides our eyes." The symbol of a mask is an apt one; it speaks to the covering up of what is real to present a false face. But we actually didn't see the same fear emerging from black and white women in our group; we saw different faces across the two groups. Lorde (1984, p. 42) also describes our individual causes of donning the mask: "In the case of silence, each of us draws the face of her own fear—fear of contempt, of censure, or some judgment, or recognition, of challenge, of annihilation. But most of all, I think, we fear the visibility without which we cannot truly live."

Black and white women in our group expressed different reasons for donning the mask, different sources of fear. For black women, we talked about being fearful of letting white women in because there could be dire consequences for us in relation to our professional safety. So when white women reach out to black women, they may "not respond to friendly overtures by white women for fear that they will be betrayed." hooks (1994) talks about black women's fear of betrayal from white women—that at some unpredictable moment, white women will assert their power and privilege. So black women do not open up and let their white colleagues in. As Scully concluded, "a lot is at stake if the feared risks of letting down one's guard to form a friendship actually materialize. At stake is the black woman's job and livelihood—a livelihood that may support an extended family given the persistent socioeconomic disparities by race in the U.S."

White women talked about fear from a different perspective. They talked about the fear of being seen as "not getting it," or not being aware of their privilege. hooks (1994, p. 107) describes white women as being fearful of exposure—fear of black women seeing "the gap between their words and their deeds, saw contradictions and inadequacies . . . that Black women have the power to see through their disguises, to see the parts of themselves they want no one to see." Thompson (1996, p. 101) described how "My fear of admitting to the reality of White skin privilege turned out to be a mask which hid how access to unearned privileges and self loathing can co-exist." In our experiences, white women in our group talked about not wanting to be perceived as racist or unaware of their privilege. As a result of their fear, they may opt not to reach out for fear of rejection or losing their friendships with black women. Although the origins of our fears were unique, we often had a common response—silence.

As we interacted with one another, we found that we were not silent about everything. In fact, we shared a great deal about our backgrounds and past experiences, positive and negative, with women across racial boundaries. We saw silence in areas where we were likely to bump into challenging dynamics—when we had to address substantive issues where we may have to confront loaded sociohistorical schemas across race.

In these charged relationships between black and white women, we see social psychological processes that engender silence. Some black woman consciously or unconsciously hide behind allegations of racism to shield themselves from criticism. For them, any critique offered from a white woman must be motivated by racism rather than the intent to share critical and necessary feedback. Wilson and Russell (1996) describe this behavioral strategy as self-protection (p. 170)—members of stigmatized groups hold on to their self-esteem by attributing criticism to the racism of others. White women, suspecting that feedback of any kind will lead to accusations of racism, engage in a kind of silence that Thomas (1989) has called "protective hesitation." This occurs when participants in a relationship characterized by different identity and power groups hold back on sharing critical information for fear of being accused of insensitivity due to racism, sexism, or some other ism.

These dynamics of self-protection and protective hesitation set in motion a dance of weariness and wariness among black and white women. For both groups, costs are associated with silence. As Fanning noted, "Black women fear letting White women in, so they build a wall. White women fear being seen as racist, so they don't fight to get in. Thus things stay as they are." There were consequences for our team of not speaking out and letting fear silence us. The white women experienced the feeling that silence kept them alone and farther from that "warm blanket" that the black women had wrapped around themselves. For the white women, silence also meant that they could not locate each other. Fanning wondered "if I didn't speak up because I was worried that if I were skeptical or disagreed, it would be disregarded as a result of my white privilege or innate racism. . . . But I feel like I am not getting a true sense of my feelings in relation to other white women because I am not speaking up and neither did it appear the majority of white women in our group were." For black women, the silence implied fear or uncertainty among the white women regarding a discussion of race. Proudford noted that white women's silence also left black women with "the familiar feeling of black women taking the lead during the conversation about race."

Beyond the conversations of our small group of black and white women, silence has larger implications for professional relationships between black and white women in general. From the fear of speaking comes silence and loneliness, where no one truly can be wrapped in a warm blanket. Silence inhibits women from forming relationships, which in the professional realm means white and black women are missing out on potentially strong alliances. Gloria Anzaldúa (1987) describes the Borderlands as being "physically present wherever two or more cultures edge each other, where people of different races occupy the same territory...where the space between two individuals shrinks with intimacy." Silence in the face of race does not allow black or white women to inhabit the Borderlands. In fact, when black and white women are separated from one another, through the dynamics of protective hesitation and self-protection that accompany fear and silence, our ability to act as allies and supporters for one another is hindered. It is challenging to go to the mat for the sister whom you do not fully know—we are not able to vouch for one another in crucial ways.

Making Friends, Forming Allies

I knew of no intimacy, no deep closeness, no friendship between Black and White women. Though never discussed, it was evident in daily life that definite barriers separated the two groups, making close friendship impossible.

—hooks (1994, p. 94)

As our discourse evolved, we discovered a significant challenge to forming relationships between black and white women at work. Namely, the white women appear to be more interested in forming relationships with their black peers than the reverse. The black women in our group were unanimously uninterested in forming friendships with white women at work. In contrast, the white women wanted at least to make alliances with black women, if not form full-fledged friendships with them. In addition, the white women were shocked to learn that black women were not interested in forming cross-race friendships, and some were quite hurt to learn how one-sided the desire for friendship was.

Digging deeper, we turned to the question of allies, wondering if black women sought white women as allies in their organizations. Again, the answer was no. In fact, many of the black women had had such negative experiences in the past—being used, ignored, or insulted by white women—that they did not form alliances with white women at work. Furthermore, the reality is that in the majority of organizations in the United States, white men hold the most significant positions of power. Given this, black women, like white women, turn to white men as allies to help them navigate their careers and progress in the organization's hierarchy. In fact, many of the black women felt that they were competing to some extent for access to white men's power. The white women, on the other hand, were more likely to take their access to white men for granted. Hurtado (1989, p. 834) underscores this competition for access to white men, "The conflicts and tensions between White feminists and feminists of Color are viewed too frequently as lying solely in woman-to-woman relationships. These relationships, however, are affected in both obvious and subtle ways by how each of these two groups of women relate to White men." Our differential relationship to white men has implications for our relationships with one another. As Hurtado (1989, p. 843) notes, "White men use different forms of enforcing oppression of White women and women of Color. As a consequence, these groups of women have different political responses and skills, and at times these differences cause the two groups to clash."

As we thought more about how to breach this divide, we began to wonder about an alternative way to think about it. Rather than seeking strategies to help black and white women want to become friends, we realized that making connections with each other is important. By associating with each other in our organizations, we build strength for ourselves, each other, and the organization. So it is essential to consider the obstacles preventing white and black women from really bonding, both personally and professionally, at work. We identified two major hurdles to making this connection. First, both black and white women face risks when forming friendships with one another, though those that blacks encounter are greater. The second hurdle can best be described as a subtle power shift that we observed occurring in black/white women's friendships, leaving both parties in unfamiliar territory. Understanding how these barriers manifested for ourselves and our black/white counterparts is crucial if we are to move forward together.

During our conference call, the black women agreed that building relationships with their white counterparts in the workplace poses significant hazards. One colleague mentioned, "One strike you're out; for black people, one mistake and it's hard to recover." The white women had difficulty visualizing these risks and found their existence surprising. Scully said, "I just realized as I was writing this that I am not exactly sure what the feared risks look like in detail." Our discussions revealed that black women's lack of trust of white women is deeply embedded. Black women are taught at an early age to beware of white women/people; they also have a host of experiences to support the wariness. As Scully stated, "The black woman, necessarily aware of the risks of opening up to friendship at work, may scan the scene to see how the white women relate to each other. Will a white woman be a loyal ally? Let's see how she relates to other white women. Will a white woman stick up for me when the going gets tough? Let's see if white women have each other's backs." It is clear that white women hold the power in the professional realm, which was reinforced by Scully's statement, "The corporate world is a white woman's world." That realization, coupled with the existing wariness, speaks volumes about the level of risk black women perceive in building friendships with white women. As a result, black women focus on their professional lives while in the workplace and form "invisible fences" as a form of protection from the perceived risks. In some cases, white women are either completely unaware or unconscious of how these factors dictate the actions of black women in the workplace. "White women see Black women as distrusting and distant. Black women, however, see themselves as occupied with a unique set of concerns that White women will not understand" (Proudford, 2002, p. 2).

The gains of women are really the gains of white women—the "whitewash dilemma" (Betters-Reed & Moore, 1995). Black women feel the pressure of having to work twice as hard to prove themselves and advance in their careers. The frustration of seeing their hard work primarily benefit white women exacerbates the risks of forming cross-race friendships. Additionally, literature on workplace social networks (Combs, 2003) has shown that informal social networks (reactions to opportunities and problems of the work environment) are imperative to career advancement. However, Combs stated, "The Catalyst (1999) study reports that 40 percent of the African American women surveyed stated that their advancement is inhibited by a lack of informal networks and social systems in the workplace" (Combs, 2003, p. 385). Black women do not perceive white women to be supportive or helpful in the workplace; the perception is that white women are self-focused and only interested in advancing their own careers.

LaRoche's personal experience reflected that perception. "Over time I saw that the woman [a senior white woman] was only interested in her career. She did nothing to bring up other women or support them; all of our projects benefited her and we got no capital back from them. I began to feel used. Slowly our relationship deteriorated and she moved on to others that could help her." White women do not extend the professional channels to black women; in turn, black women are less likely to allow white women into their personal realm.

Black women are concerned about the potential threat to their career should they allow white women into their world. The perceived risks can manifest themselves in different ways depending on the organization, but they will most certainly make the black women's jobs more difficult or threaten their job security. This lack of trust, due in part to past experiences, has created uncertainty about white women's actions if the invisible fences are removed. Seeing the benefits of cross-race relationships is difficult for black women, because they do not perceive their white peers as allies in their career advancement, though the white women have more power in the professional realm.

Although some white people may be reluctant to admit it, they face risks in reaching across race as well. When white women confront issues of racism, they risk repercussions from other white people (Bailey, 1998; Segrest, 1994). Many white people are consciously or unconsciously invested in protecting their racial privilege. They might find it threatening to see other white people working to break down (rather than maintain) barriers between white and black women. In this era of 360-degree reviews and upward and downward feedback, white women might feel that reaching out to black women at work poses risks to their careers. In fact, one white woman in our team experienced this sort of backlash as a result of initiating a conversation about race in her job. Afterward, someone anonymously contacted her calling her a "race traitor," because in that person's opinion, as a white woman her allegiance should be to other white people first.

White women also face the risk of exposing their own privilege and racism when they form friendships with black women. As Hunt described it, "Because whiteness and privilege are a part of me in ways that are not apparent to me, I'm afraid sometimes to speak because my privilege and racism will surface unknowingly." Scully added another perspective, "What we did not mention, and again is rather taboo, is that...in subtle ways, we check out whether a black woman might be amenable to connection or will lecture us about our racism."

In our conversation, we observed an unexpected power shift between black and white women. Although white women hold infinitely more power than their black peers in the professional domain, in interpersonal relationships, black women hold the power to accept or reject white women's friendship. As Blake-Beard stated,

> in the relational dance that happens between white and black professional women's personal relationships, the power dynamic is different. I feel as if black women have this power to withhold their friendship and connection. Two caveats are that they withhold because they may have been burned in the past, or they just got the message, "You can't trust white people," over and over again passed on from lips of great grandmother to grandmother to mother. The second caveat is that this withholding is not without cost to the black woman.

Scully reinforced this power shift with her observation that "in the interpersonal realm, it is white women who are 'proving themselves.'"

Keeping this power in perspective, however, is important. As Scully put it, "In the whole scheme of life, it is just an eye-dropperful of power." However, we need to consider this power shift to understand the challenges white and black women face in making connections with one another. White women often feel they need to prove themselves to black women—prove that they "get it" and understand their own privilege. As a result, they can appear to be overeager in their attempts to connect with black women (Wilson & Russell, 1996). Black women, on the other hand, perceive so many risks to friendship with white women, that they can come off as uninterested and undereager to make connections. This creates a cycle in which white women fear rejection and either stop trying to connect or never even start, which reinforces black women's perceptions that white women are indifferent or don't value their contributions, personally or professionally.

A double bind results from this dynamic. Black women keep white women at a distance to protect themselves in the workplace, but it has a significant impact on all women. Turnbull stated, "having relationships at work is risky because performance is tied to success. If it goes awry, the cost is hefty. However, not having relationships at work is also risky, because it diminishes the effectiveness of women in the workplace and prevents us from unleashing our power as a group." We inhibit ourselves from being a stronger, more influential group in the workplace. Furthermore, maintaining the invisible fences exhausts black women. It requires a daily effort to take protective measures, and this diminishes personal effectiveness. We can learn so much from each other and have incredible resources to share to support everyone's career advancement. Blake-Beard shared a powerful visual of the impact of the double bind.

> An image of black and white women walking on parallel paths, each with obstacles and hurdles in the way . . . At some places, the paths are actually close enough so that one could jump out and reach the other. But she doesn't because she is scared she is going to fall into the gap—it doesn't matter that the gap is only three feet; she's been conditioned to know that to jump is a sure way to pain. . . . This image makes me so sad—because in fact, there are times when the black woman could really use the white woman over there on her parallel path. Sometimes, the white woman could use a tip or strategy from her black counterpart. So they can't share important information, strategies, and support with one another.

Early in our process, the team talked about the benefits of working with the opposite race; the responses were positive, encouraging, and powerful. We talked about "the additional perspective gained from interacting with a woman of the opposite race. There was a focus on what could be learned, what she would learn about herself, and access gained to that world." Yet instead of working together, black and white women turn to white men as the logical allies. This means women of both races are competing for the same allies. Overall, organizational effectiveness continues to decline because women are working in a disjointed way due to cross-race divides. As the workforce becomes more diversified, strong cross-race relations are becoming imperative. Organizations will not be able to succeed without drastic improvement in this area.

To break the cycle, we need to create a world where white and black women share the power in professional and personal realms. They each bear burdens as members of their individual groups. Yet they also bear a collective burden as women. Given the competitive nature of organizations, particularly at higher levels, black and white women must start making connections and easing each others' burdens early in their careers. Doing so will allow them to build a bridge between white and black women, so that when they—we—get to those high levels, we can pull each other up instead of shutting each other down. Understanding the risks and barriers to building those friendships is crucial to overcoming them.

INSIGHTS FROM OUR COLLECTIVE WISDOM

One of the most powerful aspects of this project was the opportunity to be with one another and to learn from and draw on our collective wisdom to understand and posit conditions for successful support of relationships between black and white women. We found from our research, our experiences, and the literature that several practices support white and black women in their efforts to connect with one another.

Entering the Space: Declaring Our Intentions

Because of the history between black and white women, one thing that we acknowledged early on was the importance of our willingness to enter into this work with one another. Because of the way the invitation was expressed and the identity of the person issuing it, we started from a basis of willingness to engage and consider trust that rarely accompanies cross-race relationships in organizational contexts.

Hunt visualized our beginning conversations and the ensuing bonds that we built with one another as a "circle of trust" (see Figure 8.2). She identified three components that contributed to building relationships across dimensions of diversity—respect, communication, and relationship. Because no particular entry point into the circle exists, breaking in is challenging. Respecting people allows one to trust them enough to enter into relationship. Communicating with them should engender additional respect, trust, and so on. All three elements (respect, communication, and relationship) seem to be necessary (based on our responses) to build trust. A way to overcome the barriers to the creation of a circle of trust is to focus on a common objective or passion. Many of us described our positive relationships with black/white women within the context of a pursuing a common purpose. In those relationships we respected each other and communicated effectively. We moved beyond the visible differences to another level that enabled us to learn from and trust each other. Fanning put

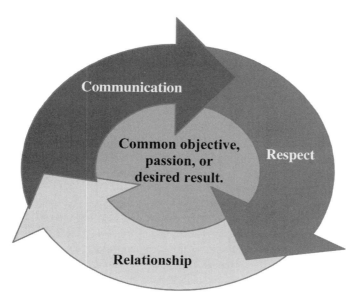

FIGURE 8.2.   Circle of trust.

this insight into concrete terms: "I will force myself to leave my comfort zone and talk about race in terms of differences, similarities, and opportunities. [I will] engage people to consider learning from past experiences to form stronger interracial relationships."

Working Together through Our Differences

Our tendency in doing this work as black and white women is to focus on our similarities. But rather than suppressing our differences as black and white women, we can also learn from them. Holvino (2005) suggests that the four skills enabling white women and women of color to work together are inquiring and disclosing, asking difficult questions, making differences explicit (confronting), and showing support and seeking common ground. Our group used each of these skills to build our strong connections. We started with inquiry; at each stage of our research, we asked and answered questions posed by our group. And our group responded immediately with a level of disclosure and sharing that we each recognized as a rare, invaluable invitation. In reaction to one of our early group conference calls, Porter shared her response, "I'm impressed by how open each one of us was, including sharing some difficult moments, personal challenges, and, for many of us, self-doubt." We also asked one another difficult questions. When we recognized the pattern of black women being very vocal and the white women being more muted, we challenged each other to unpack this dynamic. What did we learn about ourselves individually and as a community as we looked at differences between black and white women in the modes and frequency of communication?

Once differences are examined and confronted, black and white women can shift their attitude toward each other. LaRoche wrote, "I have been humbled and thrilled to know that there are white people in the world who look at race on a [regular] basis. . . . These four women have permanently altered my view of white people and what it means to be white."

Attending to the Structural

Holvino (2005) is unequivocal in advocating for acknowledgment of the systemic and societal dimensions of difference. Though it is important for black and white women to be able to connect with one another on an individual level, really working across differences requires more than this micro-level discourse. If we act as advocates, allies, and mediators for one another, we also will need to acknowledge structurally supported differential treatment. For black and white women to be committed to working together, we must also be willing to interrupt dynamics of institutionalized racism and sexism when we see this particularly virulent combination bearing down on our sisters. Blake-Beard was recently a participant in a train-the-trainer session on a particular experiential process for group work. When she raised an issue about how she, as a woman of color who is a trainer, might need to interact with this process using different tools than the white male facilitators at the front of the room, her questions and concerns were summarily dismissed. The dismissal, which is a common occurrence but no less painful, was only bearable because a white woman in the room took up her question, challenging the white male facilitators. Although this white ally also was dismissed, she had stood up—she had identified herself as an advocate willing to address the very systems that benefit her as a white woman. Both white and black women will need to take action and move beyond the traditional bystander role that we often take in cross-race interactions. A measure of courage and willingness to take risks is necessary as black and white women act as advocates, allies, and mediators for one another. As Segrest (2002, p. 221) says, "birthing such new structures will require both great patience and great impatience."

Acknowledging Our Simultaneity

As we worked together, we were cognizant of and sensitive to the multiple identities that each one of us brought to our interaction. Holvino (2005) describes this aspect of working across difference as simultaneity. "Simultaneity means that we each belong to many social groups at the same time, which complicates our identities and the fluid quality of our advantages and disadvantages within same-race and same-ethnicity groups and with other racial and ethnic groups" (Holvino, 2005, p. 4). Our multiple identities add another layer of complexity to the task of building relationships between black and white women. For example, to the extent that black women are not aware of their complex identities, they may speak from a "race" perspective; conversely, white women may be aware of other identities and thus see themselves in that context, although rarely from a race perspective. Proudford explains how multiple identities have affected her perception of connecting with white women.

> I was also thinking about our complex identities as we talked. For example, I am from a middle-class background. That influences what I do, how I do it, etc. It feels fine to me to "own" that. People from a working-class background might get quite frustrated with me because I don't always "get" class in the same way they do... thinking about myself in this complex way helps me connect to white women. Our conversation helped me take that complexity seriously.

CONCLUSION

We see the distinctions identified between black and white women as critical, a creative and necessary force for change. Holvino (2005) notes that the most effective way for women to achieve power, support each other, and make our organizations better is by engaging our differences both within and across race. We need to be able to both build on our similarities and not be afraid to step into our differences.

But engaging these differences is not easy work—or as Bell et al. share (2003, p. 410), "there are no easy papers on race." Our team definitely found this statement to be true; working virtually underscored the challenge of this collaboration. The process in which we engaged was marked by tense silences, hard questions, and tender vulnerabilities—a challenging translation of the issues that hurt and heal us. As Lorde (1984, p. 127) notes, "for it is in the painful process of this translation that we identify who are our allies with whom we have grave differences, and who are our genuine enemies."

Through analysis of our conversations (those held through electronic means and via conference calls) and the literature review, we identified several critical factors that get in our way and that enable us—the ties that bind and separate. The factors that separate us include challenging intergroup and intragroup dynamics, fear, and silence. Those that bind us together are processes of building a circle of trust to hold challenging conversations, taking risks in transforming our working relationships to friendships, and identifying allies and advocates across race. We entered this dialogue with one another from a place of hope—as Porter said, "by staying silent we just feed into the cycle of distrust, fear, and misunderstanding. I realize now that the risks of trying to connect and being rejected are much less significant than the risk of never connecting at all."

REFERENCES

Anzaldúa, G. E. (1987). *Borderlands: La frontera—The new mestiza*. San Francisco: Aunt Lute Books.

Anzaldúa, G. E., & Keating, A. (2002). *This bridge we call home: Radical visions for transformation*. New York: Routledge.

Ayvazian, A., & Tatum, B. D. (1994). *Women, race and racism*: A *dialogue in black and white. Work in Progress #65*. Wellesley, MA: Stone Center Working Paper Series.

Bailey, A. (1998). Locating traitorous identities: Towards a view of privilege-cognizant white character. *Hypatia, 13*(3), 27–42.

Bell, E. L. J., Meyerson, D., Nkomo, S., & Scully, M. (2003). Interpreting silence and voice in the workplace: A conversation about tempered radicalism among black and white women researchers. *Journal of Applied Behavioral Science, 39*(4), 381–414.

Bell, E. L. J., & Nkomo, S. (2001). *Our separate ways: Black and white women and the struggle for professional identity*. Boston, MA: Harvard Business School Press.

Betters-Reed, B., & Moore, L. L. (1995). Shifting the management paradigm for women. *Journal of Management Development, 14*(2), 15–30.

Blake, S. (1999). At the crossroads of race and gender: Lessons from the mentoring experiences of professional black women. In A. J. Murrell, F. J. Crosby, & R. J. Ely (Eds.), *Mentoring dilemmas: Developmental relationships within multicultural organizations* (pp. 83-104). Mahwah, NJ: Lawrence Erlbaum Associates.

Breines, W. (1996). Sixties stories' silences: White feminism, black feminism, black power. *NWSA Journal*, 8(3), 101–122.

Byrne, D. (1971). *The attraction paradigm*. New York: Academic Press.

Catalyst. (2004). *The bottom line: Connecting corporate performance and gender diversity*. New York: Catalyst.

Combs, G. M. (2003). The duality of race and gender for managerial African American women: Implications of informal social networks on career advancement. *Human Resource Development Review*, 2(4), 385–405.

Connolly, M. L., & Noumair, D. A. (1997). The white girl in me, the colored girl in you, and the lesbian in us: Crossing boundaries. In M. Fine, L. Weis, L. C. Powell, & L. M. Wong (Eds.), *Off white: Readings on race, power and society*. New York: Routledge.

Dumas, R. G. (1985). Dilemmas of black females in leadership. In A. D. Coleman, & M. H. Geller (Eds.), *Group Relations Reader 2* (pp 323–334). Jupiter, FL: A. K. Rice Institute.

Dunbar, P. L. (1913). We wear the mask. *The complete poems of Paul Lawrence Dunbar*, New York: Dodd, Mead.

Ely, R. J. (1995). The power in demography: Women's social constructions of gender identity at work. *Academy of Management Journal*, 38(3), 589–634.

Eng, P. (1999). *Warrior lessons: An Asian American woman's journey into power*. New York: Pocket Books.

Giddings, P. (1984). *When and where I enter: The impact of black women on race and sex in America*. New York: Bantam.

Granger, D. (2002). Friendships between black and white women. *American Behavioral Scientist*, 45(8), 1208–1213.

Holvino, E. (2005). *Commentary #5: Women in organizations: Why our differences matter and what to do about it*. Boston, MA: Center for Gender in Organizations, Simmons School of Management.

hooks, b. (1981). *Ain't I a woman: Black women and feminism*. Boston, MA: South End Press.

hooks, b. (1989). *Talking back: Thinking feminist, thinking black*. Boston, MA: South End Press.

hooks, b. (1994). Holding my sister's hand: Feminist solidarity. *Teaching to transgress: Education as the practice of freedom*. New York: Routledge.

Hurtado, A. (1989). Relating to privilege: Seduction and rejection in the subordination of white women and women of color. *Signs, 14*, 833–855.

Hurtado, A. (2003). *Voicing chicana feminisms: Young women speak out on sexuality and identity*. New York: New York University Press.

Kanter, R. M. (1977). *Men and women of the corporation*. New York: Basic Books.

Lorde, A. (1984). *Sister outsider*. Freedom, CA: The Crossing Press.

Moraga, C., & Anzaldua, G. (1983). *This bridge called my back: Writings by radical women of color*. New York: Kitchen Table/Women of Color Press.

Poe, R., & Courter, C. L. (1994). Women against women. *Across the Board, 31*(3).

Proudford, K. L. (2002). *Insights #14: Asking the question: Uncovering the assumptions that undermine conversations across race*. Boston, MA: Center for Gender in Organizations, Simmons School of Management.

Rindfleish, J. (2000). Senior management women in Australia: Diverse perspectives. *Women in Management Review*, 15(4), 172–183.

Segrest, M. (1994). *Memoir of a race traitor*. Boston, MA: South End Press.

Segrest, M. (2002). *Born to belonging: Writings on spirit and justice*. New Brunswick, NJ: Rutgers University Press.

Thomas, D. A. (1989). Mentoring and irrationality: The role of racial taboos. *Human Resource Management, 28*, 279–290.

Thompson, B. (1996). Time traveling and border crossing: Reflections on white identity. In B. Thompson, & S. Tyagi (Eds.), *Names we call home: Autobiography on racial identity* (pp 93–109). New York: Routledge.

Thompson, B. (2001). *A promise and a way of life: White antiracist activism*. Minneapolis: University of Minnesota Press.

U.S. Equal Employment Opportunity Commission. (2003). Occupational employment in private industry by race/ethnic group/sex and by industry, United States. http://www.eeoc.gov/stats/jobpat/2003/national.html.

Wallace, M. (1979). *Black macho and the myth of the superwoman*. New York: Dial.

Wilson, M. & Russell, K. (1996). *Divided sisters: Bridging the gap between black women and white women*. New York: Anchor Books.

9

Black Women in Management

Ancella Livers

Once asked, the question generally hangs in the air, taking on a life of its own, corrupting the relationships of the past and the future by the sheer volume of assumptions, perspectives, and lack of awareness that are embedded in the words.

"So are you a woman first or black first?"

The assumption is that these aspects of self can be pulled apart, separated as if they have no relationship to each other. Inherent in this question is the belief that one or the other of these characteristics must predominate—race or gender—and the other must necessarily be subsumed. Yet the experiences of women of color belie these assumptions. They are "both/and," not "either/or."[1]

The stories of African American women managers are stories that are born in the nexus of race and gender and tempered in the workplace. They are the stories of both/and as women, black women, slowly find a place in the corporate managerial ranks. In a July 2003 report, the Equal Employment Opportunity Commission stated that 195,784 or 3.3 percent of African American women employed in the private sector held official or managerial positions. This percentage shows a change in the number of black women managers from 1990, when 111,318 black women were officials and managers, to 2001 when the number grew to 195,784. Although the sheer number of African American women managers is the largest of all of the female minority racial groups recorded in the report, the percentage of other minority women managers is growing at a faster rate.[2] Furthermore, though it is difficult to find statistics comparing the pay of black and white women managers and those of black male and female managers, annual earnings comparisons indicate that black women earn less than either their white female or black male counterparts. Statistics compiled by the National Committee on Pay Equity show that in 2003 black men earned an annual average of $32,241 compared to white women, who earned $31,169, and black women, who earned $26,965. All three groups earned less money than white males, who earned an annual average of $41,211.[3] This pay disparity is clear evidence that the combination of race and gender has a different impact than the experience of race or gender alone. "I would like to think that my performance plays a larger role than my race and gender," said Deborah Raleigh, a vice president at a major manufacturing conglomerate, "but I don't know that for a fact, and I don't think I will ever know that."[4]

This combination of race and gender, or perhaps the lack of awareness of it, helps create the specific kind of environment, miasma, in which black women managers must work. *Miasma* is "the murky atmosphere of misperception and distortion" in and through which many nontraditional leaders have to navigate in their work life. Akin to a low-lying fog that makes the environment difficult and at times treacherous for maneuvering, miasma speaks to the stereotypes, perceptions, misinterpretations, and general baggage that people who are different from the mainstream must manage. When nontraditional leaders work in organizations that have a low tolerance for difference, the miasma can become quite dense, as relationships, trust, and communication are degraded. In organizations where tolerance and inclusion flourish, the miasma is generally less problematic and more easily managed.[5]

The characteristics of miasma for women managers, in general, may include stereotypes about women being emotional or irrational. They may also include concerns about the impact of pregnancy and child care on workplace efficiency and competency and a vague but pervasive question about the appropriateness of women in certain jobs.

The aspects of miasma for African American managers also include concerns that others question their competence, goodness of fit, and emotionality. Added to this are lingering beliefs in employers' minds that blacks may not have a particularly strong work ethic and that they may get unfairly promoted because of affirmative action policies.

Black women managers bear the burdens of all of these perceptions with added nuances. "We're always challenged around credibility and competency," said Margaret Stone, the director of diversity at a national financial institution. She also believes that co-workers wonder, "How did they get this information? This job? How much power do they really have?" Referring to the miasma each group faces, she said, "I don't think it is different for white women or African-American males. I think the degree is magnified [for black women]."

According to a 2004 Catalyst report, African American women believe they face significant barriers to their organizational advancement. The most common barriers the women report are not having mentors or sponsors, poor informal networks, lack of same race/ethnic group role models, and few high-visibility projects. They also say that they must deal with others' negative stereotypes of black women, endure increased scrutiny, challenges to authority, questioning of their credibility, and continual questions of fit.[6]

As they tell their own stories, black women managers acknowledge the challenges and tensions that often underlie their work life; yet they also talk about their strength and ability to survive. It is not unusual for these women to speak of the lessons learned from their families and the formative experiences that they believe help them succeed. Based on a series of interviews with black women managers, this chapter looks at the way black women see themselves and how they believe others see them. The chapter will also talk about the women's challenges, fears, and coping mechanisms.

Nine women were interviewed. Their names have been changed to give them enough anonymity to speak freely about their work lives. Most are managers, many at the director level and higher. They tend to work for large national and international for-profit corporations, although one works for a big-city hospital and another for a not-for-profit. Almost all have worked for twenty or more years; the youngest is thirty-seven and the oldest is fifty-eight. The women live in numerous communities, large and small, representing the East, South, Midwest, and Southwest. Although their personal life and work experiences are varied, their perceptions of what it is like to be an African American woman manager are parallel and strongly resemble those of black women profiled in other studies. Furthermore, beyond noting how these women see themselves, the chapter will also look at some of the similarities in how others see them.

One of the most common comments about black women is that they are often too direct in their dealings at work. In the Center for Creative Leadership's African American Leadership Program, black women managers regularly report they are perceived as being too straightforward. One woman, Jan Henry, a manager in a chemical corporation said that in her work "I tend to be very, very direct about how I understand things or questions that I ask." She noted that in her organization there are about fifteen other black professional women, all of whom have very different personalities yet all of whom have been told at some point in their careers that they are too direct.[7]

Although others may consider this characteristic to be a fault, many black women embrace directness, seeing it as an asset rather than a detriment. Elizabeth Scott, a training manager for an international shipping firm said, "I am very direct, very competent, and very knowledgeable." She continued. "I've had people who've said 'you can't say that. They won't understand.' But my thing is that's more on them than on me." Scott also said that she would guess that 99 percent of those who report directly to her love their relationship. "I allow them to be the people they need to be and to do the job they need to do."

Stone also believes that black women are more direct than many of their other female colleagues because they are not accustomed to being taken care of and are willing to confront, "to have the corporate fight." This willingness to ask the difficult questions is often necessary, she said, because so many corporate cultures "make nice." "We do it in a professional way," said Stone, "We are professional, but we see it as a disservice to not name the issues and have the tough discussions."

Julianne Street, who works as a director of human resources in a global information media company, said she is perceived as being a "very strong, outspoken person," adding, "One of the things people describe me as is a straight talker and being fearless about saying the truth." Though Street said she will confront issues others will not, she has learned through difficult experience that "most people don't want to confront issues." Consequently, she now picks her battles more carefully, choosing to be vocal on issues she considers to be critically important to her job or the organization. "Everything is built on relationships and it's hard enough to build relationships to just keep my job," she said.

Paula McPherson, manager of executive development at a major financial institution, said that because she is a psychologist, her job and education also allow her to say what's on her mind. "I can speak the unspoken and have it not be as detrimental to me as it would be to someone else."

Grace Evans, vice president of human resources for a national cable organization, said, "I am willing to speak up and have the unpopular comment. If my heart is right, I'm OK with that."

Because they are black and women and somewhat rare in the organizational hierarchy, these managers often feel disconnected from the mainstream. This disconnection, along with cultural influences, allows and sometimes pushes them to question the system in ways others may not feel as comfortable doing. Many of these women have been raised to resist the labels and stereotyping of larger society. As children or young women, they were often taught that those who succeeded in life were responsible to help change the system and to give voice to the voiceless.[8] For example, Cayenne Jackson, a senior vice president of diversity for a national firm in the retail industry, said she wanted to make sure to accomplish as much as she could for her organization and community. It is important to her to make a significant contribution to her company, a retail industry firm for which she has worked for several decades. Making systemic changes is also important to her. "I see the opportunity to help the doors be more readily opened for people who have been disenfranchised in this particular industry," Jackson said, "coupled with the opportunity to give something back in my community."

Frances Montana, an executive director of a private, nonprofit educational job-training center in a small town, said she is a role model. Because she is one of the few black leaders in her community, Montana said black parents "bring their children through the doors just to see me. That's still an important thing for them because their children's teachers are still white; their principal is white; the store managers are still white. Everybody is white." Everybody is white but Montana, and she sees her role as being a mentor and opening doors for those whom others may overlook.

Furthermore, as people who are often outside of the power structure, some black women feel that they are already marginalized and have less to lose within the organizational hierarchy than their colleagues. "We are not intimidated by the system," Stone said. "I can make a successful living doing many things. I don't have to work here to live."

Because they are so aware of being outsiders, some women feel they have to gird themselves against the racial slights they fear are inevitable. Scott, for example, talked of working as a bank manager. At one point one of the tellers had a problem and needed to speak to the manager—Scott. The teller said to one of her co-workers, "What can that monkey do for me?" referring to Scott. The co-worker shared the comment with Scott, who went to the original teller, did not confront her on her comment, but helped her work through the problem. In spite of the teller's racist views, Scott said she was able to handle the situation. Though racial incidents have occurred in her career, Scott said race has never really been a hindrance to it. Yet when she discusses her greatest fear, she said it is that someone, probably a yet unknown white male manager who will be her boss at some future date, will make a problematic racial comment to her. "I'd probably lose my job, for a minute anyway and then I'd get it back." She added, "I know it's going to happen one day," referring to the possible comment and her response.

Mercedes Esterhaus, marketing director for a professional services and consulting firm, said she, too, believes the potential for racist comments or attitudes are possible in any situation. "I always know that they're there," she said referring to racist attitudes. "You always know that question [about black competency] is always there. I try not to spend a lot of time focusing on it, but I know as I go about doing my job it could be there."

For Esterhaus, the impact of always being prepared for battle is a part of the stress of the corporate workplace. Though she says concerns about race are not in the forefront of her mind, they do have an effect on her ability to trust people, particularly whites. "I have never been, am not in, and will never be in an environment where I can say 'I trust you, you have my back.' You have to always be watchful."

Montana said black people have to deal with race as an issue every day of their lives. "As a black person in America, you're always confronted with the question 'is it a matter of race?' she said, adding, "when they see you in America, they see black first."

WHITE WOMEN

Race may come even more to the fore when gender is held constant. Specifically, many black women feel there is significant distrust or tension between black and white women. Often, they say white women neither understand nor try to understand that black women must navigate through a different set of biases and assumptions than do their white female colleagues. Consequently, the natural bond of gender, for many black and white women, may not be so natural.[9]

Stone said there is tension because white women are often in denial about the treatment they receive compared to the treatment black women receive. She went on saying white women are often "acknowledged quicker, sooner, and more often than women of color. They are invited to the table sooner. They get more stretch assignments. Women of color more often have to prove their credibility." Stone said white women's denial or unawareness is what causes the tension. "They actually think they got where they got without special privileges. From a gender perspective they [as women] are treated differently [in the workplace], but from a race perspective, they are treated better."

McPherson said she has experienced "distinct tension" with white women since she entered corporate America. "With white women," she said, "it's almost as if we can't hear each other." She wondered if each group makes assumptions about how the others would behave based on their own understanding of womanhood; beyond womanhood, however, race adds a confounding factor that neither group knows how to interpret appropriately. "With white men there is no assumption of similarity," added McPherson. "We're so different it almost leaves us open to explore."

Speaking personally, McPherson said part of the problem with the underlying tension between black and white women is the potentially insidious effect on the rapport with her white female colleagues. If she finds that something is not going well with her female colleagues and if the problem is not discussed, McPherson said her relationships can be undermined. "In the absence of information, I have noticed an increased tendency in myself to assume malintent." Because she recognizes the behavior, McPherson said she has become proactive in managing it. "If I find there is less than supportive behavior and I find myself being impacted, I go and talk about it."

Esterhaus says she, too, has experienced the tension and suggests that white women "feel threatened by the way we communicate, come across, and dress."

Grace Evans said she thinks the issue is one of distrust, not tension. The distrust, though, is hers, not her white colleagues'. She said her experiences have taught her to be careful and not to believe that white women will help her out of difficult situations. When she was in high school, Evans ran for a student office. As she recalled the event, some white female students had initially supported her; however, the election had ended in a tie and had to be rerun. "They jumped ship to the other side," she said, "I knew where they would go when it all came down." For Evans, the incident still feeds her distrust of whites in general and white women in particular. "They may not be there for me; I need to be aware of that," she said.

Street said working with white women can be a "nightmare." She went on to say, "They have a constant inability to take directions from somebody who is black." She added that she has several white women who report to her and who have worked actively to undermine her authority. In her experience, she said, it has not been unusual for white women whom she has managed to try to determine if she has organizational support. "If they perceive any weakness or if you're not supported at the highest level, they'll come after you." Street added, though, that white women who are peers are often more collegial. "That's because the higher up you go, there are fewer women," she said. She concluded that the impact of hierarchical movement is sometimes to make gender a more salient issue than race.

Although many black women experience feelings of tension or distrust when dealing with white women, others say their relationships with white women have not been problematic. "I see it in just women, period," said Kelly Carter about problems between female colleagues, "it doesn't have to be white women." Carter, a clinical research coordinator at a large women's hospital, acknowledged, though, that many black women don't trust white women.

Montana said that she has never experienced any particular difficulties with white women either. "Most of the women, I would say I've met," she said, "were all struggling to find level ground with the men."

The feelings many black women have toward white women often seem to spring from personal experience, vestigial historical recollection, different cultural styles, and racial stereotypes held by both groups. Many black women believe that white women do not acknowledge that their pain of nonacceptance is akin to but different from that of white women and, furthermore, that white women don't recognize their own complicity in creating some of that pain.[10]

The relationship between black and white women also speaks to the fragility of trust and the assumption of mal-intent on the parts of both black and white women. Certainly these disconnects are quite present in black women's retelling of past hurts and possibly in the stories of white women as well. These conditions make it difficult for women to "hear" each other, as McPherson suggested, and may continue to lay the groundwork for further misunderstandings.

ALLIES

In spite of the tension some black women feel about white women and often, white men, many of those interviewed also listed representatives from these groups among their closest professional allies. The apparent inconsistency seemingly goes unnoticed as the nuances of racial relationships retreat to the background in the face of personal friendships.

Evans said one of her allies is a white woman with whom she has become fairly close. "She was excluded from the white group for whatever reason," Evans said speaking of her friend. "She kind of attached herself to me." Evans also noted that because her friend is white, she often hears comments and gathers and shares information to which Evans might not normally be privy. "I also bring her into projects where I think she would do well. It's not that she is not good," Evans said reassuringly, "it's her personality. She's a library type, and she makes the guys uncomfortable."

Evans said she also has allies among her direct reports, who help keep her informed of events around the office. In addition, she considers her boss, a white male, to be a supporter. I've seen him go to bat for something I want to push through the organization," she said. "I sometimes think 'why's he doing this?' Part of it is just him, and part of it is having a woman of color makes him look good. And I do think that part of my job is to make him look good."

Montana said her mentors have both been white men. She said her first mentor was an older man who said, "You know, you're going to be good. Don't let anybody shake your resolve. If you need anything from me, give me a call." She added, "I was so hurt that a black man didn't say anything to me. They wanted to play games." Her other mentor was a minister whom she said has "always remained faithful to me." Both men were people she could ask for advice and who would speak up for her when she wasn't in the room to speak up for herself. She said their words and support helped her believe she could be successful in the organizational environment.

Others interviewed also talked about the variety of allies and supporters they had. Scott noted that she had four people with whom she could discuss anything. Her support group consisted of three men, two black and one white, and a black female. Stone said she had senior leaders, women of color, gays, and lesbians as allies. "I have many allies across teams because of the work I do," said the diversity director. Carter said an older white woman in her office saw she was "sharp, a quick learner, good, and had a good personality" and so began sharing experiences to help her acclimate to a new job.

Having allies, supporters, mentors, and coaches is particularly important for African Americans who, in general, tend to describe a workplace that is frequented by more hardships and fewer challenging tasks than the workplace described by their white counterparts. Although many studies have suggested that blacks have fewer workplace mentors than their white colleagues, a 2003 report, "Key Events and Lessons for Managers in a Diverse Workforce," from the Center for Creative Leadership suggests that the internal supportive relationships blacks do have may be of particular significance as they maneuver through the corporate environment. When asked to describe the key or major events in their managerial careers, African Americans were more likely than their white counterparts to mention the impact that mentors and other allies had on their work lives.[11] Although it is unlikely that blacks in the center's study truly had more mentoring experiences than whites, it seems probable that the mentors they did have had a more significant effect on their careers because, in general, their need for an advocate was greater and their chances of getting one lower. Consequently, the study's black respondents often credited their mentors with opening doors or giving them opportunities when no one else would.

The Catalyst study reports that 38 percent of the African American women they surveyed had mentors. In fact, of the three racial groups detailed (Latinas, Asians, and African Americans), black women were more likely than the other groups to have mentors. Those mentors tended to be either black or white with 32 percent being black men, 22 percent black women, and 29 percent white men. Black women reported that white women were least likely (at 16 percent) to be mentors.[12]

Though many black women report having internal mentors, many also say they get their main support for work outside of the workplace. McPherson said she's always had a good external support system made of other professional women. "My challenge," she said, "is that I do not have a good support network internally." Though she said her internal support was not strong, she distinguished that from internal allies that she said she did have. Similar to the experience of others, McPherson had allies who sought her out because they saw she was taking on challenging tasks. McPherson sees both allies and supporters as important in the corporate world. In her view, supporters are people with whom she can discuss problems and concerns, personal or professional. Allies, on the other hand, are people who help push through initiatives or who help create professional opportunities.

Street also feels that allies are important, particularly when a situation is difficult to manage. "I usually have information others don't have," Street said, "so I try to share information. That's my barter. That's what I have to trade." She called her current environment "politically treacherous" and though she has some allies, she said her support is largely garnered from people outside of the office. "Here, it's been hard to find people to trust," Street said. She relies on a friends and former colleagues to help her navigate in the corporate workplace. "I have support from other people with whom I've worked. I have a previous boss and we've been friends for fifteen years."

"I think my husband is my biggest ally," said Evans. "He gives me a man's perspective." Carter also noted that her husband was one of her strongest supporters. "You have to have family members who know you completely," she said, "and when you're bloody, they clean you up and send you back in there and let you know you'll be all right."

The women interviewed did not take their supporters and allies for granted. In fact, often the women seemed surprised to have them. Always, they were grateful as they described the positive impact these people had on their careers. What might seem a little more unusual considering their descriptions of themselves as proactive is the fact that so many of these women said their mentors and allies had made the initial move. Only a few of the women said they had actively sought allies. Though the data are inconclusive, perhaps the women, who typically see themselves as estranged from the organizational power structure, make no assumptions that those within it will help them. Consequently, when help does come, those who are able to embrace it find the relationships very important to their careers.

MANAGING PERCEPTIONS

One of the strongest coping mechanisms black women display is that of managing the perceptions others may have of them. "You always have to manage perceptions, all of the time," said Carter. As a black woman, Carter said she must always be alert because, "I am culturally different and visually different and people don't know how to take that."

McPherson agreed. "Yes, definitely," she said about managing perceptions. "That's not new to this environment. I always have felt this way." As someone who has typically been one of the younger people in her workplace, she said, "I have to manage how I'm perceived because of age, then race and gender." McPherson said she began working as a psychologist at age twenty-nine, and people always assumed she was too inexperienced. She said her struggles around age were then overlaid with the stereotypes she was facing around race and gender. She remembered one job interview when the hiring manager, a white male, had not read her résumé. During the meeting, her interviewer said, "'We had an elder statesman in mind for the job,' *code, code, code*," said McPherson, alluding to her belief that the term "elder statesman," was really code meaning older white male. "As we went through the interview," she continued with her story, "it was interesting to watch him because he became increasingly uncomfortable as I broke his stereotypes."

Concerning perceptions, Montana said she absolutely had to manage them. "You have to be above reproach," she said. "You have to carry yourself in such a way that they recognize you're not a joke." She said that it was very difficult having to work daily to gain respect. "It took years and years," she said, noting that she never had a mentor or anyone who would open doors for her. "I don't know if it would have been easier if I had been in a large community. I had trouble with black men, the white community, and females. All of them had these perceived stereotypes that you had to contend with and knock down one by one."

As did the others, Street said she has always had to manage perceptions of herself. She noted though that because she is a light-skinned black woman, how she is perceived in New York City is very different than how she is perceived when she is working in the South. "I'm light-skinned," she said, "and on the face of it, I could be Cuban, Puerto Rican, or many things. Here, though, I am not white, and that's what I have to manage." Street said that her work also has her interacting with a lot of people from the South. "In the South, they know what black people look like. They know the difference between a Mexican, a Puerto Rican, and light-skinned black people." She said that in the South she has many more perceptions to manage and overcome. "They are much more difficult to deal with. They challenge me a lot more. They go over my head a lot more. It takes me a lot more time to manage my relations with them." In the "city," she said, the treatment is not as blatant, but it exists. "There is still a big difference in New York from being white and not white." Street was careful to underscore that her viewpoint stems from her being light-skinned. "I see black-skinned sisters, and it's very different for them," she said suggesting that their overt blackness may cause them to be challenged differently and more frequently than she.

Except for two of the most senior women in this interview who felt they had earned a respected place in their organizations, the sense that black women had to manage perceptions of themselves regularly was pervasive among those interviewed. Indeed, even the two women who felt they no longer had to maintain a vigil over their behaviors admitted that earlier in their careers they also had to pay attention to how they were perceived.

Grace Evans said about handling how others see her, "Yes, all of the time I have to manage that [perceptions]. Part of my job is to be my own PR person." She continued, saying that she has to manage the perceptions that she is competent and that she "gets it," meaning "I understand how these things [work issues] connect and impact our customers." She noted that she also had to make sure that the view of herself as a professional aligned with her core values and beliefs.

Esterhaus said she, too, has to pay attention to how others see her at work. She is quite aware that she presents one face in the work environment and another when she is in more comfortable social settings. At work, she said, "they see the serious side of me getting things done. There's a certain level of comfort I don't let everyone see because I'm concerned about what they'll do with that information." Esterhaus went on to tell a story based on the differences between the hair care needs of black and white women and how she believes sharing some personal information eventually hurt her. She began her tale by communicating some basic facts about black female hair care. Black women who wear their hair artificially straightened usually have weekly beauty appointments, she said. Many black women feel wearing their hair in a straightened fashion is important to their acceptance at work. For example, of the women surveyed in the Catalyst 2003 study, 86 percent said they feel they have to "often or always conform to corporate standards of appearance."[13]

Rather than paying for each beautician visit, Esterhaus pays an annual fee to ensure she always has a weekly appointment, even if that appointment must be juggled because of her busy schedule. "A year ago at a real busy time with my job, I found a time I could go to see her [the beautician] at 8 a.m. on Wednesday. I got into the office at 10 a.m. My week is a forty-hour week. I got called to task because I had a weekly appointment." Esterhaus said. Although this issue may seem quite shallow, for her it was very important. She did not feel she was short-changing her employer or ignoring her work by keeping an appointment with her hairdresser during working hours.

Although her workweek is supposed to be a forty-hour week, Esterhaus said she typically works sixty hours. In addition, while she's at the hairdresser, she is usually reading materials for work. She is also answering emails on her handheld computer. Yet in spite of her conscientious efforts to manage both her personal and work needs, Esterhaus believes she was inappropriately chastised for her actions. She feels that her white employer does not understand that black women can't manage their hair as white women do. "Black hair care is very different. She [Esterhaus's boss] saw it [the hair appointment] as very fru fru. She made an assumption when she needed to ask for clarification. My experience is that we do have to work harder," she said. "You have to do more to prove yourself so you're not perceived as being lazy."

Many blacks believe issues of hair—how it is worn—are significant predictors of how they will be perceived and received in the workplace. As one woman quoted in the Catalyst report said, "You're proud of your black heritage. Anything you do that shows your blackness is something that makes them uncomfortable. Part of the problem whites have with the braids is their perception that you're radical or too bold. They translate that into your work. Braids mean power to the people."[14]

One reason the women interviewed say they have to work so hard to manage perceptions is because there are so few professional African American women. Esterhaus believes she is one of the first black women at her level with whom many of her colleagues have worked. "At times, it is tiring," she said, "when you wish you didn't have to fight these battles. I'm tired of being the first, tired of fighting these battles. Unfortunately, I'm still educating people."

Carter agreed, saying that her white colleagues have most often come in contact with nonprofessional African Americans. These colleagues, therefore, assume that they have little in common with any blacks. "They may not invite you into conversations about things that are socially enlightening or involved such as plays etc.," she said. "People don't know how to place you." Carter said she enters into these conversations and talks about the kinds of activities in which she is involved. "I want people to know what level I'm operating on," she said. To be seen as a colleague, "I need them to see me at that level." Like Esterhaus, Carter believes she must be the teacher.

McPherson said it is often up to blacks or other people of difference to take the first step in building relationships or in helping others overcome their own stereotypes or biases. She said she has learned "how to initiate interactions with people and how to make friends." In situations where there are biases, "I've had to learn how to get around them." Though she recognizes that she takes most of the initiative in the early stages of relationship building, she says, "Culturally, in the United States, that's just the way it is." Even in diversity workshops, she said, the people of color are often asking questions and leading discussions. "The people of color are doing the work and telling their stories."

For many black women professionals, managing perceptions means paying close attention to the ways that others may interpret their behaviors. These women also manage perceptions by working actively to assuage the concerns about capability that often swirl around them. In fact, each woman seemed to take pride in saying that others saw her as being competent. Beyond their work product, though, these women also take on the role of relationship initiator and teacher as they try to get their colleagues to see beyond race or, more importantly, to see beyond their own assumptions of race.

FAMILY LESSONS

Many of the women interviewed discussed the importance of their families and the lessons they learned as children that continue to play out in their lives as adults and managers. Often these lessons were explicit guides on how to maneuver in a society in which race could become an issue at any time. Evans said as a black girl growing up in Mississippi, she was taught early on that in the minds of whites, there were acceptable and nonacceptable black people. "You didn't want to go in the nonacceptable group," she said. "You knew if you were going to aspire to anything you had to go through them [whites]. If you weren't acceptable, you would have a really, really hard time."

Evans said if you were acceptable, though, doors opened up for you. Consequently, she learned to be acceptable. "It's almost innate," she said. "Part of that is who I am. It's part of my upbringing. 'When you go in there,'" she said, quoting her mother, "'you're going to put on your best face and you're going to behave.'" Evans said she carries her mother's voice with her and she can still hear it. "'When you go to work,' the voice will say, 'you want to go there and you don't want to be stereotyped.'"

During her childhood years Evans first learned to make cultural adaptations to manage others' perceptions of her. Today, she says, she thinks about the way that she gives feedback to her employees and the sports analogies she uses to be understood. "It [the feedback] has to be rooted in good logic, not feeling," said Evans, who works mostly with men. "Even if I want to use feeling words, I have to use good baseball analogies to make my point even though these are not words I usually use." Scott said she was always taught to be a leader. She told a story of her childhood when her parents received news from her fourth-grade teacher that Scott was bossy. Because her father had more flexible hours than her mother, he went to the school and talked to the teacher who said if Scott didn't want to do what the other children were doing, she would go off on her own and do something else. Often the other children would decide to come and play her game, abandoning their original one. Scott said her father asked the teacher, "You're saying that if she doesn't like what the other children are doing, she does what she wants? She doesn't stop them from what they're doing. She doesn't take anything from them, and she doesn't impede what they're doing in any way?"

When the teacher said "yes," Scott's father responded "Good, that's what we've taught her." Scott said her family always encouraged her to think and act on her own. She said she was also told to speak her piece. Her father told her to "say what you think. Say it nicely, and when you walk away it will slap them in the face." Both of these lessons, she says, play out in her work style today. "Once I take a stance and I think it's the right stance, you can't budge me. I tell people very nicely, very professionally that this is what it is."

The most pervasive lessons the women reported learning from their families was that of survival. In her own way, each woman talked about tapping a wellspring of strength that helped her endure organizational life. "My grandmother always repeated the story of the little engine that could," said Jackson. "'I think I can, I think I can.' That's been somewhat of a life mantra for me."

Montana said she came from a family of strong women who always had to "take care of business." Saying she had been stabbed in the back by her work associates more times than she could count, she added defiantly, "I will take them on in a minute. It's because of my background. I am a survivor. I have had to survive." In the workplace, she reiterated, "I've survived by saying, 'You can't overlook me.' I'm going to fight my way through until I get recognized."

Street was raised to believe she could be just as good as anyone else. "I have a lot of confidence," she said. "I've never met a black woman who didn't have confidence. You have to have it just to show up." Because of the difficulties they regularly encounter in the workplace, Street said African American women managers are survivors. "Being a black woman and facing the regular stuff of being a black woman means you're not intimidated and you can't be intimidated. Every black woman in corporate America is strong."

"You have to have a willingness to speak up for yourself," said Stone, "in a way that can be heard, in a way that isn't bragging and is not less than positive." She said black women were taught to survive in their childhoods. "It was the way you were brought up," she said. "You were taught you could do anything you wanted to do. You have to be attuned, ready for the opportunity when it comes."

Esterhaus said her mother, who had been a day worker in the South, jumped at the opportunity to get into a technical training program as a way of bettering her and her family's lives. Because of her motivation, her mother became one of the first black operating room technicians in her state. "When the opportunity presented itself," Esterhaus said, "that's what she did. That's the kind of environment I come from. It made me a stronger person. I can overcome anything."

Evans agreed with that sentiment, saying her personal life experiences have put her professional challenges into perspective. "As a black woman, issues come up at work that are very do-able as compared to the issues that come up within our personal lives. This," she said, talking about work, "is easy."

NAVIGATING THE ENVIRONMENT

Another of the themes that came through the interviews was these women's strong awareness of their environment. Perhaps because so many of them found the workplace less than welcoming, they learned to compensate by finding ways to maneuver through the many pitfalls they perceive.

"I'm pretty good at reading the environment," McPherson said, but she added that it was a skill she is constantly trying to improve. She noted that regardless of how good she might be, she has always felt she had to get better. "Maybe because there are so many extra variables that I have to interpret, I feel this will always be a growth area for me."

Evans said she very consciously surveys rooms when she enters them to determine how she should approach the event. "I scan the room to assess the situation," she said. "There are certain people in the room that I may want to go over to see. There are others that I don't want to go over to see."

Saying that she believes being strategic is a pattern for black women, Stone said of herself, "I am observant. I watch very carefully. I then make a decision on how I will handle a situation. I am very deliberate in reading the workplace." She said by paying attention, black women decide whether they will enter a situation and determine how to pace themselves if they do. She added that part of reading the environment is to help black women be ready to "pivot" or "move in the ways you want." This means that black women need to see opportunities as they arise and be willing to take advantage of them when they present themselves.

Many women did not talk directly about reading their environment. Instead, they discussed readiness and the critical need for black women to push against a system that seeks to cloak them in invisibility. Embedded in this notion, though, is that black women must have a thorough enough understanding of their environment to enable them to know if they are being rendered invisible and to help them determine ways to be seen and respected. Stone spoke to this phenomenon, advocating that black women understand their own worth in the organization. "I began to measure for myself the value I bring to the company," Stone said, "I had to always be willing to appropriately insert or acknowledge the work I've done."

Montana, too, strongly proffered the idea that to advance within the system, black women had to be seen and respected. "You have to let them know you stand your ground. You can't let them walk past you and negate your existence," she said. "You can't let them shut you out."

Many black women have a need to be aware of their environment and to have those in their environment be aware of them. This need is strongly driven by the difficulties created by being at the nexus of race and gender, which often causes their strengths and challenges to become invisible or unimportant.

Throughout the interviews, the women's comments were laced with references around their credibility. Montana, for instance, said earlier in this chapter that black women could not allow others to take them as a joke. Stone repeatedly talked about speaking up so she and other black women could be seen.

"My biggest fear," said Esterhaus, "is that they will not take me seriously. That they will always see the color of my skin and that will prevent them from seeing me and hearing my message and understanding the value I bring to the organization."

Evans echoed a similar statement: "I want them to know I'm just as competent, just as knowledgeable. That I add value. That I am good."

CONCLUSION

The African American women interviewed for this chapter echo the experiences of African American women managers around the country. Organizational life for many of them is fraught with frustration as they battle invisibility and perceptions of incompetence. They see themselves as capable professionals but are unsure if others do. They recognize themselves as culturally different, yet believe their difference is a double-edged sword. Though many embrace their direct communication style, they have often received feedback that the characteristic is intimidating. And though they love their heritage, they often receive messages that displaying that heritage through behavior, dress, or hairstyle may cause misunderstanding for those around them.

In spite of the many challenges they face, the women interviewed believed that being black women is a positive force that informs and improves their ability to navigate the work environment. Often they note that their sensitivity to the pain of others is increased because of the problems they have suffered. "As I look at my work life as a whole," said Carter, "and as an African American female, I realize that part of being black is empathy for other people, clients, and partners." Esterhaus noted something similar when she said, "Because of the adverse situations I've encountered, it makes me more sensitive, more sympathetic to see the other sides of things and to get a total picture of something." McPherson said her life experiences help her better manage and unite a team.

As individuals, these women do not claim to be without flaws or developmental needs. Like others, they have likes and dislikes, strengths, and imperfect skill sets. Yet as they speak, they do so from a wealth of experiences that is often undermined and underutilized. These are the skills they wish to bring to the workplace. "We've had to be very creative to come through some situations," said Evans. "Imagine if we could use our creativity, adaptability, and flexibility at work. Imagine how competitive it would make you."

NOTES

1. Ella Bell and Stella Nkomo, *Our Separate Ways: Black and White Women and the Struggle for Professional Identity* (Boston: Harvard University Business School Press, 2001), p. 257.

2. *Women of Color: Their Employment in the Private Sector*, U.S. Equal Employment Opportunity Commission (2003), pp. 8, 12.

3. Information Please Database, © 2005 Pearson Education, Inc. *Source:* National Committee on Pay Equity. Available online at www.infoplease.clm/ipa/A0882775.html.

4. Ancella B. Livers and Keith A. Caver, *Leading in Black and White: Working across the Racial Divide in Corporate America* (San Francisco: Jossey-Bass, 2003), p. 86.

5. Ibid., p. 18.

6. "Advancing African-American Women in the Workplace: What Managers Need to Know" Catalyst (2004): 12.

7. Livers and Caver, *Leading in Black and White*, p. 79.

8. Bell and Nkomo, *Our Separate Lives*, pp. 182–84.

9. Catalyst, p. 16.

10. Bell and Nkomo, *Our Separate Lives*, pp. 235–37.

11. Christina A. Douglas, *Key Events and Lessons for Managers in a Diverse Workforce* (Greensboro: Center for Creative Leadership, 2003), pp. 9–10.

12. Catalyst, p. 23.

13. Ibid., 15.

14. Ibid.

———— 10 ————

Latinas at Work: Issues of Gender, Ethnicity, and Class

Irene Browne and Rachel Askew

Who are Latinas and how are they faring in the U.S. labor market? Are Latinas plagued by the triple jeopardy of gender, race/ethnic, and class inequality? Are the daughters of migrants from Latin America experiencing upward mobility and approaching the American dream, or are they stuck in the low-wage jobs of the new economy? Are educated Latinas capturing the boost in wages and opportunities generated by the increase in demand for skilled workers? This chapter addresses these questions. We begin our review by considering the term *Latina*, highlighting the problems and challenges inherent in defining Latinas as an ethnic group. Keeping the definitional limitations in mind, we provide a statistical portrait of subgroups of Latinas in terms of employment, occupations, and wages. We show that Latinas continue to experience disadvantage in the labor market in comparison to white women and coethnic men.[1] In the third section of the chapter, we discuss explanations for the labor market disadvantage of Latinas, focusing on debates regarding labor market opportunities, human capital attributes, and systematic gender and ethnic inequalities. We then explore the complex intersections of gender, race/ethnicity, and class in shaping the economic fortunes of Latinas in the United States by highlighting two occupational niches: domestic work and professional employment.

WHO ARE LATINAS?

Latinas are usually defined as women whose ethnic origin or heritage includes Mexico, countries in Central and South America, Cuba, Puerto Rico, or the Dominican Republic.[2] Women who migrated to the United States from Latin America as children or adults can fall under the category Latinas, as can women born in the United States whose parents or grandparents hail from Latin American countries. Definitions of who is included within the category Latina vary over time and across studies. For instance, in 1970, the U.S. Census Bureau defined Spanish ethnicity differently depending on state of residence. Individuals living in New York, New Jersey, or Pennsylvania were counted as "persons of Spanish heritage" if they or one of their parents came from Puerto Rico. Individuals living in California or Southwestern states were classified as "persons of Spanish heritage" if they reported a Spanish surname or their primary language was Spanish. In the 2000 census, official counts for the Hispanic population were based on a self-defined ethnic identity category. Thus, a woman who self-identified as Latina because her maternal grandmother migrated from Mexico to Ohio would be counted as Latina in 2000 but not in 1970. The term *Latinas* (or *Hispanic*) encompasses such a diverse group that some scholars argue that any generalization or aggregate picture of Latinas provides vacuous information and promotes a false universalism.[3]

Despite the vague and shifting boundaries defining Hispanic ethnicity, Latina (and Latino) represents an increasingly salient identity category in the United States that carries political currency. In Los Angeles, where almost half of the population is comprised of Hispanics, the Latino constituency wielded a potent force in the mayoral election of March 8, 2005, helping elect Antonio Villagairosa, the city's first Latino mayor since 1872.[4]

Nationally, the Latina population in the United States is growing dramatically, fueled by immigration from Mexico and Central America and relatively high fertility.[5] According to recent census figures, the representation of Latinos in the U.S. population exceeds that of African Americans (about 14 percent). Hispanics are now the largest ethnic minority in the United States.[6] The majority of Latinas in the United States continue to be of Mexican origin, although the number of women (and men) arriving from Central and South America has expanded rapidly over the past fifteen years. The previous decade also witnessed a growing geographic dispersion of Latinos, with Latino communities burgeoning in traditionally black/white areas of the South as well as in cities, suburbs, and rural areas of the American heartland.[7] For example, according to the U.S. census, the number of Hispanics rose almost 400 percent in Atlanta, Georgia, and almost 200 percent in Columbus, Ohio.[8] Precise estimates of the number of Latinas and Latinos in the United States are difficult to obtain, however. Unauthorized migrants from Latin America, whose numbers are surging, are often reluctant to identify themselves to census takers or survey researchers.[9]

In tandem with demographic diversity and geographic dispersion, the Latina population in the United States tends to be characterized by economic disadvantage. The extent and shape of the economic disadvantage of particular groups of Latinas vary considerably depending on nativity and citizenship status, country of ethnic origin, the structure of the local labor market, the opportunities and resources available within the local community, and individual human capital attributes.[10] Among those with the same country of origin stand important differences based on nativity and time of arrival to the United States. A young woman arriving in Los Angeles from Mexico faced a very different set of job opportunities in 1970 and 2000.[11] We now turn to the question of current labor market conditions for Latinas in the United States.

HOW ARE LATINAS FARING IN THE LABOR MARKET?

Data

To address the question of how Latinas are faring in the labor market, we use data collected in March 2002 from the monthly outgoing rotation group file of the Current Population Survey (CPS), a nationally representative probability sample conducted by the Census Bureau for the Bureau of Labor Statistics.[12] We compare subgroups of Latinas in the United States with white women and coethnic men in assessing current patterns of employment, occupational distribution, and wages. We present information on Mexicans, Puerto Ricans, Cubans, Central or South Americans, and "other Latinas" (or those that self-identify as of Hispanic origin but do not indicate a country of origin) living in the United States. The number of individuals listing their ethnicity as "other Hispanic" rose sharply from the 1990 census to the 2000 census, and researchers are unclear about who makes up the "other Hispanic" category.[13] Guzman and McConnell remark that the decision to check the panethnic identity of Hispanic or Latino rather than a particular country of origin might reflect respondents' self-identification with more than one ethnicity.

For all analyses, we restricted our sample to adults aged sixteen to sixty-five who are not full-time students. We further limited our sample to employed adults who average $1 or more per hour for our analyses of occupational distribution. Finally, for analyses of wages and wages gaps, we restricted the sample even further to consider only full-time workers (those who average thirty-five or more hours per week) because part-time workers often earn lower hourly wages than full-time workers.[14] We weighted the data in all analyses to provide a representative picture of the U.S. population in 2002.

These limitations allow us to construct only a partial picture of the labor market position of Latinas. For example, many Latinas who are considered out of the labor market or among the part-time employed actually work several jobs, often in the informal sector, which falls outside traditional Bureau of Labor Statistics categories.[15]

Employment and Unemployment

The CPS data count any person who is involved with any part-time, temporary, or full-time work as employed. Persons are classified as unemployed if they do not have a job, have actively looked for work in the four weeks prior to data collection, and are currently available for work. Persons are considered not in the labor force if they are neither employed nor looking for work.

White, non-Latina women in the United States are more likely to be employed, less likely to be unemployed, and less likely to have opted out of the labor force than are Latinas living in the United States (see Table 10.1). Seventy percent of white non-Latina women are employed, whereas Latinas' employment rate ranges from a low of 56.3 percent (Puerto Ricans) to a high of 63.8 percent (Central or South Americans). Similarly, Latinas' unemployment rate ranges from a low of 4.4 percent (Cubans) to a high of 5.1 percent (Puerto Ricans), whereas the rate of unemployment for white non-Latinas is just 3.1 percent.

Occupational Distribution

For employed Latinas working in the United States, the three highest occupational categories are service (26.0 percent), administrative support (22.2 percent), and managerial or professional occupations (19.5 percent), respectively. Examples of service occupations include child-care workers, housekeepers, waitstaff at restaurants, hairdressers, and nurses' aides. Receptionists, secretaries, payroll specialists, and bank tellers are examples of administrative support occupations. Professional occupations include teachers, lawyers, physicians, and registered nurses, and examples of managerial occupations include financial managers and public administrators such as government officials.[16]

A considerably higher percentage of white non-Latinas work in managerial and professional occupations (39.2 percent) compared to the percentages of subgroups of Latinas employed in such occupations (see Table 10.2). The percentages of various subgroups of Latinas working in the better paid, more prestigious managerial and professional occupations ranges from a low of 17.0 percent (Mexicans) to a high of 27.5 percent (other Latinas).

Not surprisingly, the type of occupations in which U.S. women work are associated with their level of educational attainment. The top two occupational groups in which white and Latina women with only a high school degree work are administrative support and service occupations, regardless of their ethnicity (see Table 10.3). In contrast, the majority of women (both Latinas and white non-Latinas) in the United States with a college degree work in managerial or professional occupations.

Wages and Wage Gaps

Table 10.4 presents the average hourly wages of white and Latino men and women employed full-time in the United States in March 2002, disaggregated by gender and Hispanic origin type. Also depicted in Table 10.4 is the gender wage gap between men and women of the same ethnicity (or race, when

TABLE 10.1. Employment Status of U.S. Latinas and White, Non-Latinas Aged 16 through 65

Employment Status[a]	Total		Mexican		Puerto Rican		Cuban		Central and South American		Other Latina		White, Non-Latina	
	Number	Percent	Number	Percent	Number	Percent	Number	Percent	Number	Percent	Number	Percent	Number	Percent
Not in Labor Force	29,832	26.9	2,803	36.9	542	38.7	146	34.0	699	31.8	347	31.9	25,295	26.7
In Labor Force														
Employed	77,677	70.0	4,379	58.1	793	56.3	266	61.6	1,410	63.8	711	63.2	70,118	70.2
Unemployed	3,512	3.2	370	5.0	70	5.1	19	4.4	108	4.5	50	4.9	2,895	3.1
Total	111,021	100	7,552	100	1,405	100	431	100	2,217	100	1,108	100	98,308	100

[a]$\chi^2 = 643242.1$, $df = 10$, $p < 0.001$.

TABLE 10.2. Occupation of Employed U.S. Latinas and White, Non-Latinas Aged 16 through 65

Occupational Group[a]	Total		Mexican		Puerto Rican		Cuban		Central and South American		Other Latina		White, Non-Latina	
	Number	Percent	Number	Percent	Number	Percent	Number	Percent	Number	Percent	Number	Percent	Number	Percent
Managerial and Professional	24,467	36.5	669	17.0	175	25.3	65	27.4	240	20.2	180	27.5	23,138	39.2
Technical	2,944	4.3	102	2.5	30	3.9	4	2.0	27	2.1	27	4.4	2,754	4.6
Sales	7,200	11.2	412	11.1	72	10.0	32	13.9	130	11.0	62	11.2	6,492	11.2
Administrative Support	16,331	24.4	837	22.6	202	28.5	62	26.5	190	15.6	151	23.6	14,889	24.8
Service Occupations	9,769	14.7	1,062	25.5	137	19.1	46	18.4	422	34.2	146	23.9	7,956	12.9
Precision Production/ Craft	1,215	1.8	140	3.5	15	2.0	7	3.2	38	2.5	11	1.5	1,004	1.7
Operators/Laborers/ Transport	4,059	6.4	625	15.3	83	10.5	19	8.5	195	14.2	43	7.3	3,094	5.2
Farming/Forestry/ Fishing	424	0.7	85	2.5	4	0.7	1	0.1	4	0.2	4	0.6	326	0.5
Total	66,409	100	3,932	100	718	100	236	100	1,246	100	624	100	59,653	100

[a]$X^2 = 2568239.6$, $df = 35$, $p < 0.001$.

TABLE 10.3. Occupation of Employed U.S. Latinas and White, Non-Latinas Aged 16 through 65, by Educational Attainment

Occupational Group by Educational Attainment	Total		Mexican		Puerto Rican		Cuban		Central and South American		Other Latina		White, Non-Latina	
	Number	Percent	Number	Percent	Number	Percent	Number	Percent	Number	Percent	Number	Percent	Number	Percent
High School Graduates[a]														
Managerial and Professional	3,220	15.3	145	10.5	36	14.7	5	7.4	35	8.9	25	11.2	2,974	16.1
Technical	599	2.9	32	2.4	9	3.3	1	1.9	5	1.3	8	4.2	544	3.0
Sales	3,001	14.2	190	13.8	30	11.2	12	15.6	57	14.9	28	14.6	2,684	14.3
Administrative Support	7,023	33.0	410	29.7	83	30.7	26	36.7	68	17.3	61	28.6	6,375	33.8
Service Occupations	4,539	20.7	358	23.8	64	23.5	15	19.9	154	39.2	59	27.4	3,889	19.7
Precision Production/ Craft	590	2.8	60	4.2	7	2.2	4	5.9	13	3.3	6	3.2	500	2.6
Operators/Laborers/ Transport	2,208	10.5	214	14.5	40	13.9	9	12.8	72	15.0	20	9.2	1,853	9.8
Farming/Forestry/ Fishing	158	0.7	14	1.1	1	0.5	—	—	1	0.1	3	1.6	139	0.7
Total	21,338	100	1,423	100	270	100	72	100	405	100	210	100	18,958	100
College Graduates[b]														
Managerial and Professional	15,015	73.4	260	67.4	84	66.1	50	63.4	150	59.2	96	71.6	14,375	73.9
Technical	757	3.6	12	3.4	7	5.3	2	3.1	9	2.4	10	7.7	717	3.5
Sales	1,414	7.1	17	4.6	2	1.4	8	10.5	16	7.1	6	5.4	1,365	7.2
Administrative Support	2,192	10.8	42	12.2	18	16.2	9	12.2	27	9.9	13	9.8	2,083	10.7
Service Occupations	724	3.6	30	7.8	8	7.6	6	6.7	44	18.5	4	3.1	632	3.2
Precision Production/ Craft	106	0.5	3	0.7	2	1.5	1	1.4	4	0.7	2	0.4	94	0.5
Operators/Laborers/ Transport	155	0.8	13	3.5	4	2.0	2	2.8	7	2.1	2	1.9	127	0.6
Farming/Forestry/ Fishing	58	0.3	1	0.4	—	—	—	—	—	—	—	—	57	0.3
Total	20,421	100	378	100	125	100	78	100	257	100	133	100	19,450	100

[a]$X^2 = 2354275.6$, $df = 35$, $p < 0.001$.
[b]$X^2 = 2875353.0$, $df = 35$, $p < 0.001$.

comparing white men and women), or women's average hourly wage to every $1 of coethnic men's hourly wage.

Put simply, both gender and ethnicity matter substantially in terms of wages. In terms of gender, men from every Latino subgroup earn more per hour than do their female counterparts, and white men make over $4 an hour more than white women (see Table 10.4). Whether we compare male and female high school or college graduates (see Table 10.5), or males and females of the same immigration status (refer to Table 10.8), U.S. women are disadvantaged relative to their male peers.

Being of Latino ethnicity also proves a substantial disadvantage in the labor market for both men and women. The ethnic wage gap refers to the pay disparity between white non-Latino employees and those (both male and female) of Hispanic origin. The ethnic wage gap is measured as Latinos' hourly wage for every $1 of whites' hourly wage. White non-Latino men averaged more per hour than each of the Latino subgroups, and white non-Latina women earned more, on average, than each of the Latina subgroups (see Tables 10.4 and 10.6). White non-Latino men averaged more than $3 an hour above the highest-earning Latino subgroup (other Latinos), and white non-Latina women earned more than $2 an hour, on average, above the highest-earning Latina subgroup (Cuban women; see Table 10.4). Latinas working in the U.S. labor market are therefore doubly disadvantaged. They suffer from both gender and ethnic wage inequalities.

Some of the ethnic wage inequality that exists between Latinas and non-Latinas can be attributed to differences in educational attainment. A greater percentage of white non-Latinas attended or graduated from college than did

TABLE 10.4. Average Hourly Wages and Gender Wage Gaps of U.S. Full-Time Latino and White, Non-Latino Employees Aged 16 through 65, by Sex

Hispanic-Origin Type[a]	Average Hourly Wage (Men)	Average Hourly Wage (Women)	Gender Wage Gap (Women's Average Hourly Wage to Every $1 of Co-ethnic Men's Hourly Wage)
Mexican	$12.68 ($n = 5,678$)	$11.39 ($n = 3,135$)	0.90
Puerto Rican	$16.30 ($n = 654$)	$13.74 ($n = 601$)	0.84
Cuban	$15.86 ($n = 254$)	$14.09 ($n = 200$)	0.89
Central or South American	$13.72 ($n = 1,430$)	$12.32 ($n = 989$)	0.90
Other Latino	$17.11 ($n = 609$)	$13.58 ($n = 501$)	0.79
White, Non-Latino	$20.46 ($n = 57,672$)	$16.33 ($n = 46,359$)	0.80

[a]$F = 900.5$, $df = 12$, $p < 0.001$.

TABLE 10.5. Average Hourly Wages and Gender Wage Gaps of U.S. Full-Time Latino and White, Non-Latino Employees Aged 16 through 65, by Sex and Educational Attainment

Hispanic-Origin Type by Educational Attainment	Average Hourly Wage (Men)	Average Hourly Wage (Women)	Gender Wage Gap (Women's Average Hourly Wage to Every $1 of Men's Hourly Wage)
High School Graduates[a]			
Mexican	$12.70 ($n = 1,904$)	$10.77 ($n = 1,153$)	0.87
Puerto Rican	$14.95 ($n = 240$)	$11.61 ($n = 227$)	0.78
Cuban	$12.35 ($n = 112$)	$10.09 ($n = 65$)	0.82
Central or South American	$12.22 ($n = 436$)	$10.15 ($n = 318$)	0.83
Other Latino	$14.72 ($n = 233$)	$11.31 ($n = 169$)	0.77
White, Non-Latino	$16.39 ($n = 19,239$)	$12.74 ($n = 14,532$)	0.78
College Graduates[b]			
Mexican	$21.54 ($n = 402$)	$18.64 ($n = 324$)	0.87
Puerto Rican	$23.36 ($n = 92$)	$19.79 ($n = 118$)	0.85
Cuban	$21.77 ($n = 69$)	$20.00 ($n = 66$)	0.92
Central or South American	$21.57 ($n = 220$)	$18.70 ($n = 218$)	0.87
Other Latino	$25.87 ($n = 119$)	$20.01 ($n = 106$)	0.77
White, Non-Latino	$27.03 ($n = 19,181$)	$21.51 ($n = 15,925$)	0.80

[a]$F = 304.0$, $df = 12$, $p < 0.001$.
[b]$F = 198.8$, $df = 12$, $p < 0.001$.

TABLE 10.6. Ethnic Wage Gaps of U.S. Full-Time Latino and White, Non-Latino Employees Aged 16 through 65, by Sex and Educational Attainment

Hispanic-Origin Type by Educational Attainment	Ethnic Wage Gap, Men (Latino Hourly Wage to Every $1 of White Men's Hourly Wage)	Ethnic Wage Gap, Women (Latino Hourly Wage for Every $1 of White Women's Hourly Wage)
All Full-Time Employees		
Mexican	0.62	0.70
Puerto Rican	0.80	0.84
Cuban	0.78	0.86
Central or South American	0.67	0.75
Other Latino	0.84	0.83
High School Graduates		
Mexican	0.77	0.85
Puerto Rican	0.91	0.91
Cuban	0.75	0.79
Central or South American	0.75	0.80
Other Latino	0.90	0.89
College Graduates		
Mexican	0.80	0.87
Puerto Rican	0.86	0.92
Cuban	0.81	0.93
Central or South American	0.80	0.87
Other Latino	0.96	0.93

their Latina equivalents (see Table 10.7). For example, 64.0 percent of white women employees attended and/or graduated from college, compared to just 33.0 percent of Mexican women who did so. When comparing average wages of white and Mexican women who completed the same numbers of years of education, the ethnic wage gap is smaller than that between all full-time white women and Mexican women employees. For example, college-educated Mexican women earn 87 cents for each dollar that white women with the same education make. The gap widens to 70 cents on the dollar when comparing all full-time white and Mexican female workers, as Table 10.6 shows. Thus, differences in education levels explain some of the ethnic wage gap. Indeed, additional education is associated with both higher absolute wages for all subgroups of Latinas and smaller ethnic and gender wage gaps. Put another way, more education is linked with lower wage inequity between Latinas and white women and between Latinas and Latinos and is also associated with higher earnings.

One final dimension along which Latinas' and Latinos' wages vary is that of immigration status. Latinos and Latinas native to the United States earn more than their nonnative counterparts regardless of country of origin (see Table 10.8). Moreover, recent immigrants (those who immigrated between 1998 and 2002—the five years prior to data collection) are at a larger disadvantage relative to Latinas and Latinos born in the United States than nonnatives who immigrated prior to 1998. This is consistent with the findings of previous studies.[17]

LATINAS IN THE U.S. WORKFORCE BY COUNTRY OF ORIGIN: A SNAPSHOT OF DIFFERENCE AND SIMILARITY

Cubans

The immigration of Cubans to the United States was spearheaded by the revolution and Castro's rise to power in 1958. Middle-class and elite Cubans arrived in Miami in the 1960s and received financial assistance from the U.S. Cubans established vibrant enclave economies in Florida, which provided entrepreneurial opportunities and employment for subsequent generations.[18] New waves of immigration from Cuba to the United States have brought a more diverse group of workers.[19] However, the strong economic base and the economic advantages that Cubans enjoyed following the revolution have translated into a more advantaged labor market status overall relative to other groups of Latinos.

Cuban women enjoy the lowest unemployment rate of the Latina subgroups. Their unemployment rate of 4.4 percent is second only to white women's low unemployment rate (3.1 percent, see Table 10.1). More Cuban women work in managerial and professional occupations (27.4 percent) than in any others (see Table 10.2); the percentage of Cuban women working in

TABLE 10.7. Educational Attainment of Employed U.S. Latinos and White, Non-Latinos Aged 16 through 65

Educational Attainment[a]	Total		Mexican		Puerto Rican		Cuban		Central and South American		Other Latino		White, Non-Latino	
	Number	Percent	Number	Percent	Number	Percent	Number	Percent	Number	Percent	Number	Percent	Number	Percent
No High School Diploma	4,256	7.3	1,240	30.7	103	14.7	22	9.6	319	24.7	94	14.9	2,478	4.3
High School Graduate	21,338	32.2	1,423	36.3	270	35.3	72	31.2	405	32.1	210	33.0	18,958	31.7
Some College	20,394	30.2	891	23.6	220	31.8	64	26.7	265	21.8	187	31.0	18,767	31.1
College Graduate	20,421	30.3	378	9.4	125	18.2	78	32.5	257	21.4	133	21.1	19,450	32.9
Total	66,409	100	3,932	100	718	100	236	100	1,246	100	624	100	59,653	100

[a]$\chi^2 = 51518844.6$, $df = 15$, $p < 0.001$.

TABLE 10.8. Average Hourly Wages and Gender Wage Gaps of U.S. Full-Time Latino Employees Aged 16 through 65, by Sex and Immigration Status

Hispanic-Origin Type by Immigration Status	Average Hourly Wage (Men)	Average Hourly Wage (Women)	Gender Wage Gap (Women's Average Hourly Wage to Every $1 of Co-ethnic Men's Hourly Wage)
Native (born in U.S.)[a]			
Mexican	$15.63 $(n = 2,011)$	$12.88 $(n = 1,692)$	0.82
Puerto Rican	$17.16 $(n = 336)$	$14.06 $(n = 325)$	0.82
Cuban	$18.85 $(n = 68)$	$15.95 $(n = 60)$	0.85
Central or South American	$16.38 $(n = 134)$	$15.67 $(n = 147)$	0.96
Other Latino	$18.21 $(n = 421)$	$15.27 $(n = 342)$	0.94
Nonnative (1998–2002)[b]			
Mexican	$8.96 $(n = 835)$	$7.81 $(n = 228)$	0.87
Puerto Rican	$12.18 $(n = 39)$	$11.44 $(n = 20)$	0.94
Cuban	$9.25 $(n = 35)$	$7.53 $(n = 23)$	0.81
Central or South American	$10.84 $(n = 255)$	$10.22 $(n = 135)$	0.94
Other Latino	$12.14 $(n = 28)$	$9.23 $(n = 20)$	0.76
Nonnative (Prior to 1998)[c]			
Mexican	$11.58 $(n = 2,832)$	$9.83 $(n = 1,215)$	0.85
Puerto Rican	$15.84 $(n = 279)$	$13.47 $(n = 256)$	0.85
Cuban	$16.02 $(n = 151)$	$14.34 $(n = 117)$	0.90
Central or South American	$14.03 $(n = 1,041)$	$11.99 $(n = 707)$	0.85
Other Latino	$15.81 $(n = 160)$	$10.86 $(n = 139)$	0.69

[a]$F = 24.1$, $df = 9$, $p < 0.001$.
[b]$F = 8.9$, $df = 9$, $p < 0.001$.
[c]$F = 49.7$, $df = 9$, $p < 0.001$.

administrative support jobs (26.5 percent) is nearly as high. Cuban women living in the United States are the best-educated Latinas (see Table 10.7). Approximately two in five Cubans are college educated, which is the same as the percentage of white women who have completed college, and fewer than one in ten Cuban women did not finish high school.

Overwhelming majorities (77.8 percent) of Cuban women live and work in the South (see Table 10.9). The top two groups in which Cubans in the South are employed are administrative support (27 percent) and managerial/professional occupations (23.5 percent). Administrative and managerial/professional occupations are the most common for Cuban women in other regions as well (see Table 10.10).

At $14.09 an hour, Cuban women make the highest average hourly wage of all the Latina subgroups. Nevertheless, Cuban women working in the United States remain considerably disadvantaged compared to whites and Cuban men. Their average hourly wage is 86 percent of their white non-Latina counterparts', 89 percent of the average wage earned by Cuban men, and 69 percent of the average wage earned by white men. Thus, although compared to other groups of Latinas, Cuban women in general fare better in the labor market, they still encounter ethnic and gender barriers. A wage gap exists between Cuban and white women, and the former experience pay disparities compared to both Cuban and white men.

Though the majority of most Latina subgroups were born in the United States, only one-third of Cubans were. Not only did a greater percentage of Cubans immigrate to the United States, a greater percentage than other Latinas immigrated recently, in the five years before data collection in 2002 (see Table 10.11).

Cuban women's slight workforce advantage, on average, over their Latina sisters masks the fact that Cuban women working in the United States are not a homogenous group. To be sure, those native to the United States, those who immigrated prior to 1998, and those with a college degree enjoy a relatively high average wage compared to their Latina counterparts. Nevertheless, Cuban women who recently immigrated (Table 10.8) and those with only a high school degree (Table 10.5) earn the *lowest* average wage of all the Latina subgroups.

Mexican-Origin Women

Over two-thirds of the Hispanics living in the United States are of Mexican origin.[20] Mexican-origin women include U.S. citizens whose families laid roots in states that were former Mexican territories, such as Texas and California. Joining these longtime residents are older migrants as well as new arrivals from Mexico, who make up the largest share of Latina immigrants to the United States.[21] Though the majority of Mexican-origin women still reside in the West and Southwest, a growing number of new immigrants are arriving in the South and Midwest.[22]

Mexican-origin women are the least well educated of all the Latina subgroups; less than 10 (9.4) percent of Mexican women in the United States earned college degrees, and nearly a third (30.7 percent) did not finish high school (see Table 10.7). Majorities of Mexican-origin women in the U.S. workforce live and work in the West (see Table 10.9), and the top occupational group in which they are employed is service. Only in the Midwest do more Mexican-origin women work in an occupational group other than service. There, 30.2 percent of these women toil in operator, laborer, or transportation positions, and only 18.3 percent work in service jobs (see Table 10.10).

Mexican-origin women earn the lowest hourly wage ($11.39 on average) of all the Latina subgroups. Although the majority of full-time female U.S. employees who self-identify as Mexican were born in the United States

TABLE 10.9. Geographic Distribution of Employed U.S. Latinos and White, Non-Latinos Aged 16 through 65

Region[a]	Total		Mexican		Puerto Rican		Cuban		Central and South American		Other Latino		White, Non-Latino	
	Number	Percent	Number	Percent	Number	Percent	Number	Percent	Number	Percent	Number	Percent	Number	Percent
Northeast	15,688	20.5	100	2.4	416	56.0	28	10.8	411	30.0	134	25.0	14,599	21.5
Midwest	18,261	25.8	546	11.2	60	8.6	8	3.6	73	4.8	44	6.9	17,530	28.5
South	16,904	32.3	1,076	34.3	190	30.4	170	77.8	386	35.8	133	29.7	14,949	31.8
West	15,556	21.3	2,210	52.2	52	5.1	30	7.8	376	29.5	313	38.3	12,575	18.2
Total	66,409	100	3,932	100	718	100	236	100	1,246	100	624	100	59,653	100

[a]$X^2 = 44869571.5$, $df = 15$, $p < 0.001$.

TABLE 10.10. Occupation of Employed U.S. Latinos and White, Non-Latinos Aged 16 through 65, by Region

Occupation Group by Region[a]	Total		Mexican		Puerto Rican		Cuban		Central and South American		Other Latino		White, Non-Latino	
	Number	Percent	Number	Percent	Number	Percent	Number	Percent	Number	Percent	Number	Percent	Number	Percent
Northeast[a]														
Managerial and Professional	6,025	37.9	25	24.6	93	24.0	12	44.0	75	20.2	32	21.6	5,788	39.5
Technical	685	4.4	2	1.1	20	4.3	—	—	3	0.5	3	2.1	657	4.7
Sales	1,639	10.5	5	6.8	42	10.0	3	12.1	38	10.3	12	8.7	1,539	10.6
Administrative Support	3,790	24.5	10	8.5	111	27.8	7	21.8	64	15.7	23	19.3	3,575	24.9
Service Occupations	2,279	15.0	33	32.3	77	18.0	5	18.7	128	33.2	42	33.4	1,994	13.7
Precision Production/Craft	263	1.5	5	4.8	9	1.8	—	—	14	2.3	3	1.8	232	1.5
Operators/Laborers/Transport	940	5.7	19	20.9	60	12.9	1	3.5	88	17.6	19	13.1	753	4.7
Farming/Forestry/Fishing	67	0.4	1	1.0	4	1.2	—	—	1	0.1	—	—	61	0.4
Total	15,688	100	100	100	416	100	28	100	411	100	134	100	14,599	100
Midwest[b]														
Managerial and Professional	6,509	35.2	82	15.0	11	18.1	2	21.3	16	22.6	17	39.2	6,381	36.2
Technical	836	4.5	15	2.7	2	3.2	—	—	3	3.1	1	0.5	815	4.6
Sales	1,891	10.6	46	9.0	4	6.9	—	—	3	3.9	6	13.6	1,832	10.7
Administrative Support	4,638	24.9	99	19.1	24	39.1	4	58.3	11	16.9	7	16.3	4,493	25.0
Service Occupations	2,633	14.5	108	18.3	10	18.2	1	9.9	23	33.2	8	19.0	2,483	14.3
Precision Production/Craft	369	2.0	28	5.1	1	1.7	—	—	3	4.4	1	1.6	336	1.9
Operators/Laborers/Transport	1,287	7.7	163	30.2	8	12.6	1	10.5	12	13.6	3	8.1	1,100	6.8
Farming/Forestry/Fishing	98	0.5	5	0.5	—	—	—	—	2	2.2	1	1.7	90	0.5
Total	18,261	100	546	100	60	100	8	100	73	100	44	100	17,530	100

(continued)

TABLE 10.10. (Continued)

Occupation Group by Region[a]	Total		Mexican		Puerto Rican		Cuban		Central and South American		Other Latino		White, Non-Latino	
	Number	Percent	Number	Percent	Number	Percent	Number	Percent	Number	Percent	Number	Percent	Number	Percent
South[c]														
Managerial and Professional	6,429	37.2	185	16.7	57	29.0	42	23.5	87	21.4	32	23.3	6,026	40.3
Technical	763	4.3	25	2.5	8	4.0	4	2.6	7	1.6	9	7.0	710	4.6
Sales	1,908	11.7	119	11.6	18	11.0	25	14.8	48	12.1	24	17.2	1,674	11.6
Administrative Support	4,142	24.5	242	23.0	57	28.9	45	27.0	51	14.0	28	21.8	3,719	25.0
Service Occupations	2,240	13.6	312	29.0	34	18.8	30	17.9	139	35.4	32	25.5	1,639	11.1
Precision Production/Craft	320	1.9	42	3.7	4	2.5	7	4.1	9	2.7	—	—	258	1.7
Operators/Laborers/Transport	995	6.1	137	12.4	12	5.8	17	10.0	45	12.7	8	5.2	776	5.2
Farming/Forestry/Fishing	107	0.7	14	1.2	—	—	—	—	—	—	—	—	93	0.6
Total	16,904	100	1,076	100	190	100	170	100	386	100	133	100	14,949	100
West[d]														
Managerial and Professional	5,504	35.6	377	17.2	14	29.4	9	45.3	62	18.3	99	32.4	4,943	41.5
Technical	660	3.9	60	2.6	—	—	—	—	14	4.0	14	4.7	572	4.3
Sales	1,762	11.7	242	11.5	8	10.4	4	13.3	41	11.5	20	7.6	1,447	11.9
Administrative Support	3,761	23.8	486	23.8	10	15.8	6	13.6	64	17.2	93	29.0	3,102	24.0
Service Occupations	2,617	16.2	609	24.5	16	33.8	10	26.7	132	33.8	64	17.3	1,786	12.9
Precision Production/Craft	263	1.8	65	3.0	1	1.9	—	—	12	2.2	7	2.5	178	1.5
Operators/Laborers/Transport	837	5.8	306	13.7	3	8.9	—	—	50	12.8	13	5.0	465	3.3
Farming/Forestry/Fishing	152	1.2	65	3.8	—	—	1	1.2	1	0.3	3	1.4	82	0.5
Total	15,556	100	2,210	100	52	100	30	100	376	100	313	100	12,575	100

[a] $X^2 = 4669344.4$, $df = 35$, $p < 0.001$.
[b] $X^2 = 4669697.2$, $df = 35$, $p < 0.001$.
[c] $X^2 = 9806083.8$, $df = 35$, $p < 0.001$.
[d] $X^2 = 10953962.3$, $df = 35$, $p < 0.001$.

TABLE 10.11. Immigration Status of U.S. Full-Time Latino Employees Aged 16 through 65

Immigration Status[a]	Total		Mexican		Puerto Rican		Cuban		Central and South American		Other Latino	
	Number	Percent	Number	Percent	Number	Percent	Number	Percent	Number	Percent	Number	Percent
Native (Born in U.S.)	2,564	48.2	1,690	55.6	325	56.2	60	31.1	147	15.0	342	62.5
Nonnative												
Immigrated 1998–2002	427	7.3	228	6.7	20	2.9	23	11.0	136	13.1	20	3.1
Immigrated prior to 1998	2,441	44.5	1,218	37.7	256	40.9	117	57.9	710	71.9	140	34.4
Total	5,432	100	3,136	100	601	100	200	100	993	100	502	100

[a]$\chi^2 = 5801054.7$, $df = 8$, $p < 0.001$.

239

(55.6 percent), that alone does not seem to give them a workplace advantage over other Latinas. Indeed, whereas native women from the other Latina subgroups earn between $14 and $16 an hour on average, the comparable figure for native Mexican women workers is only $12.88 per hour (see Table 10.8).

Education certainly matters to Mexican-origin women's wages in the United States. College-educated Mexican-origin women earn an average wage of $18.64 per hour, compared to just $10.77 an hour for those with only a high school degree. Education seems to matter less to Mexican-origin women than to white women and to other subgroups of Latinas, however. For example, although Mexican-origin women with a high school degree earn slightly more per hour than equally educated Central/South American and Cuban women, among women with a college degree, Mexican-origin women earn the lowest wage of all the Latina subgroups (see Table 10.5).

Central/South Americans

Women from Central and South America represent the smallest group of Latinas proportionally, but they show some of the largest increases among recent immigrants. Beginning in the 1980s, the number of women (and men) from Central America living in the United States increased rapidly as individuals fled war and political violence in their home countries.[23] Although much of the violence has abated, the economic and social disruption in countries such as Guatemala, El Salvador, and Nicaragua has fueled continued migration to the United States.[24] Though many Central Americans settled in California in the 1980s, more recent immigrants have located in a diverse range of cities and towns, particularly in the South and the Midwest.

With 63.8 percent of Central/South American Latinas participating in the labor force, Central/South American women living in the United States have the highest labor force participation of all the Latina subgroups. A plurality of Central/South American women works in service occupations in all regions of the U.S. (see Table 10.10). Among Central/South American women workers with a high school degree, the percentage employed in service occupations is especially high: 39.2 percent. Among women with a college degree, more than twice as many Central/South American women (18.5 percent) are employed in service occupations as are their Latina and white equivalents (see Table 10.3).

Although one in four Central or South American women employees working in the United States did not graduate from high school (24.7 percent), one in five graduated from college (21.4 percent, see Table 10.7). Average wages of high school- versus college-educated Central/South American women differ markedly, but Central/South American workers' average hourly wage is lower than that of most other Latina subgroups working in the United States regardless of their level of educational attainment (see Table 10.5; the only subgroup whose average wage is lower than that of Central/South American women is Mexican women).

Central/South American women employed in the United States are the least likely of all the Latina subgroups to have been born there; only 15 percent are natives. The vast majority immigrated before 1998 (71.9 percent), although an additional 13.1 percent of Central/South American women workers immigrated more recently (see Table 10.11). Unlike self-identified Mexican women who were born in the United States, the small percentage of Central/South American women who are native to the United States earn a relatively high wage compared to other Latinas born in the United States (see Table 10.8). The average of $15.67 an hour that Central or South American women native to the United States earn is second only to that of Cuban women who were born in the States (and earn an average of $15.95 an hour). Central/South American women who immigrated recently also enjoy a relative wage advantage compared to many other subgroups of recent Latina immigrants, but women who immigrated to the United States from Central or South America before 1998 do not enjoy such an advantage (see Table 10.8).

Puerto Ricans

Puerto Ricans are the second largest group of Latinos in the United States and remain concentrated primarily in New York, Chicago, and Miami.[25] Individuals from the Commonwealth of Puerto Rico are U.S. citizens and are therefore not represented among the immigrant population. Economic policies shifting the Puerto Rican economy from agriculture to manufacture in the 1950s and 1960s created high unemployment and poverty among residents of the island. This accelerated Puerto Ricans' migration to the United States, where they face multiple disadvantages.[26]

Nearly 39 percent of Puerto Rican women who live in the United States opt out of the labor force voluntarily; thus their participation rate is lower than white women's and lower than all other Latinas' rates. Furthermore, their unemployment rate exceeds white women's (3.1 percent) and is also higher than each of the other Latina groups' rates (see Table 10.1).

The top two groups in which Puerto Rican women are employed are administrative support (28.5 percent) and managerial and professional occupations (25.3 percent). Another 19.3 percent of Puerto Rican women employees work in service occupations. A higher percentage of Puerto Rican women are employed in administrative positions than in any other occupational group in every region of the country except the West, where more Puerto Rican women work in service occupations (33.8 percent) than in either managerial/professional (29.4 percent) or administrative support categories (15.8 percent, see Table 10.10).

Puerto Rican women living in the United States are in a unique position compared to other Latina subgroups in that everyone born in Puerto Rico is a U.S. citizen. Nevertheless, Puerto Ricans' nativity pattern is closest to that of Mexican women. Fifty-six percent of Puerto Rican women working in the United

States were born there (just as 55.6 percent of Mexican women workers were born in the States; see Table 10.11). An additional 40.9 percent of Puerto Rican women employed in the United States immigrated prior to 1998; only 2.3 percent immigrated from 1998 to 2002. Unlike their Latina peers who gravitate toward the Southern and Western parts of the country, the majority of Puerto Rican women working in the United States live and work in the Northeast (56.0 percent, see Table 10.9).

Puerto Rican women make a relatively high average wage compared to other Latina subgroups working in the United States. They earn $13.74 an hour, on average, which is more than their Mexican ($11.39) and Central or South American peers ($12.32) make. They also have a higher average wage than the heterogeneous group of other Latinas ($13.58). Among Latinas, only Cuban women ($14.09) earn more. Puerto Rican women are the top earners among Latinas with only a high school education (see Table 10.5) and those who recently immigrated to the United States (see Table 10.8).

WHAT EXPLAINS THE CONTINUED DISADVANTAGE OF LATINAS IN THE LABOR MARKET?

The labor market opportunities for Latinas in the United States occur within the context of globalization and the restructuring of the U.S. economy. Industrial restructuring has shifted the economic landscape, expanding opportunities within the service sector, closing or relocating manufacturing jobs, and creating a growing disparity between workers with little schooling and those with college degrees.[27] Recent Latina immigrants in particular sit at the vortex of the global economy, where a growing number of professional white women in the United States need the domestic services of low-wage women workers, and some local communities have increased their demand for cheap labor in garment, meatpacking, and canning industries.[28] Thus economic opportunities for Latinas and competition for jobs vary greatly across local labor markets. For immigrants and native Latinas alike, the "first job" is important for occupational mobility across the life course.[29] Thus, young, unskilled Latinas entering the labor market now face fewer advancement opportunities compared to older cohorts of Latina workers.[30]

Although economic restructuring makes earning a living difficult for all low-skilled workers, Latina employees in the United States face additional challenges.[31] Scholars identify human capital, the gender system, and discrimination as major factors underlying Latinas' labor market disadvantage relative to non-Hispanic white men and women.[32] Though not unique to Latinas, these barriers are at the core of debates regarding race/ethnic and gender stratification in the U.S. labor market more generally.[33] Immigration policy is an additional impediment to geographic and economic mobility for many Latinas.[34]

Similar to debates regarding the disadvantaged status of African American women in the U.S. labor market, the literature on Latina workers often focuses on the extent to which economic opportunities are distributed unequally based on race/ethnicity and gender. In particular, some scholars argue that low levels of human capital and aggregate labor demand explain almost all gaps in wages and employment between Latinas and non-Hispanic white women.[35] Others contend that systematic inequality by gender, race/ethnicity, and their intersections permeate all social institutions, restricting opportunities for Latinas within the labor market both indirectly through access to resources and social capital and directly through discrimination.[36]

With the exception of Cuban women, Latinas fall substantially behind on human capital attributes compared to non-Hispanic white women. Over 25 percent of Latinas did not graduate from high school, compared to 4 percent of white women (Table 10.7). Recent immigrants from Mexico and Central/South America in particular tend to have very low levels of education.[37] Their children have more schooling than they do and therefore experience some inter-generational upwardly mobility.[38] However, high school completion rates in the United States are lower among native-born Latinos than among whites, and the former also are less likely to graduate from college than their white counterparts.[39] Also, because Latina employees, on average, tend to be younger, they have less employment experience, which also serves to lower human capital.[40] Latinas immigrating to the United States often arrive with little or no proficiency in English, which carries an additional human capital deficit. Many are thus reliant on networks of relatives and friends—social capital—to find steady employment.

Across all levels of human capital, Latinas enter a labor market that is characterized by occupational segregation by gender. Within gender-segregated occupations, Latinas are further concentrated in a smaller range of jobs (what Catanzarite dubs "brown-collar jobs").[41] There is some evidence that the percent female *and* the percent Latina in a job lowers wages, above and beyond the effects of human capital.[42] The gender system that circumscribes the economic fortunes of Latinas extends beyond the labor market. Women's responsibilities for raising children and tending the house can limit their labor market options. Latinas also must negotiate gender dynamics within the family, which are suffused with ideologies regarding women's "role" in regard to marriage, motherhood, and work. These ideologies differ depending on social class, nativity, a woman's country and town of origin, and her birth cohort, so that the gender system intersects with ethnicity, class, and generation.[43]

The segregation of occupations by gender and race/ethnicity can assume a self-perpetuating character, as jobs become sex- and race-typed. Employers will then associate a particular type of worker with a job.[44] Many economists argue that market competition militates against employers selecting workers based on ascribed characteristics, such as gender and ethnicity, rather than hiring the most productive worker for a job.[45] Yet employers clearly hold stereotypes of their potential workforce based on gender and ethnicity. For example, Latinos are considered to be hard workers, particularly in comparison to African Americans.[46] These stereotypes may open doors to low-wage jobs, but they do not necessarily produce opportunities for mobility. Indeed, studies indicate that in some workplaces, native-born Latinas are assumed to be immigrants and are therefore passed over for jobs.[47] Nevertheless, evidence documenting the prevalence of discrimination is difficult to obtain; employers are often unaware that their perceptions are based on stereotypes or biases, and employer attitudes are not closely coupled with their actions.[48] We draw on the examples of domestic work and Latinas in the professions to illustrate the complexity of these issues.

DOMESTIC WORK

In all regions except the Midwest, over one-fourth of Latina workers are employed in the service sector (Table 10.10). Many labor as maids or cleaning staff in hotels and restaurants.[49] A sizable number of Latinas toil in private houses as domestic workers, tending children and cleaning. Employment in private households is plentiful for Latinas, particularly if they are undocumented. However, the conditions of domestic employment that create ample opportunities for work simultaneously produce fertile ground for exploitation. Indeed, as Glenn and others have argued, domestic work is based on and reproduces social hierarchies of gender, race/ethnicity, and class.[50] Raising children and cleaning house are considered women's work. Thus, rather than sharing parental and housecleaning responsibilities with their husbands, many middle-class (predominantly white) women hire women of color to perform the "duties of motherhood."[51] Rollins argues that racial/ethnic and class hierarchies are reinforced as white female employers feel a sense of racial superiority over their domestic workers, treating them as "unfortunate others" or rendering them invisible. Although racial and class domination were perpetuated through the employers' "maternalistic" behavior in Rollins's study, Pierrette Hondagneu-Sotelo found a different dynamic that was no less alienating. Many of the live-in domestic workers interviewed reported insufficient personal contact and communication between themselves and their employers. They felt dehumanized at work, because they were treated as "servants" or "employees."[52]

In addition to the perpetuation of racial/ethnic hierarchies, class hierarchies between live-in domestic workers and their employers are literally reproduced, as live-ins are often paid extremely low wages and expected to work long hours. "Room and board" is usually considered part of the live-in's compensation, justifying wages far below the minimum. Often, the hours and conditions of work are not clearly specified, so the domestic may be always on call. For instance, some domestics in Hondagneu-Sotelo's study were required to sleep near the bedroom of their employer's children, in case a child awakened in the night and needed care. For those live-in domestics who had left their own children to the care of others in her country of origin, the conditions of work extracted a high emotional cost.[53] As Hondagneu-Sotelo emphasizes, labor laws regulate the work conditions of domestic employees, but they are often ignored. Negotiating for better working conditions can prove difficult, particularly for Latinas who are undocumented or native-born women with few other options and an absolute need for a paycheck.

Domestic workers who live outside their employers' homes exercise greater control and autonomy and receive higher wages and better working conditions than live-in domestics.[54] Latinas who are self-employed cleaning houses are in the most advantageous position, particularly compared to live-in or live-out domestics who both tend children and clean house for their employer. Self-employed Latinas are not dependent on any one employer; they can determine their own hours and wage rates (within the limits of the market). They can leave situations they find unpleasant or unjust. Furthermore, cleaning does not require the additional emotional labor of meeting children's demands.

Research on Latina domestic employees also reveals how their type of work can reinforce or challenge gender inequalities in the labor market and the family. For instance, in her study of Mayan immigrants in Texas, Hagan found that the gendered division of labor and conditions of domestic work served to disadvantage women and advantage men.[55] Domestic work was the predominant form of employment among the Mayan women in the sample, whereas the Mayan men worked on maintenance teams in a large company. The geographic and social isolation of domestic work severely restricted women's access to employment contacts and information that could lead to better jobs, particularly among those who were live-ins. In contrast, the men had access to information through other men on their teams; their jobs were attached to mobility ladders; and they acquired new skills on the job. Furthermore, the men participated in recreational activities such as soccer teams on the weekends, which expanded their contacts with weak social ties and thus elevated their social capital. In contrast, the women worked six days per week and had limited chances to socialize on Sundays (their day off).[56]

The differences in access to social capital provided to the men and women in the study also led to disparities in their ability to acquire legal status in the United States. When the Immigration Reform and Control Act passed in 1986 allowing undocumented workers to apply for legal residency in the United States, obtaining documentation of residency (such as rent receipts and utility bills) and employment (pay stubs), and a letter of verification from a U.S. citizen was easier for the men. The women in the study who were working as live-in domestics did not have documentation of residency because they had been compensated with room and board and cash payments. Employers of domestics were reluctant to sign affidavits of employment and residence for their employees, fearing that the Internal Revenue Service would be notified.

According to Hagan,[57] this gender disparity in mobility opportunities, access to social resources, and legal status increased men's power relative to women in the community and the family. Menjívar's research reveals that domestic employment and the gender division of labor can also influence gender marital dynamics through challenging or affirming gender ideologies. In her study of women who had migrated to California from El Salvador and Guatemala,[58] Menjívar found that the women who worked as domestics were exposed to new ideas of gender roles in the homes of their white North American employers. Their husbands, on the other hand, worked among other men from Central America, who reinforced their traditional ideas about gender. The men often resisted their wives' attempts to change power relations in their marriage.

Menjívar also found that the ways that a woman's employment influenced power and gender relations in the family depended on the gender ideologies and work histories that they brought from their home countries.[59] The women could easily find domestic work in the United States, whereas men were more likely to be unemployed. The indigenous Guatemalan men viewed their wives' employment opportunities and wages as an opportunity for the couple to get ahead. The Latino Guatemalan men and the Salvadoran men saw their wives' paid work as a threat to their sense of masculinity. The tension between these latter two groups was particularly acute within couples where the husband was unemployed.

LATINAS IN THE PROFESSIONS

The literature on Latinas in low-wage jobs continues to burgeon, informing debates over the overall status of low-wage workers in the United States and enriching feminist theories of the intersections of gender, race/ethnicity, and class.[60] In contrast, much less is known about the experiences of Latinas in the professions.

Indeed, Latinas are severely underrepresented in managerial and professional occupations, many of which require a college diploma or an advanced degree (Table 10.2). For example, only 9 percent of Mexican-origin women, 18 percent of Puerto Rican women, and 21 percent of Central/South American women have college diplomas, compared to 33 percent of white women (Table 10.7). The educational gap grows even wider with more years of schooling. In 2001, Latinas accounted for only 2 percent of all doctorates earned in the sciences and engineering, and not quite 5 percent of all the science and engineering doctorates that were awarded to women (sciences include the social sciences).[61] In contrast, white women earned 32 percent of all science and engineering doctorates awarded in 2001, and black women earned slightly more than 2 percent.

Why do Latinas lag so far behind non-Hispanic white women in obtaining the postsecondary schooling necessary to enter the professions? A recent study by the Pew Hispanic Center finds that part of the Hispanic-white disparity arises from the "selective pathways" that Latinos take into higher education.[62] Compared to white students, even the academically best-prepared Latinos are more likely to attend two-year colleges and nonselective four-year colleges.[63] Gradu-ation rates for all groups tend to be lower at these colleges. In addition, Latinos graduate at lower rates than whites within all types of institutions, with one exception. The best-prepared Latino students at the most selective colleges and universities, who are a very small group, have graduation rates on par with whites.

The large numbers of working-class and poor Latino families and relatively few elite Latinos also contribute to disadvantage in attaining the education that can lead to professional careers. Latinas from working-class or poor backgrounds who aspire to attend college cannot rely on their parents for the advice and financial assistance that is often available to their white middle-class peers.[64] Even when they do achieve academic success and progress into graduate pro-grams and academic positions, Latinas often encounter a "hidden curriculum" that tends to highlight the accomplishments of white men and favors a con-servative, "male, Euro-centric epistemology."[65] For instance, in her study of Chicana (Mexican-origin) professors, Denise Segura finds that the academy represents a distinct world that Chicana academics must learn to navigate.[66] Because there are so few Latina academics, their efforts are often quite visible to their colleagues, and their workload is increased. Similar to African American women in the academy, Latina professors face pressures to serve on multiple committees and to advise and mentor large numbers of students of color.[67]

Studies of Latinas in nonacademic professions also describe the difficulties they face as racial/ethnic minorities and women in fields that are predominantly Anglo and male. As tokens in their workplaces, Latinas can find themselves subject to negative stereotyping by employers and co-workers. Latinas working in professional or white-collar jobs report that Anglo co-workers question their abilities and competence. To counter these doubts, Latinas must "prove them-selves more" than their Anglo colleagues.[68]

CONCLUSION

Latinas' experiences in graduate programs and the professions suggest that the overall picture of labor market disadvantage found among Mexican-origin, Puerto Rican, and Central/South American women is not simply due to the large numbers of recent immigrants and low-wage workers in their ranks. In-stead, Latinas appear to be caught in intersecting and multiple disadvantages of gender, ethnicity, race, and social class. The ways in which these multiple di-mensions of disadvantage play out to determine economic fortunes vary con-siderably between and within different subgroups of Latinas, however.

Understanding the position of different groups of Latinas requires analyses at multiple levels of social, political, and economic life. At the macro level, the global economy is key in determining employment opportunities and barriers for all groups of workers.[69] On the national level, the enactment and enforcement of immigration laws and economic policies are particularly salient for Latina im-

migrants.[70] Local labor markets, community resources, and political mobilization also create constellations of inequality and opportunity for native-born and
immigrant Latinas.[71] Even at the micro level, the household is a key economic
unit that must be considered.[72] At all these levels, race/ethnicity, gender, and
class combine to shape the economic fortunes of Latinas and their families.

NOTES

1. Throughout this chapter, "white" refers to non-Hispanic white individuals.

2. Roberto de la Cruz Ramirez and Patricia de la Cruz Ramirez, *The Hispanic
Population in the United States: March 2002* (Washington, DC: U.S. Census Bureau,
2003).

3. Heather Antecol, "Why Is There Interethnic Variation in the Gender Wage
Gap? The Role of Cultural Factors," *Journal of Human Resources* 36(1) (2001).

4. Patrick McGreevy, "Latinos, Flexing Political Muscle, Come of Age in L.A.; a
New Generation of Leaders Now Debates How to Use Its Power to Shape Public Policy,"
Los Angeles Times, June 27, 2005. Scholars note that nationwide, the political participation of Latinos falls far behind their representation in the population (Nicole Gaou-
ette, "The Nation: Latino Clout at Polls Lagging, Study Says," *Los Angeles Times*, June
28, 2005).

5. Betsy Guzman and Eileen Diaz McConnell, "The Hispanic Population: 1990–
2000 Growth and Change," *Population Research and Policy Review* 21(1–2) (2002);
Sonia M. Perez and Cecilia Munoz, "Latino Low-Wage Workers: A Look at Immigrant
Workers," in Richard Kazis and Marc S. Miller, eds., *Low-Wage Workers in the New
Economy* (Washington, DC: Urban Institute Press, 2001).

6. Pew Hispanic Center, *Hispanic Trends: A People in Motion* (Washington, DC:
Pew Hispanic Center, 2005).

7. Guzman and McConnell, "The Hispanic Population"; Rakesh Kochhar, Roberto
Suro, and Sonya Tafoya, *The New Latino South: The Context and Consequences of Rapid
Population Growth* (Washington, DC: Pew Hispanic Center, 2005).

8. Roberto Suro and Audrey Singer, "Latino Growth in Metropolitan America:
Changing Patterns, New Locations," in *Brookings Institution Survey Series* (Washington,
DC: Brookings Institution, 2002).

9. Jeffrey S. Passel, "Estimates of the Size and Characteristics of the Undocumented Population," in *Pew Hispanic Center Report* (Washington, DC: Pew Hispanic
Center, 2005).

10. Frank Bean and Marta Tienda Bean, *The Hispanic Population of the United
States* (New York: Russell Sage Foundation, 1987); Alejandro Portes and Ruben G.
Rumbaut, *Immigrant America: A Portrait*, 2nd ed. (Berkeley: University of California
Press, 1996); Alejandro Portes, "Immigration Theory for a New Century: Some Problems
and Opportunities," *International Migration Review* 31(4) (1997): 120.

11. Marta Lopez-Garza and David R. Diaz, eds., *Asian and Latino Immigrants in a
Restructuring Economy: The Metamorphosis of Southern California* (Stanford: Stanford
University Press, 2001).

12. Bureau of Labor Statistics, U.S. Department of Labor, *Handbook of Methods*
(Washington, DC: Government Printing Office, 2003).

13. Guzman and McConnell, "The Hispanic Population."

14. Marlene Kim, "Women Paid Low Wages: Who They Are and Where They Work," *Monthly Labor Review* 123(9) (2000).

15. Marta Tienda and Rebecca Raijman, "Immigrants' Income Packaging and Invisible Labor Force Activity," *Social Science Quarterly* 81(1) (2000).

16. U.S. Census Bureau, *1980 Census of Population Classified Index of Industries and Occupations* (Washington, DC: Government Printing Office, 1980).

17. Dowell Myers and Cynthia J. Cranford, "Temporal Differentiation in the Occupational Mobility of Immigrant and Native-Born Latina Workers," *American Sociological Review* 63(1) (1998); Roger Waldinger and Cynthia Feliciano, "Will the New Second Generation Experience 'Downward Assimilation?' Segmented Assimilation Reassessed," *Ethnic and Racial Studies* 27(3) (2004).

18. Alejandro Portes and Robert L. Bach, *Latin Journey: Cuban and Mexican Immigrants in the United States* (Berkeley: University of California Press, 1985).

19. Sylvia Pedraza and Ruben Rumbaut Pedraza, *Origins and Destinies: Immigration, Race, and Ethnicity in America* (Belmont, CA: Wadsworth, 1996).

20. Ramirez, "The Hispanic Population."

21. Jeffrey S. Passel, Jennifer Van Hook, and Frank D. Bean, *Estimates of Legal and Unauthorized Foreign Born Population for the United States and Selected States, Based on Census 2000* (Washington, DC: Urban Institute, 2004; available online at www.sabresys.com/i_whitepapers.asp).

22. Kochhar, Suro, and Tafoya, *The New Latino South.*

23. Julie Shayne, *The Revolution Question in Feminism* (New Brunswick, NJ: Rutgers University Press, 2004).

24. Cecilia Menjívar, "The Intersection of Work and Gender: Central American Immigrant Women and Employment in California," *American Behavioral Scientist* 42(4) (1999).

25. Bean and Bean, *The Hispanic Population of the United States.*

26. Ibid.

27. Leslie McCall, *Complex Inequality: Gender, Class and Race in the New Economy* (New York: Routledge, 2001).

28. Sandra Charvat Burke and Willis J. Goudy, "Immigration and Community in Iowa: How Many Have Come and What Is the Impact?" Conference paper delivered at the Annual Meeting of the American Sociological Association, Chicago, IL, 1999; Denise Segura, "Walking on Eggshells: Chicanas in the Labor Force," in Stephen Knouse, Paul Rosenfeld, and Amy L. Culbertson, eds., *Hispanics in the Workplace* (Newbury Park, CA: Sage, 1992).

29. Myers and Cranford, "Temporal Differentiation."

30. Vilma Ortiz, "The Mexican Origin Population," in Roger Waldinger and Mehdi Bozorgmehr, eds., *Ethnic Los Angeles* (New York: Russell Sage Foundation, 1996).

31. Perez and Munoz, "Latino Low-Wage Workers."

32. Ibid.

33. Delores Aldridge, "African American Women since the Second World War: Perspectives on Gender and Race," in Alton Hornsby Jr., ed., *A Companion to African American History* (Malden, MA: Blackwell, 2005); Irene Browne, Leann Tigges, and Julie Press, "Inequality through Labor Markets, Firms, and Families: The Intersection of Gender and Race-Ethnicity across Three Cities," in Chris Tilly, Alice O'Connor, and

Larry Bobo, eds., *Urban Inequality: Evidence from Four Cities* (New York: Russell Sage Foundation, 2001).

34. Cynthia Bansak and Steven Raphael, "Immigration Reform and the Earnings of Latino Workers: Do Employer Sanctions Cause Discrimination?" *Industrial and Labor Relations Review* 54(2) (2001); Pierrette Hondagneu-Sotelo, *Domestica: Immigrant Workers Cleaning and Caring in the Shadows of America* (Berkeley: University of California Press, 2001); Perez and Munoz, "Latino Low-Wage Workers."

35. Claudia Alejandra Gonzalez, "Cost of Labor Force Participation and Racial Discrimination" (Ph.D. diss., University of Wisconsin, 2003).

36. Pierrette Hondagneu-Sotelo, *Gendered Transitions: Mexican Experiences of Immigration* (Berkeley: University of California Press, 1994); Denise Segura, "Navigating between Two Worlds: The Labyrinth of Chicana Intellectual Production in the Academy," *Journal of Black Studies* 34(1) (2003); Maria Angelina Soldatenko, "Made in the USA: Latinas/Os? Garment Work and Ethnic Conflict in Los Angeles' Sweatshops," *Cultural Studies* 13(2) (1999).

37. Myers and Cranford, "Temporal Differentiation."

38. Ibid.; Waldinger and Feliciano, "Will the New Second Generation Experience 'Downward Assimilation?'"

39. Pew Hispanic Center, "Educational Attainment: Better than Meets the Eye, but Large Challenges Remain," in *Fact Sheet* (Washington, DC: Pew Hispanic Center, 2002).

40. U.S. Census Bureau, "Race and Hispanic or Latino Origin by Age and Sex for the United States: 2000." Report PHC-T08 (Washington, DC: Government Printing Office, 2000).

41. Browne et al., "Inequality through Labor Markets"; Lisa Catanzarite and Michael Bernabe Aguilera, "Working with Co-Ethnics: Earnings Penalties for Latino Immigrants at Latino Jobsites," *Social Problems* 49(1) (2002).

42. Browne et al., "Inequality through Labor Markets"; Catanzarite and Aguilera, "Working with Co-Ethnics"; Carolyn Aman Karlin, Paula England, and Mary Richardson, "Why Do 'Women's Jobs' Have Low Pay for Their Educational Level?" *Gender Issues* 20(4) (2002).

43. Irene Browne and Joya Misra, "The Intersection of Gender and Race in the Labor Market," *Annual Review of Sociology* 29 (2003); Jennifer S. Hirsch, "En El Norte La Mujer Manda: Gender, Generation, and Geography in a Mexican Transnational Community," *American Behavioral Scientist* 42(9) (1999); Menjívar, "The Intersection of Work and Gender."

44. Lisa Catanzarite, "Brown-Collar Jobs: Occupational Segregation and Earnings of Recent-Immigrant Latino Workers," *Sociological Perspectives* 43(1) (2000).

45. See Paula England, *Comparable Worth: Theories and Evidence* (New York: Aldine de Gruyter, 1992) for a review of the economic theory underlying the debates on discrimination.

46. Philip I. Moss and Chris Tilly, *Stories Employers Tell: Race, Skill, and Hiring in America* (New York: Russell Sage Foundation, 2001).

47. Richard Wright, Adrian Bailey, Ines Miyares, and Alison Mountz, "Legal Status, Gender and Employment among Salvadorans in the U.S.," *International Journal of Population Geography* 6 (2000).

48. Devah Pager and Lincoln Quillian, "Walking the Talk? What Employers Say Versus What They Do," *American Sociological Review* 70(3) (2005).

49. Alan B. Krueger and Jonathan M. Orszag, "Hispanics and the Current Economic Downturn: Will the Receding Tide Sink Hispanics?" in *Pew Hispanic Center Study* (Washington, DC: Pew Hispanic Center, 2002).

50. Evelyn Nakano Glenn, "From Servitude to Service Work: Historical Continuities in the Racial Division of Paid Reproductive Labor," *Signs* 18(1) (1992); Mary Romero, *Maid in the USA* (New York: Routledge, 1992).

51. Mary Romero and Phyllis Palmer, "Domesticity and Dirt: Housewives and Domestic Servants in the United States, 1920–1945," *NWSA Journal* 3(1) (1991).

52. Pierrette Hondagneu-Sotelo, *Domestica*, 2001.

53. Pierrette Hondagneu-Sotelo and Ernestine Avila, "'I'm Here, but I'm There': The Meanings of Latina Transnational Motherhood," *Gender and Society* 11(5) (1997).

54. Ibid.

55. Jacqueline Maria Hagan, "Social Networks, Gender, and Immigrant Incorporation: Resources and Constraints," *American Sociological Review* 63(1) (1998).

56. Weak ties are social connections to acquaintances and "friends of friends." Strong ties are social connections to family members and close friends. In his classic paper, Granovetter argues that the information about labor market opportunities provided by weak ties is more diverse and far-ranging than the information provided by strong ties. Weak ties have access to social networks and information about opportunities that are unknown to a job seeker. Strong ties, on the other hand, tend to be connected to the same networks of individuals as the job seeker, and thus provide a smaller range of information and contacts. See Mark S. Granovetter, "The Strength of Weak Ties," *American Journal of Sociology* 78(6) (1973).

57. Hagan, "Social Networks."

58. Menjívar, "The Intersection of Work and Gender."

59. Ibid.

60. Browne and Misra, "The Intersection of Gender and Race."

61. National Science Foundation, Division of Science Resources Statistics, Survey of Earned Doctorates, 1994–2001.

62. Richard Fry, "Latino Youth Finishing College: The Role of Selective Pathways," in *Pew Hispanic Center Report* (Washington, DC: Pew Hispanic Center, 2004).

63. Ibid.

64. Segura, "Navigating between Two Worlds."

65. Eric Margolis and Mary Romero, "'The Department Is Very Male, Very White, Very Old, and Very Conservative': The Functioning of the Hidden Curriculum in Graduate School Departments," *Harvard Educational Review* 68(1) (1998); Segura, "Navigating between Two Worlds."

66. Segura, "Navigating between Two Worlds."

67. Ibid.

68. Denise A. Segura, "Chicanas in White-Collar Jobs: 'You Have to Prove Yourself More,'" *Sociological Perspectives* 35(1) (1992).

69. Saskia Sassen, *Globalization and Its Discontents: Essays on the New Mobility of People and Money* (New York: New Press, 1998).

70. Portes and Rumbaut, *Immigrant America.*

71. McCall, *Complex Inequality.*

72. Tienda and Raijman, "Immigrants' Income Packaging."

11

Unearned Privilege: Issues of Race, Gender, and Social Inequality in U.S. Organizations

Ashleigh Shelby Rosette

Management textbooks and business trade journals usually do not have the words *"unearned privileges"* printed in their index or glossaries, but many organizational actors will report that they exist and admit that organizations need to take heed of operating systems of privilege. Although most organizations are based on merit and performance, non–merit-based social structures work in tandem with traditional performance-based establishments. Specifically, social systems in organizations that give opportunity and advantage to people based on their ability and talents coexist with social systems that bestow advantage based on nonmeritorious characteristics such as class, race, gender, religion, and a host of additional categorical variables. When demographics and related categorical distinctions are considered in organizational settings, the attention is frequently given to disadvantaged groups rather than to those who are advantaged or privileged because of social inequalities.

This disregarded side of organizations warrants attention because to only consider social inequalities from the perspective of disadvantaged groups captures a mere portion of organizational experiences. When unearned privileges are ignored, organizational settings may be breeding grounds for skewed understandings of social inequalities. Accordingly, the goal of this chapter is to examine unearned privileges in organizations as related to race, gender, and social inequality. First, distinctions between unearned and earned privileges are made, and potential explanations for the focus on unfair disadvantage as opposed to unearned privilege when studying social inequality in organizations are considered. Second, the principal tenets of unearned privileges are described. Specifically, unearned privilege is often invisible to its holder and is frequently considered a social norm. Next, examples of white privilege and male privilege are given, and empirical evidence that substantiates these types of unearned privileges is provided. Finally, attribution theory is offered as a theoretical frame for the study of unearned privilege.

UNEARNED PRIVILEGE DEFINED

A privilege is an advantage, benefit, or reward that is not available to everyone.[1] Privileges accrue to particular people and are withheld from others. In an organizational context, privileges are sometimes earned. They are based on achieved status, which is a social position that reflects a significant measure of personal ability and competence.[2] Earned privileges accrue to people with achieved status. For example, when a computer salesperson sells more laptops than any of her colleagues, she may be rewarded with a reserved parking spot or a monetary token of appreciation. Her rewards, the parking spot and bonus, are based on her achievement, namely, selling the most computers. Accordingly, her privilege is earned because it is based on her performance. This type of privilege is expected in U.S. organizations because most are presumed to be meritocracies whereby advancements and rewards are perceived to be based on individual merit and accomplishment.[3]

Not all privileges in the workplace, however, are earned. Many are bestowed on organization members because of ascribed status.[4] Ascribed status is a social position attained by categorical distinctions or demographics.[5] Unearned privileges accrue to members with ascribed status because of groupings such as race, gender, sexual orientation, religion, class, and physical ability. These distinctions are not merit-based but are haphazardly determined by external factors mostly beyond the individual's immediate control. They are established outside of the organization but have substantial impact on the individual's experience within the organization. Consequently, the privileges that people accumulate due to these categorical distinctions are unearned.

Although a host of unearned privileges could be considered when examining organizational experiences, the categorical distinctions of interest in this chapter are race and gender. This chosen emphasis does not reflect a biased or slanted perception of social inequality in organizations, nor does it maintain that certain demographics are more important than others. It does, however, reflect the emphasis in social inequality research. A wealth of empirical and theoretical literature exists regarding the attitudes and behaviors between underrepresented minorities and whites and between men and women in organizational contexts. In addition, the political and social milieu of the United States is such that the relationships between underrepresented minorities and whites and between men and women have played a major role in shaping organizational interactions as evidenced by public policy and legislation (e.g., the Civil Rights Act of 1964, affirmative action, *Brown v. Board of Education*). Also, the majority of complaints filed with the Equal Employment Opportunity Commission (EEOC), the federal agency responsible for complaints of inequality in the workplace, reference race and gender.[6] Therefore, understanding the relationship between race and gender, on one hand, and corresponding unearned privileges, on the other hand, is the primary focus of this chapter.

Organizational Framing of Social Inequity

Unearned privileges are not frequently considered under the broad category of racial and gender inequality in organizations and accordingly are not often reported in organizational research. Impressive sets of literature in sociology, psychology, and organizational studies examine these organizational inequalities;[7] however, the focus is generally on the disadvantaged and not the privileged. For example, when proportional representation of the diverse workforce is considered, the emphasis is mainly on the increase of underrepresented minorities and women as opposed to a decrease in the number of whites and men. In addition, results of inequality studies are most commonly presented as how underrepresented minorities and women experience difficulty as they attempt to progress up the corporate ladder as opposed to the simplicity and ease that may be more familiar to whites and men. For example, when reporting existing wage disparities, the phrase "minority workers are underpaid relative to their white counterparts" is more likely to be used than the phrase "white workers are overpaid relative to minorities." Similarly when reporting statistics, it is far more common to see the phrase "women's salaries are only 76 percent of men's salaries" than it is to see the report that "men earn $1.32 for each dollar that women earn." These differences are not mere semantics; they direct the way racial and gender inequality is examined in organizational settings.

When topics of race and gender inequalities arise in organizations, they generally fall under the umbrella of diversity issues. It is usually presumed that racial issues encompass concerns of African Americans, Hispanics, Asians, Native Americans, or other racial minorities. Far less frequently are the concerns of whites included as a subcategory within the context of diversity issues in organizations. A similar classification concern occurs when gender-based issues are considered in organizations. It is presumed that gender issues are relegated only to the problems and concerns of women. Male issues, concerns, and perspectives are not frequently considered except as an implied reference category. Accordingly, when considering racial and gender inequality in an organizational setting, focus and attention remain on the concerns and issues of the subordinated group as opposed to considering the role played by those with advantage. This does not presume that in all organizations women and minorities are subordinated, nor does it presume that racial and gender inequalities are analogous. It does presuppose that this type of social hierarchy is more likely than not.

However, focusing on only one side of the inequality equation prevents the complete understanding of organizational hierarchies and their related social systems. Specifically, if it is agreed that at times one group is unfairly disadvantaged, then by all calculations, it follows that another group is unfairly advantaged. The two groups are parallel, and one does not exist without the other. One reason that social inequality is viewed through a lens of disadvantage as opposed to advantage is probably because of the legal doctrines that govern organizations.

Legal Depiction of Discrimination

Racial and gender inequality in organizations is most frequently governed by the legal depiction of discrimination. This legal definition implies negative behavior, which may indirectly preclude the consideration of unearned advantage in an organizational context.

When referencing society at large, absent the boundaries imposed by organizational form, discrimination is defined as classifying people into different groups and according the members of each group distinct and typically unequal treatments, rights, and obligations.[8] Thus discrimination in its most simplistic form is differentiation among persons. When considered from this communal perspective, valence is not assigned to the act of discriminating. Accordingly, discrimination in society at large can connote a positive or negative distinction.

When considering discrimination within the confines of organizations, a narrower legal definition is usually applied. This definition is the most widely used conceptualization of discrimination because of the laws that govern many organizations' continuation and livelihood (i.e., organizations with more than fifteen employees).[9] Discrimination in federal civil rights laws is considered to be unfavorable or unfair treatment of a person or class of persons in comparison to others because of specific categorical or demographic distinctions, such as race and gender. Accordingly, the 80,000 complaints received annually by the EEOC were not submitted by complainants who benefited from unequal treatment. Instead, they were tendered due to unfair, negative, or unfavorable behavior.

The legal conceptualization of racial and gender inequality as negative treatment is likely a principle driver of the frame in which inequality is viewed in organizations. Consequently, undeserved disadvantage receives substantial attention and unearned advantage is often ignored. Understanding the conceptualization of discrimination in organizations allows for better appreciation of the reasons why those who study organizations have rarely examined unearned privileges. Unearned privileges are by-products of deliberate negative actions, which are infrequently addressed in the legal conceptualization of employment discrimination and, consequently, rarely considered in any social study of organizational experiences. This is not to say that the concept of unearned advantage has not been broached when studying and examining societal experiences at large, but far less frequently is the concept considered or studied empirically within an organizational context.

Individual Motivations

In addition to the organizational and legal justifications for not frequently examining unearned privileges in an organizational context, individual motivations also exist. Thinking about unearned privilege from the perspective of those who are advantaged in organizations requires the contemplation of sensitive topics because specific categories of unearned privilege must be considered. When unearned privileges are attached to specific categories such as race and gender, the resulting terms are *white* privilege and *male* privilege. When these terms are used to describe existing social inequalities, they are frequently associated with prejudice or animosity against others that is connoted by racism or sexism. For example, the term *white privilege* conjures up images of white supremacy, an ideology which holds that the white race is superior to others, and the term is most often thought of in connection with anti–African American racism and anti-Semitism. The association of privilege with superiority and racism and sexism precludes an in-depth understanding of unearned privilege in organizations because subsequent discussion could lead to the application of the dreaded racist or sexist label. One need only look in the popular press to see the adverse consequences of making disparaging remarks based on race or gender.[10] Thus, discussions of unearned privileges may prove to be risky due to resulting discomfort and even fear because people may not know how to talk about unearned privilege and may feel vulnerable to culpability. Accordingly, individual motivations in a society that is charged by political correctness may preclude a frank consideration of unearned privileges. The key to reducing the risk is a better understanding of differences.

The discussion of unearned privilege is risky not only for those who benefit from the privilege but also for those who may find it to be detrimental. In U.S. organizations, individual accomplishments and autonomy are highly valued;[11] hence, it may be very difficult to avoid the negative judgments attached to undeserved disadvantage. In particular, because individual accomplishments are so highly valued and rewarded, "just world beliefs" often follow. Living in a just world means that those who work hard professionally and personally will succeed in life.[12] Alternatively, those who are lazy and work poorly will fail. This notion assumes that people are motivated to believe that they live in a just world where each person gets what he or she deserves.[13] Any evidence that this is not the case threatens the underlying mindset of a just or fair world and elicits efforts to eliminate that threat. A psychological defense to the threat is re-interpretation of the cause, which means rationalizing that the victim caused the suffering and was deserving of the consequence. Derogation of those who are undeservedly disadvantaged may occur, making their shortcomings appear as if they were deserved. Hence, people who are unfairly disadvantaged may be quite comfortable talking about unearned privilege among others who are similar to them, but less likely to initiate such discussions in more heterogeneous groups because of the negative judgments that may follow.[14]

INVISIBILITY OF UNEARNED PRIVILEGE

Because unearned privilege is not often considered in organizational contexts, it sometimes remains invisible to its holders. The invisibility of unearned privilege was made famous in Peggy McIntosh's seminal essay, "Unpacking the Invisible Knapsack."[15] According to McIntosh, invisibility implies that people with unearned privilege are unable or unwilling to acknowledge that they receive benefits because of their privileged group membership. Thus, these unearned benefits remain unseen by those who hold the privileged category distinction.

In U.S. society, many with unearned privilege go through life wearing blinders and do not recognize how their privileged distinction is accompanied by advantage. This invisibility is mimicked in U.S. organizations, most of which are meritocracies where unearned privileges have a negative meaning. Thus, it is counter to many organizational values, which presume a meritocracy, for employees to admit that one group of workers may have an unearned advantage over another due to race or gender. People resist acknowledging that they may be benefactors of unearned privilege because doing so may cause others to view their work performance less favorably. Thus, unearned privilege becomes normalized.

Unearned privilege allows those who hold it to experience their customary routines as the social norm.[16] Holders of privilege may not perceive it as something bestowed on them. Instead it appears simply as the way things are. The privileged group receives unearned benefits because of its categorical distinction and may be oblivious to its groups' advantages and benefits that simply seem normal or customary. Alternatively, others who are not privileged have a lack, an absence, a distinction.

Kimmel and Ferber used e-mail addresses to provide a poignant example of the normalization of privilege.[17] Many people in the United States have an e-mail address and many send e-mails to friends and colleagues in the United States and abroad. A distinction exists between the e-mails sent to friends within versus outside of the United States. Domestic e-mail addresses generally end with ".edu" for an educational institution or ".gov" for a governmental organization. However, e-mails going to other nations end in a country code such as ".nl" for The Netherlands or ".uk" for the United Kingdom. Most e-mails going to and from the United States, however, do not reference a country code. The use of country codes as a distinction for other nations is a social norm to which most U.S. citizens are accustomed. Just as the United States is the normative reference category to which all other countries are compared, whites and men are the implied referent to which minorities and women, respectively, are compared in U.S. organizations.

The invisibility of unearned privilege often depends on the demographics of the perceiver. Underrepresented minorities typically agree that white people enjoy white privilege, but whites often deny they have it and disagree about the concept's existence.[18] Women generally acknowledge that men have certain advantages, but men do not see how women's disadvantage is directly or indirectly related to their gains.[19] Even if whites and men acknowledge their unearned privilege, it may be compared to unearned privilege granted to minorities and women through affirmative action programs, although these types of unearned privileges are rarely invisible. These reactions are defensive mechanisms because acknowledging unearned privilege can be threatening to the self-esteem and self-efficacy of its beneficiaries.

Alternatively, underrepresented minorities and women are more likely to recognize the benefits that they see granted to whites and men because doing so provides a potential explanation for subpar performance and failures. Just like those who benefit from unearned privileges, those who do not are motivated to view themselves and their capabilities in the most positive light, and pointing out unearned privileges allows them to maintain a positive self-concept.

WHITE PRIVILEGE AND MALE PRIVILEGE

Whether acknowledged or denied, the most apparent race-based privilege in most organizations is white privilege, because whites are the most advantaged labor market.[20] White privilege is an advantage or immunity granted to or enjoyed by white persons beyond the common advantage of others.[21] McIntosh listed forty-six examples of white privilege that occurred at work, including (a) being able to associate with people of her own race most of the time; (b) performing well in challenging situations without being called a credit to her own race; (c) being able to go home from most organizational meetings feeling somewhat tied in, rather than isolated and out of place; (d) thinking about social or professional options without having to ask whether a person of her race would be accepted or allowed to do it; (e) never being asked to speak for all people that make up her racial group; and (f) not needing to ask if a negative occurrence or situation at work has racial overtones.[22]

Maier and Johnson separately composed similar lists with regard to male privilege, which results from a gender-based hierarchy.[23] Examples from their lists include (a) not being mistaken as "just a spouse" at social functions, (b) not having limited social networking opportunities because of gender, (c) being held to a lower standard than women in professional and upper-level occupations, (d) controlling conversations and being allowed to get away with it, (e) not being slotted into a narrow range of lower-tiered occupations identified with their gender, (f) expecting that representation in government and ruling circles of corporation will share their gender, and (g) expecting that their gender will not be used to determine if they fit in at work.

From reading the examples of unearned privileges, three points should be clear. First, unearned privileges do not have to come about because of a deliberate or conscious set of decisions or actions. However, they likely evolve from the continuation of social norms and are not likely to cease unless the norms are challenged. Organizational members may not give very much thought to these unearned advantages, nonetheless, they continuously accrue and manifest such that organizational level impact is profound and racial and gender-based inequality thrives. People in organizational settings are drawn to people who look like themselves;[24] thus, women and minorities may be undeservedly disadvantaged (i.e., not promoted up the organizational ladder or included in important social networks) simply because they are dissimilar to the decision makers or do not fit an expected prototype.[25] Hence, deliberate choice may not lead to the perpetuation of unearned privileges in organizational settings; instead it may be a function of social categorization that lays out a path of least resistance and allows people to function in their own comfort zone.[26] For example, the top-ranked barrier among many persisting racial and gender obstacles reported by 72 percent of human resource managers at 304 organizations responding to a survey was that "traditional managers (white males) are already in place, limiting access to women and people of color because they have greater comfort with their own kind."[27]

The second point that should be clear about the examples of unearned white and male privileges is that they are more likely to occur in core as opposed to peripheral organizations. In particular, one can think of organizations where white privilege and male privilege are not very salient, such as minority-owned or women-owned businesses. Organizations whose owners and managers are African American disproportionately employ African American workers.[28] Similarly, women-owned businesses are more likely than male-owned businesses to employ women.[29] In these types of organizations, being a minority or a woman may be advantageous. However, these firms make up only a small percentage of all U.S. organizations and do not represent the social structure of most; thus they are peripheral. According to the Survey of Minority-Owned Businesses, a study that the U.S. Census Bureau conducted for the five-year period from 1992 to 1997, approximately 85 percent of all U.S. businesses were owned by whites, and these companies collected approximately 97 percent of all gross receipts.[30] Similarly, according to the Survey of Women-Owned Businesses, approximately 74 percent of all U.S. firms were not solely owned by women; of those owned by women, approximately half had receipts of less than $10,000.[31] Thus, white privilege and male privilege are more likely to be the norm as opposed to the exception in many core U.S. organizations. Even in U.S. organizations that are white- or male-owned and -operated and employ large numbers of minorities and women, whites and males are more likely than not to be concentrated in upper management jobs where unearned privileges continue to accrue, and minorities and women will be more strongly represented in lower-tier jobs.[32]

The third point that should be clear is that unearned privileges can lead to superior performance, exclusive networks, and advancement opportunities. This can be demonstrated by reviewing studies that match whites and African Americans and women and men on similar characteristics. Sufficient empirical studies exist that compare the experience of African Americans to whites and women to men and suggest that whites and males benefit from unearned privileges. Much of this research demonstrates that when African Americans and whites and women and men are matched on similar characteristics and qualifications, a bias exists that favors whites and men and disadvantages African Americans and women. The focus on African Americans as opposed to other minorities does not reflect that one minority group is more important than the other; however, much of the research on racial inequality in U.S. organizations examines the social, political, and historical relationship between whites and African Americans.

An audit study using African American and white job seekers with matched qualifications (fields of study, degrees, schools attended, and grade point averages) found that white applicants progressed better than African American applicants about 20 percent of the time.[33] In another study using matched fictitious résumés, job applicants with names that are common to whites, such as Emily and Greg, were 50 percent more likely to receive calls for interviews than were applicants with names that are common to African Americans, such as Lakisha and Jamal.[34]

Unearned privileges not only limit access to organizations but also affect the organizational experience. Utilizing a meta-analysis consisting of 74 studies and over 17,000 participants, Kraiger and Ford examined race effects in performance evaluations.[35] The findings showed that same-race supervisor/subordinate relationships resulted in a more positive evaluation of the subordinate. Because an overwhelming majority of the executives and managers in the U.S. workforce is white,[36] this biased effect is likely to advantage white workers more than African American workers. In addition, Thomas showed that same-race mentoring relationships provided more social-psychological support than did cross-race mentoring relationships.[37] Because white mentees were frequently paired with white mentors, they did not have to seek support from outside of their departments, whereas African American mentees did.

Maume used the term *glass ceiling* to reference the experience of African American men in corporate settings and the term *glass escalator* to describe the experience of white men in corporate settings.[38] Using a comprehensive longitudinal data set, Maume showed that when personal and job-related factors were controlled, white men were 52 percent more likely to attain a managerial position than were African American men. In addition, Maume found evidence that supported earlier assertions that African Americans are often concentrated in jobs such as community relations, public relations, and personnel, which are not considered preparatory roles for chief leadership positions.[39] Another study showed that the difference between African American and white men was not limited to access to managerial positions but also substantially affected their wages and employment rate. Wage discrimination increased the employment rate of white men to 122 percent of African American men's employment rate.[40]

Although not in an organizational setting, perhaps the most compelling evidence supporting the unearned privilege that accrues to whites is provided by the Implicit Association Test (IAT). In the IAT, participants classify stimuli representing racial groups (i.e., African American and white faces) and evaluate attributes (e.g., pleasant and unpleasant words) using two separate response keys. Participants typically perform the task more quickly and easily when pleasant attributes share the same response key with white than African American faces and unpleasant attributes share the same key with African American than white faces.[41] These experiments have demonstrated a strong positive evaluation of whites and a relatively negative evaluation of African Americans. Although researchers have not yet administered the IAT in organizational settings, given the preponderance of empirical organizational evidence that already exists exhibiting a bias in favor of whites, it is likely that the IAT findings are likely to be applicable to an organizational context as well.

Studies matching women and men on comparable characteristics and experiences show a similar pattern to the empirical evidence on race. Greenhaus and Parasuraman examined how biased performance evaluations negatively influence women.[42] They surveyed more than 700 managers and found that among highly accomplished employees, men's successful job performance was more likely to be attributed to ability than women's. When Lyness and Thompson matched women and men in the financial services industry on their organizational position, performance ratings, and pay level, they found that although compensation was comparable, men had more authority, received more stock options, and were more satisfied with their future career opportunities than women.[43] In a follow-up study that matched comparable men and women executives, Lyness and Thompson found that women were more likely to emphasize the importance of successful and distinguishing accomplishments, such as turning a troubled business around or managing downsizing, than were men executives.[44] This emphasis suggests that the women executives had to accomplish major business feats to be successful. In addition, they found that men executives did not have to circumvent barriers to career advancement that were erected for women. Men did not report that they experienced negative consequences, such as exclusion from informal networks and lack of culture fit, to the extent that women did.

In an interview study, Davies-Netzley interviewed corporate presidents and chief officers and found that men leaders did not report barriers such as being excluded from important social networks.[45] Women interviewed in the study noted that opportunities are often blocked for women and that external barriers exist, whereas the men attributed their accomplishments to hard work and personal abilities. Ibarra showed that in four Fortune 500 firms, when controlling for occupation and hierarchical rank, men had more same-gender business relationships than women, and fast-track or high-potential men did not rely on relationships outside of their subunits. Fast-track or high-potential women, on the other hand, had to go outside of their immediate subgroups and establish relationships for career advancement.[46]

Roach matched women and men in-house attorneys in the financial services and manufacturing industries.[47] She found that men were located in large legal departments that offered career advancement and high-paying salaries, whereas women were concentrated in medium-sized legal departments with fewer opportunities to move up the corporate ladder. In addition, she attributes this disparity to the company's hiring practices and job assignments and not to the attorneys' individual choices.

The studies reviewed here are a very small subset of those that have examined racial and gender inequality in organizations. Some show that racial and gender parity exist in organizational settings, and others indicate that under certain circumstances, a bias may exist that favors women and minorities.[48] However, the studies are likely to be representative of the experiences that occur in core organizations and could very easily directly or indirectly map on to the sample list of unearned advantages described by McIntosh, Maier, and Johnson. Accordingly, unearned advantages can shape the experience of organization members.

The existence of unearned privilege does not mean that those who possess it do not work hard or that credit and accolades are not deserved. However, it implies that an additional asset is possessed that makes it more likely that whatever talent and skills they have will be showcased, recognized appropriately, and rewarded; however, the same may not be true with regard to those people without it. For example, consider that whites and males are nearly the only ones who have been able to penetrate the persistent barrier to top management. According to the Glass Ceiling Commission Report, 97 percent of the senior managers of Fortune 500 companies are white, and 95 percent are male.[49] Statistics for the Fortune 2000 industrial and service companies are comparable. Whites and males represent 95 percent and 96 percent, respectively, of the senior-level management positions. In contrast, women and minorities represent approximately 60 percent of the working population.

THEORETICAL FOUNDATION OF UNEARNED PRIVILEGE

Attribution theory, one of the most significant theories in social research, can provide a solid theoretical frame for analyzing white privilege, male privilege, and the principal tenet of invisibility. In its simplest form, the theory seeks to explain the way people make inferences about themselves and others. Attribution theory looks at how people make sense of their environment by ascribing cause and effect to personal dispositions or situational characteristics of the environment.[50]

A main finding related to attribution theory is that people tend to take more credit than is deserved for success and less than is warranted for failure.[51] Accordingly, when a reward is bestowed or success is achieved, people are less likely to attribute it to an external cause and more likely to attribute it an internal cause (i.e., their own ability, talent, or merit).[52] This occurs because success can potentially enhance the self-concept. People desire specific explanations for success and are sufficiently motivated to create the necessary attributional conditions to be able to come to desired conclusions.[53] Motives can bias reasoning, and in an organizational setting that values meritocracy and individual accomplishment, personal responsibility for successful performance may provide sufficient motivation for positive attributions.[54] However, race and gender often serve as proxies for ability, and competence and should not be so easily discarded in favor of positive personal attributions.

Certain demographics, specifically being male and white, are loaded with performance undertones or expectations, and unearned privileges are awarded because of them.[55] Specifically, when people make distinctions based on race and gender, these differences will be used when developing performance expectations. Regardless of whether the distinctions are relevant to the task or job assigned, they will be used when assessing performance effectiveness; advantages will accrue accordingly. These benefits are initially unearned because they are based on demographics, not the individual's demonstrated merit or ability. Unearned privileges based on categorical distinctions may include opportunity, favorable appraisals, high regard, and even power.[56]

This pattern of positive internal attributions made for the performance of whites and males may then lead to negative internal attributions made for underrepresented minorities and women. Accordingly, unearned privileges emerge because people suspect positive causes for the performance of whites and men, and negative causes for the performance of underrepresented minorities and women. Negative causes attributed then lead to negative evaluations which support inequality.

When whites and males acknowledge their privileged position and recognize that benefits accruing to them in their organization result from both earned and unearned advantages, privilege awareness may occur. Getting people to acknowledge that they benefit from unearned privileges is likely to be quite difficult. However, if mechanisms that may overcome self-serving biases to facilitate privilege awareness are identified, changes in attributions toward themselves and those without unearned privilege may occur.

Perhaps an intersection of unearned privilege from the viewpoints of the advantaged and disadvantaged may serve as an impetus because social hierarchies are interlocking; no group is privileged or disadvantaged on every continuum of unearned privilege. In the late 1980s, when McIntosh sought to examine male and white privilege in her women's studies academic curriculum, she noticed that her male colleagues often willingly acknowledged the women's disadvantage but seldom recognized their own privilege.[57] As she pondered what seemed to be a blatant injustice, she realized that because hierarchies in society are interlinked, there must also be a phenomenon of white privilege as well. The intersection of her disadvantage as a woman in her women's studies curriculum helped reveal her unearned privileges as a white person.

In a counseling psychology study, Ancis and Szymanski noted the influence of the intersection of privileged and nonprivileged state on counseling trainees.[58] They read McIntosh's article listing forty-six advantages available to her as a white person that were unavailable to her African American co-workers, friends, and acquaintances. The trainees were instructed to select one or more of these advantages and provide a written reaction. Excerpts from some of their responses indicate that the overlap of unearned privilege with disadvantaged categories may facilitate privilege awareness. One female student wrote, "I feel that there are a great many barriers to success for me because of my gender. What I had neglected to consider was the experiences of women of color, the effect of being doubly discriminated against. How I could have missed this, I don't know."[59] A second female student wrote, "Although I cannot know whether options will be open to me as a woman, I do know that women of color must consider many more barriers and prejudice than I do when looking for a job, getting promoted, and being seen as worthy in general."[60]

The excerpts indicate that people are embedded within myriad categories and no group or individual is completely privileged or nonprivileged in most social settings. The experience of nonprivilege in one setting, however, may help reveal unearned privilege in another. Observations of students who examined the privileges associated with their multiple socio-identities with respect to gender and race and articulated an understanding of unearned privilege and its impact on others suggest that an intersection of unearned privilege and disadvantage may assist in making unearned privileges visible.

CONCLUSION

The role of unearned privilege in organizational contexts should not remain in the background when examining racial and gender inequalities because its consideration may potentially contribute much to our understanding of organizational experiences. Unearned privileges should be moved to the forefront to gain a more comprehensive understanding of the considerable fissures that exist because of race and gender. These gaps will not be bridged by only considering a portion of the disparity equation. The ideas proposed with regard to privilege awareness are in their infancy, and just as an intersection of privilege may serve to increase privilege awareness, under certain conditions it may also decrease such awareness. A better understanding of what motivates acknowledgment of unearned privileges versus denial is needed, and other antecedents, such as individual ideologies, beliefs, and personal experiences, should be considered. Awareness of unearned privileges will not solve the problem of racial and gender inequality in U.S. organizations; however, it may be an innovative step toward a better understanding of difference and warrants attention in organizational research.

NOTES

1. S. M. Wildman, "Privilege in the Workplace: The Missing Element in Anti-discrimination Law," in S. M. Wildman, ed., *Privilege Revealed: How Invisible Preference Undermines America* (New York: New York University Press, 1996).

2. R. Linton, *The Study of Man* (New York: D. Appleton-Century, 1936).

3. L. J. Griffin and A. L. Kalleberg, "Stratification and Meritocracy in the United States: Class and Occupational Recruitment Patterns," *British Journal of Sociology* 32(1) (1981): 1–38.

4. A. S. Rosette and Leigh L. Thompson, "The Camouflage Effect: Separating Achieved Status and Unearned Privilege in Organizations," in Margaret A. Neale, Elizabeth A. Mannix, and Melissa Thomas-Hunt, eds., *Research on Managing Teams and Groups* (Stanford, CA: Stanford University Press, 2005), pp. 259–81.

5. Linton, *The Study of Man.*

6. Equal Employment Opportunity Commission Report, Charge statistics: FY 1992 through FY 2004. Available online at www.eeoc.gov/stats/charges.html.

7. See B. Reskin and P. Roos, *Job Queues, Gender Queues* (Philadelphia: Temple University Press, 1990); Robert L. Dipboye and Adrienne Colella, *Discrimination at Work: The Psychological and Organizational Bases* (Mahwah, NJ: Lawrence Erlbaum Associates, 2005); P. M. Blau, *Inequality and Heterogeneity* (New York: Free Press, 1977); R. M. Kanter, *Men and Women of the Organization* (New York: Basic Books, 1977).

8. J. Jones, *Prejudice and Racism* (New York: McGraw-Hill, 1997).

9. Title VII of the 1964 Civil Rights Act.

10. See examples in Sam Dillon, "Harvard Chief Defends His Talk on Women," *New York Times*, January 18, 2005, p. 16; Brian Davis, "OU Coach Resigns," *DallasNews.com*, May 2, 2005. Available online at www.dallasnews.com/s/dws/spt/colleges/oklahoma/stories/050205dnspooucoach.2326e5010.html.

11. G. Hofstede, *Culture's Consequences: International Differences in Work-Related Values* (Beverly Hills, CA: Sage, 1980).

12. M. J. Lerner, *The Belief in a Just World: A Fundamental Delusion* (New York: Plenum, 1980).

13. M. J. Lerner, D. T. Miller, and J. G. Holmes, "Deserving and the Emergence of Forms of Justice," in L. Berkowitz and E. Walster, eds., *Advances in Experimental Social Psychology: Equity Theory, Toward a General Theory of Social Interaction* (New York: Academic Press, 1976).

14. B. D. Tatum, *Why Are All the Black Kids Sitting Together in the Cafeteria?* (New York: Basic Books, 1999).

15. P. McIntosh, "White Privilege and Male Privilege: A Personal Account of Coming to See Correspondences through Work in Women's Studies," Working paper no. 189, Wellesley College Center for Research on Women (1988).

16. S. M. Wildman and A. D. Davis, "Making Systems of Privilege Visible," in S. Wildman, ed., *Privilege Revealed: How Invisible Preference Undermines America* (New York: New York University Press, 1996).

17. M. Kimmel and Abby Ferber, *Privilege* (Cambridge, MA: Westview Press, 2003).

18. B. Lowery, Eric David Knowles, and Miguel M. Unzueta, "Framing Inequality Safely: The Motivated Denial of White Privilege," in *Academy of Management Annual Meetings* (Honolulu: Academy of Management, 2005).

19. McIntosh, "White Privilege and Male Privilege."

20. P. Dressel, "Patriarchy and Social Welfare Work," *Social Problems* 34 (1987): 294–309.

21. P. S. Rothenberg, *White Privilege: Essential Readings on the Other Side of Racism* (New York: Worth Publishers, 2002).

22. McIntosh, "White Privilege and Male Privilege."

23. M. Maier, "Invisible Privilege," *Diversity Factor* Summer (1997): 28–33; A. G. Johnson, *Privilege, Power, and Difference* (New York: McGraw-Hill, 1997).

24. P. Tharenou. "Going Up? Do Traits and Informal Social Processes Predict Advancing in Management?" *Academy of Management Journal* 44(5) (2001): 1005–17; David A. Thomas, "The Impact of Race on Managers' Experiences of Developmental Relationships," *Journal of Organizational Behavior* 11(6) (1990): 479–92.

25. R. M. Kanter, *Men and Women of the Organization* (New York: Basic Books, 1977); James D. Westphal and Laurie Milton, "How Experience and Network Ties Affect the Influence of Demographic Minorities on Corporate Boards," *Administrative Science Quarterly* 45(2) (2000): 366–98.

26. Johnson, *Privilege, Power, and Difference*.

27. A. M. Morrison, C. T. Schreiber, and K. T. Price, *A Glass Ceiling Survey: Benchmarking Barriers and Practices* (Greensboro, NC: Center for Creative Leadership, 1995), p. 42.

28. W. J. Carrington and K. R. Troske, "Interfirm Segregation and the Black/White Wage Gap," *Journal of Labor Economics* 16 (1998): 231–60.

29. W. J. Carrington and K. R. Troske, "Gender Segregation in Small Firms," *Journal of Human Resources* 30 (1994): 503–33.

30. "Survey of Minority-Owned Business Enterprises," U.S. Department of Commerce, Census Bureau, 2001. Available online at www.census.gov/csd/mwb.

31. "Survey of Women-Owned Business Enterprises," U.S. Department of Commerce, Census Bureau, 2001. Available online at http://www.census.gov/csd/mwb.

32. E. W. Jones, "Black Managers: The Dream Deferred," *Harvard Business Review* 64 (1986): 84–93; Reskin and Roos, *Job Queues, Gender Queues*.

33. M. Bendick, C. Jackson, and V. Reinsoso, "Measuring Employment Discrimination through Controlled Experiments," *Review of Black Political Economy* 23 (1994): 25–48.

34. M. Bertrand and S. Mullainathan, "Are Emily and Greg More Employable Than Lakisha and Jamal? A Field Experiment on Labor Market Discrimination," University of Chicago Graduate School of Business Working Paper (2003).

35. K. Kraiger and J. K. Ford, "A Meta-Analysis of Ratee Race Effects in Performance Ratings," *Journal of Applied Psychology* 70(1) (1985): 56–65.

36. U.S. Department of Labor, 2000. Statistics report available at www.bls.gov.

37. D. A. Thomas, "The Impact of Race on Managers' Experiences of Developmental Relationships," *Journal of Organizational Behavior* 11(6) (1990): 479–92.

38. D. J. Maume, "Glass Ceilings and Glass Escalators," *Work and Occupations* 26(4) (1999): 483–509.

39. Jones, "Black Managers."

40. M. L. Baldwin and W. G. Johnson, "The Employment Effects of Wage Discrimination against Black Men," *Industrial and Labor Relations Review* 49(2) (1996): 302–16.

41. N. Dasgupta, D. E. McGhee, A. G. Greenwald, and M. R. Banaji, "Automatic Preference for White Americans: Eliminating the Familiarity Explanation," *Journal of Experimental Social Psychology* 36 (2000): 316–28; A. G. Greenwald, D. E. McGhee, and J. L. Schwartz, "Measuring Individual Differences in Implicit Cognition: The Implicit Association Task," *Journal of Personality and Social Psychology* 74 (1998): 1464–80.

42. J. Greenhaus and S. Parasuraman, "Job Performance Attributions and Career Advancement Prospects: An Examination of Gender and Race Effects," *Organizational Behavior and Human Decision Making Processes* 55(2) (1993): 273–97.

43. K. S. Lyness and D. E. Thompson, "Above the Glass Ceiling? A Comparison of Matched Samples of Female and Male Executives," *Journal of Applied Psychology* 82 (1997): 359–75.

44. K. S. Lyness and D. E. Thompson, "Climbing the Corporate Ladder: Do Female and Male Executives Follow the Same Route?" *Journal of Applied Psychology* 85(1) (2000): 86–101.

45. S. A. Davies-Netzley, "Women above the Glass Ceiling: Perceptions on Corporate Mobility and Strategies for Success," *Gender and Society* 12(3) (1998): 339–55.

46. H. Ibarra, "Paving an Alternative Route: Gender Differences in Managerial Networks," *Social Psychology Quarterly* 60(1) (1997): 91–102.

47. S. L. Roach, "Men and Women Lawyers in in-House Legal Departments: Recruitment and Career Patterns," *Gender and Society* 4(2) (1990): 207–19.

48. See C. L. Aberson and T. E. Ettlin, "The Aversive Racism Paradigm and Responses Favoring African-Americans: Meta-Analytic Evidence of Two Types of Favoritism," *Social Justice Research* 17(1) (2004): 25–46; A. S. Tsui and B. A. Gutek, "A Role Set Analysis of Gender Differences in Performance, Affective Relationships, and Career Success of Industrial Middle Managers," *Academy of Management Journal* 27(3) (1984): 619–35.

49. U.S. Glass Ceiling Commission, *Good for Business: Making Full Use of the Nation's Human Capital* (Washington, DC: U.S. Government Printing Office, 1995).

50. F. Heider, *The Psychology of Interpersonal Relations* (New York: Wiley, 1958).

51. M. Zuckerman, "Attribution of Success and Failure Revisited, or the Motivational Bias Is Alive and Well in Attribution Theory," *Journal of Personality* 47 (1979): 245–85.

52. L. Ross, "The Intuitive Psychologist and His Shortcomings: Distortions in the Attribution Process," in L. Berkowitz, ed., *Advances in Experimental Social Psychology* (New York: Academic Press, 1977), pp. 174–221.

53. J. M. Riggs, "Self-Handicapping and Achievement," in A. K. Boggiano and T. S. Pittman, eds., *Achievement and Motivation: A Social-Developmental Perspective* (New York: Cambridge University Press, 1992).

54. Z. Kunda, "The Case for Motivated Reasoning," *Psychological Bulletin* 108 (1990): 480–98.

55. D. G. Wagner and Joseph Berger, "Status Characteristics Theory: The Growth of a Program," in J. Berger and M. Zelditch, eds., *Theoretical Research Programs*, (Stanford, CA: Stanford University Press, 1993), pp. 23–63; J. Berger, B. P. Cohen, and M. Zelditch, "Status Characteristics and Social Interaction," *American Sociological Review* 37(3) (1972): 241–55.

56. M. Webster and J. E. Driskell, "Status Generalization: A Review and Some New Data," *American Sociological Review* 43 (1978): 220–36.

57. McIntosh, "White Privilege and Male Privilege."

58. J. R. Ancis and D. M. Szymanski, "Awareness of White Privilege among White Counseling Trainees," *Counseling Psychologist* 29(4) (2001): 548–69.

59. Ibid., p. 559.

60. Ibid.

12

Gender Inequality in the U.S. Labor Market: Evidence from the 2000 Census

Jongsung Kim

Working women have been an important component of the U.S. society, becoming more essential to our economy's advancement. Women composed 30 percent of the U.S. workforce in 1950; fifty years later, they made up 47 percent of the labor force.[1] During this time, women's labor market status has greatly improved due to changes in the social climate and passage of laws such as Title VII of the Civil Rights Act of 1964.[2] Over the past fifty years, women's labor force participation rate has steadily increased from 33.9 percent in 1950 to 59.2 percent in 2004, whereas that of men has declined from 86.4 percent to 73.3 percent during the same period. This leads to a remarkable lessening of the gender gap in labor force participation rates from 52.5 percentage points in 1950 to 14.1 percentage points in 2004.[3]

Due to the substantial rise in women's gainful employment since the 1950s, the average contemporary young woman expects to work after completing formal schooling, a belief shared by many women at all educational levels and racial and ethnic groups. An increase in women's educational attainment, the lower fertility rates, the availability of new household technologies and the emergence of flexible work schedules have encouraged women to enter the labor market.[4]

Women have made tremendous strides in all occupations, and notables such as former Supreme Court Justice Sandra Day O'Connor, Secretary of Sate Condoleezza Rice, and former Hewlett-Packard CEO Carly Fiorina epitomize the advancement and success of women in U.S. society.[5] Though some women have made progress on their own merits, gender equality in the U.S. labor market has not been achieved despite the Title VII's impact in providing employment opportunities for women. Many employed women still encounter disadvantages; they earn less and work in lower-status occupations than male peers with comparable credentials.

Although educational attainments are believed to enhance workers' productivity and status in the labor market, gender inequality persists even among college-educated workers.[6] Given the importance of women and the rapidly changing demographic characteristics in the U.S. labor market, this chapter investigates the current labor market status of women in earnings and occupations across four major ethnic groups: white and black women born in the United States and Hispanic and Asian immigrant women.[7]

Consideration of foreign-born population in this chapter mirrors the growing importance of immigrants in all aspects of U.S. society. In particular, race and ethnicity have long played an important role in shaping employment opportunities and labor market outcomes.[8]

Data used in this chapter are drawn from the 2000 Census 5 percent Public Use Microdata Sample (PUMS). The sample includes civilians who were sixteen to sixty-five years old, participated in the labor force, and did not reside in group quarters in 1999.[9] To obtain accurate estimates, using a large representative sample with detailed individual background information on variables such as education, occupation, geographic location, age, hours worked per week, weeks worked per year, and salary earnings is necessary. Census PUMS satisfies all these criteria and provides a large number of observations, essential for the analyses of ethnic minorities.

Sample descriptive statistics for socioeconomic variables are listed in Tables 12.1 and 12.2. Due to the large number of observations, a 20 percent random sample was used for white workers, and 100 percent samples were used for black, Hispanic, and Asian workers. Because men tend to work more weeks per year and more hours per week than women, an annual salary comparison between males and females is misleading. This chapter uses the hourly wage, obtained by dividing the annual salary income by the product of weeks worked per year and hours worked per week. Observations with missing values of hourly wage were dropped. The top and bottom 1 percent of the hourly wage were excluded to minimize the bias that could occur if the outliers were included.

Among those participating in the labor force with imputed hourly wage, white workers are slightly older than the rest of the sample. White men are the oldest, with a mean age of 39.2 years, and Hispanic men, with a mean age of 35.3 years, are the youngest. Across all racial and ethnic groups, men are found to work longer hours per week and more weeks per year. Consequently, men earn higher annual income. Men also earn higher hourly wages when controlling for hours worked per week and weeks worked per year. White and Asian workers report higher educational attainments than black and Hispanic workers in terms of number of years in schooling and the proportion with college and graduate degrees. Women report slightly higher number of years in school than men, except among Asian workers. Although no particular gender differences exist in the location of residence, black workers are heavily concentrated in the South (i.e., over 60 percent for both men and women), and Asian workers in the West. The percentage of men in management equals or exceeds that of women for all racial and ethnic groups.

TABLE 12.1. Characteristics of Native-born Workers (Standard Deviation in Parentheses)

	White Female*	White Male*	Black Female	Black Male
Age	39.05	39.22	37.35	37.59
	(12.27)	(12.22)	(11.80)	(11.98)
Married	0.612	0.634	0.374	0.472
	(0.482)	(0.481)	(0.484)	(0.499)
Annual salary income	24,578	41,122	22,207	27,457
	(19,175)	(39,749)	(17,146)	(21,640)
Hourly wage	13.73	18.83	12.92	14.50
	(8.81)	(14.99)	(9.06)	(10.19)
Hours worked a week	36.98	43.39	37.88	40.74
	(11.28)	(11.52)	(10.16)	(11.15)
Weeks worked a year	45.99	47.75	44.33	45.02
	(11.32)	(9.95)	(13.06)	(12.81)
Years of education	13.75	13.61	13.24	12.82
	(2.31)	(2.51)	(2.22)	(2.33)
Less than high school	0.092	0.123	0.156	0.207
	(0.289)	(0.328)	(0.363)	(0.405)
High school	0.290	0.298	0.295	0.344
	(0.449)	(0.457)	(0.456)	(0.475)
Some college (no degree)	0.265	0.241	0.301	0.257
	(0.441)	(0.428)	(0.459)	(0.437)
Associate degree	0.090	0.069	0.072	0.056
	(0.286)	(0.254)	(0.258)	(0.229)
Bachelor's degree	0.182	0.177	0.120	0.098
	(0.386)	(0.382)	(0.325)	(0.297)
Master's degree	0.071	0.059	0.045	0.028
	(0.257)	(0.237)	(0.206)	(0.164)
Professional degree	0.014	0.021	0.008	0.007
	(0.117)	(0.142)	(0.086)	(0.083)
Doctorate degree	0.006	0.011	0.003	0.004
	(0.077)	(0.106)	(0.058)	(0.061)
Managerial**	0.075	0.112	0.049	0.049
	(0.263)	(0.315)	(0.218)	(0.217)
Professional	0.107	0.132	0.099	0.081
	(0.309)	(0.338)	(0.299)	(0.273)
Technical	0.198	0.067	0.134	0.045
	(0.398)	(0.251)	(0.341)	(0.208)
Service	0.556	0.281	0.581	0.373
	(0.499)	(0.449)	(0.493)	(0.484)
Farming	0.003	0.011	0.002	0.009
	(0.051)	(0.102)	(0.044)	(0.093)
Manual	0.061	0.298	0.100	0.275
	(0.239)	(0.457)	(0.301)	(0.447)
Moving	0.021	0.099	0.032	0.166
	(0.142)	(0.299)	(0.177)	(0.372)
Northeast	0.205	0.198	0.131	0.125
	(0.404)	(0.399)	(0.337)	(0.331)
Midwest	0.283	0.282	0.175	0.171
	(0.450)	(0.449)	(0.379)	(0.377)
South	0.327	0.332	0.610	0.610
	(0.469)	(0.471)	(0.488)	(0.489)
West	0.185	0.188	0.084	0.097
	(0.389)	(0.391)	(0.278)	(0.296)
Number of observations	409,184	457,327	285,086	228,845

Source: 2000 Census 5 percent Public Use Microdata Sample.

*20 percent random sample.

**Broadly defined occupational categories are based on 471 occupations used in the 2000 Census PUMS.

TABLE 12.2. Characteristics of Foreign-born Workers (Standard Deviation in Parentheses)

	Hispanic Female	Hispanic Male	Asian Female	Asian Male
Age	37.01 (11.23)	35.31 (11.27)	38.97 (11.24)	38.91 (11.31)
Married	0.587 (0.492)	0.614 (0.487)	0.689 (0.463)	0.697 (0.459)
Annual salary income	16,985 (14,231)	22,193 (17,883)	28,256 (23,753)	42,997 (45,536)
Hourly wage	10.58 (7.87)	11.84 (8.74)	15.96 (11.73)	21.15 (18.74)
Hours worked a week	37.59 (10.46)	42.01 (10.32)	38.42 (11.78)	42.35 (12.11)
Weeks worked a year	43.18 (13.52)	45.26 (11.71)	45.29 (12.05)	46.64 (10.92)
Years of education	11.11 (4.33)	9.92 (4.46)	13.91 (3.71)	14.54 (3.79)
Less than high school	0.413 (0.492)	0.556 (0.497)	0.159 (0.366)	0.140 (0.347)
High school	0.210 (0.408)	0.201 (0.400)	0.159 (0.366)	0.140 (0.347)
Some college (no degree)	0.169 (0.375)	0.121 (0.326)	0.166 (0.372)	0.160 (0.367)
Associate degree	0.062 (0.240)	0.033 (0.179)	0.077 (0.266)	0.059 (0.236)
Bachelor's degree	0.101 (0.301)	0.056 (0.231)	0.295 (0.456)	0.263 (0.440)
Master's degree	0.028 (0.165)	0.016 (0.126)	0.093 (0.291)	0.143 (0.349)
Professional degree	0.014 (0.117)	0.013 (0.112)	0.032 (0.176)	0.041 (0.199)
Doctorate degree	0.004 (0.065)	0.004 (0.061)	0.018 (0.134)	0.052 (0.222)
Managerial	0.039 (0.194)	0.039 (0.196)	0.059 (0.235)	0.099 (0.298)
Professional	0.061 (0.239)	0.044 (0.205)	0.170 (0.376)	0.266 (0.442)
Technical	0.096 (0.295)	0.027 (0.161)	0.174 (0.379)	0.098 (0.297)
Service	0.548 (0.498)	0.309 (0.462)	0.446 (0.497)	0.306 (0.461)
Farming	0.034 (0.181)	0.062 (0.242)	0.004 (0.061)	0.004 (0.064)
Manual	0.179 (0.383)	0.398 (0.489)	0.134 (0.341)	0.179 (0.383)
Moving	0.043 (0.203)	0.119 (0.324)	0.014 (0.116)	0.049 (0.216)
Northeast	0.168 (0.374)	0.132 (0.338)	0.207 (0.405)	0.231 (0.421)
Midwest	0.065 (0.247)	0.078 (0.268)	0.106 (0.308)	0.110 (0.313)
South	0.278 (0.448)	0.301 (0.459)	0.200 (0.400)	0.208 (0.406)
West	0.488 (0.499)	0.489 (0.499)	0.487 (0.499)	0.450 (0.498)
Number of observations	138,154	232,659	82,632	93,280

Source: 2000 Census 5 percent Public Use Microdata Sample.

Another notable pattern in the occupational distribution is the heavy representation of women in the service occupation categories. Approximately 55 percent of women in the white, black, and Hispanic samples report that their occupations are service-related. Asian women are most highly represented in professional occupation categories with 45 percent reporting their occupations as service-related.

The proportion of males employed full-time (at least thirty-five hours per week and forty weeks per year) is the highest for white men at 82.3 percent. The lowest is for black men at 74.3 percent, whereas Asian and Hispanic men rank 79.5 percent and 76.6 percent, respectively. Women work fewer hours than men in paid employment. The proportion of full-time female workers is the highest for Asian women at 69.5 percent and lowest for Hispanic women at 63.2 percent. Black and white women come in at 68.2 percent and 65.8 percent, respectively.

Blacks are less likely to be married than workers in other groups. Only 37.4 percent of black women are married, which is the lowest proportion for any group. Black females may be more likely to head single-parent households than those in other ethnic or racial groups.[10]

Two notable patterns emerge in terms of number of observations in the sample. Hispanic men are substantially overrepresented, with 68.5 percent more Hispanic males than females, and black men are underrepresented, with 19.7 percent fewer black males than females.[11] Black men's underrepresentation is interesting, given that men in general tend to participate and work more actively in the labor market. Among blacks, women tend to be overrepresented in the labor force; one important reason for this is that black women traditionally have been more committed to the labor force than white women.[12]

EARNINGS

Although recent years have seen some narrowing of the long-standing gender earnings gap, women still receive substantially less than men. Women's median income was 60.5 percent of that of men in 1980 and rose to 76.3 percent in 2003.[13] If this pattern of narrowing gender earnings gap continues, it will still take another forty to fifty years for women to attain earnings equality with men. At this rate, even young women just starting their careers may not be able to see the earnings parity while they remain in the labor market.[14]

What are the sources of the gender earnings gap in the U.S. labor market? Much research has been and continues to be conducted to answer this question. Predominant theories about the gender earnings gap pertain to human capital and labor market discrimination. Human capital theory postulates that differences in relative levels of human capital such as education and work experience are responsible for the gender earnings gap and other gender-related labor market inequalities, such as occupational segregation. However, a significant portion of gender earnings gap cannot be explained by the human capital theory.[15]

This remaining portion is generally attributed to varying degrees of discrimination against women. Though overt and blatant discrimination stemming from prejudice now occur less frequently due to social climate changes and the enforcement of antidiscrimination laws, statistical discrimination or subtle discrimination are still common in the U.S. labor market. Statistical discrimination against women occurs when employers have limited information about their skills and other labor market–related characteristics, such as turnover propensity. In this situation, employers have an incentive to use easily observable characteristics such as gender to discriminate against women.

2000 Census PUMS Evidence of Gender and Racial Earnings Gap

Race and ethnicity have long played an important role in shaping employment opportunities and labor market outcomes. Table 12.3 presents the pattern of hourly wage for white, black, Hispanic, and Asian workers. White and Asian women (men) earn relatively higher average hourly wages of $13.73 ($18.83) and $15.96 ($21.15) respectively, whereas black and Hispanic women (men) earn relatively lower hourly wages of $12.92 ($14.50) and $10.58 ($11.84), respectively.

Table 12.3 presents the gender and racial earnings gap. For both men and women, white and Asian workers earn more than black and Hispanic workers. However, the gender wage ratio is higher for black and Hispanic workers. Although this finding may prima facie appear to reflect the better position of black and Hispanic women, a more accurate interpretation can be found in the lower hourly wages of black and Hispanic men. In other words, though black and Hispanic workers of both sexes earn less than white and Asian workers, the wage gaps are bigger for men. Table 12.3 shows that black and Hispanic men earn 77 percent and 63 percent, respectively, of what white men earn, whereas black and Hispanic women earn 94 percent and 77 percent of white women's wages, respectively.

TABLE 12.3.   Hourly Wage, Gender Wage Ratio, and Racial Wage Ratio

	White	Black	Hispanic	Asian
Hourly wage for women	$13.73	$12.92	$10.58	$15.96
Hourly wage for men	$18.83	$14.50	$11.84	$21.15
Gender wage ratio	0.729	0.891	0.894	0.755
Racial and ethnic wage ratio				
Women	1*	0.941	0.771	1.162
Men	1	0.770	0.629	1.123

Source: 2000 Census 5 percent PUMS.
*White is the base group for racial and ethnic wage ratio.

Age is an important factor in determining workers' earnings and wages. As workers age, they accumulate more job market experiences, which should be reflected in higher wages. However, men's and women's wages may not increase in the same manner as this occurs. Table 12.4, which lists the gender wage ratio across five equally divided age cohorts, depicts the effects of age on the gender wage ratio.[16]

In most cases, except for black men and Asian women, workers' hourly wages reaches a peak when they are between forty-six and fifty-five years old. Black men earn the highest wage between ages fifty-six and sixty-five, and Asian women between thirty-six and forty-five. For native-born citizens, white men at ages forty-six to fifty-five earn the highest hourly wage at $23.13; black women at ages sixteen to twenty-five earn the lowest hourly wage at $8.75. Among immigrants, Asian men at ages forty-six to fifty-five earn the highest hourly wage at $23.26 and Hispanic women at ages sixteen to twenty-five earn the lowest at $8.32, which is the lowest hourly wage for all groups.

Although workers earn more as they age, the wage gaps between age groups sixteen to twenty-five and twenty-six to thirty-five is the largest for all racial and ethnic groups. One reason is because some workers in the sixteen to twenty-five years age group have not completed high school. The lack of a high school diploma and lack of job experiences due to their youth may lead workers in this age cohort into working in occupations that command low wages.

How are gender wage ratio and age related? Figure 12.1 shows the patterns of gender wage ratios of all racial and ethnic groups across five age cohorts. Across all age cohorts and racial and ethnic groups, women earn less than men. Another noteworthy pattern is the relationship between age and wage. As workers age, the gender wage ratios become lower in all cases, except for black

TABLE 12.4. Hourly Wage and Gender Wage Ratio across Age Cohorts

	16–25	26–35	36–45	46–55	56–65
White women	$8.67	13.77	15	15.69	14.45
White men	9.78	16.81	21.05	23.13	22.28
Wage ratio	0.887	0.819	0.713	0.678	0.649
Black women	$8.75	12.42	13.94	15.67	14.67
Black men	9.3	13.8	15.73	17.5	17.65
Wage ratio	0.941	0.900	0.886	0.895	0.831
Hispanic women	$8.32	10.41	11.29	11.74	11.38
Hispanic men	8.72	11.42	13.42	14.16	13.82
Wage ratio	0.954	0.912	0.841	0.829	0.823
Asian women	$11.41	16.87	17.12	16.11	15.54
Asian men	12.92	20.81	22.99	23.26	22.77
Wage ratio	0.883	0.811	0.745	0.693	0.682

Source: 2000 Census 5 percent PUMS.

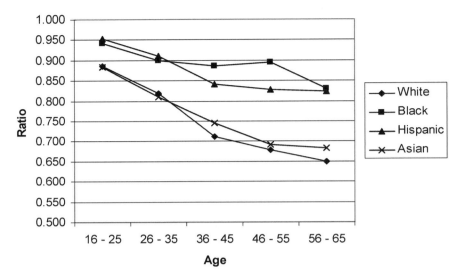

FIGURE 12.1.   Gender wage ratio by age cohort.
Source: 2000 Census 5 percent PUMS.

workers ages forty-six to fifty-five, suggesting that the gender wage gap widens for older workers. Thus, older women seem doubly disadvantaged. As Gregory succinctly states, "women get old at a younger age than men."[17] White and Asian workers have similar gender wage ratios with respect to age cohorts; so do black and Hispanic workers. Again gender wage gaps are smaller for black and Hispanic workers than for white and Asian workers for all age cohorts.

Education and Earnings

Education is one of the most important factors in enhancing employees' productivity at work and marketability in the labor market. A Census Bureau report shows that in 2003, for the second year in a row, women had a higher rate of high school completion (85 percent) than men (84 percent). Over the past decade, women also made greater strides in college education. Women experienced an increase of nearly 7 percentage points in the proportion with a bachelor's degree in the past decade, reaching 26 percent, whereas men experienced an increase of about 4 percentage points, reaching 29 percent. The proportions having completed some college (or more education) were more similar—52 percent of women and 53 percent of men.[18]

In U.S. society, where individual ability is the most valuable criterion, education has been regarded as the key to opportunity and success. In particular, obtaining a college education is considered crucial in determining an individual's eventual location in the social class system and therefore has even more important implications for intergenerational mobility.[19] Because no convincing evidence shows that intergenerational mobility has improved over time, children of low-wage workers without a college education also may lack an undergraduate degree and therefore also earn low wages.[20]

Tables 12.1 and 12.2 list detailed information about the educational attainments of racial and ethnic groups. For both men and women, white and Asian workers' educational attainments are higher than those of black and Hispanic workers. Hispanic workers' educational levels are the lowest for both men and women at ten and eleven years, respectively, which are insufficient for high school diplomas. Table 12.5 and Figure 12.2 show the gender wage gap by eight detailed education categories across racial and ethnic groups.

Although women's progress in educational attainment in recent decades partly explains the narrowing gender wage gap, at every education level, however, women continue to earn less than similarly educated men. Educational gains have not yet translated into full equity for women in the labor market.

Among women, whites and Asians are more likely to have a college degree than blacks and Hispanics. In all race categories except Hispanic, the percentage having a college degree, excluding graduate degrees, is slightly higher

TABLE 12.5.   Gender Wage Gap by Educational Categories

	Edu1	Edu2	Edu3	Edu4	Edu5	Edu6	Edu7	Edu8
White women	$8.66	10.98	12.37	14.53	17.91	21.91	22.72	23.92
White men	11.82	15.26	17.19	18.78	25.04	29.38	40.37	32.34
Wage ratio	0.732	0.720	0.720	0.774	0.715	0.746	0.563	0.740
Black women	9.39	10.87	12.5	14.31	17.96	23.23	23.23	25.1
Black men	11.12	13.01	14.89	16.71	20.32	24.47	27.74	27.01
Wage ratio	0.844	0.836	0.839	0.856	0.884	0.949	0.837	0.929
Hispanic women	8.62	9.86	11.29	12.04	14.39	19.22	16.43	21.94
Hispanic men	10.24	11.48	13.59	14.44	17.97	22.16	19.8	24.98
Wage ratio	0.842	0.859	0.831	0.834	0.801	0.867	0.829	0.878
Asian women	9.98	11.44	12.98	15.66	19.31	23.26	27.08	24.58
Asian men	11.82	13.41	15.54	17.92	23.84	31.04	39.87	32.47
Wage ratio	0.844	0.853	0.835	0.874	0.810	0.749	0.679	0.757

Source: 2000 Census 5 percent PUMS.
Edu1: Less than high school.
Edu2: High school.
Edu3: Some college (no degree).
Edu4: Associate degree.
Edu5: Bachelor's degree.
Edu6: Master's degree.
Edu7: Professional degree.
Edu8: Doctorate degree.

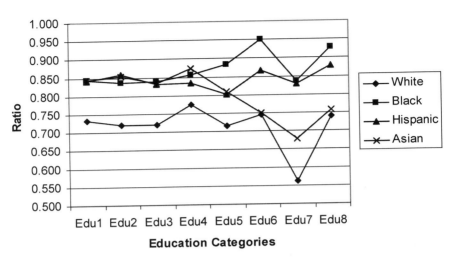

FIGURE 12.2. Gender wage gap by education.
Source: 2000 Census 5 percent PUMS.

for women than for men. The gender gap in college education is significant for the Hispanic sample, 10.5 percent for women versus 5.6 percent for men.

As expected, women with college degrees earn more than those without. For example, on an hourly wage basis in the 2000 Census PUMS data, white women with four-year college degrees (Edu5) earn approximately 65 percent more than the hourly wage of white women with high school education (Edu2), $17.91 versus $10.98. The college premium of approximately 65 percent higher hourly wage also applies to black ($17.96) and Asian women ($19.31). For Hispanic women, the college premium is much smaller at 45 percent, mainly because the college-educated Hispanic educated women earn at least 25 percent less, at $14.39, than comparably educated women in other races.

Figure 12.2 shows downward spikes in the gender wage ratio for the professional degree category that includes some of the most lucrative occupations.[21] This suggests the presence of a glass ceiling, in which women with relatively high earnings and positions still cannot reach the top due to remaining barriers.

Inspection of the 2000 Census PUMS data reveals that for all age cohorts and across all racial and ethnic groups, educational attainments in the form of number of years in school and the proportion of college degree are the highest for age cohort twenty-six to thirty-five. The details are listed in Table 12.6. Interestingly, women surpass men in college education at the age cohort twenty-five to thirty-six for all racial and ethnic groups. Black and Hispanic workers are found to be less likely to have college degrees. Given the importance of a college education, it is almost certain that racial earnings gap will persist into the future.

Workers in the age cohort twenty-six to thirty-five will most likely remain in the labor market for another twenty to thirty years, or longer as life expectancies

TABLE 12.6.   Educational Attainment and Proportion of College
Graduates for Age Cohort 26–35

	Years of Education	Proportion of College Graduates
White women	14.2	0.26
White men	14.1	0.23
Black women	13.5	0.15
Black men	13.1	0.12
Hispanic women	11.5	0.12
Hispanic men	10.1	0.06
Asian women	14.7	0.34
Asian men	15.1	0.31

Source: 2000 Census 5 percent PUMS.

improve and more people continue to work into their seventies. When this happens, questions to be answered include: How large will the gender wage gap be for these young workers? Will women's greater educational attainment relative to men in the age twenty-six to thirty-five cohort help narrow the gender wage gap in the future? Will women's educational advantage cancel out the widening of the gender wage gap that typically occurs as workers get older? The prognosis here is still uncertain because more factors must be considered to properly answer such questions. If a greater proportion of women than men earn college degrees, other things equal, women's earnings should increase. However, this may not happen because what women study in college[22] and what they do in the labor market may be more important than how long they stay in school.[23]

Women's statistical dominance among college students is expected to continue. According to a report by American Association of University Women, 56 percent of undergraduates in the United States were women in 2000, up from 42 percent in 1970. The proportion of women graduate students grew from 39 to 58 percent during this period. The most dramatic change occurred in professional programs such as medicine, law, and business, where the proportion of women shot up from 9 percent in 1970 to 47 percent in 2000.[24]

Although Asian workers report more years of education and a higher proportion of college degree than the rest of workers, some may have attended college outside the United States. Foreign college degrees may not necessarily translate into higher earning in the U.S. labor market. Approximately 28 percent of Asian women and 37.3 percent of Asian men of age cohort twenty-six to thirty-five are believed to have received their college education outside the United States.[25]

Regardless of gender, those with college degrees enjoyed a real increase in purchasing power between 1973 and 2001. Women without these credentials saw little or no improvement, and men with a high school education or less saw a decline in the purchasing power of their earnings. Nevertheless, though women with a college degree earn considerably more than those without it, females still earn less than males with similar educational backgrounds. In fact, in the data used for this chapter, men are found to earn more than women in all categories of educational attainment across all racial and ethnic groups.

Besides increasing earnings power in the current generation, having a college degree has long-term implications. High school graduates whose parents have no post–high school education are three times less likely to enroll in a four-year college than their counterparts with a parent who graduated from college.[26]

Because Hispanic workers are less likely to earn a college degree than any other group, their income potential and opportunities are severely curtailed. Moreover, their communities and the nation lose the benefit of their full parti-cipation. Because power and success are so closely linked to educational attain-ment, our notion of U.S. society as an equitable place is severely challenged when a significant population group has an obviously limited educational achievement.[27] To the extent that Hispanic workers are least likely to have obtained a college education, their low wages will most likely persist in the future.

The percent of black women who are single heads of households may be another concern. Earning less than all male workers and all other female workers except Hispanic women, black women comprise 31.6 percent of single-mother households. The economic hardship they experience may adversely affect their children's educational attainment, thereby perpetuating low eco-nomic status in the future.

OCCUPATIONS

A survey by Catalyst, an organization to promote women in upper-level jobs, shows that although women made up 47 percent of the U.S. workforce in 2000, they held only 11.7 percent of board of director positions in Fortune 500 com-panies. Furthermore, only 12.5 percent of the corporate officers of those firms were women. According to a projection based on the average rate of increase in appointments of women to corporate offices, more women than men will be employed in the workforce in 2020. But even then, men will still hold nearly 75 percent of such positions in Fortune 500 companies.[28] Barriers to women's ad-vancement are not restricted to the corporate hierarchies in the U.S. labor market. Even at the United Nations, which advocates issues of international peace and justice, including gender equality, women still face obstacles in reaching senior management and professional positions. In 2004, women formed 83.3 percent of staff at the lowest professional level, P-1, but 16.7 percent of the highest staff level, the Under-Secretaries-General.[29]

Gender occupational segregation is another important factor at the heart of debates about gender inequality in the U.S. labor market.[30] Women are often segregated into a small number of female-dominated occupations, thereby making their proportion in those occupations much higher than the ratio of women in the entire labor market. A side effect of occupational segregation is that most of those predominantly female occupations, labeled as women's jobs, pay low wages, even controlling for measured personal characteristics of workers and a variety of characteristics of occupations.[31]

Gender occupational segregation has been considered to be responsible for the gender earnings gap. Persistent occupational segregation may lead women entering the job market or in early career stages to wrongly conclude that women's lower position in the occupational distribution is legitimate. Occupational choice is often the product of tradition and culture. Because tradition dies hard, the persistence of gender occupational segregation may discourage young women from developing their full potential in terms of education and job training even before they enter the labor market. This may perpetuate gender inequalities in the future by positioning many women only at lower levels of the career ladder.

From the demand perspective, taste-based discrimination against women has been blamed as a causal factor in gender occupational segregation. Even without this type of blatant discrimination, statistical discrimination, which was defined earlier, also may have contributed to occupational segregation. An argument often made from the supply side is that women generally anticipate shorter, less continuous careers and are forced to choose jobs that are compatible with household and family duties perceived to be theirs. This type of situation, described as societal discrimination by Blau and colleagues, leads women to take occupations that require smaller human capital investment and have lower penalties for breaks in the careers.[32]

As Table 12.7 shows, the gender wage gap is prevalent in every occupational category across all racial and ethnic groups, ranging from a 3.1 percent gap for Hispanic women in the farming category, to 32.5 percent for white women in managerial occupations. Gender wage gaps generally seem less severe in such labor-intensive categories as farming and moving and also are less pronounced for black and Hispanic than for white and Asian women. This does not mean that black and Hispanic women's labor market positions are better than those of white and Asian counterparts because black and Hispanic men fare less well than white and Asian men. Though black and Hispanic women earn 94 and 77 percent of what white women earn, the pay gap by race is wider for male workers. Black and Hispanic men earn only 76 and 57 percent, respectively, of white men's pay.

Most of the top fifteen female-dominated occupations, in which at least 500,000 workers are employed, are secondary, meaning that they assist other workers in higher positions.[33] Also many, except for nursing, neither pay well nor lead workers into a promotion track. Two of the most highly female-dominated occupations are secretaries and administrative assistants and receptions and information clerks. Employers routinely engage in ageism, favoring younger women for positions in these occupations.[34]

TABLE 12.7. Gender Wage Ratio across Racial and Ethnic Groups and Occupational Categories

	Managerial	Professional	Technical	Service	Farming	Manual	Moving
White women	$18.88	17.98	17.45	11.21	8.35	11.24	10.76
White men	27.95	24.93	24.13	15.92	10.51	16.09	14.19
Wage ratio	0.675	0.721	0.723	0.704	0.794	0.699	0.758
Black women	18.56	17.42	16.88	11.12	8.76	11.35	11.39
Black men	21.38	19.94	19.27	12.58	9.2	14.39	13.25
Wage ratio	0.868	0.874	0.876	0.884	0.952	0.789	0.860
Hispanic women	15.87	15.87	14.72	9.74	8.03	8.92	8.75
Hispanic men	18.64	18.84	18.43	10.74	8.29	11.54	11.24
Wage ratio	0.851	0.842	0.799	0.907	0.969	0.773	0.778
Asian women	20.86	22.04	22.39	12.22	9.07	10.84	10.94
Asian men	30	28.03	29.64	14.46	11.75	15.05	13.74
Wage ratio	0.695	0.786	0.755	0.845	0.772	0.720	0.796

Source: 2000 Census 5 percent PUMS.

Nursing, though a female-dominated occupation, does not have the same disadvantages in earnings and opportunity associated with other such occupations. The nursing profession requires special training and pays higher wages than nearly all top fifteen female-dominated occupations. However, even within nursing, the 2000 Census PUMS revealed that men earn more than women across all racial and ethnic groups.[35] For preschool teachers, another occupation in which women predominate, females earn less than males; the earnings gap ranges from 2 percent for Hispanics to 37 percent for whites.

Although gender occupational segregation has been believed to be a major source of gender earnings inequality, women who work in occupations where segregation is not particularly severe still encounter a gender wage gap. Two of the most prestigious occupations in terms of social status are lawyers and medical doctors (physician and surgeon); women represented 29.4 of job holders in both in 2004.[36] Even in these relatively integrated, elite occupations for which a professional graduate degree is a prerequisite, women still earn less than men across all racial and ethnic groups according to 2000 Census PUMS. This is partly because white male medical doctors and lawyers earn the highest wages in comparison with white women and all other racial and ethnic groups; thus the gender wage gaps are the largest for white workers in these occupations. For lawyers, gender wage ratios are 68 percent for whites, 92.4 percent for blacks, 90.2 percent for Hispanics, and 89.2 percent for Asians. For physicians and surgeons, gender wage ratios are 50.6 percent for whites, 81.1 percent for blacks, 84.4 percent for Hispanics, and 66.4 percent for Asians.

The different impact of education on men's and women's earnings has been neglected in the debate about the effects of educational attainment on the gender earnings gap and occupational segregation. Women's presence in professional programs, such as business, law, and medical schools, is rising. However, even when a woman has equivalent qualifications as her male peers, her advancement in narrowly defined occupational categories where old boy networks flourish is, unfortunately, not ensured. Therefore, physicians who are female still earn less than their comparably trained male peers.

The findings from the data that indicate that even the most highly educated and trained women still encounter a gender wage gap have the following implications. First, although educational attainment enhances a worker's wage, the pattern differs between the sexes and is skewed in men's favor. Second, the findings may be due to the presence of internal segregation within such broadly defined occupations as lawyers and medical doctors, where many specialties and subspecialties exist.

The percentage of women partners at America's largest law firms slightly increased from 15.7 percent in 1998 to 17.1 percent in 2004. However, these numbers may equalize in the future because 48 percent of JD enrollment in 2004 were women, and the proportion of female associates at large law firms grew from 39 percent in 1998 to 47.8 percent in 2004.[37]

The gender gap persists, however. The typical female physician received $55,000 less in total compensation than her male counterpart. One reason typically cited is that women are more likely to choose lower-paying specialties or those in less demanding fields.[38] For example, few women are invasive cardiologists or orthopedic or thoracic surgeons. Women physicians also tend to work fewer hours than their male colleagues.[39]

Women medical doctors earn less than male doctors based on a survey for ten categories. Gender earnings gaps are larger for specialties with higher earnings. Two specialties with the highest earnings are invasive cardiology and orthopedic surgery, where gender earnings ratios based on median earnings in 2001 were 79.2 and 66.3 percent, respectively. Two specialties with the lowest earnings are family practice without obstetrics and internal medicine, where gender earnings ratio are 83.4 and 84.3 percent, respectively.[40] One factor contributing to disparity is that female doctors may prefer not to be self-employed.[41] Many believe that hospitals offer greater job security and recognize that at most urban hospitals, there is no need to be on call twenty-four hours a day as in private practice. Thus, physicians who avoid self-employment would have more flexibility to attend to family or other concerns.

The lower wages of women lawyers and physicians are due to vertical segregation, which refers to the distribution of men and women within the same occupation when one sex is more likely to be at a higher grade or level. As women's educational attainment rises, so do their earnings. A recent report shows that approximately half of the incoming students in medical schools and law schools are women. After graduation, with proper training and licenses, they surely will earn more than men without such qualifications. Female lawyers will make more than male paralegals; female physicians will be paid more than male nurses. This implies that education and training may reduce horizontal gender occupational segregation, which exists across occupations but will not necessarily lessen vertical segregation.

Although the negative impact of gender occupational segregation on the wage gap is well established, these two aspects of gender inequalities are related in a more complex manner than normally assumed. In some male-dominated occupations, women may earn as much as men due to the skill-based nature of compensation. However, even in nursing, one of the most female-dominated occupations, a gender wage gap favoring men still exists. In the relatively integrated occupations such as lawyer and physician, women are paid less than men despite their professional degrees and training. These findings suggest that more factors must be considered to understand the relationship between gender occupational segregation and the gender earnings gap.

Despite the changes in the notion of women's role at home and in society, many women still ponder over noneconomic factors, such as raising children, dealing with family concerns, deciding whether to work, and choosing occupations. To identify sources of occupational segregation and wage gap, more efforts should be focused on analyzing the sociological and psychological aspects of the decision-making process of women in the labor market.

Perception of gender roles, which is important in determining the women's future career path, develops in the very early stages of work. Consequently employees encounter gender inequality in the labor market as early as in their teens. Based on a Dutch data set, boys and girls with almost identical backgrounds seem to accumulate different human capital in the earliest stage of their labor market careers. Even within the highly homogenous groups, boys earn substantially more than girls. Furthermore, the earnings gap cannot be explained by differences in participation rates and hours of work or by gender wage gaps within job types. Rather, it occurs because girls work more in job types with relatively low wages, in particular, baby-sitting.[42] Though these findings are based on Dutch data, similar anecdotal evidence supports the existence of gender differences in teens' compensation in the United States.

CONCLUSION

Title VII has had an enormous impact in providing employment opportunities for women and allowing them to advance. Now, four decades after Title VII, gender inequality in the U.S. labor market persists across racial and ethnic groups, raising the question of whether true gender-based workplace equality is possible. Amartya Sen, a Nobel Prize laureate in economics, believes that "gender inequality can take many different forms, not being a homogeneous phenomenon, but a collection of disparate and interlinked problems." He argues that "informed and critical agency" is important in combating gender inequality of every kind.[43]

Due to the changes in the social climate and the enforcement of anti-discrimination laws, identifying and addressing the blatantly overt discrimination against women in the labor market is less problematic. The covert and subtle discrimination, however, remains difficult to prove. Because much gender discrimination emanates from a false presumption about women's ability and work ethic, reducing it will be possible only after ascertaining accurate data about women's qualifications and the changing views of women in the labor market. Public education beginning at a young age may positively affect the latter, but early socialization experiences, which parents and other caregivers strongly influence, are also important.

Despite the fact that occupational segregation and gender earnings gap still persist even among highly educated women, the progress of women depends heavily on educational attainment. College and higher education are increasingly important to women's success in the labor market. Policy attention should be focused not only on encouraging female students, especially young minority women, to attend and graduate from college but also on urging them to study subjects that are traditionally known as male fields (such as engineering) that are associated with higher pay, while noting that educational parity alone does not ensure the elimination of gender gap.

With the foreign-born population steadily rising, discussion of the gender and race inequality issues is incomplete without considering immigrant workers. Between 2000 and 2100, the non-Hispanic white percentage of the U.S. population is expected to drop from 72 to 40 percent and will continue to fall after 2100. In contrast, the Hispanic share will jump from 12 to 32 percent and will continue to rise. Although the Asian population is expected to grow from 4 to 13 percent, non-Hispanic blacks will grow marginally from 13 to 15 percent.[44]

Mainly due to the lower educational attainment, Hispanic workers, Mexican immigrants in particular, report low economic status in the U.S. labor market.[45] Issues surrounding gender inequality are very complex, especially in the era of racial and ethnic diversity. To address labor market inequalities across gender, race, and ethnic groups, policy should focus on problems that differ across racial and ethnic groups. Although all groups of women suffer from horizontal and vertical segregation, the latter is a more prevalent problem for white and Asian women than for black and Hispanic women. Though gender wage gaps are smaller for black and Hispanic workers, this is due to the lower economic performance of black and Hispanic men.

For Hispanic workers, the ethnic wage gap seems more common than the gender wage gap. Due to much economic hardship among Hispanic workers without high school diplomas, returning to school is almost impossible for them. An alternative to the regular day school is the community-based night school where English language education can be offered to improve workers' communication skills. This will in turn enhance their marketability and may eliminate their current status as the lowest socioeconomic group.

Many women's educational achievements and occupational choices reflect influences of the culture in which they were raised. Therefore, understanding and projecting gender inequalities in Hispanic and Asian communities require a thorough knowledge about male-dominated Asian and Hispanic culture.

Although some women may voluntarily choose to work in low-paying, low-status positions in return for a more flexible work schedule to fulfill family and other obligations, society has not pressured men to make such decisions.[46]

Many women are literally forced into accepting their "choices" due to lack of better alternatives. Strong public commitment to parental leave for men and women, removal of the stigma associated with using it, and reliable child care policies may address some of these concerns.

In addition to being a form of social injustice, gender occupational segregation reflects inefficient use of human resources and rigidities in the labor market and society.[47] Meritocracy is highly valued in the United States and has been a basis for fulfillment of the American dream. What workers know and can do in the labor market should take precedence over their gender, race, and ethnicity.

NOTES

1. "Gender Inequality at Work," UWA Research Bulletin, Summer 2003. Available online at www.uaw.org/publications/jobs_pay/index2003.cfm.

2. Title VII is the short name given to various provisions contained in the Civil Rights Act of 1964 and later amended by the Equal Employment Act of 1972. It is the broadest-based and most comprehensive legislation in the area of antidiscrimination. Title VII makes it unlawful for an employer to fail to hire, refuse to hire, to discharge, to classify, to segregate, to deprive of employment opportunities, or otherwise discriminate or adversely effect the status of the employee or the compensations, terms, conditions or privileges of the employee on the basis of the employee's race, color, religion, gender, or national origin. Raymond F. Gregory, *Women and Workplace Discrimination: Overcoming Barriers to Gender Equality* (New Brunswick, NJ: Rutgers University Press, 2003).

3. For 1950 data, see *Economic Report of the President 2000*, Table B-37. For 2004 data, see *Economic Report of the President 2005*, Table B-39.

4. Francine D. Blau, Patricia Simpson, and Deborah Anderson, "Continuing Progress? Trends in Occupational Segregation in the United States over the 1970s and 1980s," NBER Working Paper no. 6716, 1998.

5. In 1952, after Sandra Day O'Connor graduated third in her class from Stanford Law School—a year early—she could not even find work in private practice as a female attorney. Three decades later, Justice O'Connor began her journey to be the first woman appointed to the U.S. Supreme Court in 1981, serving in that position until 2005.

6. Whether education enhances worker's productivities or is just a sheepskin has been a hot topic of many debates. Even if education does not make workers more productive, many employers still consider education a strong signal of worker's productivity because it takes dedication, perseverance, and intelligence to complete school

successfully, especially four-year college. College-educated workers are also believed to be more adaptable and quick to respond to the always changing high-technology work environments. Paul G. Keat and Philip Young, *Managerial Economics*, 5th ed. (New York: Prentice Hall, 2006).

7. An immigrant is defined to be a person who was born outside the United States.

8. Over the past three decades, the proportion of foreign-born population, or immigrants, in the United States increased from 4.7 percent in 1970 to 11.1 percent in 2000. This is the highest record since 1930, when 11.6 percent of the population was foreign-born. The 31.1 million immigrants reported in Census 2000 represent a 57 percent increase over the 1990s, which exceeds 40 percent in 1980s and 47 percent in 1970s. *Profile of the Foreign-Born Population in the United Sates: 2000*, P23–206, December 2001, U.S. Census Bureau.

9. Workers who are older than sixty-five are excluded because there is a risk that nonrandom mortality would bias the sample of older workers in favor of the more healthy.

10. In March 2000, there were 9,681,000 total single mothers. The proportions of white, black, and Hispanics were 49.2 percent, 31.6 percent, 16.2 percent, respectively (Jason Fields and Lynne Casper, *Current Population Report P20–537: America's Families and Living Arrangements*, 2001, Table 4). The remaining 3.1 percent is assumed to apply for Asian and other omitted groups. According to a census report, the racial and ethnic composition of the United States in 2000 was as follows: 75.1 percent white, 12.3 percent black, 12.5 percent Hispanics, and 3.6 percent Asian. The reason that the sum of the proportions exceed 100 percent is some individuals were counted in more than one category (Elizabeth Grieco and Rachel Cassidy, *Overview of Race and Hispanic Origin 2000*, Census 2000 Brief, March 2001, C2KBR/01-1, Table 1). The comparison between the racial/ethnic composition of the U.S. population and the proportion of single mothers implies that black women may be more likely to head single-parent households than those in other ethnic or racial groups.

11. For white and Asians groups, there are more men than women at 11.7 percent and 12.9 percent, respectively.

12. Mary Corcoran, "The Economic Progress of African American Women," in Irene Browne, ed., *Latinas and African American Women at Work* (New York: Russell Sage, 1999). For the most part, black women throughout history have been forced to work outside their homes—forced first by slave holders and then by the threat of poverty that plagued their families after emancipation (Jacqueline Jones, *Labor of Love, Labor of Sorrow: Black Women, Work, and the Family from Slavery to the Present* [New York: Basic Books, 1985], p. 323).

13. The figures are based on money income of year-round full-time workers. For 1980 data, see *Economic Report of the President 2000*, Table B-31. For 2003 data, see *Economic Report of the President 2005*, Table B-33.

14. The gender wage ratio varies significantly by demographic group. The ratio was about 88 percent for both blacks and Hispanics in 2003; for whites it was 79 percent; and for Asians it was 78 percent. *Highlights of Women's Earnings*, Report no. 978, U.S. Department of Labor Bureau of Labor Statistics, 2004.

15. Francine Blau argues that human capital variables (actual labor market experience, education in years, whether the person has a college diploma, whether the person has an advanced degree) explain 32 percent of gender wage gap in 1988 data. On

the other hand, Solomon Polachek argues that depending on methods, the proportion of gender wage gap explained by human capital varies from less than 7 percent to anywhere between 85 and 95 percent. ("Why Is There a Gender Wage Gap and Why Is It Shrinking?" Debate between Solomon Polachek and Francine Blau at the Center for the Study of Inequality, Cornell University on March 2003); Available online at www .inequality.com/events/papers/Contorversies%20About%20Inequality%20Debate%20 Series/CAIDebate2.PDF.

16. Because the data used here are cross-sectional, the results in Table 10.4 fail to show the dynamics between age and gender wage ratio. In other words, the gender wage ratio of white workers age sixteen to twenty-five will not necessarily be 0.713, which is the gender wage ratio of white workers in age cohort thirty-six to forty-five, after they spend another twenty years in the labor market.

17. Gregory, *Women and Workplace Discrimination.*

18. "Some college" includes respondents who have completed some college but have no degree and those who have completed an associate's degree; Nicole Stoops, *Educational Attainment in the United States: 2003*, Current Population Reports, P20–550, 2004.

19. Sharlene Nagy Hesse-Biber and Gregg Lee Carter, *Working Women in America: Split Dreams*, 2nd ed. (Oxford: Oxford University Press, 2005), p. 137.

20. Gottschalk used Panel Study of Income Dynamics (PSID) to find that of those who were in the lowest quintile of incomes in 1974, 42.1 percent were still in the same position in 1991. Of those individuals who managed to escape the lowest quintile, most did not make a significant progress, with the largest group moving to the next quintile. Only 7.8 percent were able to move up to the top quintile. Peter Gottschalk, "Inequality, Income Growth, and Mobility: The Basic Facts," *Journal of Economic Perspectives* 11 (1997): 21–40.

21. Examples of professional degree are MD, DDS, DVM, and JD. MBA is included in graduate degree. *Census 2000 Summary File 3 Technical Documentation*, SF3/ 15 (RV), March 2005.

22. According to Lois Joy, "Encouraging women to complete college and major in traditionally male-dominated fields has, in the past, contributed to the closing of the wage gap, but the evidence suggests that educational parity alone does not ensure labor market parity." Lois Joy, "Salaries of Recent Male and Female College Graduates: Educational and Labor Market Effects," *Industrial and Labor Relations Review* 56(4) (2003): 606–21.

23. Changes in labor market experiences have been more important than changes in education in closing the gender wage gap. Blau and Kahn indicate that changes in accumulated experience have been far larger and explain a much larger share of the increase in female/male wages than do changes in education; Francine D. Blau and Lawrence M. Kahn, "Swimming Upstream: Trends in the Gender Wage Differential in the 1980s," *Journal of Labor Economics* 15(1) (1997): 1–42.

24. National Center for Education Statistics, *Digest of Education Statistics* (Washington, DC: U.S. Department of Education, 2002).

25. Census PUMS does not provide information about the place of college education. I used the available information on age and years of entry to the United States to impute the number of individual who were believed to receive their college education outside the United States, assuming that college education was received by age twenty-four.

26. *The Condition of Education 2002*, NCES 2002–25 (Washington, DC: U.S. Government Printing Office, 2002).

27. Alana M. Zambone and Margarita Alicea-Sáez, "Latino Students in Pursuit of Higher Education: What Helps or Hinders Their Success?" in Valentina Kloosterman, ed., *Latino Students in American Schools: Historical and Contemporary Views* (Westport, CT: Praeger, 2003).

28. "2000 Catalyst Census of Women Corporate Officers and Top Earners," Catalyst Fact Sheet, available online at www.catalystwomen.org.

29. Global Policy Forum 2004, available online at www.globalpolicy.org/soceecon/inequal/gender/2004.

30. Gender occupational segregation refers to the tendency for men and women to be employed in different occupations.

31. Francine C. Blau and Lawrence M. Kahn, "Gender Difference in Pay," *Journal of Economic Perspectives* 4(4) (2000): 75–99.

32. Francine D. Blau, Patricia Simpson, and Deborah Anderson, "Continuing Progress? Trends in Occupational Segregation in the United States over the 1970s and 1980s," NBER Working Paper no. 6716, 1998. Some evidence exists to counter this notion. Women spend more time in the workforce than ever before. Sixty-one percent of women with children under the age of two and 78 percent of mothers with school-age children remain in the workforce (*Pay Equity*, American Association of University Women; available online at www.aauw.org/issue_advocacy/actionpages/positionpapers/PDFs/payequity.pdf).

33. Table 11, Employed persons by detailed occupation, sex, race, and Hispanic or Latino ethnicity, available online at www.bls.gov/cps/cpsaat11.pdf.

34. Gregory, *Women and Workplace Discrimination*, p. 50.

35. 77.8 percent for white, 87 percent for black, 90.1 percent for Hispanic, and 86 percent for Asian.

36. Table 11, Employed persons by detailed occupation, sex, race, and Hispanic or Latino ethnicity; available online at http://www.bls.gov/cps/cpsaat11.pdf.

37. See www.emplawyernet.com/jobfront/jf1200.cfm. For 2004 law school enrollment statistics, see www.abanet.org/legaled/statistics/fall2004enrollment.pdf. See *Women and Attorneys of Color at Law Firms—2004*, by Association for Legal Career Professionals, available online at www.nalp.org/content/index.php?pid=253.

38. Wayne J. Guglielmo, "Physicians' Earnings: Our Exclusive Survey." *Medical Economics* (September 19, 2003): 80.71; available online at www.memag.com/memag/article/articleDetail.jsp?id=112482.

39. David J. Bashaw and John S. Heywood, "The Gender Earnings Gap for U.S. Physicians: Has Equality Been Achieved?" *Labour* 15(3) (2001): Table 1. Alicia Sasser also wrote that "women physicians sharply reduced their hours of work after marrying/having children" (Alicia C. Sasser, "Gender Differences in Physician Pay: Tradeoffs between Career and Family," *Journal of Human Resources* 40[2] [2005]: 477–504).

40. Male doctors' median earnings are $371,655 for invasive cardiology, $356,225 for orthopedic surgery, $157,412 for internal medicine, and $153,282 for family practice without obstetrics; Robert Lowes, "Earnings Survey: More Hours, More Patients, No Raise?" *Medical Economics* 22 (2002): 76; available online at www.memag.com/memag/article/articleDetail.jsp?id=116509.

41. Sharmistah Dev, "Income Disparities between Male and Female Physicians," *Journal of Pre-Health Affiliated Students* 4(1) (2005); available online at www2.uic.edu/orgs/jphas/journal/vol4/issue1/research_sd.shtml.

42. Peter Kooperman, "The Persistent Segregation of Girls into Lower-Paying Jobs while in School," IZA Discussion Paper no. 1535, 2005.

43. Amartya Sen, "Many Faces of Gender Inequality," 2005; available online at www.nu.or.cr/pnud/docs/Sen-man.pdf.

44. Leon Kolankiewicz, *Immigration, Population, and the New Census Bureau Projections*, Backgrounder,Center for Immigration Studies, 2000.

45. In 2000, people of Mexican origin were the largest Hispanic group in the United States, representing 59.3 percent of the country's total Hispanic population and 7.4 percent of the overall U.S. population. Sixty-four percent of Mexican Americans are immigrants. Approximately 46 percent of foreign-born Hispanics entered the United States between 1990 and 2000. About 29 percent arrived between 1980 and 1990. The proportion of those who have attained at least a bachelor's degree is the lowest for Mexicans. Roberto R. Ramirez, *We the People: Hispanics in the United States: Census 2000 Special Reports*, CENSR-17 (Washington, DC: U.S. Census Bureau, 2004).

46. The notion of a trade-off between home and work and a need to balance the two applies less to black women. Shortly after emancipation, black women were expected to be employed. In addition to their works, black women have been responsible for household work and child care. Sharon Harley, Francille Rusan Wilson, and Shirley Wilson Logan, "Historical Overview of Black Women and Work," in Sharon Harley, ed., *Sister Circle: Black Women and Work* (New Brunswick, NJ: Rutgers University Press, 2002), pp. 1–10.

47. Richard Anker, "Theories of Occupational Segregation by Sex: An Overview," *International Labour Review* 136(3) (1997); available online at www.ilo.org/public/english/support/publ/revue/articles/ank97-3.htm.

Index

Page numbers followed by f or t indicate figures or tables.

About the Editor and Contributors

Margaret Foegen Karsten is Professor in the Department of Business and Accounting and Coordinator of the Print Business Administration Distance Program at the University of Wisconsin-Platteville, where she teaches management and human resource management courses. She developed a *Management, Gender, and Race* course and has taught it for many years. Her books include *Management, Gender, and Race in the 21st Century* (2005) and *Management and Gender: Issues and Attitudes* (1994), in addition to over twenty other professional publications. She has presented at many national and regional conferences, has received several grants, and has held various administrative positions. Her current research interests include career paths of executive women and the impact of intellectual distance between students and professors on learning.

Nancy J. Adler is Professor of International Management at McGill University in Montreal, Canada, and has consulted and conducted extensive research on global leadership and cross-cultural management. She is the author of more than 100 articles as well as the books *International Dimensions of Organizational Behavior*, *Women in Management Worldwide*, *Competitive Frontiers: Women Managers in a Global Economy*, *Women Managing Worldwide*, and *From Boston to Beijing: Managing with a Worldview*. Nancy is also an established artist whose paintings increasingly enrich her work as a global business consultant and leadership expert.

Rachel Askew is a doctoral candidate in sociology at Emory University and received a master's in sociology from Rutgers University. Her research interests focus on women's and children's well-being. Recent publications include "Race, Ethnicity, and Wage Inequality among Women: What Happened in the 1990s and Early 21st Century?" in *American Behavioral Scientist* with Irene Browne, and "Stress and Somatization: A Sociocultural Perspective" from *Psychology of*

Stress with Corey L. M. Keyes. Her current research emphasis is on diagnosis and treatment within healthcare systems.

Stacy Blake-Beard is Associate Professor of Management at the Simmons College School of Management, where she teaches organizational behavior. She is also part of the research faculty in the Center for Gender in Organizations at Simmons. Prior to joining Simmons, Blake-Beard was a faculty member at the Harvard University Graduate School of Education. She also has worked in sales and marketing at Procter & Gamble and in the corporate human resources department at Xerox. Her research focuses on the challenges and opportunities offered by mentoring relationships, with a focus on how they may be changing as a result of increasing workforce diversity. Blake-Beard has published research on gender, diversity, and mentoring in several publications, including the *Journal of Career Development*, the *Academy of Management Executive*, the *Journal of Management Development*, and the *Journal of Business Ethics*.

Irene Browne is Associate Professor of Sociology and Women's Studies at Emory University. Her research interests focus primarily on economic inequality by race and gender, particularly in the labor market. In this work, she investigates theories of intersections of gender, race, and class. She is editor of *Latinas and African American Women at Work: Race, Gender and Economic Inequality*, and her work is published in a range of journals and edited volumes, including the *American Sociological Review, Social Forces*, and *Sociological Quarterly*.

Jane Carlson grew up in the north of England and, after fifteen years in the British Civil Service, started her own business consulting for a variety of organizations, including the British Potato Council. On her emigration to the United States, she founded a second business specializing in editing and writing documents for professionals in business, academia, and medicine. Her current projects include research and writing for books on hurricanes and coastal erosion and on transportation engineering.

Kelly Fanning is Internal Consultant at Blue Cross Blue Shield of Massachusetts. Before joining the Business Consulting Group in September 2005, Fanning worked within the nonprofit sector. As an Education and Program Coordinator for SmithBucklin, she developed and managed the program content for four national associations and strategically managed and implemented educational programs, including regional seminars, online Web-casts, and annual national conferences. As Program Manager for the Congressional Award Foundation in Washington, D.C., Fanning worked with members of Congress to direct national ceremonies honoring over 100 youth and led the public relations and marketing of the program across the Eastern United States. She cofounded the Net Impact Chapter while earning her MBA from Simmons School of Management.

Jeanie Ahearn Greene is founder and sole proprietor of Ahearn Greene Associates, a social science research and consulting firm dedicated to research-based writing and publication as a way to advocate for and support the rights and needs of discriminated-against adults, children, and their families. She focuses her work on giving voice to the disenfranchised, un(der)served, and unheard, particularly women and children, and lives in metropolitan Washington, D.C. She is the author of *Blue-Collar Women at Work with Men: Negotiating the Hostile Environment* (Praeger 2006).

Lisa Gundry is Professor of Management and Director of the Leo V. Ryan Center for Creativity and Innovation at DePaul University. Her work focuses on innovative processes in organizations and entrepreneurial growth strategies.

Laurie Hunt is a management consultant specializing in mentoring, diversity, and leadership communication with over twenty years of international marketing, communications, and human resources experience. She designs, develops, and implements formal mentoring programs for organizations and has a special interest in supporting the advancement of women and people of color. Hunt is a consulting affiliate with the Center for Gender in Organizations at Simmons College and is also is a professional coach, assisting clients with leadership development, career change, and transitions. At Nortel Networks she held positions in new product introduction, marketing communications, sales, diversity, and employee relations. At the Humphrey Group Hunt was responsible for business development, working with companies to design custom leadership development and communications programs.

Gillian P. S. Khoo is a certified Professional Integral Coach through New Ventures West and is President of Windom International, an executive coaching firm with offices in San Francisco and Washington, D.C. A seasoned executive coach with over fourteen years of domestic and international coaching experience, Khoo has assessed and coached hundreds of senior executives and is intimately familiar with the barriers and critical success factors to building effective leadership.

Jongsung Kim is Associate Professor of Economics at Bryant University in Rhode Island. In addition to gender earnings gap and occupational segregation, his research interests include various labor market issues about inequalities and the foreign-born workers in the U.S. labor market. He is the author of *Labor Supply and Occupational Structure of Asian Immigrants in the U.S. Labor Market* (2000).

Gina LaRoche is the Managing Director of INSPIRITAS, a consulting and training firm advancing leadership practice with executive programs that challenge leadership teams to accelerate results using vision, strategy, and accountability.

Her recent clients include Miller Brewing, Harvard University, American Student Assistance, and Stamford Hospital. She has eighteen years of experience in sales, marketing, and training at high-tech and emerging growth companies. Currently a visiting professor in Simmons School of Management's executive education program, LaRoche has worked with many organizations as a consultant, coach, and trainer to develop strategic business and marketing plans and execute on them to achieve breakthrough results. Gina began her career as a sales professional at IBM, where she received numerous excellence awards.

Ancella Livers is Group Manager in Open Enrollment for the Center for Creative Leadership in Greensboro, NC, and is global manager of the Center's flagship offering, the Leadership Development Program. She also oversees the African American Leadership, Coaching for Development and Women's Leadership Programs and delivers custom programs tailored to public, private, and nonprofit sector clients' needs. Livers is a certified feedback coach providing assessment, feedback, and coaching to senior-level executives in various organizations. Before joining CCL, she was Assistant Professor in the School of Journalism at West Virginia University. Earlier, she was acting business editor and Capitol Hill reporter for the Gannett News Service and a regular guest on the Baltimore public affairs television show *Urban Scene*. She is coauthor of *Leading in Black and White: Working across the Racial Divide in Corporate America* (2003) and the 2002 *Harvard Business Review* article "Dear White Boss," and author of "Coaching Leaders of Color," a chapter in the center's *Handbook of Leadership Coaching*.

Laurel Ofstein is Assistant Director of the Ryan Center for Creativity and Innovation at DePaul University. She has contributed to textbooks on entrepreneurship and created cases for student use.

Patricia S. Parker is Associate Professor of Communication Studies at the University of North Carolina at Chapel Hill, where she is a Burress fellow at the Institute for the Arts and Humanities, a research fellow at the Institute of African American Research, and a 2005 scholar in residence at the Center for Urban and Regional Studies. Her research and teaching focus on critical and feminist studies of race, gender, class, and culture in organizational processes and emphasize career socialization, leadership, and empowerment for women and girls. Recent publications include *Race, Gender, and Leadership: Re-envisioning Organizational Leadership from the Perspectives of African American Women Executives* (2005) and several articles and book chapters on race, gender, and organizational communication. Her current work focuses on leadership development and empowerment for African American teen girls in low-income neighborhoods.

Jessica L. Porter is Research Associate at Harvard Business School. She is currently working on a study examining the microdynamics of work in the professional services industry. Prior to earning her MBA from Simmons School of Management, Porter founded the Association of Labor Assistants and Childbirth Educators, a nonprofit organization that supported childbearing women by training independent doulas and educators across North America.

Margaret Posig is Associate Professor and Director of the Leadership and Change Management concentration in the Charles H. Kellstadt Graduate School of Business at DePaul University. Her major research interests are in the areas of organizational leadership and workplace stress, and she has published articles on women in leadership, leadership trust, servant leadership, and empowerment.

Elizabeth Powell is Assistant Professor in Management Communication at the Darden Graduate School of Business, University of Virginia. She is currently working on projects related to leadership, reputation, and professional identity formation.

Karen L. Proudford is Associate Professor of Management at the Graves School of Business and Management, Morgan State University, and is an affiliated faculty member at the Center for Gender in Organizations, Simmons School of Management. Her research, writing, and consulting interests include group and intergroup dynamics, leadership, diversity, and conflict. Prior to beginning her career in academia, she held positions at Honeywell and IBM. Her work has appeared in such publications as *Group and Organization Management, Journal of Labor and Employment Law, Diversity Factor*, and *International Review of Women and Leadership*; the volume *Addressing Cultural Issues in Organizations: Beyond the Corporate Context*; and most recently, the *Handbook of Workplace Diversity*.

Ashleigh Shelby Rosette is Assistant Professor at the Fuqua School of Business at Duke University, where she teaches courses in managerial effectiveness and negotiations. A Certified Public Accountant in Texas, she previously was a consultant with Arthur Andersen in its Houston and Atlanta offices. Her research on organizational diversity focuses on systems of privilege and workplace discrimination, and recent work on negotiation deals with the influence of intercultural differences and the strategic use of emotion on negotiated outcomes. Rosette has conducted and presented research in the United States, France, Spain, Portugal, Hong Kong, South Africa, and Canada and has published book chapters and research articles in journals such as *Organizational Behavior* and *Human Decision Processes*. Her many awards and grants include the Academy of Management's Best Paper Based on a Dissertation and State Farm Insurance's Education Grant. She also has provided consulting services for various groups across the United States.

Maureen A. Scully is a faculty member at the College of Management at the University of Massachusetts, Boston, and an affiliated faculty member at the

Center for Gender in Organizations at the Simmons School of Management. Her research investigates how inequality in the workplace is sometimes legitimated by the idea of meritocracy but sometimes contested by grassroots employee groups that see departures from meritocracy. She has studied a variety of corporate change efforts regarding diversity, ethics, teamwork, and reward systems Her work has appeared in *Journal of Applied Behavioral Science*, *Journal of Management Inquiry*, and *Organization Science* and has been funded by the Ford Foundation and the National Science Foundation.

Cheryl A. Smith is Associate Professor in the Adult Learning Division of Lesley University and a member of the university's Undergraduate Curriculum Committee, Academic Technology and Center for Academic Technology's Grants and Advisory committees. In addition, she is a member of the Advanced Graduate Council, which oversees the doctoral program in Educational Studies and the Women's Studies Task Force of the Women's Resource Group. She is the author of *Market Women: Black Women Entrepreneurs: Past, Present, and Future* (Praeger 2005).

Suzette Turnbull is Associate Director of the MBA Program at Simmons College School of Management (SOM). Within the SOM community, she is an Assurance of Learning/AACSB Accreditation committee member, advisor to the Women of Color and International Student Clubs, and a member of the newly launched Entrepreneurship Certificate Program Taskforce. She is an alumna of the Partnership and a board member for New England Citybridge. Her expertise lies in staff and volunteer management, fundraising, and program administration. Turnbull earned her B.S. in business management from Florida Atlantic University and her MBA from Simmons College School of Management.

Linda Sue Warner is currently Associate Vice-Chancellor for Academic Affairs at the Tennessee Board of Regents in Nashville. She is a member of the Comanche Tribe of Oklahoma and has over thirty-five years of experience as an educator working in public schools in Missouri and Bureau of Indian Affairs schools in Alaska, New Mexico, Kansas, and Arizona. Her research at the graduate level centers on educational policy and leadership, and her teaching areas deal with the principalship and education law. Warner has had teaching and research appointments at the University of Kansas, Pennsylvania State University, and the Harry S Truman Center for Public Policy at the University of Missouri-Columbia. She currently serves on President Bush's National Advisory Council for Indian Education.

Patricia H. Werhane is Wicklander Professor of Business Ethics and Executive Director of the Institute for Business and Professional Ethics at DePaul University with a joint appointment at the Graduate School of Business, University of Virginia. She is a member of the Academic Advisory Committee for the

Business Roundtable for Corporate Ethics. Werhane has written extensively on business ethics and organizational ethical issues in health care.

Deborah A. Woo, a sociologist, has been Professor in Community Studies at the University of California, Santa Cruz, since 1984. Awarded a grant by the federal Glass Ceiling Commission to explore the glass ceiling among Asian Americans, she is author of *The Glass Ceiling and Asian Americans: The New Face of Workplace Barriers.* Although her primary research interest deals with workplace inequities, Woo has also written more broadly about the politics of culture as it has shaped policies or practices toward Asian Americans in higher education, health, law, and the workplace. More recent publications include writings on the cultural defense, corporate culture and leadership, and cultural issues in the delivery of health services.